Advanced BASIC
The Peter Norton Programming Series

Who This Book Is For

Intermediate to advanced BASIC programmers who want to extend their programming expertise and add new performance to their programs.

What's Inside

- More than 100 ready-to-run programs that show the best ways to work with windows, pull-down menus, animation, the mouse, and new fast routines

- Expert tips to increase program speed and finesse

- A learn-by-doing approach to programming that shows code in action in a direct, highly readable style

About the Peter Norton Microcomputer Libraries from Brady

All of the volumes in the Peter Norton Libraries, written in collaboration with Peter Norton Computing, provide clear, in-depth discussions of the latest developments in computer hardware, operating systems, and programming. Fully tested and rigorously reviewed by the experts at Peter Norton Computing, these libraries deserve a special place on your bookshelf. These libraries are comprised of two series:

The Peter Norton Hardware Library gives you an insider's grasp of your computer and the way it works. Included are such best-selling classics as *Inside the IBM PC*, *Inside the Apple Macintosh*, and *The Hard Disk Companion*.

The Peter Norton Programming Library focuses on creating programs that work right away and offers the best tips and techniques in the industry. It includes *Advanced Assembly Language*, *C Programming*, *C++ Programming*, *QBasic Programming*, *Advanced DOS*, and more.

Advanced BASIC

Steven Holzner with Peter Norton Computing

Brady

New York   London   Toronto   Sydney   Tokyo   Singapore

 **Brady**

A Division of Simon & Schuster, Inc.
15 Columbus Circle
New York, NY 10023

Manufactured in the United States of America

10 9 8 7 6 5 4 3 2 1

Library of Congress Cataloging-in-Publication Data

Norton, Peter.
    Advanced BASIC / Peter Norton, Steven Holzner.
        p.cm.
    Includes index.
    1. BASIC (Computer program language) I. Holzner, Steven
II. Title.
    QA76.73.B3H68   1991
    005.26'2--dc20   90-24638
                                                              CIP

ISBN 0-13-658758-5

Contents

Introduction

BASIC Makes a Comeback

For many long years, BASIC was the language not of programmers, but of dilettantes. BASIC (or BASICA or GWBASIC) was the language that came free with your computer. Originally intended as a learning language, it became the language that let you scroll "Hello" up on the screen to show you what your new computer was good for. However, if you attempted any substantial programming, you found that the results were invariably slow and prone to awkward errors ("Redo from start"). To professionals, BASIC was the Dick and Jane of programming.

Circumstances can change, however, and nowhere faster than in computing. And BASIC did change. It gained a new, unexpected vitality with the introduction of superfast compilers. Compilers that produce tight, efficient code gave BASIC a shot in the arm.

Among these compilers were the Microsoft BASIC products, including Quick-BASIC, with which this book is designed to be used. The executable code these compilers began to produce was, while not the fastest, at least good. And program speed began to improve with later releases. Programmers at Microsoft began to write important pieces of code in BASIC. These and other developments impressed the PC programming community, and BASIC began to make its comeback.

As run times decreased, programmers began to notice once again the major asset of the language: its enormous number of instructions, unrivaled in practically any language for the PC today. Even the very earliest version of MS BASIC supported no less than 160 built-in functions, statements, and commands. What might take lines and lines of code in other languages was often one single statement in BASIC.

During its time in the wings, BASIC borrowed much from other languages. For example, it took the SELECT CASE structure from Pascal, the COMMON statement from FORTRAN, the rudimentary use of pointers — VARPTR, VARSEG, SSEG, SADD, SSEGADD and others — from C. BASIC got better.

The notorious one-line IF statement had been improved to an IF THEN...ELSE...END IF structure. Data types became user defined. Support for reaching the operating system directly was added (with INTERRUPT( ) and INTERRUPTX( )). The language that once had everything seemed to have everything once again.

The BASIC Professional Development System

In November 1989, a significant milestone was reached with the release of Microsoft BASIC 7.0, also known as the BASIC Professional Development System (PDS). This package is intended as a serious programming tool (matched by a serious price), and it indicates the level of Microsoft's commitment to BASIC. Special libraries have been added, including financial functions and some advanced formatting functions. An entire toolbox kit was also included, filled with tools for matrix math, presentation graphics, and an advanced user interface — and we'll dig into that toolbox in this book.

In addition, a whole new type of file structure was added for databases — ISAM files. Referenced by pointers, ISAM records can be sorted quickly and easily, and they provide support for professional database applications. BASIC just continues to grow: The language itself, *before* including these add-ons, now supports no less than 252 built-in functions, statements, commands, metacommands, and routines. And the number of BASIC programmers also continues to grow.

In short, BASIC has once again become a premiere programming language. BASIC is back.

BASIC Taken Seriously

Now that BASIC is being used by serious programmers and professionals, books on BASIC have to follow the trend. No longer will you find chapter-long expositions on checkbook balancing programs. No longer will you see books that plod through the BASIC instruction set alphabetically as though you were reading a dictionary and not a learning tool. Instead, BASIC books today have to provide real value, significantly enhancing the reader's knowledge. Programmers will settle for nothing less.

This is even more true of a book on advanced BASIC because only people serious about programming will read it — and they want to use their time profitably, not waste it. For that reason, we're going to fill this book with the hottest programming topics available today. We'll work through all the tricks a professional programmer has, from adding mouse support to programs to showing how fast animation works and from adding pull-down menus to interfacing assembly language directly into BASIC for raw computing power. We'll even use some of BASIC's own internal subprograms to make our job easier.

As we work our way through advanced BASIC, we'll also explore many of the tools that the powerful BASIC Professional Development System has to offer. In fact, we devote one chapter (Chapter 6, *Databasing*) exclusively to PDS programming; in that chapter we create a database program using the new ISAM file system. Readers that have the BASIC PDS will find just how far they can go.

All in all, we'll make a complete survey of up-to-the-minute BASIC in this book. We're not going to have much time to get boring — not with as much power as we can generate in today's BASIC. Let's take a look at what's coming.

What's in This Book

We stress *examples* in this book and develop them incrementally so you can see what's going on. We'll use arrows to show you where we are in a certain piece of code. In addition, this book will also present a wealth of special tips that are designed to give you out-of-the-ordinary hints about BASIC programming. We'll also include some special notes when there is something of historical or machine-related interest that we should know about.

Here's a list of the chapters in this book, and a little information about each one. You might take a few seconds to skim this overview:

Introduction What you're reading now. Provides an overview and explains what you'll need to run the programs in this book.

Chapter 1: Professional Input
This is the perfect place to start — with the input to our programs. We'll see how to handle input in a professional way, and add a few enhancements that BASIC left out (such as a custom version of INKEY$ that doesn't echo struck characters on the screen).

Chapter 2: Windows
Here's where we develop our window system. This chapter has plenty of examples, and we see how to set up a window, show it on the screen, print to it, move it around, resize, or hide it. The Professional Development System (PDS) offers some built-in window functions as well here.

Chapter 3: The Mouse
In this chapter we add support for the mouse through interrupt &H33. We see how to turn the mouse cursor on and off, and to read information from it with a few easy calls. For those with the PDS, we'll look at the built-in mouse interface.

Chapter 4:   Pull-down Menus
             Here we put windows and the mouse together and come up
             with pull-down menus. We'll see how easy it is to set up a
             mouse- or keyboard driven menubar and find what selection
             was made. Again, the PDS offers some menu tools, and we'll
             take a look at them too.

Chapter 5:   Graphics
             In this chapter, we see how to augment BASIC's graphics
             capabilities by writing our own paint program. Among other
             things, we design and use graphics sprites in this chapter, and
             look into the PDS' presentation graphics, as well as animation.

Chapter 6:   Databasing
             In Chapter 6, we'll start putting together a database program.
             We'll see how using PDS ISAM files makes database
             programming a snap.

Chapter 7:   A Tour of BIOS and DOS
             In this chapter, we make use of some of the assets that DOS
             and BIOS give us. Among other things, we see how to
             determine what equipment is in the computer, how much
             space there is on a disk, and how to search through a hard
             disk for files that match a given file specification (including
             wildcards).

Chapter 8:   Advanced Data Handling and Sorting
             If you have an array full of data that you want to sort, this
             chapter is for you. Just pass it to one of the quick sorting
             routines here and you're all set. In addition, we'll explore just
             about all the ways there are of organizing data in BASIC, and
             develop a fast data search program.

Chapter 9:   Debugging
             This chapter gives us an introduction to the fundamentals of
             debugging, both under QuickBasic and with the CodeView
             standalone debugger.

Chapter 10: Welcome to Assembly Language
             This primer gives us some exposure to assembly language.
             Advanced programmers often need real speed and compact

code, and there's nothing that can compete with assembly language. Here we take a look at assembly language fundamentals so we'll be able to interface it to BASIC in the next chapter.

Chapter 11: Connecting to Assembly Language
In this chapter, we see how we can tie assembly language routines into BASIC, making them look exactly like FUNCTIONs or SUBs. We make use of the new simplified segment directives in MASM 5.1 or later versions.

Appendix: DOS and BIOS Reference
This appendix lets you tap the power of DOS and BIOS. Throughout the book, we'll make use of DOS and BIOS services, and we'll list them all in this appendix.

What You'll Need

That's it. We're just about ready to start. To make use of the programs in this book, you'll need a Microsoft BASIC product, such as the Microsoft BASIC compiler (BC.EXE), QuickBASIC (QB.EXE or extended QuickBASIC, QBX.EXE), or the BASIC PDS (BC.EXE Version 7.0, 7.10, or later).

In addition, if you want to make use of the material in Chapters 10 and 11 on powering up your BASIC programs with assembly language, you'll need the Microsoft macro assembler (MASM.EXE), Version 5.1 or later. We are going to use this or later versions because they support the simplified segment directives, which have made changes in mixed-language programming nothing short of revolutionary.

You should also know that many of the programs in this book access BIOS and DOS directly with the INTERRUPT( ) and INTERRUPTX( ) routines. By doing this, we unlock a vast reserve of computing power — just about everything the computer can do can be done with these routines. If you're using QuickBASIC (QB.EXE or QBX.EXE), however, you must use the /L switch like this with programs that use INTERRUPT( ) or INTERRUPTX( ):

```
QB PROG /L
or
QBX PROG /L
```

This switch loads the Quick libraries QB.QLB or QBX.QLB into memory. When we work with assembly langauge near the end of the book, we'll even see how to make our own Quick libraries out of assembly language procedures.

In addition, those programs using INTERRUPT( ) or INTERRUPTX( ) — and the assembly language modules we'll write — will not work in OS/2 protected mode (although the other programs in this book will). This is because they use the interrupt structure of BIOS and DOS. These programs will work, however, under the OS/2 DOS compatibility mode.

And that's all there is to it. We're ready to enter the world of advanced BASIC programming. Let's begin by turning to Chapter 1, *Professional Input*.

Professional Input

IN THIS CHAPTER, we're going to explore BASIC's keyboard input capabilities — but we won't stop there. We'll augment those functions and add a few of our own by operating at the lowest level and interfacing directly to DOS.

In addition, we'll see what kind of bulletproof input routines are needed in real applications by developing a professional style input routine that reads integers from the keyboard. And, before we're done, we'll take a look at parsing keyboard input by putting together our own reverse polish calculator.

This chapter is the natural starting point for our book — working through the ways we can get some input for our programs. And we'll see just about every way of receiving keyboard input that there is under BASIC. Let's start by reviewing what BASIC itself provides.

The INPUT Statement

Listing 1-1 shows the first example program of the book.

Listing 1-1.   Averaging Program.

```
PRINT "This program takes the average of three numbers."
INPUT "The numbers"; A!, B!, C!
PRINT "Thank You. The average is:";(A! + B! + C!)/3.0
```

In this example, we use the INPUT statement to read three values and place them into the three single-precision variables—A!, B!, and C!. We specify the prompt we want typed out in the INPUT statement, and then list the variables to fill with input (see Listing 1-1).

Unfortunately, the INPUT statement should be avoided by professional programmers. One problem is that it places a mandatory question mark after the prompt string. Assume our program had looked like Listing 1-2.

Listing 1-2.   Averaging Program Variation.

```
INPUT "Please type three numbers"; A!, B!, C!
PRINT "Thank You. The average is:";(A! + B! + C!)/3
```

Then the prompt on the screen would look like this:

```
R:\     INPUT
Please type three numbers?
```

It looks more like a plea than a prompt. The real problem, however, is that INPUT produces the "Redo from start" error message if the values typed do not fit into the variable list provided or if the values are not separated by valid delimiters such as commas. For example, we'd get this response if we left out the delimiters:

```
R: > INPUT
This program takes the average of three numbers.
The numbers? 3 3 3 ← type this.

Redo from start
The numbers?
```

This doesn't exactly match the idea of user friendliness, nor does it promote a professional image.

The INPUT$ Function

Although the INPUT$( ) function is usually used to read strings from files, you can use it to read keys from the keyboard as well. Unfortunately, you have to specify *exactly* how many characters to read. Here's an example, where we read (exactly) 10 characters and find the first occurrence of the letter e:

```
PRINT "Please type a string of 10 characters."
Instring$ = INPUT$(10) 'Note: no echoing on screen.
VALU% = INSTR(Instring$,"e")
IF VALU% = 0 THEN
        PRINT "Thank you. There was no 'e' in that string."
ELSE
        PRINT "Thank you. The first 'e' was character" VALU%
END IF
```

TIP: One of INPUT$ chief advantages is that it does not echo characters on the screen, providing an alternate method of input from the rest of the BASIC statements and functions.

First we print out our prompt ("Please type a string of 10 characters."), and then read the input string:

```
PRINT "Please type a string of 10 characters."
Instring$ = INPUT$(10) 'Note: no echoing on screen.
:
```

Now we can search the string for the first e, if there was one, and print out its location:

```
PRINT "Please type a string of 10 characters."
Instring $ = INPUT$(10) 'Note: no echoing on screen.
→    VALUE% = INSTR(Instring$,"e")
     IF VALUE% = 0 THEN
          PRINT "Thank you. There was no 'e' in that string."
ELSE
          PRINT "Thank you. The first 'e' was character" VALU%
END IF
```

However, requiring a specific number of characters (carriage returns do not terminate input) is a big drawback. And, even though you can read input without echoing it on the screen, INPUT$( ) cannot return extended ASCII codes. That rules out function keys, arrow keys, Alt keys, and so on.

NOTE: See our function InKeyNoEcho$( ), developed a little later on, for a solution to these problems.

The LINE INPUT Statement

On the other hand, the LINE INPUT statement is a very useful one. All it does is to read a string of characters from the keyboard. The string is terminated once you type a carriage return. Here's an example:

```
LINE INPUT "Please type a string:";Instring$
PRINT "Thank you. That string was";LEN(Instring$);"characters long."
```

In this case we print out a prompt ("Please type a string:") — note that no annoying question mark is added — and then we receive our input string. We can work with that string as we please, including parsing it (as we do at the end of this chapter).

TIP: If you want to read strings, the LINE INPUT statement provides the easiest solution. It is easier than INKEY$( ) and more reliable than INPUT or INPUT$.

Still, LINE INPUT doesn't give you character-by-character control; nor does it handle extended ASCII codes. For those capabilities, we have to turn to INKEY$.

INKEY$

For real control, INKEY$ is the programmer's favorite.
Everybody's familiar with INKEY$; here's an example:

```
PRINT "Type a character."

DO
InChar$ = INKEY$
LOOP WHILE InChar$ = ""

PRINT "Thank you. That character was:";InChar$
```

In this case, we're just waiting for a character to be typed. Because INKEY$ returns whatever's in the keyboard buffer immediately, we have to loop, calling it continuously until something's there:

```
  PRINT "Type a character."
→ DO
  InChar$ = INKEY$
  LOOP WHILE InChar$ = ""

  PRINT "Thank you. That character was:";InChar$
```

INKEY$ has three types of return values: (a) strings of length zero (null strings, ""), (b) length one, and (c) length two. If the return string is one character long, it's just a single character, like d or q.

TIP: Use the LEN( ) function to determine the length of the string returned by INKEY$. If it's one character long, you're all set; if it's two characters long, INKEY$ is returning an extended ASCII code.

If, however, the return string is two characters long, then it represents an *extended ASCII code*. The first character in this string is ASCII 0; that is, CHR$(0). The second character is the key's *scan code*. There is a unique scan code for each key or legal key combination (such as Alt-k) on the keyboard, and you can look them up in the tables in your BASIC documentation. (Use RIGHT$( ), LEFT$( ), or MID$( ) to separate out the first and second characters in the returned string.)

Although many programmers aren't familiar with scan codes, using them can add a lot of power to your programs; let's take a look at how to put them to work. In the following example, we set up a function that indicates which arrow key was pressed.

GetArrowKey$—Reads Arrow Keys

In this example, let's write a function to read the arrow keys on the computer's numeric keyboard and return their values in an easy-to-interpret way. For example, if the right arrow key was pressed, the return value might be r. If the up arrow key was pressed, we could return a value of u. This lets us use the arrows keys easily in our programs, without having to memorize scan codes. Here are the possible return values from GetArrowKey$( ):

r	Right arrow key pressed
l	Left arrow key pressed
u	Up arrow key pressed
d	Down arrow key pressed
h	Home key pressed
e	End key pressed

GetArrowKey$( ) can be used like any other function. When you use it, it waits for an arrow key to be pressed and then returns the corresponding letter. Let's pass an argument called WarningBeep% to GetArrowKey$( ). If you set WarningBeep% to a nonzero value, GetArrowKey$( ) will beep when you press any key but an arrow key.

This function is pretty simple. We start by setting up a continuous loop, waiting for keys:

```
FUNCTION GetArrowKey$ (WarningBeep%)
        DO
          :
          :
        LOOP WHILE 1
```

Now we can accept input from INKEY$:

```
FUNCTION GetArrowKey$ (WarningBeep%)
        DO

          DO
                InStr$ = INKEY$
          LOOP WHILE InStr$ = ""
                :
                :
        LOOP WHILE 1
```

The outer loop, DO...LOOP WHILE 1, loops forever; the inner loop waits until a key has been pressed. After INKEY$ returns a key, we get its ASCII code and then check to make sure the length of the incoming string is two; if not, and if WarningBeep% is nonzero, we beep:

```
FUNCTION GetArrowKey$ (WarningBeep%)

        DO
            DO
                            InStr$ = INKEY$
            LOOP WHILE InStr$ = ""

→           Code = ASC(RIGHT$(InStr$, 1))
            IF LEN(InStr$) = 2 THEN
                        :
                [check for arrow key]
                        :
            ELSE
→           IF WarningBeep% THEN BEEP
            END IF
        LOOP WHILE 1
```

Now we can check to see which arrow key, if any, has been pressed. That looks like Listing 1-3, using a SELECT CASE statement (and getting the scan code values from the BASIC documentation). That's it; if an arrow key has been pressed, we return the correct character, and, if not, we look back to the beginning and wait for another one (after beeping if we're supposed to).

Listing 1-3. Get Arrow Key$ Function.   1 of 2

```
FUNCTION GetArrowKey$ (WarningBeep%)

        DO
            DO
            InStr$ = INKEY$
            LOOP WHILE InStr$ = ""

            Code = ASC(RIGHT$(InStr$, 1))
            IF LEN(InStr$) = 2 THEN
→               SELECT CASE Code
                    CASE &H4D
                        GetArrowKey$ = "r"
                        EXIT FUNCTION
                    CASE &H4B
                        GetArrowKey$ = "l"
                        EXIT FUNCTION
                    CASE &H48
                        GetArrowKey$ = "u"
                        EXIT FUNCTION
                    CASE &H50
```

```
Listing 1-3.   Get Arrow Key$ Function.                          2 of 2
                        GetArrowKey$ = "d"
                        EXIT FUNCTION
                    CASE &H47
                        GetArrowKey$ = "h"
                        EXIT FUNCTION
                    CASE &H4F
                        GetArrowKey$ = "e"
                        EXIT FUNCTION
  →             END SELECT
                IF WarningBeep% THEN BEEP
            ELSE
                IF WarningBeep% THEN BEEP
            END IF
        LOOP WHILE 1

END FUNCTION
```

This is one way to use the scan codes you can read from INKEY$. As we can see, INKEY$ is a versatile function. For most purposes, we can put together a good input routine using INKEY$.

However, there are some times when INKEY$ might not be quite right. We've seen that the INPUT$( ) function does not echo on the screen, but that it also can't return extended ASCII codes.

TIP: If you use scan codes frequently, it's easiest write a small BASIC program to print data out. For example, to find the right arrow's scan code, you would run your program and type that key; the program would print the scan code it got from INKEY$.

Fortunately, we can put together our own version of INKEY$ that won't echo on the screen, but which will handle extended ASCII codes. And, since that process will introduce us to the INTERRUPT( ) routine (which is going to be used very often in the rest of the book), let's do that right now.

InKeyNoEcho$

Here we can develop our own variation on INKEY$ that operates just as INKEY$ does, but does *not* echo typed characters on the screen.

Our function InKeyNoEcho$( ) should not wait for input, just as INKEY$ does not. And it should return values exactly as you'd expect them from INKEY$ as a null string,

(""), which means that no character was waiting; a single character that holds the ASCII value of the struck key; or a double character, which means that an extended ASCII code was necessary:

Length of returned string	Means that the output is
0	Null string (" "). No character has been typed since the keyboard was last checked.
1	The ASCII code of a struck key. For example, if the q key was struck, IKeyNoEcho$ would equal q.
2	Extended ASCII code. These keys don't normally echo on the screen anyway (such as arrow keys or function keys). The first character is CHR$(0) and the second is the keys's scan code (check BASIC documentation for a list of scan codes).

Now, since no such function exists in BASIC, we're going to have to put it together ourselves. We can't use any of the input functions that already exist in BASIC to build our function because they all echo on the screen or suppress scan codes. That means we'll have to start from scratch, and one way of doing that is interfacing to DOS itself through the *interrupt* system.

Using BIOS and DOS Interrupts

By far the strongest way of augmenting the power of BASIC is to use the resources available to us in the computer's operating system, and we're going to use them frequently. Each interrupt is a prewritten program already in memory, ready for us to use. The commands you use at DOS level (e.g., COPY, TIME, VER, XCOPY, or FORMAT) all make use of the built-in interrupts — and now we, as BASIC programmers, can too. It's like adding a whole new language to our programming capabilities.

The way we pass and receive data to and from interrupt routines is by using the BASIC INTERRUPT( ) routine, and the 80 x 86's *registers*. The microprocessor handles data in 16-bit registers, and you can think of them as the computer's built in variables. The ones we'll see most are named ax, bx, cx, and dx, and they store data in the computer's CPU (see Figure 1-1).

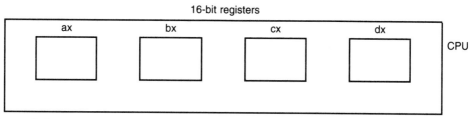

Figure 1-1

Each interrupt examines the way we've loaded some or all of these registers, and takes action accordingly. For a complete listing of each interrupt service and how to load the registers, look at the appendix of this book; it shows you what must be in each register before calling INTERRUPT( ) or INTERRUPTX( ), and what kinds out output you can expect to find.

TIP: INTERRUPT( ) and INTERRUPTX( ) are the same, except that INTER-RUPTX( ) allows you to use a few more registers. Use INTERRUPTX( ) to give you more control.

Since each register is 16 bits long, it is exactly like a BASIC INTEGER, and we can load integer values into them like 53, 3251, or -219 (see Figure 1-2).

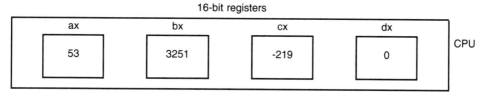

Figure 1-2

To the computer, however, each register can also be thought of as two bytes, so you can also break up these registers into a high 8-bit register and a low 8-bit register. For example, the high 8-bit part of ax (bx, cx ...) is called ah (bh, ch ...), and the low 8-bit part of ax (bx, cx ...) is called al (bl, cl ...) (see Figure 1-3).

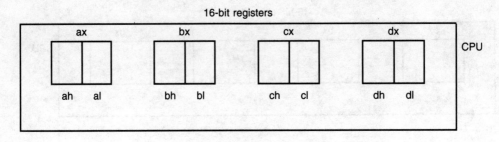

Figure 1-3

Frequently, we'll have to load one of these 8-bit registers, such as ah, with a particular value to use an interrupt. When we work with registers, we'll use hexadecimal values. (Hexadecimal, of course, is just base 16, where digits go from 0 to 9 and then from &HA to &HF.)

Hexadecimal is handy because a 16-bit binary number — the size of each full register — makes up four hexadecimal digits. That means that the values we can place in the 80 x 86's registers go from 0 to &HFFFF (65535) (Figure 1-4).

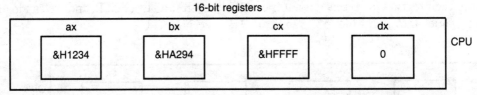

Figure 1-4

In addition, 8 bits (a byte) make up exactly two hex digits — &H12 or &H34 — so a byte can hold values from 0 to &HFF (255). Because we can divide registers like ax into ah and al, the top byte in a 16-bit word like ax is simply the first two hex digits, and the bottom byte is the bottom two. For example, if ax held &H1234, then ah contains &H12 and al contains &H34 (Figure 1-5).

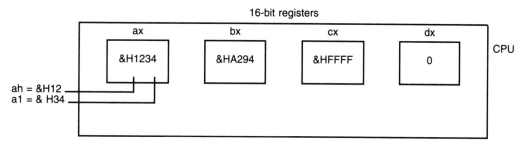

Figure 1-5

To reach the 80 x 86's registers from BASIC, we first have to set up two data structures, InRegs and OutRegs, as type RegType. That type is defined this way:

```
TYPE RegType
      ax     AS INTEGER
      bx     AS INTEGER
      cx     AS INTEGER
      dx     AS INTEGER
      bp     AS INTEGER
      si     AS INTEGER
      di     AS INTEGER
      flags AS INTEGER
END TYPE
```

Now we'll be able to refer to registers like ax as InRegs.ax, bx as InRegs.bx, and so on. Note that we had to set aside space for four new registers here bp, si, di, and the flags register (see Figure 1-6).

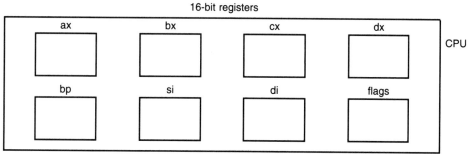

Figure 1-6

> **NOTE:** The high and low bytes of these new registers cannot be addressed separately; for example, si does not split into sh and sl.

With the exception of the flags register, we won't see these new registers until we start to deal with assembly language. The bp register is normally used in manipulating stack data, and we'll use it in Chapter 11. The si and di registers are used by the 80 x 86 to manipulate strings, and we'll see them in Chapter 10. However, we will see more of the *flags register* in this chapter.

There are nine flags common to all 80 x 86 processors (there are 13 flags in the 80 x 86); these flags usually report the status of mathematical operations. For example, there is a zero flag that is set if the result of an operation was zero. The carry flag is normally set if the last operation resulted in a carry. The lower bits of InRegs.flags hold the nine common 80 x 86 flags, and here they are, bit by bit:

InRegs.flag bit	Flag
11	Overflow Flag
10	Direction Flag
9	Enable Interrupts Flag
8	Trap Flag
7	Sign Flag
6	Zero Flag
4	Auxiliary Carry Flag
2	Parity Flag
0	Carry Flag

Now that we've defined our TYPE RegType, we're free to use INTERRUPT( ). For example, to print a character on the screen, we first check the appendix to find that interrupt &H21 service 2 is the one we want. INT &H21, service 2 character output on screen, is shown below:

Input

ah=2
dl=Character's ASCII code.

Because interrupt &H21 can do many things, it's divided up into services; service 2 is the one that lets us print on the screen. (See the Appendix for INTERRUPT & H21's Services.) To select a service from an interrupt, load that number into the ah register (the top eight bits of ax).

Since we're restricted to working with integers, we'll have to do that by loading 2 into the top byte of ax (recall that the first two digits in a four digit hex number make up the top byte):

```
    DIM InRegs AS RegType, OutRegs AS RegType
→  InRegs.ax = &H0200
    :
```

We also see that we have to place the character's ASCII code into the dl register, the lower 8 bits of dx. Let's print out an A:

```
    DIM InRegs AS RegType, OutRegs AS RegType
    InRegs.ax = &H0200
→  InRegs.dx = ASC("A")
    :
```

Next, we issue the call to INTERRUPT( ), which executes the interrupt. We have pass the number of the interrupt we want to use, &H21, and the variable of type RegType that holds values we want placed in the registers, which we've called InRegs. Interrupt services can also return output values, and we'll receive those values in OutRegs:

```
    DIM InRegs AS RegType, OutRegs AS RegType
    InRegs.ax = &H0200
    InRegs.dx = ASC("A")
→  CALL INTERRUPT(&H21, InRegs, OutRegs)
    :
```

And that's it: the character A is printed on the screen at the current cursor location. Now we've interfaced BASIC to DOS with the INTERRUPT( ) routine.

TIP: All programs that use INTERRUPT( ) or INTERRUPTX( ) must be loaded with the /L switch if you're using QuickBASIC (QB.EXE or QBX.EXE) like this: QB PROG /L or QBX PROG /L.

A DOS Keyboard Service

In InkeyNoEcho$( ), we'll rely on a DOS service, namely interrupt &H21 service 6. This service does exactly what we want; it reads keys from the keyboard but does not echo them on the screen. INT &H21, service 6 console I/O without echo, is shown below (also see the appendix):

Input		Output
ah = 6		
dl = &HFF	→	Zero flag set if no character was ready. Otherwise, al holds character's ASCII code.
dl < &HFF	→	Type ASCII code in dl on screen.

To use this service, we have to load ah with 6 and dl with &HFF. If we load dl with any value but &HFF, this service becomes a printing service; DOS treats the value in dl as an ASCII code and prints it on the screen. In this case, however, we want to receive input, so we place &HFF in dl. The call to INTERRUPT( ) looks like this:

```
DIM InRegs AS RegType, OutRegs AS RegType
InRegs.ax = &H0600
InRegs.dx = &HFF
CALL INTERRUPT(&H21, InRegs, OutRegs)
    :
```

This service has a variety of return values. If the zero flag of the 80 x 86 is set on return, then no key was waiting to be read. The zero flag is one of the nine flags internal to the 80 x 86; from our previous list, we can see that it's bit 6 in OutRegs.flags:

OutRegs.flag bit	Flag
11	Overflow Flag
10	Direction Flag
9	Enable Interrupts Flag
8	Trap Flag

OutRegs.flag bit	Flag
7	Sign Flag
→ 6	Zero Flag
4	Auxiliary Carry Flag
2	Parity Flag
0	Carry Flag

That means we can check whether a character was waiting like this:

```
DIM InRegs AS RegType, OutRegs AS RegType
InRegs.ax = &H0600
InRegs.dx = &HFF
CALL INTERRUPT(&H21, InRegs, OutRegs)

REM No character ready if zero flag set

→ IF (OutRegs.flags AND 2^6) THEN
     InKeyNoEcho$ = ""
        :
        :
```

If no character was waiting (i.e., if the zero flag bit was set), then OutRegs.flags AND 2^6 will be nonzero, and we assign a null string to InKeyNoEcho$, just as you've expect to get from INKEY$.

On the other hand, if a key was waiting, we have to examine its value, which is returned in the al register (the bottom eight bits of OutRegs.ax). If it's nonzero, then it's the ASCII value of the struck key, and we have to turn it into a one character BASIC string before returning:

```
DIM InRegs AS RegType, OutRegs AS RegType
InRegs.ax = &H0600
InRegs.dx = &HFF

CALL INTERRUPT(&H21, InRegs, OutRegs)

REM No character ready if zero flag set

IF (OutRegs.flags AND 2^6) THEN
     InKeyNoEcho$ = ""
ELSE
→    IF (OutRegs.ax AND &HFF)
        InKeyNoEcho$ = CHR$(OutRegs.ax AND &HFF)
     :
     :
```

Again, this is just what you'd expect from INKEY$. Finally, if the ASCII code in al is 0 after the call to this service, it indicates that the pressed key has an extended ASCII value. In this case, we have to make a second call to service 6 to receive the key's scan code. We then make up a two-character string from ASCII 0 (i.e., CHR$(0)) and the key's scan code like this:

```
DIM InRegs AS RegType, OutRegs AS RegType
InRegs.ax = &H0600
InRegs.dx = &HFF

CALL INTERRUPT(&H21, InRegs, OutRegs)

REM No character ready if zero flag set

IF (OutRegs.flags AND 2'6) THEN
    InKeyNoEcho$ = ""
ELSE
    IF (OutRegs.ax AND &HFF) <> 0 THEN
        InKeyNoEcho$ = CHR$(OutRegs.ax AND &HFF)
    ELSE 'Need one more call
        InRegs.ax = &H0600
        InRegs.dx = &HFF
        CALL INTERRUPT(&H21, InRegs, OutRegs)
        InKeyNoEcho$ = CHR$(0) + CHR$(OutRegs.ax AND &HFF)
    END IF
END IF
```

This is also just what you'd expect from INKEY$ if an extended ASCII code was to be returned. In this way, InKeyNoEcho$( ) mimics what you'd see from INKEY$, except that nothing is echoed on the screen as the user is typing.

TIP: Use this function, InKeyNoEcho$( ), when in graphics mode or typing a password. Since it doesn't echo, nothing will appear on the screen.

Listing 1-4 shows the whole function.

Listing 1-4. InKeyNoEcho$( ) Function.		1 of 2

```
TYPE RegType
        ax        AS INTEGER
        bx        AS INTEGER
        cx        AS INTEGER
        dx        AS INTEGER
        bp        AS INTEGER
        si        AS INTEGER
        di        AS INTEGER
```

Listing 1-4. InKeyNoEcho$( ) Function.   2 of 2

```
        flags   AS INTEGER
END TYPE

DECLARE SUB INTERRUPT (IntNo AS INTEGER, InRegs AS RegType, OutRegs AS RegType)

FUNCTION InKeyNoEcho$

    DIM InRegs AS RegType, OutRegs AS RegType
    InRegs.ax = &H0600
    InRegs.dx = &HFF

    CALL INTERRUPT(&H21, InRegs, OutRegs)

    REM No character ready if zero flag set

    IF (OutRegs.flags AND 2^6) THEN
        InKeyNoEcho$ = ""
ELSE
        IF (OutRegs.ax AND &HFF) <> 0 THEN
            InKeyNoEcho$ = CHR$(OutRegs.ax AND &HFF)
        ELSE    'Need one more call
            InRegs.ax = &H0600
            InRegs.dx = &HFF
            CALL INTERRUPT(&H21, InRegs, OutRegs)
            InKeyNoEcho$ = CHR$(0) + CHR$(OutRegs.ax AND &HFF)
        END IF
END IF

END FUNCTION
```

With InkeyNoEcho$( ), we're getting more advanced. We've made use of a DOS service, and that's a step ahead. So far, we've worked through the standard BASIC keyboard input statements and functions: INPUT, INPUT$, LINE INPUT, and INKEY$, and now we've even added an input function of our own, InKeyNoEcho$( ).

The next step is to build on these elementary functions. In professional programs, input routines have to be pretty bulletproof, and we'll see just how that looks when we develop the code to read integers next.

Writing a Professional Input Function

Let's see what a professional input function that reads integer values from the keyboard might look like. We can call it, say, GetInteger%( ); this function should screen numeric input to avoid mistakes, along with the embarassing consequences (e.g., "Redo from start"). That means that it has to check for possible overflows and only accept legal characters.

If an inappropriate number was typed, we can design GetInteger%( ) to simply erase that number and start over, moving the cursor back to where it was when GetInteger%( ) was called. If we've set up the screen in some careful way, this function won't ruin it. Also, like our function GetArrowKey$( ), we can pass a parameter named WarningBeep%. If WarningBeep% is nonzero, we can have GetInteger%( ) beep if a noninteger is entered.

Let's write this function. First, we save the present cursor position and then set up a DO...LOOP WHILE 1 loop, which loops forever (the only way to leave GetInteger%( ) is by typing an integer):

```
FUNCTION GetInteger% (WarningBeep%)

    CursorRow% = CSRLIN
    CursorCol% = POS(0)
→   DO
        :
        :
    LOOP WHILE 1
```

At the beginning of the loop, we read an input string and name it InString$. In this outer loop, we'll loop over these typed-in strings until we get one that we can decode into an integer:

```
FUNCTION GetInteger% (WarningBeep%)

    CursorRow% = CSRLIN
    CursorCol% = POS(0)
    DO
        LINE INPUT InString$ ←
        :
        :
    LOOP WHILE 1
```

We can make a preliminary check on the size of the number by looking at its length; if it's more than six characters, we should start over (the maximum length an integer can be is six characters — five digits and a sign). Let's put in a subroutine named StartOver to do just that:

```
FUNCTION GetInteger% (WarningBeep%)

        CursorRow% = CSRLIN
        CursorCol% = POS(0)
        DO
            LINE INPUT InString$

            IF LEN(InString$) < = 6 THEN
            :
            [Number may be ok]
            :
            ELSE
→               GOSUB StartOver
            END IF 'IF LEN(InString$) < = 6...

        LOOP WHILE 1

StartOver:
        IF WarningBeep% THEN BEEP
        LOCATE CursorRow%, CursorCol%
        PRINT SPACE$(LEN(InString$));
        LOCATE CursorRow%, CursorCol%
        RETURN
```

Now we have to loop over every character in the input string InString$. If it's between 0 and 9 we add it to the running total that will result in the final integer value. The + and - signs are okay *only* if they're the first character in the string. If not, or if we've received any incorrect characters, we have to blank the string on the screen and reset the cursor back to the original position. This is how we check each character:

```
FUNCTION GetInteger% (WarningBeep%)
    CursorRow% = CSRLIN
    CursorCol% = POS(0)
    DO
        LINE INPUT InString$

        IF LEN(InString$) < = 6 THEN
→           FOR i = 1 TO LEN(InString$)
                Char$ = MID$(InString$, i, 1)
                IF Char$ <   = "0" AND Char$   = "9" THEN
                    :
                    Add this digit to running total
                    :
                ELSE
                    :
                    Check if it's a + or a - (ok in the first position)
                    :
                END IF
            NEXT i
        ELSE
            GOSUB StartOver
        END IF 'IF LEN(InString$) < = 6...
    LOOP WHILE 1
```

```
StartOver:
        IF WarningBeep% THEN BEEP
LOCATE CursorRow%, CursorCol%
PRINT SPACES(LEN(InString$));
LOCATE CursorRow%, CursorCol%
RETURN
```

If the character is acceptable, we have to add it to the running total, check if we've had an overflow (we should keep the running total in a LONG integer to avoid upsetting BASIC), and, if so, start over. Let's set up the running total in a variable named SUM& like this:

```
FUNCTION GetInteger% (WarningBeep%)

    CursorRow% = CSRLIN
    CursorCol% = POS(0)
    DO
        LINE INPUT InString$

        NegFlag% = 0
        SUM& = 0
        IF LEN(InString$) < = 6 THEN
            FOR i = 1 TO LEN(InString$)
                Char$ = MID$(InString$, i, 1)
                IF Char$ > = "0" AND Char$ < = "9" THEN
  →                 SUM& = SUM& + (ASC(Char$)-ASC("0"))*10^(LEN(InString$)-i)
                    :
                    :
                END IF
            NEXT i
        ELSE
            GOSUB StartOver
        END IF 'IF LEN(InString$) < = 6...
    LOOP WHILE 1

StartOver:
        IF WarningBeep% THEN BEEP
        LOCATE CursorRow%, CursorCol%
        PRINT SPACES(LEN(InString$));
        LOCATE CursorRow%, CursorCol%
        RETURN
```

TIP: You can convert letters into digits by subtracting the ASCII code for 0; for example, ASC(0) - ASC(0) is 0, ASC(1) - ASC(0) is 1, and so on.

For each digit, we check SUM&. If it's over the limit for INTEGERs, we beep (if required) and start again:

```
FUNCTION GetInteger% (WarningBeep%)

    CursorRow% = CSRLIN
    CursorCol% = POS(0)
    DO
        LINE INPUT InString$

        NegFlag% = 0
        SUM& = 0
        IF LEN(InString$) < = 6 THEN
            FOR i = 1 TO LEN(InString$)
                Char$ = MID$(InString$, i, 1)
                IF Char$ > = "0" AND Char$ < = "9" THEN
                    SUM& = SUM& + (ASC(Char$)-ASC("0"))*10^(LEN(InString$)-i)
        →           IF SUM& > 32767 THEN         'Overflow?
        :               GOSUB StartOver
                        EXIT FOR
                    END IF
                        :
                        :
                END IF
            NEXT i
        ELSE
            GOSUB StartOver
        END IF 'IF LEN(InString$) < = 6...
    LOOP WHILE 1

StartOver:
        IF WarningBeep% THEN BEEP
        LOCATE CursorRow%, CursorCol%
        PRINT SPACES(LEN(InString$));
        LOCATE CursorRow%, CursorCol%
        RETURN
```

Otherwise, we have to check if we've reached the end of the input string. If so, we're done; we set GetInteger% to SUM& and exit the function:

```
FUNCTION GetInteger% (WarningBeep%)

    CursorRow% = CSRLIN
    CursorCol% = POS(0)
    DO
        LINE INPUT InString$

        NegFlag% = 0
        SUM& = 0
        IF LEN(InString$) < = 6 THEN
            FOR i = 1 TO LEN(InString$)
                Char$ = MID$(InString$, i, 1)
                IF Char$ > = "0" AND Char$ < = "9" THEN
                    SUM& = SUM& + (ASC(Char$)-ASC("0"))*10^ (LEN(InString$)-i)
```

```
                        IF SUM& < 32767 THEN        'Overflow?
                            GOSUB StartOver
                            EXIT FOR
                        END IF
     →                  IF i = LEN(InString$) THEN
     :                      IF NegFlag% THEN SUM& = -SUM&
     :                      GetInteger% = SUM&
                            EXIT FUNCTION
                        END IF
                ELSE
                        :
                        :
                END IF
            NEXT i
        ELSE
            GOSUB StartOver
        END IF 'IF LEN(InString$) < = 6...
    LOOP WHILE 1

StartOver:
        IF WarningBeep% THEN BEEP
        LOCATE CursorRow%, CursorCol%
        PRINT SPACE$(LEN(InString$));
        LOCATE CursorRow%, CursorCol%
        RETURN
```

TIP: You can assign variables of two different types to each other in BASIC, as in the statement: GetInteger% = SUM&. In this case, the value in SUME& is truncated (its upper bits are lost) so that it fits into the integer GetInterger%.

So far, we've only taken characters that are ASCII digits. Now we have to check if the current character is a + or -. For any other character, we have to start over. Let's check for + or -. These sign characters are acceptable in integers only if they're the *first* character. We check that this way:

```
FUNCTION GetInteger% (WarningBeep%)

    CursorRow% = CSRLIN
    CursorCol% = POS(0)
    DO
        LINE INPUT InString$

        NegFlag% = 0
        SUM& = 0
        IF LEN(InString$) < = 6 THEN
            FOR i = 1 TO LEN(InString$)
                Char$ = MID$(InString$, i, 1)
                IF Char$ > = "0" AND Char$ < = "9" THEN
                    SUM& = SUM& + (ASC(Char$)-ASC("0"))*10^ (LEN(InString$)-i)
```

```
                        IF SUM& > 32767 THEN        - 'Overflow?
                            GOSUB StartOver
                            EXIT FOR
                        END IF
                        IF i = LEN(InString$) THEN
                            IF NegFlag% THEN SUM& = -SUM&
                            GetInteger% = SUM&
                            EXIT FUNCTION
                        END IF
                    ELSE
  →                     IF (Char$ = "-" OR Char$ = "+") AND i = 1 THEN
                            :
                        [Character is an acceptable sign]
                            :
                        END IF
                    END IF
                NEXT i
            ELSE
                GOSUB StartOver
            END IF 'IF LEN(InString$) < = 6...
        LOOP WHILE 1

StartOver:
        IF WarningBeep% THEN BEEP
        LOCATE CursorRow%, CursorCol%
        PRINT SPACE$(LEN(InString$));
        LOCATE CursorRow%, CursorCol%
        RETURN
```

If the sign is -, then we note that by setting the negative flag (NegFlag%) to 1 so we can return -SUM& later. Note that we also have to make sure that, even if the sign is the first character, there are more characters to come (i.e. the digits). Otherwise, + or - by itself would be an acceptable input. We check that this way, making note of a negative sign if we have to:

```
FUNCTION GetInteger% (WarningBeep%)
    CursorRow% = CSRLIN
    CursorCol% = POS(0)
    DO
        LINE INPUT InString$

        NegFlag% = 0
        SUM& = 0
        IF LEN(InString$) < = 6 THEN
            FOR i = 1 TO LEN(InString$)
                Char$ = MID$(InString$, i, 1)
                IF Char$ > = "0" AND Char$ < = "9" THEN
                    SUM& = SUM& + (ASC(Char$)-ASC("0"))*10^(LEN(InString$)-i)
                    IF SUM& > 32767 THEN         'Overflow?
                        GOSUB StartOver
                        EXIT FOR
```

```
                        END IF
                        IF i = LEN(InString$) THEN
                            IF NegFlag% THEN SUM& = -SUM&
                            GetInteger% = SUM&
                            EXIT FUNCTION
                        END IF
                    ELSE
      →             IF (Char$ = "-" OR Char$ = "+") AND i = 1 THEN
      :                 IF LEN(InString$) = 1 THEN
      :                     GOSUB StartOver
                            EXIT FOR
                        END IF
                        IF Char$ = "-" THEN NegFlag% = 1
                    ELSE
                        :
                        Character was not "0"-"9" or "+" or "-" -- start over.
                        :
                    END IF
                END IF
            NEXT i
        ELSE
            GOSUB StartOver
        END IF 'IF LEN(InString$)< = 6...
    LOOP WHILE 1

StartOver:
        IF WarningBeep% THEN BEEP
        LOCATE CursorRow%, CursorCol%
        PRINT SPACES(LEN(InString$));
        LOCATE CursorRow%, CursorCol%
        RETURN
```

Now we're left with characters that are illegal; they're not 0 to 9, nor are they valid signs. In that case, we beep (if required) and start over:

```
FUNCTION GetInteger% (WarningBeep%)

CursorRow% = CSRLIN
CursorCol% = POS(0)
DO
    LINE INPUT InString$

    NegFlag% = 0
    SUM& = 0
    IF LEN(InString$) < = 6 THEN
        FOR i = 1 TO LEN(InString$)
            Char$ = MID$(InString$, i, 1)
            IF Char$ > = "0" AND Char$ < = "9" THEN
                SUM& = SUM& + (ASC(Char$)-ASC("0"))*10^(LEN(InString$) - i)
                IF SUM& > 32767 THEN        'Overflow?
                    GOSUB StartOver
                    EXIT FOR
                END IF
```

```
              IF i = LEN(InString$) THEN
                   IF NegFlag% THEN SUM& = -SUM&
                   GetInteger% = SUM&
                   EXIT FUNCTION
            END IF
         ELSE
            IF (Char$ = "-" OR Char$ = "+") AND i = 1 THEN
                IF LEN(InString$) = 1 THEN
                GOSUB StartOver
                EXIT FOR
            END IF
            IF Char$ = "-" THEN NegFlag% = 1
         ELSE
            GOSUB StartOver
            EXIT FOR
         END IF
      END IF
   NEXT i
 ELSE
   GOSUB StartOver
 END IF 'IF LEN(InString$) < = 6...
LOOP WHILE 1

StartOver:
      IF WarningBeep% THEN BEEP
      LOCATE CursorRow%, CursorCol%
      PRINT SPACE$(LEN(InString$));
      LOCATE CursorRow%, CursorCol%
      RETURN
```

And we're done. You can see that accepting bulletproof INTEGER input is not necessarily an easy task, but now that task is done for us. Listing 1-5 shows the whole function.

TIP: Use this function, Get Integer% ( ), to replace INKEY$ or LINE INPUT when numerical input is required, as in spreadsheet, calculator, or accounting programs.

Listing 1-5. Get Integer% Function. 1 of 2

```
DECLARE FUNCTION GetInteger% (WarningBeep%)

FUNCTION GetInteger% (WarningBeep%)

CursorRow% = CSRLIN
CursorCol% = POS(0)
DO
    LINE INPUT InString$

    NegFlag% = 0
```

Listing 1-5.   Get Integer% Function.   **2 of 2**

```
      SUM& = 0
      IF LEN(InString$) < = 6 THEN
         FOR i = 1 TO LEN(InString$)
             Char$ = MID$(InString$, i, 1)
             IF Char$ > = "0" AND Char$ < = "9" THEN
                SUM& = SUM& + (ASC(Char$)-ASC("0"))*10^(LEN(InString$) - i)
                IF SUM& > 32767 THEN 'Overflow?
                    GOSUB StartOver
                    EXIT FOR
                  END IF
                IF i = LEN(InString$) THEN
                    IF NegFlag% THEN SUM& = -SUM&
                    GetInteger% = SUM&
                    EXIT FUNCTION
                END IF
             ELSE
                 IF (Char$ = "-" OR Char$ = "+") AND i = 1 THEN
                 IF LEN(InString$) = 1 THEN
                    GOSUB StartOver
                    EXIT FOR
                 END IF
                 IF Char$ = "-" THEN NegFlag% = 1
             ELSE
                 GOSUB StartOver
                 EXIT FOR
             END IF 'IF legal sign
         END IF 'IF Char$ > = "0" AND Char$ < = "9"...
      NEXT i
   ELSE
             GOSUB StartOver
   END IF 'IF LEN(InString$) < = 6...

   LOOP WHILE 1
StartOver:
         IF WarningBeep% THEN BEEP
         LOCATE CursorRow%, CursorCol%
         PRINT SPACES$(LEN(InString$));
         LOCATE CursorRow%, CursorCol%
         RETURN

         END FUNCTION
```

Now we've advanced even more. We've built a fairly rugged input routine out of the primitive BASIC input functions. The next step up is to accept and work with even more complicated input. For example, we can break our input up into manageable components by *parsing* it.

Interpreting Our Keyboard Input

Our parsing example is going to be pretty simple. We're just going to write a reverse Polish calculator program. It will accept and calculate problems of variable length, such as these:

2 3 + 4 -   [Answer: 1]
3.1 2.1 - 10 * 5 + [Answer: 6]

In other words, in the first example, 2 3 + 4 -, 2 is placed on the calculator's *stack*, then 3 is added to it, giving 5. Next, 4 is subtracted from that value, leaving 1.

Let's see how to make this work. Our parsing example is not going to be exactly bulletproof. In a real program, parsers must be able to tolerate multiple spaces, different delimiters, upper and lower case characters, trailing or leading spaces, and any number of other difficulties. However, that would make our parsing example very long; all we want to demonstrate here is the essential idea of parsing, which is to break input up into its component parts. In this program, we're just going to place the input into a string and parse it in an elementary way by peeling successive terms off from the left.

TIP:	After you put together a good parsing routine once, you can use it in all programs that read input.

Let's put this together. First, we get the expression to compute from the keyboard, and we can name it CurrentString$:

```
→ LINE INPUT "Expression to calculate:"; CurrentString$
    :
    :
```

We can add some minimal error checking by making sure that CurrentString$ is at least five characters long, which is the absolute minimum (e.g., 2 3 +):

```
LINE INPUT "Expression to calculate:"; CurrentString$
IF LEN(CurrentString$) >= 5 THEN        Five characters is absolute min.
    :
    :
END IF
```

Next, we can call the function that actually does the parsing NextTerm$( ). For example, if CurrentString$ was equal to 2 3 + 4 -, NextTerm$(CurrentString$) should return 2, and CurrentString$ would be truncated to 3 + 4 -. If CurrentString$ was 3.1 2.1 - 10 *

5 +, NextTerm$(CurrentString$) would return 3.1, and CurrentString$ would be truncated to 2.1 - 10 * 5 +.

Let's get the first term (i.e., the 2 in 2 3 +) and load it into a variable named RPStack! as the reverse Polish calculator's stack value. We can convert the string returned by Next Term$( ) into a numeric value with the BASIC function VAL( ):

```
→ DECLARE FUNCTION NextTerm$ (StringToParse$)

  LINE INPUT "Expression to calculate:"; CurrentString$

  IF LEN(CurrentString$) >= 5 THEN              'Five characters is absolute min.
→         RPStack! = VAL(NextTerm$(CurrentString$)) 'Get 1st term.
          :
          :
  END IF

  PRINT "Result:", RPStack!
```

Now we should get the next term, followed by an operator, and perform the operation. Then we have to keep going as long as there are still characters in CurrentString$, so let's set up a loop that will continue WHILE CurrentString$ < > "":

```
  DECLARE FUNCTION NextTerm$ (StringToParse$)

  LINE INPUT "Expression to calculate:"; CurrentString$

  IF LEN(CurrentString$) >= 5 THEN       'Five characters is absolute min.

          RPStack! = VAL(NextTerm$(CurrentString$)) 'Get 1st term.
→         DO
:                  NewTerm! = VAL(NextTerm$(CurrentString$))
:                  Operator$ = NextTerm$(CurrentString$)
                   :
→         LOOP WHILE CurrentString$ <> ""
  END IF
```

We can perform the actual operations themselves in a SELECT CASE statement:

```
  DECLARE FUNCTION NextTerm$ (StringToParse$)

  LINE INPUT "Expression to calculate:"; CurrentString$

  IF LEN(CurrentString$) >= 5 THEN       'Five characters is absolute min.

          RPStack! = VAL(NextTerm$(CurrentString$)) 'Get 1st term.
```

```
        DO
                NewTerm! = VAL(NextTerm$(CurrentString$))
                Operator$ = NextTerm$(CurrentString$)
  →             SELECT CASE Operator$
                        CASE "+"
                                RPStack! = RPStack! + NewTerm!
                        CASE "-"
                                RPStack! = RPStack! - NewTerm!
                        CASE "*"
                                RPStack! = RPStack! * NewTerm!
                        CASE "/"
                                RPStack! = RPStack! / NewTerm!
                        CASE ELSE
                                PRINT "Bad operator:"; Operator$
                                END
  →             END SELECT
        LOOP WHILE CurrentString$ <> ""
  END IF
```

| TIP: | The SELECT CASE statement in BASIC was designed to replace a "ladder" or series of IF...THEN...ELSE statements. Use SELECT CASE wherever possible instead of multiple IF statements—your code will execute faster. |

At the end of this loop over CurrentString$, we've exhausted the input string, and the result is left in RPStack!. We can print that out like this:

```
DECLARE FUNCTION NextTerm$ (StringToParse$)

LINE INPUT "Expression to calculate:"; CurrentString$

IF LEN(CurrentString$) >= 5 THEN 'Five characters is absolute min.

        RPStack! = VAL(NextTerm$(CurrentString$)) 'Get 1st term.

        DO
                NewTerm! = VAL(NextTerm$(CurrentString$))
                Operator$ = NextTerm$(CurrentString$)
                SELECT CASE Operator$
                        CASE "+"
                                RPStack! = RPStack! + NewTerm!
                        CASE "-"
                                RPStack! = RPStack! - NewTerm!
                        CASE "*"
                                RPStack! = RPStack! * NewTerm!
                        CASE "/"
                                RPStack! = RPStack! / NewTerm!
                        CASE ELSE
```

```
                                     PRINT "Bad operator:"; Operator$
                                     END
                   END SELECT
              LOOP WHILE CurrentString$ <> ""
     END IF
     PRINT "Result:", RPStack!
```

We still have to write the parsing function NextTerm$( ). Its job is to accept a string, find the first term in that string (as bounded by a trailing space), return that term and truncate the input string. We should start by finding the length of the leftmost term in the string so that we can chop it off:

```
DECLARE FUNCTION NextTerm$ (StringToParse$)

LINE INPUT "Expression to calculate:"; CurrentString$

IF LEN(CurrentString$) >= 5 THEN        'Five characters is absolute min.

     RPStack! = VAL(NextTerm$(CurrentString$)) 'Get 1st term.

     DO
              NewTerm! = VAL(NextTerm$(CurrentString$))
              Operator$ = NextTerm$(CurrentString$)
              SELECT CASE Operator$
                      CASE "+"
                              RPStack! = RPStack! + NewTerm!
                      CASE "-"
                              RPStack! = RPStack! - NewTerm!
                      CASE "*"
                              RPStack! = RPStack! * NewTerm!
                      CASE "/"
                              RPStack! = RPStack! / NewTerm!
                      CASE ELSE
                              PRINT "Bad operator:"; Operator$
                              END
              END SELECT
     LOOP WHILE CurrentString$
END IF

PRINT "Result:", RPStack!

FUNCTION NextTerm$ (StringToParse$)
→        TermLength% = INSTR(StringToParse$, "") - 1 'Find a space?
         :
         :
END FUNCTION
```

Here we've searched ahead for the first space with the BASIC function INSTR( ). For example, in the string 3.1 2.1 - 10 * 5 +, TermLength% would now be set like this:

TermLength% = 3

$\overbrace{3.1}$ 2.1 - 10 * 5 +

Now that we know where to chop off the first term, we should also figure out the length of the remaining string (so we can truncate it):

```
DECLARE FUNCTION NextTerm$ (StringToParse$)

LINE INPUT "Expression to calculate:"; CurrentString$

IF LEN(CurrentString$) >= 5 THEN          'Five characters is absolute min.

        RPStack! = VAL(NextTerm$(CurrentString$)) 'Get 1st term.

        DO
                NewTerm! = VAL(NextTerm$(CurrentString$))
                Operator $ = NextTerm$(CurrentString$)
                SELECT CASE Operator$
                        CASE "+"
                                RPStack! = RPStack! + NewTerm!
                        CASE "-"
                                RPStack! = RPStack! - NewTerm!
                        CASE "*"
                                RPStack! = RPStack! * NewTerm!
                        CASE "/"
                                RPStack! = RPStack! / NewTerm!
                        CASE ELSE
                                PRINT "Bad operator: "; Operator$
                                END
                END SELECT
        LOOP WHILE CurrentString$ <>

END IF
PRINT "Result:", RPStack!

FUNCTION NextTerm$ (StringToParse$)
        TermLength% = INSTR(StringToParse$, "") - 1 'Find a space?
→       NewStringLen% = LEN(StringToParse$)- TermLength% - 1
        :
        :
END FUNCTION
```

In the string 3.1 2.1 - 10 * 5 +, this is what the new string length would be:

TermLength% = 3

$\overbrace{3.1}$ $\underbrace{2.1 - 10 * 5 +}$

NewStringLen% = 14

However, we should also realize that if there was no space in the string, we've reached its end. In that case, we have to set the length of the first term to the length of the string, and the new length of the string after truncation to 0:

```
DECLARE FUNCTION NextTerm$ (StringToParse$)

LINE INPUT "Expression to calculate:"; CurrentString$

IF LEN(CurrentString$) >= 5 THEN        'Five characters is absolute min.

        RPStack! = VAL(NextTerm$(CurrentString$)) 'Get 1st term.

        DO
                NewTerm! = VAL(NextTerm$(CurrentString$))
                Operator$ = NextTerm$(CurrentString$)
                SELECT CASE Operator$
                        CASE "+"
                                RPStack! = RPStack! + NewTerm!
                        CASE "-"
                                RPStack! = RPStack! - NewTerm!
                        CASE "*"
                                RPStack! = RPStack! * NewTerm!
                        CASE "/"
                                RPStack! = RPStack! / NewTerm!
                        CASE ELSE
                                PRINT "Bad operator:"; Operator$
                                END
                END SELECT
        LOOP WHILE CurrentString$ <> ""
END IF

PRINT "Result:", RPStack!

FUNCTION NextTerm$ (StringToParse$)
        TermLength% = INSTR(StringToParse$, "") - 1 'Find a space?
        NewStringLen% = LEN(StringToParse$)- TermLength% - 1
→       IF TermLength% = -1 THEN 'No -- end of input string
:               TermLength% = LEN(StringToParse$)
:               NewStringLen% = 0
        END IF
        :
END FUNCTION
```

Now we're ready to chop off the first term in the input string (using LEFT$( )), and to truncate the string itself (using RIGHT$( )) as shown in Listing 1-6.

Listing 1-6. Input Parsing Function.

```
DECLARE FUNCTION NextTerm$ (StringToParse$)

LINE INPUT "Expression to calculate:"; CurrentString$

IF LEN(CurrentString$) >= 5 THEN          'Five characters is absolute min.

        RPStack! = VAL(NextTerm$(CurrentString$)) 'Get 1st term.
        DO
                NewTerm! = VAL(NextTerm$(CurrentString$))
                Operator$ = NextTerm$(CurrentString$)
                SELECT CASE Operator$
                        CASE "+"
                                RPStack! = RPStack! + NewTerm!
                        CASE "-"
                                RPStack! = RPStack! - NewTerm!
                        CASE "*"
                                RPStack! = RPStack! * NewTerm!
                        CASE "/"
                                RPStack! = RPStack! / NewTerm!
                        CASE ELSE
                                PRINT "Bad operator:"; Operator$
                                END
                END SELECT
        LOOP WHILE CurrentString$ <> ""
END IF

PRINT "Result:", RPStack!

FUNCTION NextTerm$ (StringToParse$)
        TermLength% = INSTR(StringToParse$, "") - 1 'Find a space?
        NewStringLen% = LEN(StringToParse$)- TermLength% - 1
        IF TermLength% = -1 THEN 'No -- end of input string
                TermLength% = LEN(StringToParse$)
                NewStringLen% = 0
        END IF
→       NextTerm$ = LEFT$(StringToParse$, TermLength%) 'Next term
        StringToParse$ = RIGHT$(StringToParse$, NewStringLen%)
END FUNCTION
```

   And that's all there is to it — we've chopped off the first term and truncated the string. We pass the term we've isolated back to the calling program, and it loops over them, multiplying or adding as required until all the terms are used up. At that point, we print out the result and the calculator is done.

Conclusion

That's it for our chapter on keyboard input. We've worked through the built-in resources of BASIC, seen how to add a few of our own, put together a bulletproof input routine of the kind used in real applications, and even seen some keyboard parsing at work. Now that we've made a survey of input, however, it's time to start looking at some output, and we do that with our own windows in Chapter 2.

Windows

IN THIS CHAPTER, we're going to develop a powerful set of functions and subprograms—ones that will let you add windows to your programs. With a few simple calls, you'll be able to pop a window up on the screen in the color you specify, print to it, and hide it again. This can augment your programs tremendously, giving them a professional feel. Towards the end of the chapter, we'll also see what the BASIC PDS has to offer in terms of creating our own windows. Let's get started immediately.

Designing Our Window System

We have to design our window system to be able to work with multiple windows; it's rare for a program that uses windows to use only one window. This means that we have to have some easy way of referring to a particular window. We don't want to have a different, and lengthy, subroutine for each window (i.e., CALL InitWindow1( ), CALL InitWindow2( ), CALL ShowWindow1( ), etc.).

The best way (and the way that's used by professional windows packages as well as the OS/2 Presentation Manager) is to use window *handles*; that is, a number that we can assign to each window. If we design our window system to work with up to, say, eight windows, then a window's handle will be its index number among those eight (see Figure 2-1).

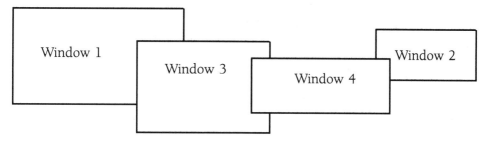

Figure 2-1

That makes the process we'll develop in this chapter simple. For example, to put a window on the screen, print "Now is the time." in it, and then make it vanish, these are the steps we'd take:

1. Get a handle for the window with the function we'll write named WindowGetHandle%( ). This function lets you design and initialize the window.

2. Call another subprogram we'll develop, named WindowShow( ), to display the window. The only argument it needs is the window's handle.

3. Call another new function WindowPrint%( ), passing it the window's handle and the text to print: "Now is the time."

4. Finally, call WindowHide( ), again passing the window's handle, to make the window vanish.

Now that we have a plan, we can start writing code. The natural place to begin is with the window initialization function, WindowGetHandle%( ).

Initializing Our Window System

The purpose of WindowGethandle%( ) is to initialize a window; this is always the necessary first call. When you set up and design a window (what size to make it, where it will be on the screen, and so on), you use WindowGetHandle%( ). This function must return the window's handle, which we can make an integer ranging from 1 to 8.

When we're programming later, we'll keep track of this handle; now we have a "name" for the window, and we'll pass this value when we make any window call. In this way, the window system knows which of the up to eight possible windows we're referring to.

Note that initializing a window does not make it appear on the screen. The standard window technique is to allow them to be invisible while we work on them, or move them around or whatever, which lets us perform actions behind the scenes. To display a window after we've initialized it, we can call WindowShow(Handle%), where Handle% is the window's handle. To hide it again, we can call WindowHide(Handle%).

To initialize a window, we'll need its screen position. Let's pass the screen coordinates of the top left corner of the window to WindowGetHandle%( ). In BASIC, (1,1) is the top left corner of the screen and (25,80) is the bottom right (see Figure 2-2).

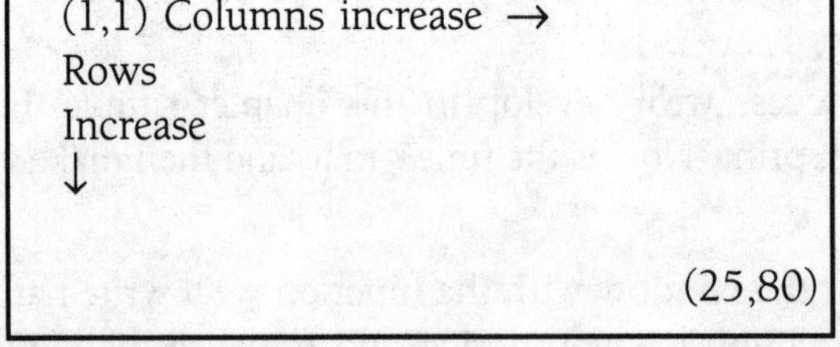

```
(1,1) Columns increase  →
Rows
Increase
↓

                                    (25,80)
```

Figure 2-2. The Screen

Also, we'll need window's size—we can pass the number of rows and columns to use. Finally, we should be able to give it a color, so let's pass a screen attribute (there is a complete discussion of screen attributes and how to use them coming up). In other words, the way we'd use WindowGetHandle%( ) is like this:

```
MyHandle% = WindowGetHandle% (TopR%, TopC%, NRow%, NCol%, Attr%)
```

where this is what each parameter means:

TopR%	INTEGER	Screen row of window's top left corner (1 = top of screen)
TopC%	INTEGER	Screen column of window's top left corner (1 = extreme left of screen)
NRow%	INTEGER	Number of rows the window is long
NCol%	INTEGER	Number of columns the window is wide
Attr%	INTEGER	Screen attribute to use displaying the window.

To use these values, WindowGetHandle%( ) is going to have to fill internal window variables with the values you've given it. All the other subprograms in the window system can then communicate through *COMMONs*, allowing them to read these variables. If you're not familiar with the idea behind the COMMON statement, it's simple: a COMMON lets the various modules in your program communicate with each other. For example, if you had three variables, A%, B%, and C%, you could share them among all your modules by including a line like this in the beginning of each one (see Figure 2-3).

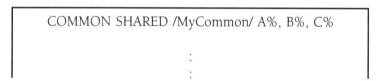

COMMON SHARED /MyCommon/ A%, B%, C%

Figure 2-3

Adding the SHARED keyword makes these variables available to all the subprograms and functions in the current module. Now, A%, B%, and C% can be used anywhere in the entire program by name. Every time you use them, you access the same memory location, so if you change A% from 3 to 5, it'll be 5 for every other part of the program too. Using COMMONs, all the window subprograms can all operate independently of each other, which means that we'll only need to link in the window functions we want to use, not the whole system. This way, we can develop our windows in a number of bite-sized subprograms, not as one huge unwieldy monster.

> **TIP:** Breaking your programs up into manageable pieces is called *Modular* programming and it makes program development and debugging much easier. The COMMON statement is the backbone of modular programming and, as such, is exceptionally powerful.

Filling the Window Arrays

Let's start setting up the arrays we'll need to hold the data for our windows. For example, we'll need an array to hold the screen attribute of each window. Let's call that array Attribute( ). If we want eight windows, the index of Attribute( ) has to range from 1 to 8. At some later date, we may want more than eight windows, so let's not make that number firm. Instead, we can start with a constant named MaxWindows, which we set to 8:

```
FUNCTION WindowGetHandle% (TopR%, TopC%, NRow%, NCol%, Attr%)

→        CONST MaxWindows = 8
         :
         :
```

Later, if we want to increase or decrease the number of windows available, this is the only number to change (there is no limit). Keep in mind, however, that we'll eat up memory if we increase it too much.

The next step is to store the data that we've been passed. There must be an array for each window variable; the index of that array ranges over the number of windows. In fact, the index will be the window's handle. If we're asked to display window 3, that window's attribute will be in Attribute(3).

An important quantity for each window is the number of rows and columns it has, and we can store those values like this:

```
FUNCTION WindowGetHandle% (TopR%, TopC%, NRow%, NCol%, Attr%)

         CONST MaxWindows = 8
→        DIM Rows(1 TO MaxWindows) AS INTEGER
         DIM Cols(1 TO MaxWindows) AS INTEGER
         :
         :
```

Next, we can store the screen coordinates of each window like this:

```
FUNCTION WindowGetHandle% (TopR%, TopC%, NRow%, NCol%, Attr%)

          CONST Max Windows = 8
          DIM Rows(1 TO MaxWindows) AS INTEGER
          DIM Cols(1 TO MaxWindows) AS INTEGER
  →       DIM Toprow(1 TO MaxWindows) AS INTEGER
          DIM TopCol(1 TO MaxWindows) AS INTEGER
          DIM BotRow(1 TO MaxWindows) AS INTEGER
          DIM BotCol(1 TO MaxWindows) AS INTEGER
          :
          :
```

Here, the top left corner of the window is (TopRow, TopCol) and the bottom right corner is (BotRow, BotCol). Following this, we can store the window's attribute, like this:

```
FUNCTION WindowGetHandle% (TopR%, TopC%, NRow%, NCol%, Attr%)

          CONST MaxWindows = 8
          DIM Rows(1 TO MaxWindows) AS INTEGER
          DIM Cols(1 TO MaxWindows) AS INTEGER
          DIM Toprow(1 TO MaxWindows) AS INTEGER
          DIM TopCol(1 TO MaxWindows) AS INTEGER
          DIM BotRow(1 TO MaxWindows) AS INTEGER
          DIM BotCol(1 TO MaxWindows) AS INTEGER
  →       DIM Attribute(1 TO MaxWindows) AS INTEGER
          :
          :
```

Now we can store the text in the window itself. Let's treat every row of the window as its own string; we can set up an array named Text(Maxwindows, 25) AS STRING to hold these strings. Assume if window 3 looks like Figure 2-4).

```
Now is the
time for all
good men to
```

Figure 2-4

Then, Text(3, 1) would equal "Now is the "; Text(3, 2) would equal "time for all"; and so on. Here's that array. (Note that we have to allow up to 25 rows for each window.)

```
FUNCTION WindowGetHandle% (TopR%, TopC%, NRow%, NCol%, Attr%)

        CONST MaxWindows = 8
        DIM Rows(1 TO MaxWindows) AS INTEGER
        DIM Cols(1 TO MaxWindows) AS INTEGER
        DIM Toprow(1 TO MaxWindows) AS INTEGER
        DIM TopCol(1 TO MaxWindows) AS INTEGER
        DIM BotRow(1 TO MaxWindows) AS INTEGER
        DIM BotCol(1 TO MaxWindows) AS INTEGER
        DIM Attribute(1 TO MaxWindows) AS INTEGER
    →   DIM Text(MaxWindows, 25) AS STRING
        :
        :
```

Note that when we hide our window again, we'll want to restore the text that was already there on the screen. This means that we have to store the text that we overwrote when we displayed our window. We can store that text in an array named OldText( ).

However, there is also a screen attribute for each position on the screen, which determines the colors of that character, and that means that besides the text we'll have to store the old screen attributes. Since the screen can be multicolored (we may even be overlapping other, colored windows), we have to store the screen attribute of *each* screen position we overwrite, as well as the character that was there. Since a screen attribute is a byte, we can store them in strings too:

```
FUNCTION WindowGetHandle% (TopR%, TopC%, NRow%, NCol%, Attr%)

        CONST MaxWindows = 8
        DIM Rows(1 TO MaxWindows) AS INTEGER
        DIM Cols(1 TO MaxWindows) AS INTEGER
        DIM Toprow(1 TO MaxWindows) AS INTEGER
        DIM TopCol(1 TO MaxWindows) AS INTEGER
        DIM BotRow(1 TO MaxWindows) AS INTEGER
        DIM BotCol(1 TO MaxWindows) AS INTEGER
        DIM Attribute(1 TO MaxWindows) AS INTEGER
        DIM Text(MaxWindows, 25) AS STRING
    →   DIM OldText(MaxWindows, 25) AS STRING
        DIM OldAttrb(MaxWindows, 25) AS STRING
        :
        :
```

And that's almost it. We've stored the window's complete specification, including its size and color. We've set up room for the text in the window, and back-up space for the text that will be overwritten, as well as the screen attributes that will be overwritten.

The final item we need is an internal variable that indicates whether the window is actually visible or not (if we didn't include this value, all windows would be on all the time). Let's add a flag indicating whether a window is visible, calling it OnFlag( ). If

OnFlag(5) equals 1, for example, window 5 is currently visible. If it's 0, the window is hidden. Here's how we can add that:

```
FUNCTION WindowGetHandle% (TopR%, TopC%, NRow%, NCol%, Attr%)

        CONST MaxWindows = 8
        DIM Rows(1 TO MaxWindows) AS INTEGER
        DIM Cols(1 TO MaxWindows) AS INTEGER
        DIM Toprow(1 TO MaxWindows) AS INTEGER
        DIM TopCol(1 TO MaxWindows) AS INTEGER
        DIM BotRow(1 TO MaxWindows) AS INTEGER
        DIM BotCol(1 TO MaxWindows) AS INTEGER
        DIM Attribute(1 TO MaxWindows) AS INTEGER
        DIM Text(MaxWindows, 25) AS STRING
        DIM OldText(MaxWindows, 25) AS STRING
        DIM OldAttrb(MaxWindows, 25) AS STRING
    →   DIM OnFlag(1 TO MaxWindows) AS INTEGER
        :
        :
```

And that's it. That's all the storage we'll need for our window system. All we have to do now is to set up the commons to communicate these arrays to other subprograms and then fill the arrays with the values passed to us.

The complete function is shown in Listing 2-1.

Listing 2-1. WindowGetHandle Function.   1 of 2

```
FUNCTION WindowGetHandle% (TopR%, TopC%, NRow%, NCol%, Attr%)

        CONST MaxWindows = 8
        DIM Rows(1 TO MaxWindows) AS INTEGER
        DIM Cols(1 TO MaxWindows) AS INTEGER
        DIM Toprow(1 TO MaxWindows) AS INTEGER
        DIM TopCol(1 TO MaxWindows) AS INTEGER
        DIM BotRow(1 TO MaxWindows) AS INTEGER
        DIM BotCol(1 TO MaxWindows) AS INTEGER
        DIM Attribute(1 TO MaxWindows) AS INTEGER
        DIM OnFlag(1 TO MaxWindows) AS INTEGER
        DIM Text(MaxWindows, 25) AS STRING
        DIM OldText(MaxWindows, 25) AS STRING
        DIM OldAttrb(MaxWindows, 25) AS STRING
    →   COMMON SHARED /WindowA/ Rows() AS INTEGER, Cols() AS INTEGER, _
    :           Toprow() AS INTEGER, TopCol() AS INTEGER, BotRow() AS INTEGER, _
                BotCol() AS INTEGER
        COMMON SHARED /WindowB/ Attribute() AS INTEGER, OnFlag() AS INTEGER, _
                Text() AS STRING, OldText() AS STRING, OldAttrb() AS STRING
```

Listing 2-1.   WindowGetHandle Function.   2 of 2

```
DECLARE FUNCTION WindowGetHandle% (TopR%, TopC%, NRow%, NCol%, Attr%)

        CONST MaxWindows = 8
        DIM Rows(1 TO MaxWindows) AS INTEGER
        DIM Cols(1 TO MaxWindows) AS INTEGER
        DIM Toprow(1 TO MaxWindows) AS INTEGER
        DIM TopCol(1 TO MaxWindows) AS INTEGER
        DIM BotRow(1 TO MaxWindows) AS INTEGER
        DIM BotCol(1 TO MaxWindows) AS INTEGER
        DIM Attribute(1 TO MaxWindows) AS INTEGER
        DIM OnFlag(1 TO MaxWindows) AS INTEGER
        DIM Text(MaxWindows, 25) AS STRING
        DIM OldText(MaxWindows, 25) AS STRING
        DIM OldAttrb(MaxWindows, 25) AS STRING
        COMMON SHARED /WindowA/ Rows() AS INTEGER, Cols() AS INTEGER, _
                Toprow( ) AS INTEGER, TopCol() AS INTEGER, BotRow() AS INTEGER, _
                BotCol( ) AS INTEGER
        COMMON SHARED /WindowB/ Attribute() AS INTEGER, OnFlag() AS INTEGER, _
                Text() AS STRING, OldText() AS STRING, OldAttrb() AS STRING
FUNCTION WindowGetHandle% (TopR%, TopC%, NRow%, NCol%, Attr%)
        WindowGetHandle% = 0

→       FOR i = 1 TO MaxWindows
:
            IF Rows(i) = 0 THEN
:               WindowGetHandle% = i
                Toprow(i) = TopR%
                TopCol(i) = TopC%
                BotRow(i) = TopR% + NRow%
                BotCol(i) = TopC% + NCol%
                Rows(i) = NRow%
                Cols(i) = NCol%
                Attribute(i) = Attr%
                OnFlag(i) = 0
                FOR j = 1 TO Rows(i)
                    Text(i, j) = SPACE$(Cols(i))
                NEXT j
            EXIT FOR
            END IF
        NEXT i

END FUNCTION
```

Note again that the window's handle is its index in the window arrays. When Win-dowGetHandle%( ) is called, we have to find the first available array index to give the new window and return as its handle. We can do that by checking Rows(i), the first of our window arrays:

```
FOR i = 1 TO MaxWindows
→    IF Rows(i) = 0 THEN
        WindowGetHandle% = i
        Toprow(i) = TopR%
        TopCol(i) = TopC%
        BotRow(i) = TopR% + NRow%
        BotCol(i) = TopC% + NCol%
        Rows(i) = NRow%
        Cols(i) = NCol%
        Attribute(i) = Attr%
        OnFlag(i) = 0
        FOR j = 1 TO Rows(i)
            Text(i, j) = SPACE$(Cols(i))
        NEXT j
    EXIT FOR
    END IF
NEXT i
```

If we find that, say, Rows(4) equals 0, there is no window 4 (you can't have zero rows), so we'll return that value as the window's handle. Then we fill the arrays with the various values (Rows(4), Cols(4), and so on).

Now we've written WindowGetHandle%( ), and stored all the necessary window data. We've taken the first step towards developing our window system. Let's see this function in action.

A Window Initializing Example

To prepare our example of WindowGetHandle%( ), let's make sure we know how to set up all the values it requires. That list looks like this:

TopR%	INTEGER	Screen row of window's top left corner (1 = top of screen)
TopC%	INTEGER	Screen column of window's top left corner (1 = extreme left of screen)
NRow%	INTEGER	Number of rows the window is long
NCol%	INTEGER	Number of columns the window is wide
Attr%	INTEGER	Screen attribute to use displaying the window.

In particular, we have to supply a *screen attribute.* we pass this as an INTEGER, but only the bottom 8 bits matter; this byte determines the colors of the window and its text. For example, we can select green characters on a blue background, or yellow character on a red background. (Note: Set bit to 1 to turn on that particular color.) A screen attribute byte looks like Figure 2-4.

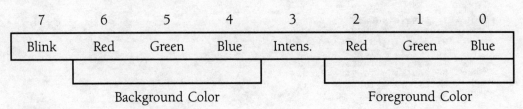

Figure 2-4

By setting the attribute byte, we can select the mix of red, green, and blue for both the foreground color (the color of the character) and the background color (the color of the widow behind the text). Also, we can set bit 3 for high intensity display, and bit 7 to make the character blink. A red foreground on a green background would have an attribute byte of 00100100 binary, or &H24 (See Figure 2-5):

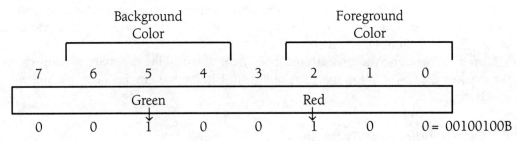

Figure 2-5

We can mix the colors too by adding the respective bit values together. Here are the bit values to add in forming the attribute byte:

Bit Value	Color Generated
1	Blue Foreground
2	Green Foreground
4	Red Foreground
8	High Intensity
16	Blue Background
32	Green Background
64	Red Background
128	Blinking

For example, to get a normal setting of white on black, we would turn on all the foreground colors (the letter itself) this way: 1 + 2 + 4 = 7. All the background colors are off, so they are set to 0. This value of 7 is the normal startup screen attribute value. If we wanted to make that high intensity, we would add 8 to give 15 = &HF. If we wanted blinking reverse video in white, we would set all the background colors on, and add 128 to make it blink: 16 + 32 + 64 + 128 = 240 = &HF0.

On monochrome screens we can't use the individual colors, but we can use the normal screen (7), high intensity (&HF), blinking normal (&H87), blinking reverse video (&HF0), and underlined, which graphics monitors don't have. To turn on underlining, use a blue foreground (making an attribute of 1). We can also have intense underlining (attribute of 9).

> **TIP:** BIOS interrupt & HIO, service 9 lets you select screen attributes for each character as you print them, giving you more control than the BASIC COLOR/ PRINT combination, where you have to select the color of the entire string you're printing. All at once.

After we pass all this information, WindowGetHandle%( ) returns the window's handle, HANDLE% (an INTEGER between 1 and 8). To display this window on the screen, we can then call WindowShow(Handle%). To hide it, we'll call WindowHide(Handle%). In other words, all we've got to pass to subprograms from now on is the window's handle. We don't have to give the dimensions, the location, or its screen attribute.

In the following example, we set up two windows, one whose top left corner is at (1,1), with five rows and columns, and screen attribute of &H24; and one whose top left corner is at (10,10), also with five rows and columns, whose screen attribute is &H61:

```
DECLARE FUNCTION WindowGetHandle% (TopRow%, TopCol%, NumRow%, NumCol%, Attr%)

Handle1% = WindowGetHandle%(1, 1, 5, 5, &H24) ←

PRINT "Window's handle is: ", Handle1%

Handle2% = WindowGetHandle%(10, 10, 5, 5, &H61) ←

PRINT "Window's handle is: ", Handle2%
```

Window 1's handle is 1, and window 2's handle is 2, and that's it. We've been able to emulate the initialization process in the professional windows packages. Let's get our window on the screen.

Displaying a Window

Now that we've set up a window with WindowGetHandle%( ), we can either work on it behind the scenes or display it directly. Let's call the subprogram that displays it WindowShow( ). To display the window (at the location and with the size you specified to WindowGetHandle%( )), we should just be able to call WindowShow(Handle%), where Handle% is the window's handle.

Let's develop this subprogram. First, we have to save the text that we're going to overwrite on the screen, and we've already set aside space for this data in the backup array OldText( ). We also have to save the current screen attributes of *every* position on the screen that the window will overwrite in the backup array OldAttrb( ). We can do both of these things by looping over the rows and columns that we'll overwrite on the screen and using the BASIC SCREEN function (which can read both text and attributes) to read what's there. Here's how we start:

```
SUB WindowShow (Handle%)

    REM Save the old section of screen

    FOR i = 1 TO Rows(Handle%)
            FOR j = 1 TO Cols(Handle%)
            :
            :
            NEXT j
    NEXT i
        :
        :
```

We can save the text and attribute data in temporary strings, temp1$ and temp2$, respectively:

```
SUB WindowShow (Handle%)

        REM Save the old section of screen
→       TR = TopRow(Handle%)
        TC = TopCol(Handle%)

        FOR i = 1 TO Rows(Handle%)
→           temp1$ = ""
            temp2$ = ""
            FOR j = 1 TO Cols(Handle%)
    →
                temp1$ = temp1$ + CHR$(SCREEN(TR + i - 1, TC + j - 1))
                temp2$ = temp2$ + CHR$(SCREEN(TR + i - 1, TC + j - 1, 1))
            NEXT j
    NEXT i
        :
        :
```

Then, for each row, we store the completed temporary strings in the backup arrays OldText( ) and OldAttrb( ):

```
SUB WindowShow (Handle%)

        REM Save the old section of screen

        TR = TopRow(Handle%)
        TC = TopCol(Handle%)
        FOR i = 1 TO Rows(Handle%)
                temp1$ = ""
                temp2$ = ""
                FOR j = 1 TO Cols(Handle%)
                        temp1$ = temp1$ + CHR$(SCREEN(TR + i - 1, TC + j - 1))
                        temp2$ = temp2$ + CHR$(SCREEN(TR + i - 1, TC + j - 1, 1))
                NEXT j
→               OldText(Handle%, i) = temp1$
                OldAttrb(Handle%, i) = temp2$
        NEXT i
                :
                :
```

When we restore the screen, we'll read the old characters and attributes out of these arrays. Now we have to place our window on the screen; we can use interrupt &H10 service 9, which lets us print both characters and their attributes at the present cursor position. We find this entry for interrupt &H10 service 9 in the appendix:

NOTE: Note: We can't use the BASIC PRINT statement, or PRINT USING, since we can't print attributes that way.

Input	Output
ah=9	Character written on screen at Cursor Position.
al=IBM ASCII code	
bh=Page Number	
bl → Alpha Modes=Attribute	
Graphics Modes=Color	
cx=Count of characters to write	

To use this service, we have to load ah with 9, al with the character's ASCII code (which we get from Text( )), and bh with the screen *page number*. We could get fancy and divide the screen output into several *pages*, but we're always going to use the default (displayed) page, page 0. We also have to load bl with the character's attribute (which we get from Attribute( )), and cx with the number of characters to print (1). To move the cursor around the screen, we can use LOCATE.

First, we establish our loop over the rows and columns of the window:

```
SUB WindowShow (Handle%)

        REM Save the old sectsion of screen

        TR = TopRow(Handle%)
        TC = TopCol(Handle%)

        FOR i = 1 TO Rows(Handle%)
                temp1$ = ""
                temp2$ = ""
                FOR j = 1 TO Cols(Handle%)
                        temp1$ = temp1$ + CHR$(SCREEN(TR + i - 1, TC + j - 1))
                        temp2$ = temp2$ + CHR$(SCREEN(TR + i - 1, TC + j - 1, 1))
                NEXT j
                OldText(Handle%, i) = temp1$
                OldAttrb(Handle%, i) = temp2$
        NEXT i

        REM Now print the new text

        LOCATE TR, TC

→       FOR i = 1 TO Rows(Handle%)
:           FOR j = 1 TO Cols(Handle%)
                :
            NEXT j
        NEXT i
```

Next, we move the cursor over the correct locations on the screen (note that we start off by saving the current cursor row and column in CurRow% and CurCol% — this is so we can restore the cursor when we're done):

```
SUB WindowShow (Handle%)

→       CurRow% = CSRLIN
        CurCol% = POS(0)

        REM Save the old section of screen

        TR = TopRow(Handle%)
        TC = TopCol(Handle%)

        FOR i = 1 TO Rows(Handle%)
                temp1$ = ""
                temp2$ = ""
                FOR j = 1 TO Cols(Handle%)
                        temp1$ = temp1$ + CHR$(SCREEN(TR + i - 1, TC + j - 1))
                        temp2$ = temp2$ + CHR$(SCREEN(TR + i - 1, TC + j - 1, 1))
```

```
                NEXT j
                OldText(Handle%, i) = temp1$
                OldAttrb(Handle%, i) = temp2$
        NEXT i

        REM Now print the new text

→       LOCATE TR, TC 'Start at top left of window

        FOR i = 1 TO Rows(Handle%)
            FOR j = 1 TO Cols(Handle%)
                        :
                    [Put the character on the screen]
                        :
→               LOCATE TR + i - 1, TC + j 'Locate next character position.
            NEXT j
→               LOCATE TR + i, TC 'Skip to next row
        NEXT i
```

Then, we set up the registers and use interrupt &H21 service 9:

```
SUB WindowShow (Handle%)

→       DIM InRegs AS RegType, OutRegs AS RegType

        CurRow% = CSRLIN
        CurCol% = POS(0)

        REM Save the old sectsion of screen

        TR = TopRow(Handle%)
        TC = TopCol(Handle%)

        FOR i = 1 TO Rows(Handle%)
                temp1$ = ""
                temp2$ = ""
                FOR j = 1 TO Cols(Handle%)
                        temp1$ = temp1$ + CHR$(SCREEN(TR + i - 1, TC + j - 1))
                        temp2$ = temp2$ + CHR$(SCREEN(TR + i - 1, TC + j - 1, 1))
                NEXT j
                OldText(Handle%, i) = temp1$
                OldAttrb(Handle%, i) = temp2$
        NEXT i

        REM Now print the new text

        LOCATE TR, TC
→       InRegs.cx = 1

        FOR i = 1 TO Rows(Handle%)
            FOR j = 1 TO Cols(Handle%)
→               InRegs.ax = &H900 + ASC(MID$(Text(Handle%, i), j, 1))
                InRegs.bx = Attribute(Handle%)
                CALL INTERRUPT(&H10, InRegs, OutRegs)
                LOCATE TR + i - 1, TC + j
            NEXT j
                LOCATE TR + i, TC
        NEXT i
```

The final step is to indicate that the window is on to other subprograms by setting OnFlag(Handle%) to 1 and then restoring the cursor from CurRow% and CurCol%.

> **TIP:** Setting flags — such as OnFlag( )—in a SHARED COMMON lets modules in a program communicate with each other *without* having to pass parameters back and forth through separate calls.

That's it. The window is now visible. Listing 2-2 shows the whole subprogram WindowShow( ).

Listing 2-2. WindowShow( ) Subprogram—Displays Windows.   1 of 2

```
DECLARE SUB WindowShow (Handle%)

TYPE RegType
        ax AS INTEGER
        bx AS INTEGER
        cx AS INTEGER
        dx AS INTEGER
        bp AS INTEGER
        si AS INTEGER
        di AS INTEGER
        flags AS INTEGER
END TYPE

DECLARE SUB INTERRUPT (IntNo AS INTEGER, InRegs AS RegType, OutRegs AS RegType)

        CONST MaxWindows = 8
        DIM Rows(1 TO MaxWindows) AS INTEGER
        DIM Cols(1 TO MaxWindows) AS INTEGER
        DIM TopRow(1 TO MaxWindows) AS INTEGER
        DIM TopCol(1 TO MaxWindows) AS INTEGER
        DIM BotRow(1 TO MaxWindows) AS INTEGER
        DIM BotCol(1 TO MaxWindows) AS INTEGER
        DIM Attribute(1 TO MaxWindows) AS INTEGER
        DIM OnFlag(1 TO MaxWindows) AS INTEGER
        DIM Text(MaxWindows, 25) AS STRING
        DIM OldText(MaxWindows, 25) AS STRING
        DIM OldAttrb(MaxWindows, 25) AS STRING
        COMMON SHARED /WindowA/ Rows() AS INTEGER, Cols() AS INTEGER, _
                Toprow() AS INTEGER, TopCol() AS INTEGER, BotRow() AS INTEGER, _
                BotCol() AS INTEGER
        COMMON SHARED /WindowB/ Attribute() AS INTEGER, OnFlag() AS INTEGER, _
                Text() AS STRING, OldText() AS STRING, OldAttrb() AS STRING

SUB WindowShow (Handle%)
```

Listing 2-2.   WindowShow( ) Subprogram—Displays Windows.   2 of 2

```
DIM InRegs AS RegType, OutRegs AS RegType
CurRow% = CSRLIN
CurCol% = POS(0)

REM Save the old section of screen

TR = TopRow(Handle%)
TC = TopCol(Handle%)
FOR i = 1 TO Rows(Handle%)
        temp1$ = ""
        temp2$ = ""
        FOR j = 1 TO Cols(Handle%)
                temp1$ = temp1$ + CHR$(SCREEN(TR + i - 1, TC + j - 1))
                temp2$ = temp2$ + CHR$(SCREEN(TR + i - 1, TC + j - 1, 1))
        NEXT j
        OldText(Handle%, i) = temp1$
        OldAttrb(Handle%, i) = temp2$
NEXT i

REM Now print the new text

LOCATE TR, TC
InRegs.cx = 1

FOR i = 1 TO Rows(Handle%)
    FOR j = 1 TO Cols(Handle%)
        InRegs.ax = &H900 + ASC(MID$(Text(Handle%, i), j, 1))
        InRegs.bx = Attribute(Handle%)
        CALL INTERRUPT(&H10, InRegs, OutRegs)
        LOCATE TR + i - 1, TC + j
    NEXT j
        LOCATE TR + i, TC
NEXT i

REM Show window is on.

OnFlag(Handle%) = 1

LOCATE CurRow%, CurCol%

END SUB
```

This is a pretty long one, although it's very easy to use. To display a particular window, you just need to call it with that window's handle. Let's put all this to work immediately with an example.

Displaying a Test Window

Here's how to display two windows on the screen (there will be no text in them). First, we initialize the windows with WindowGetHandle%( ) and then we call WindowShow( ) with the appropriate handles:

```
DECLARE FUNCTION WindowGetHandle% (TopRow%, TopCol%, NumRow%, NumCol%, Attr%)
DECLARE SUB WindowShow (Handle%)

Handle1% = WindowGetHandle%(10, 10, 5, 5, &H24)
Handle2% = WindowGetHandle%(20, 20, 3, 13, &H61)

CALL WindowShow(Handle1%) ←
CALL WindowShow(Handle2%)
```

That's all there is to it. Both windows have now appeared on the screen; the upper one is green, and the lower one brown (See Figure 2-6 below). So far, our code is a success — we've produced windows. Now let's see about hiding them.

Figure 2-6

Hiding a Window

WindowHide( ) does the reverse of WindowShow( ); it simply removes a window from the screen and restores whatever was underneath it. This does *not* stop you from working on the window. You can still move it around, print to it or whatever you like — the results just won't be visible. To hide a window, just call WindowHide( ) with that window's handle: CALL WindowHide(Handle%).

Let's develop this subprogram. We start by saving the present cursor position (because we'll be using the cursor ourselves when we restore the old text):

```
→ CurRow% = CSRLIN
  CurCol% = POS(0)

  DIM InRegs AS RegType, OutRegs AS RegType
          :
          :
  END SUB
```

Next we loop over the rows in the displayed window:

```
CurRow% = CSRLIN
CurCol% = POS(0)

DIM InRegs AS RegType, OutRegs AS RegType

REM Print the old text

LOCATE TR, TC
InRegs.cx = 1

→ FOR i = 1 TO Rows(Handle%)
      :
      :
   NEXT i
```

And then there's an inner loop over the columns. At each location, we restore the old text and attribute. We've seen how to do this in WindowPrint( ). The only difference here is that we use the backup text array OldText( ) instead of Text( ), and the array OldAttrb( ) to restore the attribute of each character position instead of Attribute( ):

```
CurRow% = CSRLIN
CurCol% = POS(0)

DIM InRegs AS RegType, OutRegs AS RegType

REM Print the old text

LOCATE TR, TC
InRegs.cx = 1

   FOR i = 1 TO Rows(Handle%)
→    FOR j = 1 TO Cols(Handle%)
         InRegs.ax = &H900 + ASC(MID$(OldText(Handle%, i), j, 1))
         InRegs.bx = ASC(MID$(OldAttrb(Handle%, i), j, 1))
         CALL INTERRUPT(&H10, InRegs, OutRegs)
         LOCATE TR + i - 1, TC + j
      NEXT j
         LOCATE TR + i, TC
   NEXT i
   :
   :
```

When we're finished with this double loop, the window has vanished from the screen. To finish up, we signal that this window is off by setting OnFlag(Handle%) to 0 and restore the old cursor position with LOCATE CurRow%, CurCol%. At this point, the window is gone, and we're done. Listing 2-3 shows the complete subprogram.

Listing 2-3.   WindowHide Subprogram—Hides Windows.

```
DECLARE SUB WindowHide (Handle%)

TYPE RegType
        ax AS INTEGER
        bx AS INTEGER
        cx AS INTEGER
        dx AS INTEGER
        bp AS INTEGER
        si AS INTEGER
        di AS INTEGER
        flags AS INTEGER
END TYPE

DECLARE SUB INTRRUPT (IntNo AS INTEGER, InRegs AS RegType, OutRegs AS RegType)

        CONST MaxWindows = 8
        DIM Rows(1 TO MaxWindows) AS INTEGER
        DIM Cols(1 TO MaxWindows) AS INTEGER
        DIM TopRow(1 TO MaxWindows) AS INTEGER
        DIM TopCol(1 TO MaxWindows) AS INTEGER
        DIM BotRow(1 TO MaxWindows) AS INTEGER
        DIM BotCol(1 TO MaxWindows) AS INTEGER
        DIM Attribute(1 TO MAXWINDOWS) AS INTEGER
        DIM OnFlag(1 TO MaxWindows) AS INTEGER
        DIM Text(MaxWindows, 25) AS STRING
        DIM OldText(MaxWindows, 25) AS STRING
        DIM OldAttrb(MaxWindows, 25) AS STRING
        COMMON SHARED /WindowA/ Rows() AS INTEGER, Cols() AS INTEGER, _
                Toprow() AS INTEGER, TopCol() AS INTEGER, BotRow() AS INTEGER, _
                BotCol() AS INTEGER
        COMMON SHARED /WindowB/ Attribute() AS INTEGER, OnFlag() AS INTEGER, _
                Text() AS STRING, OldText() AS STRING, OldAttrb() AS STRING


SUB WindowHide (Handle%)

        CurRow% = CSRLIN
        CurCol% = POS(0)

        DIM InRegs AS RegType, OutRegs AS RegType

        REM Print the old text

        LOCATE TR, TC
        InRegs.cx = 1

        FOR i = 1 TO Rows(Handle%)
            FOR j = 1 TO Cols(Handle%)
                InRegs.ax = &H900 + ASC(MID$(OldText(Handle%, i), j, 1))
                InRegs.bx = ASC(MID$(OldAttrb(Handle%, i), j, 1))
                CALL INTERRUPT(&H10, InRegs, OutRegs)
                LOCATE TR + i - 1, TC + j
            NEXT j
                LOCATE TR + i, TC
        NEXT i
        REM Show window is off
→       OnFlag(Handle%) = 0

        LOCATE CurRow%, CurCol%

END SUB
```

Again the listing is pretty long, but not as long as it was for WindowShow( ). That's because WindowHide( ) only needs to restore the old text and screen attributes; it doesn't have to store the window text before overwriting it — that text is already in the window COMMONs. Now let's see WindowHide( ) at work!

Hiding Our Test Window

In this example, we'll just take the two windows we've already created in the WindowShow( ) example program and make one disappear. First, we'll flash window 1 on the screen. Next, we'll overwrite that window with a new window, window 2, covering the message entirely. Then we hide window 2, revealing window 1 again:

```
DECLARE FUNCTION WindowGetHandle% (TopRow%, TopCol%, NumRow%, NumCol%, Attr%)
DECLARE FUNCTION WindowPrint% (Handle%, Row%, Col%, PString$)
DECLARE SUB WindowShow (Handle%)
DECLARE SUB WindowHide (Handle%)

Handle1% = WindowGetHandle%(10, 10, 5, 5, &H24)
Handle2% = WindowGetHandle%(10, 10, 3, 13, &H61)

CALL WindowShow(Handle1%)
CALL WindowShow(Handle2%)
CALL WindowHide(Handle2%)  ←
```

This use of WindowShow( ) and WindowHide( ) show the versatility of our subprograms. To display a window, just use WindowShow( ); to make it vanish, WindowHide( ). You can see how easy they are to use from a programming standpoint. Once we've worked through all the details, using them is simple.

At this point, we've initialized windows, made them appear and now dissappear; we've done a lot. On the other hand, what good is a window without text in it? Let's do a little printing.

Printing Text in a Window

Now let's do something with the windows we've created. We can develop a subprogram named WindowPrint( ) that prints text in them. This process is easy: all we really need to specify is the position in the window at which to start printing (making [1,1] the top left corner of the window), and the text we want to print.

Because a string may not fully fit in a window, there should also be some indication of success or failure. Let's make WindowPrint( ) a function: WindowPrint%( ). If it can print the string passed to it in the window, it will return a value of 1; otherwise, it will return 0.

TIP: In general, if there is the possibility of failure inside a subprogram, you should convert it to a function, which will let it report success or failure.

With that in mind, here's how we might use WindowPrint%( ):

```
→ IF WindowPrint% (Handle%, PrntRow%, PrntCol%, PrntStr$) THEN
           PRINT "String printed in window successfully."
   ELSE
           PRINT "Error. Could not print string in window."
   END IF
```

NOTE: Note: We are both using WindowPrint%( ) and checking its return value in the same line; this technique is reminiscent of programming in C.

Note the inputs in our code above:

Handle%	INTEGER	This window's handle as returned from WindowGetHandle%( ). Valid handles are nonzero and in the range 1-8.
PrntRow%	INTEGER	The row in the window at which to start printing. Use local window coordinates; i.e., the top left corner is (1, 1).
PrntCol%	INTEGER	The column in the window at which to start printing. Use local window coordinates; i.e., the top left corner is (1, 1).
PrntStr$	STRING	The string to be printed starting at location (PrntRow%, PrntCol%) in the window.

We can pass the string to print as a normal string. For example, we could print "Now is the time." like this:

```
→ PrntRow% = 1
  PrntCol% = 1
  PrntStr$ = "Now is the time."
  IF WindowPrint% (Handle%, PrntRow%, PrntCol%, PrntStr$) THEN
          PRINT "String printed in window successfully."
  ELSE
          PRINT "Error. Could not print string in window."
  END IF
```

This would generate the following output (see Figure 2-7).

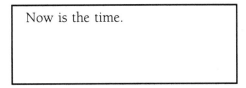

Now is the time.

Figure 2-7

Note that if the string is too long for the current row, we'll have to wrap it around to the next row. On the other hand, what if we wanted to skip to the next row intentionally? We should make some provision for including carriage returns in the string to be printed. Let's check that string for CHR$(13) characters (a carriage return); if we find one, WindowPrint%( ) should move to the first position on the next line. For example, to print we should be able to pass this string to WindowPrint%( ): "Now is the"=CHR$(13)="time."

Now is the
time.

Figure 2-8

Also note that, because we might want to work on a window behind the scenes, just printing to a window shouldn't display it. On the other hand, if the window is *already* displayed on the screen, WindowPrint( ) should update it.

Let's write this function. We start off by making non-destructive copies of the parameters passed to us: PrntRow%, PrntCol%, and PrntStr$. We also save the present cursor position (because WindowPrint%( ) might have to update the screen):

```
FUNCTION WindowPrint% (Handle%, PrntRow%, PrntCol%, PrntStr$)

        CurRow% = CSRLIN
        CurCol% = POS(0)

        WindowPrint% = 1

        REM Make non-destructive copies

→       PrintRow% = PrntRow%
        PrintCol% = PrntCol%
        PrintString$ = PrntStr$
        :
```

Now we can (optimistically) assign a return value of 1 — indicating success — to WindowPrint% itself, and set up the loop over the window's rows in which we'll insert the characters.

TIP: Success is usually indicated by non-negative values in programming.

This loop takes a little thought. Our idea here is to keep placing characters from the print string into the window as long as we do not go past the last row of the window (i.e., PrintRow% <= Rows(Handle%)), and as long as there are still characters left to print (PrintString$ <>" ").

```
FUNCTION WindowPrint% (Handle%, PrntRow%, PrntCol%, PrntStr$)

        CurRow% = CSRLIN
        CurCol% = POS(0)

        WindowPrint% = 1

        REM Make non-destructive copies

        PrintRow% = PrntRow%
        PrintCol% = PrntCol%
        PrintString$ = PrntStr$

→       DO
        :
        :
        LOOP WHILE (PrintRow% Rows(Handle%)) AND (PrintString$ <> "")
        :
        :
```

Then we have to add an inner loop that loops over the columns of the window. We can keep printing over columns in the current row as long as we're not past the edge of the window (i.e., PrintCol% <= Cols(Handle%)) and as long as there are still characters left to print (PrintString$ <> " ").

```
FUNCTION WindowPrint% (Handle%, PrntRow%, PrntCol%, PrntStr$)

        DIM InRegs AS RegType, OutRegs AS RegType

        CurRow% = CSRLIN
        CurCol% = POS(0)

        WindowPrint% = 1

        REM Make non-destructive copies

        PrintRow% = PrntRow%
        PrintCol% = PrntCol%
        PrintString$ = PrntStr$

        DO
→           DO
                :
            [Put character in window]
                :
                PrintCol% = PrintCol% + 1
            LOOP WHILE (PrintCol% Cols(Handle%)) AND (PrintString$ <> "")

            PrintRow% = PrintRow% + 1
            PrintCol% = 1

        LOOP WHILE (PrintRow% Rows(Handle%)) AND (PrintString$ "")
                :
                :
```

Notice that we increment the column at the end of every interation over columns, and increase the row (and set the column back to 1) after every iteration over rows. With these two loops, we'll loop over the columns of the present row in the window (see Figure 2-9).

Now is →

Figure 2-9

And, when we come to the end of the row, we'll skip to the next one (Figure 2-10).

Now is the time
for all →

Figure 2-10

At this point, we're ready for the character to print. Here's how we strip that character from PrintString$ and place it at (PrintRow%, PrintCol%) in the window (keep in mind that the window's text is stored in the array named Text( )):

```
FUNCTION WindowPrint% (Handle%, PrntRow%, PrntCol%, PrntStr$)

        DIM InRegs AS RegType, OutRegs AS RegType

        CurRow% = CSRLIN
        CurCol% = POS(0)
        WindowPrint% = 1

        REM Make non-destructive copies

        PrintRow% = PrntRow%
        PrintCol% = PrntCol%
        PrintString$ = PrntStr$
        DO
            DO
                Char$ = LEFT$(PrintString$, 1)
                PrintString$ = RIGHT$(PrintString$, LEN(PrintString$) - 1)
                IF ASC(Char$) = 13 THEN EXIT DO
                MID$(Text(Handle%, PrintRow%), PrintCol%, 1) = Char$
                PrintCol% = PrintCol% + 1
            LOOP WHILE (PrintCol% <=Cols(Handle%)) AND (PrintString$<>"")
            PrintRow% = PrintRow% + 1
            PrintCol% = 1
        LOOP WHILE (PrintRow% Rows(Handle%)) AND (PrintString$<>"")
            :
            :
```

In this loop, we actually insert the character into the window. Our destructive copy of the string to be printed is named PrintString$; we find the character to be printed at the current location, LEFT$(PrintString$, 1), strip it off PrintString$, and insert it into the correct row in Text(Handle%).

TIP: An easy way to strip off the first word of a string (not just its first character) is to use the INSTR( ) function like this:
FirstWord$ = LEFT$(MyString$,INSTR(MyString$, " ")-1)

We keep looping over columns until we reach the edge of the window or run out of characters to print. Note that we also have to check for carriage returns in the print string, in which case we should skip to the next row. After each row is done, we keep looping over the following rows until there's nothing left, or until we're past the end of the window.

After these loops, we've either exhausted the print string or reached the end of the window—and we must check which. If we've reached the end of the window, we have to return a value of 0, indicating that we couldn't fit all the text into the window:

```
FUNCTION WindowPrint% (Handle%, PrntRow%, PrntCol%, PrntStr$)

        DIM InRegs AS RegType, OutRegs AS RegType

        CurRow% = CSRLIN
        CurCol% = POS(0)

        WindowPrint% = 1

        REM Make non-destructive copies

        PrintRow% = PrntRow%
        PrintCol% = PrntCol%
        PrintString$ = PrntStr$

        DO
            DO
                Char$ = LEFT$(PrintString$, 1)
                PrintString$ = RIGHT$(PrintString$, LEN(PrintString$) - 1)
                IF ASC(Char$) = 13 THEN EXIT DO
                MID$(Text(Handle%), PrintRow%), PrintCol%, 1) = Char$
                PrintCol% = PrintCol% + 1
            LOOP WHILE (PrintCol% Cols(Handle%)) AND (PrintString$<>"")

            PrintRow% = PrintRow% + 1
            PrintCol% = 1

        LOOP WHILE (PrintRow% <=Rows(Handle%)) AND (PrintString$<>"")

→       IF PrintString$ <>"" THEN WindowPrint% = 0
        :
        :
```

Otherwise, we'll leave WindowPrint% set to 1, indicating success. The last thing to do is check if the window is currently visible (i.e., if OnFlag(Handle%) equals 1), in which case we have to update it on the screen. We can just borrow the code to draw the window on the screen from WindowShow( ). Listing 2-4 shows the whole function.

Listing 2-4. WindowPrint% Function—Prints Text in a Window. 1 of 3

```
DECLARE FUNCTION WindowPrint% (Handle%, PrntRow%, PrntCol%, PrntStr$)

TYPE RegType
        ax AS INTEGER
        bx AS INTEGER
        cx AS INTEGER
        dx AS INTEGER
```

Listing 2-4.   WindowPrint% Function—Prints Text in a Window.   2 of 3

```
        bp AS INTEGER
        si AS INTEGER
        di AS INTEGER
        flags AS INTEGER
END TYPE
DECLARE SUB INTERRUPT (IntNo AS INTEGER, InRegs AS RegType, OutRegs AS RegType)

        CONST MaxWindows = 8
        DIM Rows(1 TO MaxWindows) AS INTEGER
        DIM Cols(1 TO MaxWindows) AS INTEGER
        DIM TopRow(1 TO MaxWindows) AS INTEGER
        DIM TopCol(1 TO MaxWindows) AS INTEGER
        DIM BotRow(1 TO MaxWindows) AS INTEGER
        DIM BotCol(1 TO MaxWindows) AS INTEGER
        DIM Attribute(1 TO MaxWindows) AS INTEGER
        DIM OnFlag(1 TO MaxWindows) AS INTEGER
        DIM Text(MaxWindows, 25) AS STRING
        DIM OldText(MaxWindows, 25) AS STRING
        DIM OldAttrb(MaxWindows, 25) AS STRING
        COMMON SHARED /WindowA/ Rows() AS INTEGER, Cols() AS INTEGER, _
                Toprow() AS INTEGER, TopCol() AS INTEGER, BotRow() AS INTEGER, _
                BotCol() AS INTEGER
        COMMON SHARED /WindowB/ Attribute() AS INTEGER, OnFlag() AS INTEGER, _
                Text() AS STRING, OldText() AS STRING, OldAttrb() AS STRING

FUNCTION WindowPrint% (Handle%, PrntRow%, PrntCol%, PrntStr$)
        DIM InRegs AS RegType, OutRegs AS RegType

        CurRow% = CSRLIN
        CurCol% = POS(0)

        WindowPrint% = 1

        REM Make non-destructive copies

        PrintRow% = PrntRow%
        PrintCol% = PrntCol%
        PrintString$ = PrntStr$
        DO
            DO
                Char$ = LEFT$(PrintString$, 1)
                PrintString$ = RIGHT$(PrintString$, LEN(PrintString$) - 1)
                IF ASC(Char$) = 13 THEN EXIT DO
                MID$(Text(Handle%, PrintRow%), PrintCol%, 1) = Char$
                PrintCol% = PrintCol% + 1
            LOOP WHILE (PrintCol% <= Cols(Handle%)) AND (PrintString$ <> "")

            PrintRow% = PrintRow% + 1
            PrintCol% = 1

        LOOP WHILE (PrintRow% <= Rows(Handle%)) AND (PrintString$ <> "")

        IF PrintString$ <> "" THEN WindowPrint% = 0

        IF OnFlag(Handle)% THEN
```

Listing 2-4.   WindowPrint% Function—Prints Text in a Window.   **3 of 3**

```
            REM Print the new text

            TR = TopRow(Handle%)
            TC = TopCol(Handle%)

            LOCATE TR, TC
            InRegs.cx = 1

            FOR i = 1 TO Rows(Handle%)
                FOR j = 1 TO Cols(Handle%)
                    InRegs.ax = &H900 + ASC(MID$(Text(Handle%, i), j, 1))
                    InRegs.bx = Attribute(Handle%)
                    CALL INTERRUPT(&H10, InRegs, OutRegs)
                        LOCATE TR + i - 1, TC + j
                NEXT j
                    LOCATE TR + i, TC
            NEXT i

        END IF

LOCATE CurRow%, CurCol%

END FUNCTION
```

This is another fairly long listing only because we have to update the window if it's on the screen — the real meat of printing to the window is done in a dozen or so lines. Now, let's get the chance to see WindowPrint%( ) at work.

TIP: You can also use WindowPrint% ( ) to print borders in your window if you use the ASCII line drawing characters.

Printing in Our Test Window

Here's a sample program that puts WindowPrint%( ) to the test. We just print "Hello" starting at (1,1) in the window, and "Test." starting at (5,1):

```
DECLARE FUNCTION WindowGetHandle% (TopRow%, TopCol%, NumRow%, NumCol%, Attr%)
DECLARE SUB WindowShow (Handle%)
DECLARE FUNCTION WindowPrint% (Handle%, Row%, Col%, PrintString$)

Handle% = WindowGetHandle%(10, 10, 5, 5, &H24)

CALL WindowShow(Handle%)
```

```
Check% = WindowPrint%(Handle%, 1, 1, "Hello")

Check% = WindowPrint%(Handle%, 5, 1, "Test.")

IF Check% = 0 THEN PRINT "Error."
```

NOTE: The (Row, Column) coordinates we pass to WindowPrint%( ) are with respect to the window — that is, (1, 1) is the upper left-hand corner of the window.

The result of this program is a mini-window that looks like Figure 2-11.

Hello

Test.

Figure 2-11

Now we're able to set up a window, show it, print in it, and hide it. We've come pretty far. Another option we haven't explored yet, however, is moving windows around the screen. For example, we may want to move a window from the center of the screen to somewhere off on the periphery. Let's give this a try with a function we can call WindowMove%( ).

Moving a Window

Although we can set a window's initial screen position with WindowGetHandle%( ), we may not want to keep it there forever. Instead, we can set up a function named WindowMove%( ) to move windows around at will. Because moving a window may not be successful — it may end up past the edge of the screen, for example — this function should return 1 for success and 0 for failure.

And, like WindowPrint%( ), WindowMove%( ) should not make a window visible. However, if a window is *already* on the screen, we should update the screen by making the window vanish from its old position and reappear at the new one. In other words, if the window was already on the screen, and we want to move it, we'll have to go through these steps:

1. Restore area of screen covered by current window;
2. Save target area of screen; and
3. Pop window into target area of screen.

These three steps are going to make WindowMove%( ) lengthy, but keep in mind that we've already written the code for these tasks in WindowShow( ) and WindowHide( ).

TIP: Recycling your own code makes programming much faster. As you program, keep in mind all other places where you could use the same code. This also makes debugging easier.

To use WindowMove%( ), we'll have to supply the handle of the window to move and its new position (i.e., the new position of the top left corner). That might look like this if we wanted to move the window to the upper left of the screen:

```
→  NewTopRow% = 1
   NewTopCol% = 1
   IF WindowMove% (Handle%, NewTopRow%, NewTopCol%) THEN
          PRINT "Window moved successfully."
   ELSE
          PRINT "Error. Could not move window."
   END IF
```

Note the simple inputs to WindowMove%( ):

Handle%	INTEGER	This window's handle as returned from WindowGetHandle%( ). Valid handles are non-zero and in the range 1-8.
NewTopRow%	INTEGER	The new screen row (1 - 24) of the top left corner of the window after it's been moved.
NewTopCol%	INTEGER	The new screen column (1 - 79) of the topleft corner of the window after it's been moved.

Let's develop the program. We start off by doing some boundary checking — would the new location of the window put it off the screen? Here's the code:

```
WindowMove% = 1
IF NewTopRow% < 1 OR NewTopCol% < THEN
        WindowMove% = 0
        EXIT FUNCTION
END IF

IF NewTopRow% + Rows(Handle%) > 25 OR NewTopCol% + Cols(Handle%) >80 THEN
        WindowMove% = 0
        EXIT FUNCTION
END IF
:
:
```

If we're still in the function, the move is legal. To move the window, all we really have to do is to refill the location arrays in the window commons for this window, Top-Row(Handle%), TopCol(Handle%), BotRow(Handle%), BotCol(Handle%), where the window is set up like Figure 2-12.

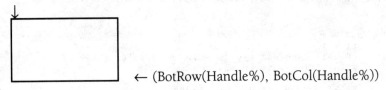

(TopRow(Handle%), TopCol(Handle%))

← (BotRow(Handle%), BotCol(Handle%))

Figure 2-12

To refill those arrays looks like this:

```
     WindowMove% = 1

     IF NewTopRow% < 1 OR NewTopCol% < 1 THEN
             WindowMove% = 0
             EXIT FUNCTION
     END IF

     IF NewTopRow% + Rows(Handle%) > 25 OR NewTopCol% + Cols(Handle%)>80 THEN
             WindowMove% = 0
             EXIT FUNCTION
     END IF
→    TopRow(Handle%) = NewTopRow%
     TopCol(Handle%) = NewTopCol%
     BotRow(Handle%) = NewTopRow% + Rows(Handle%)
     BotCol(Handle%) = NewTopCol% + Cols(Handle%)

     IF OnFlag(Handle%) = 0 THEN EXIT FUNCTION
     :
     :
```

If the window is not displayed, then we're done, and we exit the function. Otherwise, we've got a lot of work ahead of us. The bulk of the code in this program will be to move the window on the screen if it's presently visible (i.e., OnFlag(Handle%) = 1).

In that case, we have to hide the window about to be moved by restoring the old text that was there before the window was displayed. We can adapt the code in WindowHide( ) to do that for us. All we have to do is to note the original position of the window before we update its coordinates, and restore the text there like this:

```
    DIM InRegs AS RegType, OutRegs AS RegType

    CurRow% = CSRLIN
    CurCol% = POS(0)

    WindowMove% = 1

    IF NewTopRow% < 1 OR NewTopCol% < THEN
            WindowMove% = 0
            EXIT FUNCTION
    END IF

    IF NewTopRow% + Rows(Handle%)> 25 OR NewTopCol% + Cols(Handle%)>80 THEN
            WindowMove% = 0
            EXIT FUNCTION
    END IF

→ OldTopRow = TopRow(Handle%)
  OldTopCol =TopCol(Handle%)
  TopRow(Handle%) = NewTopRow%
  TopCol(Handle%) = NewTopCol%
  BotRow(Handle%) = NewTopRow% + Rows(Handle%)
  BotCol(Handle%) = NewTopCol% + Cols(Handle%)

    IF OnFlag(Handle%) = 0 THEN EXIT FUNCTION
    REM Restore old section of screen
→ TR = OldTopRow
  TC = OldTopCol
  LOCATE TR, TC
  InRegs.cx = 1
  FOR i = 1 TO Rows(Handle%)
      FOR j = 1 TO Cols(Handle%)
          InRegs.ax = &H900 + ASC(MID$(OldText(Handle%, i), j, 1))
          InRegs.bx = ASC(MID$(OldAttrb(Handle%, i), j, 1))
          CALL INTERRUPT(&H10, InRegs, OutRegs)
          LOCATE TR + i - 1, TC + j
      NEXT j
          LOCATE TR + i, TC
  NEXT i
          :
          :
  END SUB
```

Then we have to move the window. We start off by storing what's in the target area of the screen now, using code from WindowShow( ):

```
DIM InRegs AS RegType, OutRegs AS RegType

CurRow% = CSRLIN
CurCol% = POS(0)

WindowMove% = 1

IF NewTopRow% < 1 OR NewTopCol% < 1 THEN
        WindowMove% = 0
        EXIT FUNCTION
END IF

IF NewTopRow% + Rows(Handle%) > 25 OR NewTopCol% + Cols(Handle%)>80 THEN
        WindowMove% = 0
        EXIT FUNCTION
END IF

OldTopRow = TopRow(Handle%)
OldTopCol =TopCol(Handle%)
TopRow(Handle%) = NewTopRow%
TopCol(Handle%) = NewTopCol%
BotRow(Handle%) = NewTopRow% + Rows(Handle%)
BotCol(Handle%) = NewTopCol% + Cols(Handle%)

IF OnFlag(Handle%) = 0 THEN EXIT FUNCTION

REM Restore old section of screen

TR = OldTopRow
TC = OldTopCol
LOCATE TR, TC
InRegs.cx = 1

FOR i = 1 TO Rows(Handle%)
    FOR j = 1 TO Cols(Handle%)
        InRegs.ax = &H900 + ASC(MID$(OldText(Handle%, i), j, 1))
        InRegs.bx = ASC(MID$(OldAttrb(Handle%, i), j, 1))
        CALL INTERRUPT(&H10, InRegs, OutRegs)
        LOCATE TR + i - 1, TC + j
    NEXT j
        LOCATE TR + i, TC
NEXT i
REM Save the target section of screen

TR = TopRow(Handle%)
TC = TopCol(Handle%)

FOR i = 1 TO Rows(Handle%)
        temp1$ = ""
        temp2$ = ""
        FOR j = 1 TO Cols(Handle%)
                temp1$ = temp1$ + CHR$(SCREEN(TR + i - 1, TC + j - 1))
                temp2$ = temp2$ + CHR$(SCREEN(TR + i - 1, TC + j - 1, 1))
```

```
        NEXT j
        OldText(Handle%, i) = temp1$
        OldAttrb(Handle%, i) = temp2$
    NEXT i
    :
    :
```

Now we can display the window on the screen, again using code from WindowShow( ). Listing 2-5 shows the whole function:

Listing 2-5.   WindowMove% Function—Moves Windows on Screen.   1 of 3

```
DECLARE FUNCTION WindowMove% (Handle%, NewTopRow%, NewTopCol%)

TYPE RegType
        ax      AS INTEGER
        bx      AS INTEGER
        cx      AS INTEGER
        dx      AS INTEGER
        bp      AS INTEGER
        si      AS INTEGER
        di      AS INTEGER
        flags   AS INTEGER
END TYPE

DECLARE SUB INTERRUPT (IntNo AS INTEGER, InRegs AS RegType, OutRegs AS RegType)

        CONST MaxWindows = 8
        DIM Rows(1 TO MaxWindows) AS INTEGER
        DIM Cols(1 TO MaxWindows) AS INTEGER
        DIM TopRow(1 TO MaxWindows) AS INTEGER
        DIM TopCol(1 TO MaxWindows) AS INTEGER
        DIM BotRow(1 TO MaxWindows) AS INTEGER
        DIM BotCol(1 TO MaxWindows) AS INTEGER
        DIM Attribute(1 TO MaxWindows) AS INTEGER
        DIM OnFlag(1 TO MaxWindows) AS INTEGER
        DIM Text(MaxWindows, 25) AS STRING
        DIM OldText(MaxWindows, 25) AS STRING
        DIM OldAttrb(MaxWindows, 25) AS STRING
        COMMON SHARED /WindowA/ Rows() AS INTEGER, Cols() AS INTEGER, _
                Toprow() AS INTEGER, TopCol() AS INTEGER, BotRow() AS INTEGER, _
                BotCol() AS INTEGER
        COMMON SHARED /WindowB/ Attribute() AS INTEGER, OnFlag() AS INTEGER, _
                Text() AS STRING, OldText() AS STRING, OldAttrb() AS STRING

FUNCTION WindowMove% (Handle%, NewTopRow%, NewTopCol%)
        DIM InRegs AS RegType, OutRegs AS RegType

        CurRow% = CSRLIN
        CurCol% = POS(0)

        WindowMove% = 1
        IF NewTopRow% < 1 OR NewTopCol% < 1 THEN
                WindowMove% = 0
                EXIT FUNCTION
```

Listing 2-5.   WindowMove% Function—Moves Windows on Screen.   2 of 3

```
        END IF

        IF NewTopRow% + Rows(Handle%) > 25 OR NewTopCol% + Cols(Handle%)>80 THEN
                WindowMove% = 0
                EXIT FUNCTION
        END IF

        OldTopRow = TopRow(Handle%)
        OldTopCol =TopCol(Handle%)
        TopRow(Handle%) = NewTopRow%
        TopCol(Handle%) = NewTopCol%
        BotRow(Handle%) = NewTopRow% + Rows(Handle%)
        BotCol(Handle%) = NewTopCol% + Cols(Handle%)

        IF OnFlag(Handle%) = 0 THEN EXIT FUNCTION

        REM Restore old section of screen

        TR = OldTopRow
        TC = OldTopCol
        LOCATE TR, TC
        InRegs.cx = 1

        FOR i = 1 TO Rows(Handle%)
            FOR j = 1 TO Cols(Handle%)
                InRegs.ax = &H900 + ASC(MID$(OldText(Handle%, i), j, 1))
                InRegs.bx = ASC(MID$(OldAttrb(Handle%, i), j, 1))
                CALL INTERRUPT(&H10, InRegs, OutRegs)
                LOCATE TR + i - 1, TC + j
            NEXT j
                LOCATE TR + i, TC
        NEXT i
        REM Save the target section of screen

        TR = TopRow(Handle%)
        TC = TopCol(Handle%)

        FOR i = 1 TO Rows(Handle%)
                temp1$ = ""
                temp2$ = ""
                FOR j = 1 TO Cols(Handle%)
                        temp1$ = temp1$ + CHR$(SCREEN(TR + i - 1, TC + j - 1))
                        temp2$ = temp2$ + CHR$(SCREEN(TR + i - 1, TC + j - 1, 1))
                NEXT j
                OldText(Handle%, i) = temp1$
                OldAttrb(Handle%, i) = temp2$
        NEXT i
        REM Now print the new text

        LOCATE TR, TC
        InRegs.cx = 1

        FOR i = 1 TO Rows(Handle%)
            FOR j = 1 TO Cols(Handle%)
                InRegs.ax = &H900 + ASC(MID$(Text(Handle%, i), j, 1))
                InRegs.bx = Attribute(Handle%)
```

Listing 2-5. WindowMove% Function—Moves Windows on Screen. 3 of 3

```
                    CALL INTERRUPT(&H10, InRegs, OutRegs)
                    LOCATE TR + i - 1, TC + j
            NEXT j
                    LOCATE TR + i, TC
        NEXT i

        LOCATE CurRow%, CurCol%
  END SUB
```

And that's it; we've been able to move our window(s) around the screen. Let's see this in action.

Moving Our Test Window

Here's an example program, showing how to use WindowMove%( ):

```
DECLARE FUNCTION WindowGetHandle% (TopRow%, TopCol%, NumRow%, NumCol%, Attr%)
DECLARE SUB WindowShow (Handle%)
DECLARE FUNCTION WindowMove% (Handle%, NewTopRow%, NewTopCol%)

Handle1% = WindowGetHandle%(10, 10, 5, 5, &H24)
Handle2% = WindowGetHandle%(20, 20, 3, 13, &H61)

CALL WindowShow(Handle1%)
CALL WindowShow(Handle2%)

PRINT "Press any key to move window 2."
DO
LOOP WHILE INKEY$ = ""

Check% = WindowMove%(Handle2%, 5, 20) ←

IF Check% = 0 THEN PRINT "Error."
```

In this example, we put two windows on the screen, then wait for a key to be pressed. When we read a key, we move window 2 from screen coordinates (20, 20) to (5, 20) (see Figure 2-13). Note that these coordinated are the screen coordinates of top left corner of the window we're moving.

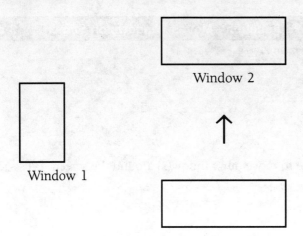

Figure 2-13

Let's take stock of our window system. At this point, we've developed a set of subprograms and functions that will let you add windows to your programs, setting them up, printing in them, and moving them around the screen freely. But how about getting rid of them? There should be some way of deleting a window and freeing its handle for later reassignment.

Deleting a Window

Let's develop a a final window subprogram to delete a window and free its handle. All we'll need is the window's handle — to delete a window, we can just call, say, WindowDelete(Handle%). This is especially valuable if you're near the maximum number of windows you can fit into memory, and you know that another part of your program is going to allocate a few windows.

NOTE: Deleting a window is more than just hiding it. The window's handle is deassigned, and you can't display the window again.

Let's develop this subprogram. We can begin by hiding the window, if it's being displayed, with code we've seen in WindowHide( ):

```
DECLARE SUB WindowDelete (Handle%)

        CurRow% = CSRLIN

        CurCol% = POS(0)

        DIM InRegs AS RegType, OutRegs AS RegType

        REM Restore old text if necessary.
  →     IF OnFlag(Handle%) THEN
  :
  :          TR = TopRow(Handle%)
             TC = TopCol(Handle%)
             LOCATE TR, TC
             InRegs.cx = 1

             FOR i = 1 TO Rows(Handle%)
                 FOR j = 1 TO Cols(Handle%)
                     InRegs.ax = &H900 + ASC(MID$(OldText(Handle%, i), j, 1))
                     InRegs.bx = ASC(MID$(OldAttrb(Handle%, i), j, 1))
                     CALL INTERRUPT(&H10, InRegs, OutRegs)
                     LOCATE TR + i - 1, TC + j
                 NEXT j
                     LOCATE TR + i, TC
             NEXT i
        END IF

        LOCATE CurRow%, CurCol%
             :
             :
END SUB
```

Now we're ready for the real business of WindowDelete( ), which is to convince
WindowGetHandle%( ) that this handle is free. The function WindowGethandle%( )
checks for free entries in the window arrays by looking at the array Rows( ), like this
(from WindowGetHandle%( )):

```
  FOR i = 1 TO MaxWindows
  →    IF Rows(i) = 0 THEN
           WindowGetHandle% = i
           Toprow(i) = TopR%
           TopCol(i) = TopC%
           BotRow(i) = TopR% + NRow%
           BotCol(i) = TopC% + NCol%
           Rows(i) = NRow%
           Cols(i) = NCol%
           Attribute(i) = Attr%
           OnFlag(i) = 0
           FOR j = 1 TO Rows(i)
               Text(i, j) = SPACE$(Cols(i))
           NEXT j
      EXIT FOR
      END IF
  NEXT i
```

In other words, to delete a window, we just have to set Rows(Handle%) equal to 0, where Handle% is the handle we've been passed. This is very easy — we only have to add one line. Listing 2-6 shows the whole subprogram.

Listing 2-6.   WindowDelete Subprogram—Deletes Window.   1 of 2

```
DECLARE SUB WindowDelete (Handle%)

TYPE RegType
        ax      AS INTEGER
        bx      AS INTEGER
        cx      AS INTEGER
        dx      AS INTEGER
        bp      AS INTEGER
        si      AS INTEGER
        di      AS INTEGER
        flags   AS INTEGER
END TYPE

DECLARE SUB INTERRUPT (IntNo AS INTEGER, InRegs AS RegType, OutRegs AS RegType)

        CONST MaxWindows = 8
        DIM Rows(1 TO MaxWindows) AS INTEGER
        DIM Cols(1 TO MaxWindows) AS INTEGER
        DIM TopRow(1 TO MaxWindows) AS INTEGER
        DIM TopCol(1 TO MaxWindows) AS INTEGER
        DIM BotRow(1 TO MaxWindows) AS INTEGER
        DIM BotCol(1 TO MaxWindows) AS INTEGER
        DIM Attribute(1 TO MaxWindows) AS INTEGER
        DIM OnFlag(1 TO MaxWindows) AS INTEGER
        DIM Text(MaxWindows, 25) AS STRING
        DIM OldText(MaxWindows, 25) AS STRING
        DIM OldAttrb(MaxWindows, 25) AS STRING
        COMMON SHARED /WindowA/ Rows() AS INTEGER, Cols() AS INTEGER, _
                Toprow() AS INTEGER, TopCol() AS INTEGER, BotRow() AS INTEGER, _
                BotCol() AS INTEGER
        COMMON SHARED /WindowB/ Attribute() AS INTEGER, OnFlag() AS INTEGER, _
                Text() AS STRING, OldText() AS STRING, OldAttrb() AS STRING

SUB WindowDelete (Handle%)
        CurRow% = CSRLIN
        CurCol% = POS(0)

        DIM InRegs AS RegType, OutRegs AS RegType

        REM Restore old text if necessary.

        IF OnFlag(Handle%) THEN

            TR = TopRow(Handle%)
            TC = TopCol(Handle%)
            LOCATE TR, TC
            InRegs.cx = 1

            FOR i = 1 TO Rows(Handle%)
```

Listing 2-6.   WindowDelete Subprogram—Deletes Window.   **2 of 2**

```
                FOR j = 1 TO Cols(Handle%)
                    InRegs.ax = &H900 + ASC(MID$(OldText(Handle%, i), j, 1))
                    InRegs.bx = ASC(MID$(OldAttrb(Handle%, i), j, 1))
                    CALL INTERRUPT(&H10, InRegs, OutRegs)
                    LOCATE TR + i - 1, TC + j
                NEXT j
                    LOCATE TR + i, TC
            NEXT i
        END IF

        LOCATE CurRow%, CurCol%

  →     Rows(Handle%) = 0          'WindowGetHandle checks only this.
  END SUB
```

That's all there is to WindowDelete( ). Now we have a tool that will let us do some housecleaning, if necessary, in our window system. Use WindowDelete( ) whenever you're approaching the maximum number of windows allowed by the system to free a few handles.

Deleting Our Test Window

Here's an example showing WindowDelete( ) in action:

```
DECLARE FUNCTION WindowGetHandle% (TopRow%, TopCol%, NumRow%, NumCol%, Attr%)
DECLARE SUB WindowShow (Handle%)
DECLARE SUB WindowDelete (Handle%)

Handle1% = WindowGetHandle%(10, 10, 5, 5, &H24)
Handle2% = WindowGetHandle%(10, 10, 3, 13, &H61)

CALL WindowShow(Handle1%)
CALL WindowShow(Handle2%)
CALL WindowDelete(Handle2%)
```

This program displays a window and covers it immediately with another window. Then it deletes the second, covering, window (which removes it from the screen since it's being displayed) and frees its handle for reassignment.

And that's it for our window system. We've designed windows, displayed them, hidden them, printed in them, moved them around the screen — and now deleted them. We've put together a formidable set of programming tools, ready for action. We should also note that the BASIC PDS has a number of window tools available; let's take the time now to see what it offers us here.

Windows in the BASIC PDS

The BASIC Professional Development System provides some window tools in its BASIC ToolBox ready for use (if you own a copy of the PDS). To see how they work, let's put together a window with the word "Hello" in it, and flash it on the screen.

Microsoft provides some preassembled assembly language routines for extra speed in displaying and hiding windows, and this code is in a file named UIASM.OBJ (which comes with the PDS). If you're using QBX.EXE, you'll have to put this .OBJ file into a Quick library before using it; if you're using BC.EXE (version 7.0 or later), you can put this .OBJ file into a library file and link it in.

Let's start with QBX.EXE. First, you have to create a Quick library, UIASM.QLB, like this:

```
LINK /Q UIASM.OBJ QBX.LIB, UIASM.QLB,, QBXQLB.LIB;
```

TIP: Making your own Quick libraries is a very powerful technique. Putting your tested and compiled modules into a Quick library means they'll all load at once, and the program as a whole will compile much faster.

If we were to call our example program WINDOWER.BAS, then we could then load it with QBX.EXE like this:

```
QBX WINDOWER /L UIASM
```

This loads WINDOWER.BAS and the quick library we just made. Before we can run the program, however, we'll have to load the PDS files MENU.BAS, GENERAL.BAS, WINDOW.BAS, and MOUSE.BAS as well — the PDS window system uses code in all these modules. After we do this, we're set, and we can run WINDOWER to make our window appear.

If you're using BC.EXE, you can create a library named UIASM.LIB to hold all the modules you'll need. This file has to contain not only the UIASM.OBJ module, but also the compiled versions of MENU.BAS, GENERAL.BAS, WINDOW.BAS, and MOUSE.BAS as well. Compile those files with BC.EXE and create the library UIASM.LIB like this:

```
LIB UIASM.LIB+UIASM.OBJ+GENERAL.OBJ+MOUSE.OBJ+MENU.OBJ+WINDOW.OBJ+QBX.LIB;
```

Now we've got everything we need. Compile WINDOWER.BAS with BC.EXE and then create the .EXE file like this:

```
LINK WINDOWER,,,UIASM;
```

At this point, we're ready to run WINDOWER.EXE, and we'll get the same result as we would under QBX.EXE.

WINDOWER.BAS—A PDS Window Program

Let's write the program WINDOWER.BAS to put a window on the screen. We have to start our program with a number of definition files, like this:

```
' $INCLUDE: 'C:\BC7\WINDOW.BI'
' $INCLUDE: 'C:\BC7\MENU.BI'
' $INCLUDE: 'C:\BC7\MOUSE.BI'
' $INCLUDE: 'C:\BC7GENERAL.BI'
        :
```

Next, just as in the code we developed ourselves, we have to set up some window commons:

```
' $INCLUDE: 'C:\BC7\WINDOW.BI'
' $INCLUDE: 'C:\BC7\MENU.BI'
' $INCLUDE: 'C:\BC7\MOUSE.BI'
' $INCLUDE: 'C:\BC7\GENERAL.BI'

COMMON SHARED /uitools/ GloMenu              AS MenuMiscType
COMMON SHARED /uitools/ GloTitle()           AS MenuTitleType
COMMON SHARED /uitools/ GloItem()            AS MenuItemType
COMMON SHARED /uitools/ GloWindow()          AS windowType
COMMON SHARED /uitools/ GloButton()          AS buttonType
COMMON SHARED /uitools/ GloEdit()            AS EditFieldType
COMMON SHARED /uitools/ GloStorage           AS WindowStorageType
COMMON SHARED /uitools/ GloWindowStack()     AS INTEGER
COMMON SHARED /uitools/ GloBuffer$()

DIM GloTitle(MAXMENU)             AS MenuTitleType
DIM GloItem(MAXMENU, MAXITEM)     AS MenuItemType
DIM GloWindow(MAXWINDOW)          AS windowType
DIM GloButton(MAXBUTTON)          AS buttonType
DIM GloEdit(MAXEDITFIELD)         AS EditFieldType
DIM GloWindowStack(MAXWINDOW)     AS INTEGER
DIM GloBuffer$(MAXWINDOW + 1, 2)
        :
```

Now we're ready to start the initialization process. Three systems have to be initalized to put a window on the screen — the window system, the menu system, and the mouse system (even though we're not using menus or the mouse):

```
' $INCLUDE: 'C:\BC7\WINDOW.BI'
' $INCLUDE: 'C:\BC7\MENU.BI'
' $INCLUDE: 'C:\BC7\MOUSE.BI'
' $INCLUDE: 'C:\BC7\GENERAL.BI'

COMMON SHARED /uitools/ GloMenu              AS MenuMiscType
COMMON SHARED /uitools/ GloTitle()           AS MenuTitleType
COMMON SHARED /uitools/ GloItem()            AS MenuItemType
COMMON SHARED /uitools/ GloWindow()          AS windowType
COMMON SHARED /uitools/ GloButton()          AS buttonType
COMMON SHARED /uitools/ GloEdit()            AS EditFieldType
COMMON SHARED /uitools/ GloStorage           AS WindowStorageType
COMMON SHARED /uitools/ GloWindowStack()     AS INTEGER
COMMON SHARED /uitools/ GloBuffer$()

DIM GloTitle(MAXMENU)              AS MenuTitleType
DIM GloItem(MAXMENU, MAXITEM)      AS MenuItemType
DIM GloWindow(MAXWINDOW)           AS windowType
DIM GloButton(MAXBUTTON)          AS buttonType
DIM GloEdit(MAXEDITFIELD)          AS EditFieldType
DIM GloWindowStack(MAXWINDOW)      AS INTEGER
DIM GloBuffer$(MAXWINDOW + 1, 2)
        CALL MenuInit               ←
        CALL WindowInit
        CALL MouseShow
        :
```

At this point, we're almost ready to display our window with the PDS subprogram WindowOpen( ). First, however, we have to figure out values for the numerous arguments we must pass to that subprogram. Here they are, in order:

Handle%   The window's number (1 for us)
Row1%, Col1%   Coordinates of upper left corner
Row2%, Col2%   Coordinates of lower right corner
TextFore%   Text foreground color (0-15)
TextBack%   Text background color (0-7)
Fore%   Window foreground color (0-15)
Back%   Window background color (0-7)
Highlight%   Color of highlighted buttons (0-15)
Movewin%   If TRUE (defined in the .BI files), window can
                     be moved
Closewin%   If TRUE, window can be closed

Sizewin%	If TRUE, window can be resized
Modalwin%	TRUE means that selecting outside the window results in a beep
Borderchar%	0 → No border
	1 → Single line border
	2 → Double-line border
Title$	Title of the window, " " → no title displayed

And here are the values we'll use for our window:

```
' $INCLUDE: 'C:\BC7\WINDOW.BI'
' $INCLUDE: 'C:\BC7\MENU.BI'
' $INCLUDE: 'C:\BC7\MOUSE.BI'
' $INCLUDE: 'C:\BC7\GENERAL.BI'

COMMON SHARED /uitools/ GloMenu              AS MenuMiscType
COMMON SHARED /uitools/ GloTitle()           AS MenuTitleType
COMMON SHARED /uitools/ GloItem()            AS MenuItemType
COMMON SHARED /uitools/ GloWindow()          AS windowType
COMMON SHARED /uitools/ GloButton()          AS buttonType
COMMON SHARED /uitools/ GloEdit()            AS EditFieldType
COMMON SHARED /uitools/ GloStorage           AS WindowStorageType
COMMON SHARED /uitools/ GloWindowStack()     AS INTEGER
COMMON SHARED /uitools/ GloBuffer$()

DIM GloTitle(MAXMENU)             AS MenuTitleType
DIM GloItem(MAXMENU, MAXITEM)     AS MenuItemType
DIM GloWindow(MAXWINDOW)          AS windowType
DIM GloButton(MAXBUTTON)          AS buttonType
DIM GloEdit(MAXEDITFIELD)         AS EditFieldType
DIM GloWindowStack(MAXWINDOW)     AS INTEGER
DIM GloBuffer$(MAXWINDOW + 1, 2)

        CALL MenuInit
        CALL WindowInit
        CALL MouseShow

→       CALL WindowOpen(1, 10, 20, 15, 30, 2, 1, 2, 1, 15, TRUE, TRUE, TRUE,
                    TRUE, 0, "")
        :
```

After we've done this, the window is on the screen. To print in it, we have to position the cursor with WindowLocate( ); then we can use the PDS subprogram WindowPrint( ) to do the actual printing (see Listing 2-7).

Listing 2-7.   Using Windows in BASIC PDS.

```
' $INCLUDE: 'C:\BC7\WINDOW.BI'
' $INCLUDE: 'C:\BC7\MENU.BI'
' $INCLUDE: 'C:\BC7\MOUSE.BI'
' $INCLUDE: 'C:\BC7\GENERAL.BI'

COMMON SHARED /uitools/ GloMenu            AS MenuMiscType
COMMON SHARED /uitools/ GloTitle()         AS MenuTitleType
COMMON SHARED /uitools/ GloItem()          AS MenuItemType
COMMON SHARED /uitools/ GloWindow()        AS windowType
COMMON SHARED /uitools/ GloButton()        AS buttonType
COMMON SHARED /uitools/ GloEdit()          AS EditFieldType
COMMON SHARED /uitools/ GloStorage         AS WindowStorageType
COMMON SHARED /uitools/ GloWindowStack()   AS INTEGER
COMMON SHARED /uitools/ GloBuffer$()

DIM GloTitle(MAXMENU)             AS MenuTitleType
DIM GloItem(MAXMENU, MAXITEM)     AS MenuItemType
DIM GloWindow(MAXWINDOW)          AS windowType
DIM GloButton(MAXBUTTON)          AS buttonType
DIM GloEdit(MAXEDITFIELD)         AS EditFieldType
DIM GloWindowStack(MAXWINDOW)     AS INTEGER
DIM GloBuffer$(MAXWINDOW + 1, 2)
        CALL MenuInit
        CALL WindowInit
        CALL MouseShow

        CALL WindowOpen(1, 10, 20, 15, 30, 2, 1, 2, 1, 15, TRUE, TRUE, TRUE, _
                 TRUE, 0, "")
→       CALL WindowLocate(1, 1)
        CALL WindowPrint(1, "Hello.")
```

In this example, we use WindowLocate( ) to position the cursor at (1,1) in the window, and then print in this window (window 1) with WindowPrint( ); at this point, "Hello." appears in our window. And that's it — the PDS window is set up. If you have the PDS, give it a try; there are many different window options, and you might find some of them that work well for you.

Conclusion

And that's it for windows. In this chapter, we've seen how to set them up, show them or hide them, print to them, move them, and delete them — and we've seen what the BASIC PDS has to offer as well. But now we're going to turn from output to input; we're going to augment BASIC by adding support for the mouse in Chapter 3, *The Mouse*.

The Mouse

IN THIS CHAPTER, we're going to add support for the mouse. We can do that by using DOS interrupt &H33 (the mouse interrupt) to reach the mouse from BASIC. There's going to be frequent use of the INTERRUPT( ) routine in this chapter.

> **NOTE:** Because all the subprograms and functions in this chapter use the INTER-RUPT( ) routine, you must load them with the /L switch if you're using Quick-BASIC — either QB.EXE or QBX.EXE.

We'll see how to initialize the mouse, read position and button information from it, and work with the mouse cursor. We'll also see examples, showing how to make use of mouse information. And, in the next chapter, we'll really put what we've learned here to use, when we combine windows and the mouse to produce pull-down menus.

Getting Started

There are two things you need to know before we start to use the mouse. First, under DOS, you must load the mouse driver software that came with your mouse before trying to use it. You can do that by running the .COM file that comes with the mouse (e.g., MOUSE.COM for a Microsoft or a Logitech mouse, or MOUSESYS.COM for a Mouse Systems mouse). You must run this driver program before any program can use your mouse. For more information, consult the mouse's documentation. Note that under OS/2 or the DOS mode of OS/2 you do not need to do this — OS/2 sets up the mouse for you.

> **NOTE:** The mouse driver program loads the code to handle the mouse interrupt, interrupt &H33.

Second, you have to initialize the mouse before using it. Just as in the window functions we developed, where we had to use WindowGetHandle%( ), you need to initialize the mouse system before putting it to work. We'll start this chapter off by developing a function named MouseInitialize%( ) to do exactly that; before you can use the mouse, you must call MouseInitialize%( ). After that, you can use any other mouse function or subprogram that we develop below in whatever order you want, as demonstrated by the examples coming up.

NOTE: MouseInitialize%( ) initializes the mouse driver software that you loaded above.

TIP: In many programs, use of a mouse is optional and depends on whether or not a mouse and mouse driver are installed. You should know that, even if a mouse is optional, you can call and use the mouse functions and subprograms here without a problem. If there is no mouse, you'll simply see no mouse "events" like cursor movements or button presses. (And you should make sure you don't loop forever, waiting for such events.) In other words, using the mouse subprograms and functions does no harm if there is no mouse.

Initializing the Mouse

Initializing the mouse is a necessary first step towards using the mouse. We can do that with interrupt &H33, service 0. If this service returns a nonzero value, the mouse is initialized; otherwise, the mouse cannot be used (because it's not installed in the computer or the mouse driver is missing). In that case, and if your program depends on the use of a mouse, you should print out an error message and quit.

Once the mouse is initialized, we're all set until the computer is turned off — we don't have to initialize it again (although doing so does no harm). Note that initializing the mouse does not display the mouse cursor: to display the cursor use the subprogram we'll develop later, named MouseShowCursor( ).

MouseInitialize% ( )

This function just uses interrupt &H33 service 0 (i.e., ah = 0) to initialize the mouse system. As mentioned, this is the necessary first step to using any other mouse function. Here's all we do: load ah with 0 and call interrupt &H33, then we set MouseInitialize% to the value returned in ax:

```
    DIM InRegs AS RegType, OutRegs AS RegType
→   InRegs.ax = 0
    CALL INTERRUPT(&H33, InRegs, OutRegs)
    MouseInitialize% = OutRegs.ax
```

If this value is not zero, the mouse was successfully intialized; otherwise the operation failed. Make sure you test this return value.

Listing 3-1 shows the whole function:

Listing 3-1.   MouseInitialize% ( ) Function.

```
DECLARE FUNCTION MouseInitialize% ( )

TYPE RegType
          ax    AS INTEGER
          bx    AS INTEGER
          cx    AS INTEGER
          dx    AS INTEGER
          bp    AS INTEGER
          si    AS INTEGER
          di    AS INTEGER
          flags AS INTEGER
END TYPE
DECLARE SUB INTERRUPT (IntNo AS INTEGER, InRegs AS RegType, OutRegs AS RegType)
FUNCTION MouseInitialize%
DIM InRegs AS RegType, OutRegs AS RegType
InRegs.ax = 0
CALL INTERRUPT(&H33, InRegs, OutRegs)
MouseInitialize% = OutRegs.ax
END FUNCTION
```

Mouse Initializing Window

Here's how to use MouseInitialize%( ):

```
REMExample of MouseInitialize

DECLARE FUNCTION MouseInitialize% ( )

LOCATE 1, 1

IF MouseInitialize% THEN
     PRINT "Mouse Initialized."
ELSE
     PRINT "Mouse driver not installed."
END IF
```

We check the value returned by MouseInitialize%( ) — if it's zero, we print out an error message ("Mouse driver not installed.") and quit. Otherwise, we print "Mouse Initialized." and then quit.

Now that we've set up the mouse system for use, let's start our use of the mouse by displaying the mouse cursor.

Making the Mouse Cursor Visible

The next step in using the mouse is to show the mouse cursor on the screen. In text mode, this cursor appears as a solid block (although you can change that with MouseSet-Cursor( ), developed later in this chapter), and in graphics mode as an arrow. Let's write a small subprogram named MouseShowCursor( ) to do the work for us.

MouseShowCursor( )

Like all the of mouse functions and subprograms we'll write, we just use another interrupt &H33 service here; in this case, we use service 1, which displays the mouse cursor:

```
    DIM InRegs AS RegType, OutRegs AS RegType
→   InRegs.ax = 1
    CALL INTERRUPT(&H33, InRegs, OutRegs)
```

When you use MouseShowCursor( ), the cursor appears on the screen. Listing 3-2 shows the whole subprogram.

```
List 3.2.   MouseShowCursor ( ) Subprogram.

DECLARE SUB MouseShowCursor ( )
TYPE Reg
        Type
        ax     AS INTEGER
        bx     AS INTEGER
        cx     AS INTEGER
        dx     AS INTEGER
        bp     AS INTEGER
        si     AS INTEGER
        di     AS INTEGER
        flags AS INTEGER
END TYPE

DECLARE SUB INTERRUPT (IntNo AS INTEGER, InRegs AS RegType, OutRegs AS RegType)

SUB MouseShowCursor

    DIM InRegs AS RegType, OutRegs AS RegType
    InRegs.ax = 1
    CALL INTERRUPT(&H33, InRegs, OutRegs)
END SUB
```

Using MouseShowCursor( )

Here's how to put MouseShowCursor( ) to work:

```
REM Example of MouseShowCursor

DECLARE FUNCTION MouseInitialize% ( )
DECLARE SUB MouseShowCursor ( )

Check% = MouseInitialize%

LOCATE 1, 1
IF Check% = 0 THEN
   PRINT "Mouse driver not installed."
ELSE
   PRINT "Mouse Initialized."
   CALL MouseShowCursor
END IF
```

Notice that we first initialize the mouse with the function MouseInitialize%( ), and, if that worked, then we display the cursor with MouseShowCursor( ).

TIP: If the mouse system is not initialized for some reason, calls to interrupt &H33 have no effect.

Now that we've displayed the mouse cursor on the screen, our next step will be to hide it.

Hiding the Mouse Cursor

Now we'll hide the mouse cursor. There are times when the mouse cursor can be a distraction on the screen, and we'll fix that problem here.

NOTE: If the mouse cursor is already off, it stays off when we hide it.

There is one more little-known — but very important — reason for hiding the mouse cursor. As the mouse cursor moves over the screen, the mouse driver software reads the character at the present screen position before displaying the mouse cursor. Then, when the mouse cursor moves on, that character is restored, attribute and all. However, if you've changed the screen display behind the mouse cursor, it will still restore the original (and wrong) character.

For example, if you move the mouse cursor to position A, the driver reads the character at position A for later restoration, and then it overwrites it with the mouse cursor. Now, before you move the mouse cursor, let's say you turn a window on there, using WindowShow( ). Next, you move the mouse cursor, and the driver software, unaware of appearance of the window, replaces the original character at position A, leaving a one-character hole in your window.

To avoid this problem, you should always turn the mouse cursor *off* when displaying a window or overwriting the mouse cursor in any way (using the subprogram we're about to write, MouseHideCursor( )), and turn it on again immediately afterwards (using MouseShowCursor( )). This solves the problem completely.

NOTE: In fact, if you look through the menu programs carefully in Chapter 4, *Pull-down Menus,* you'll see where we have to do exactly this to avoid the problem.

Let's write the subprogram to hide the mouse cursor, MouseHideCursor( ).

MouseHideCursor( )

Here we just make use of interrupt &H33 service 2, which hides the mouse cursor:

```
    DIM InRegs AS RegType, OutRegs AS RegType
→   InRegs.ax = 2
    CALL INTERRUPT(&H33, InRegs, OutRegs)
```

Listing 3-3 shows what the whole subprogram looks like, ready to roll.

Listing 3.3 MouseHideCursor Subprogram.   1 of 2

```
DECLARE SUB MouseHideCursor ( )

TYPE RegType
        ax    AS INTEGER
        bx    AS INTEGER
        cx    AS INTEGER
        dx    AS INTEGER
        bp    AS INTEGER
        si    AS INTEGER
        di    AS INTEGER
        flags AS INTEGER
END TYPE
```

Listing 3.3 MouseHideCursor Subprogram.   2 of 2

```
DECLARE SUB INTERRUPT (IntNo AS INTEGER, InRegs AS RegType, OutRegs AS RegType)

SUB MouseHideCursor

 DIM InRegs AS RegType, OutRegs AS RegType
 InRegs.ax = 2
 CALL INTERRUPT(&H33, InRegs, OutRegs)

 END SUB
```

Using MouseHide Cursor( )

The example program show in Listing 3-4 displays the mouse cursor and then hides it after you press any key:

Listing 3-4. MouseHide Cursor Program.

```
REM Example of MouseHideCursor

DECLARE FUNCTION MouseInitialize% ()
DECLARE SUB MouseShowCursor ()
DECLARE SUB MouseHideCursor ()
Check% =MouseInitialize%

LOCATE 1,1
IF Check%= 0 THEN
    PRINT "Mouse driver not installed."
ELSE
    PRINT "Mouse Initialized."
    CALL MouseShowCursor
    PRINT "Press any key to hide the mouse cursor."
    DO
    LOOP WHILE INKEY$ = ""
    CALL MouseHideCursor
END IF
```

Again, we initialize the mouse system, and, if successful, show the mouse cursor and print out the prompt: "Press any key to hide the mouse cursor." When a key is pressed, we hide the mouse cursor with MouseHideCursor( ).

At this point, we've been able to set the mouse system up, show the cursor and hide it at will. Those are good beginning steps, but now it's time to start reading information from the mouse.

For example, we may want to check the status of the mouse at some given time. Is there a button being pressed? And where is the mouse cursor? We'll work out the answer to these questions next.

Reading Immediate Mouse Information

There is one way of getting information from the mouse — interrupt &H33 service 3 returns the immediate status of the left and right buttons, as well as the row and column number of the mouse cursor's position. When you call it, it returns this information encoded in the bx, cx, and dx registers, providing us with a snapshot of what the mouse is doing now.

Here's how the registers are set on return:

bx	0 = no button down; 1 = right button down; 2 = left button down; 3 = both buttons down
cx	Screen column of mouse cursor (using pixel ranges)
dx	Screen row of mouse cursor (using pixel ranges) Let's write a subprogram to report these things to us.

MouseInformation( )

It would be ideal to have a subprogram we could call this way: CALL MouseInformation (Right%, Left%, Row%, Col%) The variables we pass could be set this way on return:

Right%	0 = Right mouse button is up; 1 = Right mouse button is down
Left%	0 = Left mouse button is up; 1 = Left mouse button is down
Row%	Current text-mode screen row of mouse cursor (Range 1 - 25)
Col%	Current text-mode screen column of mouse cursor (Range 1 - 80)

This subprogram is designed to return a snapshot of the mouse's present state. As we saw, interrupt &H33 service 3 returns button information in OutRegs.bx; if this value is 1, the left button only is down. If it's 2, the right button only is down. If 3, both are down. (And if 0, neither are down.) Here's how we can decode that information into the parameters Right% and Left%:

```
    SUB MouseInformation (Right%, Left%, Row%, Col%)

        DIM InRegs AS RegType, OutRegs AS RegType
        InRegs.ax = 3
        CALL INTERRUPT(&H33, InRegs, OutRegs)

            Right% = 0
            Left% = 0

→           SELECT CASE OutRegs.bx
:               CASE 1
:                       Left% = 1
                    CASE 2
                        Right% = 1
                    CASE 3
                        Left% = 1
                        Right% = 1
                END SELECT
                    :
                    :
```

Next, OutRegs.dx holds the present screen row in pixels, and OutRegs.cx holds the present screen column in pixels. The mouse and menu work we're going to do will usually be in text mode, however, so let's report screen row and column numbers (i.e., 1-25 and 1-80, not pixel ranges like 0-199 and 0-639). We convert from pixel ranges to the normal screen row and column ranges like this:

```
    SUB MouseInformation (Right%, Left%, Row%, Col%)

        DIM InRegs AS RegType, OutRegs AS RegType
        InRegs.ax = 3
        CALL INTERRUPT (&H33, InRegs, OutRegs)

            Right% = 0
            Left% = 0

            SELECT CASE OutRegs.bx
                CASE 1
                        Left% = 1
                    CASE 2
                        Right% = 1
                    CASE 3
                        Left% = 1
                        Right% = 1
                END SELECT

→           Row% = Out Regs.dx  8 + 1
            Col% = Out Regs.cx 8 + 1
```

And we're set. Listing 3-5 shows the whole subprogram.

Listing 3-5.   Mouse Information Subprogram.

```
DECLARE SUB MouseInformation (Right%, Left%, Row%, Col%)

TYPE RegType
        ax    AS INTEGER
        bx    AS INTEGER
        cx    AS INTEGER
        dx    AS INTEGER
        bp    AS INTEGER
        si    AS INTEGER
        di    AS INTEGER
        flags AS INTEGER
END TYPE

DECLARE SUB INTERRUPT (IntNo AS INTEGER, InRegs AS RegType, OutRegs AS RegType)

SUB MouseInformation (Right%, Left%, Row%, Col%)

 DIM InRegs AS RegType, OutRegs AS Reg Type
 InRegs.ax = 3
 CALL INTERRUPT(&H33, InRegs, OutRegs)

    Right% = 0
    Left% = 0

    SELECT CASE OutRegs .bx
        CASE 1
            Left% = 1
        CASE 2
            Right% = 1
        CASE 3
            Left% = 1
            Right% = 1
    END SELECT

    Row% = OutRegs.dx   8 + 1
    Col% = OutRegs.cx   8 + 1

END SUB
```

Finding the Mouse's Current State

This example program just reports the mouse state when you press a key:

```
REM Example of MouseInformation

DECLARE FUNCTION MouseInitialize% ()
DECLARE SUB MouseShowCursc ()
DECLARE SUB MouseInformation (Right%, Left%, Row%, Col%)

Check% = MouseInitialize%

LOCATE 1, 1
IF Check% = 0 THEN
    PRINT "Mouse driver not installed."
ELSE
```

```
    PRINT "Mouse Initialized."
    CALL MouseShowCursor
    PRINT "Position the mouse and press any key."
    DO
    LOOP WHILE INKEY$ = ""
    CALL MouseInformation (Right%, Left%, Row%, Col%)

    IF RIGHT% THEN
        PRINT "Right button down."
    ELSE
        PRINT "Right button up."
    END IF

    IF LEFT% THEN
        PRINT "Left button down."
    ELSE
        PRINT "Left button up."
    END IF

    PRINT "Row: ", Row%, "Column: ", Col%

END IF
```

Here you can see how we use MouseInformation( ) and then decode the returned values Right%, Left%, Row%, and Col%. To use this program, make sure you've loaded the mouse driver as outlined in the beginning of this chapter. When you press any key on the keyboard, this program will report the present mouse state.

The most severe limitation here is that MouseInformation( ) only provides an instant snapshot of what's going on with the mouse. If you want to use it for mouse input, you have to keep "polling" it; that is, looping over it until something happens.

TIP: A better option is the subprograms we will develop later that use other, specialized interrupt &H33 services. In them, button action is stored in a "queue," and it waits until you call for it. This is the way most mouse programming is done — with queues. You don't have to catch a button being pressed exactly as it is being pressed — you can find out about it when you're ready to deal with it.

Also, you might prefer to have the row and column numbers returned in pixel format rather than text format (i.e., in ranges like 0-199 and 0-639 rather than 1-25 and 1-80). If so, just set Row% and Col% equal to OutRegs.dx and OutRegs.cx, respectively, at the end of MouseInformation( ):

```
Row% = OutRegs.dx
Col% = OutRegs.cx
```

TIP: In text mode, the mouse cursor jumps from character position to character position anyway. The pixel value that is returned corresponds to the top left corner of the character position.

Let's continue our exploration of the mouse with service 4, which lets you move the mouse cursor at will.

Moving the Mouse Cursor

With service 4, we'll gain control over the mouse cursor. Up to this point, the only way to make the mouse cursor move was to move the mouse (as soon as you show the mouse cursor, it responds to mouse movements). However, we can develop a subprogram named MouseMoveCursor( ) to position the mouse cursor as we want it.

MouseMoveCursor( )

It would be simplest if we could position the mouse by just passing the desired screen row and column numbers like this:

```
CALL MouseMoveCursor (Row%, Col%)
```

To write MouseMoveCursor( ), we'll just make use of interrupt &H33 service 4. We have to pass the mouse cursor's new location in dx (rows) and cx (columns). Because we are using text-mode rows and columns, we first convert that location into pixel ranges like this:

```
    DIM InRegs AS RegType, OutRegs AS RegType

→   InRegs.dx = 8 * (Row% - 1)
    InRegs.cx = 8 * (Col% - 1)
    InRegs.ax = 4
    CALL INTERRUPT(&H33, InRegs, OutRegs)
```

Even if you request a position far off the screen, this service does not return an error (which is why MouseMoveCursor( ) does not produce any output); it simply places the cursor at the edge of the screen. Listing 3-6 shows the whole subprogram.

Listing 3-6.   MouseMoveCursor Subprogram.

```
DECLARE SUB MouseMoveCursor (Row%, Col%)

TYPE RegType
        ax        AS INTEGER
        bx        AS INTEGER
        cx        AS INTEGER
        dx        AS INTEGER
        bp        AS INTEGER
        si        AS INTEGER
        di        AS INTEGER
        flags     AS INTEGER
END TYPE

DECLARE SUB INTERRUPT (IntNo AS INTEGER, InRegs AS RegType, OutRegs AS RegType)

SUB MouseMoveCursor (Row%, Col%)

    DIM InRegs AS RegType, OutRegs AS RegType
    InRegs.dx = 8 * (Row% - 1)
    InRegs.cx = 8 * (Col% - 1)
    InRegs.ax = 4
    CALL INTERRUPT(& H33, InRegs, OutRegs)

END SUB
```

Moving to the Top Left of the Screen

In this example, we move the mouse cursor to screen position (1, 1) after you press a key:

```
REM Example of MouseMoveCursor

DECLARE FUNCTION MouseInitialize% ()
DECLARE SUB MouseShowCursor ()
DECLARE SUB MouseMoveCursor (Row%, Col%)

Check% = MouseInitialize%

LOCATE 1, 1
IF Check% = 0 THEN
    PRINT "Mouse driver not installed."
ELSE
    PRINT "Mouse Initialized."
    CALL MouseShowCursor
    LOCATE 10, 20
    PRINT "Press any key to move the mouse cursor to (1,1)"
    DO
    LOOP WHILE INKEY$ = ""
    CALL MouseMoveCursor (1,1)
END IF
```

You can see that it's easy to use MouseMoveCursor( ) — just pass the desired row and column number. Of course, getting no error back from this service is both a blessing and a curse. On one hand, you're not troubled by error messages; on the other, if you made a genuine error in placing the mouse cursor, you should know about it.

One reasonable change to MouseMoveCursor( ) is to check the row and column number requested. If they're out of range, you should still move the cursor, but you can pass back an error code.

The next interrupt &H33 service is among the most useful. Service 5 tells you how many times a specific button was pressed since the last time you inquired — and using this service means that we won't have to catch button presses as they happen.

Reading the Button Pressed Queue

It would be useful to develop the mouse equivalent of INKEY$. We already have MouseInformation( ), but you must catch mouse events as they happen to use it. Instead, it would be much better if they could be stored and we could read them as we require them.

We can do that with service 5. This service lets us read the number of times a specific button has been pressed since we last checked. It also gives you the row and column screen position of mouse cursor the *last* time the button was pressed. Pressing a mouse button is usually more significant than just moving the mouse cursor around the screen. For that reason, you can treat this service as the primary mouse input routine.

Let's write a subprogram called, say, MouseTimesPressed( ), to connect service 5 to BASIC. We should call MouseTimesPressed( ) when we start accepting input to clear the mouse buffer, then loop over and call it periodically to see if anything else has happened, much like INKEY$.

MouseTimesPressed( )

We need to query service 5 about the number of time a specific button — right or left — was pressed. The return values we expect are the number of times the button has been pressed, and the mouse cursor's position the last time the button was pressed. In other words, we can set up MouseTimesPressed( ) like this:

```
CALL MouseTimesPressed (Button%, NumberTimes%, Row%, Col%)
```

We can use the same designation for the variable Button% as the interrupt &H33 services themselves use — a value of 0 for the left button, and 1 for the right button. On return, we'll be able to read the other variables like this:

NumberTimes%	The number of times the specified button was pushed since the last time MouseTimesPressed( ) was called.
Row%	The screen row (1-25) of the mouse cursor the last time that button was pressed.
Col%	The screen column (1-80) of the mouse cursor the last time that button was pressed.

Using interrupt &H33 service 5 makes this subprogram pretty easy. We just place the button number (0 for the left button, 1 for the right) into InRegs.bx and call service 5:

```
    SUB MouseTimesPressed (Button%, NumberTimes%, Row%, Col%)

    DIMInRegs AS RegType, OutRegs AS RegType

→   InRegs.bx = Button%
    InRegs.ax = 5
    CALL INTERRUPT(&H33, InRegs, OutRegs)
        :
        :
```

The results come back in bx, cx, and dx. The bx register holds the number of times the specified button, left or right, was pressed since the last time service 5 was called. The dx register holds the screen (pixel) row where the button was last pushed, and cx holds the corresponding column. We can convert these to text-mode row and column ranges (1-25 and 1-80) and return:

```
    SUB MouseTimesPressed (Button%, NumberTimes%, Row%, Col%)

    DIM InRegs AS RegType, OutRegs AS RegType

    InRegs. bx = Button%
    InRegs. ax = 5
    CALL INTERRUPT(&H33, InRegs, OutRegs)

→   NumberTimes% = OutRegs.bx
    Row% =  OutRegs .dx 8 + 1
    Col % = OutRegs.cx 8 + 1
```

Listing 3-7 shows the entire code for MouseTimesPressed( ), ready to be put to work:

Listing 3-7.   MouseTimesPressed Subprogram.

```
DECLARE SUB MouseTimesPressed (Button%, NumberTimes%, Row%, Col%)
REM Button% should be 0 to return left button info, 1 for right.

TYPE RegType
        ax    AS INTEGER
        bx    AS INTEGER
        cx    AS INTEGER
        dx    AS INTEGER
        bp    AS INTEGER
        si    AS INTEGER
        di    AS INTEGER
        flags AS INTEGER
END TYPE

DECLARE SUB INTERRUPT (IntNo AS INTEGER, InRegs AS RegType, OutRegs AS RegType)

SUB MouseTimesPressed (Button%, NumberTimes%, Row%, Col%)

 DIM InRegs AS RegType, OutRegs AS RegType

 InRegs.bx = Button%
 InRegs.ax = 5
 CALL INTERRUPT(&H33, InRegs, OutRegs)

 NumberTimes% = OutRegs.bx
 Row% = OutRegs.dx 8 + 1
 Col% = OutRegs.cx 8 + 1

END SUB
```

And now we can put it to work.

Counting Button Presses

This example program shows MouseTimesPressed( ) at work. All it does is to ask you to press the right mouse button a number of times and then press any key on the keyboard. When you do, this program reports the number of times you've clicked the button, and the last position at which you did so.

```
REM Example of MouseShowCursor

DECLARE FUNCTION MouseInitialize% ()
DECLARE SUB MouseShowCursor ()
DECLARE SUB MouseTimesPressed (Button%, NumberTimes%, Row%, Col%)

Check% = MouseInitialize%

LOCATE 1, 1
IF Check% = 0 THEN
    PRINT "Mouse driver not installed."
ELSE
    PRINT "Mouse Initialized."
    CALL MouseShowCursor
    PRINT "Press the right mouse button a number of times and then any key."
    DO
    LOOP WHILE INKEY$ = ""
    CALL MouseTimesPressed(1, NumberTimes%, Row%, Col%)
    PRINT "You pressed it ";NumberTimes%;" times."
    PRINT "The last time was at (";Row%;",";Col%;")."

END IF
```

Let's go through the steps: we initialize the mouse with MouseInitialize( ), display the cursor with MouseShowCursor( ), and then read mouse information with MouseTimesPressed( ).

The limitation here is that MouseTimesPressed( ) only returns the location of the *last* time a specific button was pressed, and you still have to poll this subprogram periodically to find out what's going on with the mouse (but not as often as with MouseInformation( ), in which you have to catch the mouse event in the act).

In practice, this means that you should check MouseTimesPressed( ) frequently enough to make sure that mouse events don't get a chance to stack up in the mouse queue.

Another limitation here is that you're often more interested in when the mouse button was *released*, not pressed. For example, releasing the mouse button is important when you're dragging an object across the screen or making a menu selection. Luckily, the next interrupt &H33 service, service 6, lets us handle that.

Reading the Button Released Queue

We can use service 6 to write a subprogram that will give us button release information; let's call this subprogram MouseTimesReleased( ). It should give us information about the number of times a particular button was released since we called it, and the screen position of the mouse cursor when it was last released.

MouseTimesReleased ( )

Here's how we might call MouseTimesReleased( ):

```
CALL MouseTimesReleased (Button%, NumberTimes%, Row%, Col%)
```

Again, we set Button% to 0 if we want right button information, and to 1 for the left button. And, following MouseTimesPressed( ), this is how we can design the return values:

NumberTimes%   INTEGER   The number of times the specified button was released since the last time MouseTimesReleased( ) was called.

Row%   INTEGER   The screen row (1-25) of the mouse cursor the last time that button was released.

Col%   INTEGER   The screen column (1-80) of the mouse cursor the last time that button was released.

This subprogram is very like MouseTimesPressed( ), except that we use interrupt &H33 service 6, not 5:

```
    DIM InRegs AS RegType, OutRegs AS RegType

    InRegs.bx = Button%
→   InRegs.ax = 6
    CALL INTERRUPT(&H33, InRegs, OutRegs)
    :
    :
```

After the call, we decode the information in exactly the same way as we did for MouseTimesPressed( ):

```
    DIM InRegs AS RegType, OutRegs AS RegType

    InRegs.bx = Button%
    InRegs.ax = 6
    CALL INTERRUPT(&H33, InRegs, OutRegs)

→   NumberTimes% = OutRegs.bx
```

```
Row% = OutRegs.dx 8 + 1
Col% = OutRegs.cx 8 + 1
```

And that's it. Listing 3-8 shows the whole subprogram.

Listing 3-8.   MouseTimesReleased Subprogram.

```
DECLARE SUB MouseTimesReleased (Button%, NumberTimes%, Row%, Col%)

REM Button should be 0 to return left button info, 1 for right.

TYPE RegType
        ax    AS INTEGER
        bx    AS INTEGER
        cx    AS INTEGER
        dx    AS INTEGER
        bp    AS INTEGER
        si    AS INTEGER
        di    AS INTEGER
        flags AS INTEGER
END TYPE

DECLARE SUB INTERRUPT (IntNo AS INTEGER, InRegs AS RegType, OutRegs AS RegType)

SUB MouseTimesReleased (Button%, NumberTimes%, Row%, Col%)

    DIM InRegs ASRegType, OutRegs AS RegType

    InRegs.bx = Button%
    InRegs.ax = 6
    CALL INTERRUPT(&H33, InRegs, OutRegs)

    NumberTimes% = OutRegs.bx
    Row% = OutRegs.dx 8 + 1
    Col% = OutRegs.cx 8 + 1

END SUB
```

Now let's put it to work!

Counting Button Releases

This example program is just like the one for MouseTimesPressed( ), except that it indicates the number of times the button was released, not pressed:

```
REM Example of MouseShowCursor

DECLARE FUNCTION MouseInitialize% ()
```

```
DECLARE SUB MouseShowCursor ()
DECLARE SUB MouseTimesReleased (Button%, NumberTimes%, Row%, Col%)

Check% = MouseInitialize%

LOCATE 1, 1
IF Check% = 0 THEN
    PRINT "Mouse driver not installed."
ELSE
    PRINT "Mouse Initialized."
    CALL MouseShowCursor
    PRINT "Press the left mouse button a number of times and then any key."
    DO
    LOOP WHILE INKEY$ = ""
CALL MouseTimesReleased(0, NumberTimes%, Row%, Col%)

PRINT "You released it ";NumberTimes%; "times."
PRINT "The last time was at (";Row%;",";Col%;")."

END IF
```

Again we initialize the mouse, then show the mouse cursor and, after a key is pressed, read mouse information from MouseTimesReleased( ). That's all we have to do.

We've been following the interrupt &H33 services throughout this chapter, and there are a few more that deserve our attention. For example, the next service, service 7, allows you to restrict the mouse cursor to a specific range of columns on the screen.

TIP: Together with service 8, which restricts the row range, you can restrict the mouse cursor to a specific window on the screen if you wish, giving a very professional effect.

Restricting the Mouse Horizontally

As mentioned, service 7 restricts the mouse cursor, and therefore mouse events, to a specified range of columns. We can put together a subprogram to interface with this service like this:

```
CALL MouseHorizontalRange (Right%, Left%)
```

Where we fill the variables like this:

Right%   Right column of allowed mouse cursor range. (Range: 1-80)
Left%   Left column of allowed mouse cursor range. (Range: 1-80)

Now all that remains is to write the code.

MouseHorizontalRange( )

As we've seen, interrupt &H33 service 7 lets us restrict the mouse cursor's horizontal range by specifying the right column of that range in cx and the right column in dx. We simply convert to pixel ranges and call interrupt &H33 to make this subprogram work:

```
        DIM InRegs AS RegType, OutRegs AS RegType

    →   InRegs.cx = 8 * (Right% - 1)
        InRegs.dx = 8 * (Left% - 1)
        InRegs.ax = 7
        CALL INTERRUPT(&H33, InRegs, OutRegs)
```

And that's all there is to it (service 7 does not return any values). Listing 3-9 shows the whole subprogram.

Listing 3-9.   MouseHorizontalRange Subprogram.   1 of 2

```
DECLARE SUB MouseHorizontalRange (Right%, Left%)

TYPE RegType
        ax      AS INTEGER
        bx      AS INTEGER
        cx      AS INTEGER
        dx      AS INTEGER
        bp      AS INTEGER
        si      AS INTEGER
        di      AS INTEGER
        flags AS INTEGER
END TYPE

DECLARE SUB INTERRUPT (IntNo AS INTEGER, InRegs AS RegType, OutRegs AS RegType)

SUB MouseHorizontalRange (Right%, Left%)

   DIM InRegs AS RegType, OutRegs AS RegType

   InRegs.cx = 8 * (Right% - 1)
```

```
Listing 3-9.   MouseHorizontalRange Subprogram.                2 of 2
    InRegs.dx = 8 * (Left% - 1)
    InRegs.ax = 7
    CALL INTERRUPT(&H33, InRegs, OutRegs)

END SUB
```

Now let's see it in action.

MouseHorizontalRange( ) at Work

In this example program, we restrict the mouse cursor to the left half of the screen by passing a leftmost column of 1 and a rightmost column of 40:

```
REM Example of MouseHorizontalRange

DECLARE FUNCTION MouseInitialize% ()
DECLARE SUB MouseShowCursor ()
DECLARE SUB MouseHorizontalRange (Right%, Left%)

Check% = MouseInitialize%

LOCATE 1, 1
IF Check% = 0 THEN
    PRINT "Mouse driver not installed."
ELSE
    PRINT "Mouse Initialized."
    CALL MouseShowCursor
    PRINT "Press any key to restrict mouse to the left half of the screen."
    DO
    LOOP WHILE INKEY$ = ""
    CALL MouseHorizontalRange(1, 40)
END IF
```

TIP: Service 7 sorts out the two values (as you can imagine, the leftmost column has to be less than or equal to the rightmost column), so it actually does not matter if we call MouseHorizontalRange(40, 1) or MouseHorizontalRange(1, 40).

If you'd like to use graphics mode, you can change MouseHorizontalRange( ) to use pixel ranges rather than column ranges.

The next service does the same thing, except that it restricts vertical, not horizontal motion. Let's look into it.

Restricting the Mouse Vertically

After MouseHorizontalRange( ), MouseVerticalRange( ) is the logical next subprogram. It restricts the mouse cursor to a specified vertical range of screen rows (1-25). Together, these two subprograms can restrict mouse operation to a specific window of your choosing. Here's the way we might use it:

```
CALL MouseVerticalRange (Top%, Bottom%)
```

where these are the inputs:

Top%	Top row of allowed mouse cursor movement (Range: 1-25)
Bottom%	Bottom row of allowed mouse cursor movement (Range: 1-25)

Developing this subprogram will be easy.

MouseVerticalRange ( )

We just have to use interrupt &H33 service 8 in much the way we used service 7. Now, however, we are restricting the mouse cursor not to a specific set of columns, but to a specific set of rows:

```
    DIM InRegs AS RegType, OutRegs AS RegType
→   InRegs.cx = 8 * (Top% - 1)
    InRegs.dx = 8 * (Bottom% - 1)
    InRegs.ax = 8
    CALL INTERRUPT(&H33, InRegs, OutRegs)
```

That's all there is to it. Listing 3-10 shows the ready-to-use subprograms.

Listing 3-10. MouseVerticalRange ( ) Subprogram. 1 of 2

```
DECLARE SUB MouseVerticalRange (Top%, Bottom%)

TYPE RegType
        ax      AS INTEGER
```

```
Listing 3-10.   MouseVerticalRange ( ) Subprogram.                    2 of 2
         bx    AS INTEGER
         cx    AS INTEGER
         dx    AS INTEGER
         bp    AS INTEGER
         si    AS INTEGER
         di    AS INTEGER
         flags AS INTEGER
END TYPE

DECLARE SUB INTERRUPT (IntNo AS INTEGER, InRegs AS RegType, OutRegs AS RegType)

SUB MouseVerticalRange (Top%, Bottom%)
        DIM InRegs AS RegType, OutRegs AS RegType

        InRegs.cx = 8 * (Top% - 1)
        InRegs.dx = 8 * (Bottom% - 1)
        InRegs.ax = 8
        CALL INTERRUPT(&H33, InRegs, OutRegs)
END SUB
```

Let's see an example.

MouseVerticalRange ( ) at Work

In this program, we restrict the mouse cursor to the top half of the screen by calling MouseVerticalRange(12, 1):

```
REM Example of MouseVerticalRange

DECLARE FUNCTION MouseInitialize% ( )
DECLARE SUB MouseShowCursor ( )
DECLARE SUB MouseVerticalRange (Bottom%, Top%)

Check% = MouseInitialize%

LOCATE 1, 1
IF Check% = 0 THEN
    PRINT "Mouse driver not installed."
ELSE
    PRINT "Mouse Initialized."
    CALL MouseShowCursor
    PRINT "Press any key to restrict mouse to the top half of the screen."
    DO
    LOOP WHILE INKEY$ = ""
    CALL MouseVerticalRange(12, 1)
END IF
```

> **TIP:** Like service 7, service 8 sorts out the two values (the top row has to be less than or equal to the bottom row), so it does not matter if we call MouseVerticalRange(12, 1) or MouseVerticalRange(1, 12).

There is one more interrupt &H33 service we might be interested in. Service &HA lets us set the style of the mouse cursor itself. Let's see how that works.

Setting the Mouse Cursor

Service &HA lets us set the text-mode (only) mouse cursor to whatever ASCII character we want. To use it, we have to define two "masks": the *screen mask* and the *cursor mask*. Each mask consists of both a character and attribute byte, and understanding how to use them takes some time and experimentation.

How to Use Screen and Cursor Masks

The screen mask determines how much of a character's ASCII code to keep when the mouse cursor lands at its screen position. This mask is ANDed with that character's ASCII code and with the character's attribute. For example, to keep the character at that screen position intact, use a *screen mask character* of &HFF and a *screen mask attribute* of &HFF. To overwrite it entirely, use a screen mask character and attribute of 0.

The cursor mask then determines what the cursor will look like. The *cursor mask character* and *cursor mask attribute* are XORed with the result of ANDing the present character and attribute with the screen mask to produce the mouse cursor.

Let's see how this works in practice. We might call this subprogram MouseSetCursor, and call it like this:

```
CALL MouseSetCursor (SMaskChar%, SMaskAttr%, CMaskChar%, CMaskAttr%)
```

Here are the inputs:

SMaskChar%   Screen mask ASCII character

SMaskAttr%		Screen mask attribute; the screen mask character and attribute are ANDed with the character and attribute already the on the screen. For example, to overwrite the character on the screen, set SMaskChar% = SMaskAttr% = 0. To preserve it, SMaskChar% = SMaskAttr% = &HFF.
CMaskChar%	INTEGER	Cursor mask ASCII character
CMaskAttr%	INTEGER	Cursor mask attribute; the cursor mask character and and attribute are XORed with the result of ANDing the character at the present position with the screen mask. That is, the cursor mask determines the shape of the mouse cursor.

For example, to use a particular ASCII character as the mouse cursor, overwrite the existing screen character entirely by setting SMaskChar% and SMaskAttr% to 0. Then load the ASCII code of the character you want as the mouse cursor (such as an up-arrow, ASCII 24) into CMaskChar%, and the desired mouse cursor attribute (such as 7 for white on black) into CMaskAttr%.

TIP: You can have your mouse cursor *color invert* characters on the screen by setting SMaskChar% to &HFF, which preserves the ASCII code of the character on the screen, and SMaskAttr% to &HFF to preserve its attribute byte. Then set CMaskChar% to 0, which will XOR the character with 0 and thus preserve it, and CMaskAttr% to &H77 to invert its attribute with XOR (use &H77, not &HFF, to avoid turning the blinking and intensity bits on). If you just want to invert the character and not the background behind it, set CMaskAttr% to 7.

In this subprogram, we're going to use interrupt &H33, service &HA. To set the mouse cursor, we have to load 0 into bx, the full screen mask (attribute and character bytes) into cx, and the cursor mask (attribute and character bytes) into dx. The main difficulty is loading these two bytes into OutRegs.cx and OutRegs.dx.

Because of the way BASIC keeps track of negative numbers (i.e., with two's complement math — see Chapter 11 for an explanantion), you can't let the top bit of an integer change as the result of a math operation. If you do, BASIC generates an overflow error.

This is a problem for us because we want to load SMaskAttr% into ch, the top byte of InRegs.cx, but we can't just say InRegs.cx = 2^8 * SMaskAttr%. If, for example, SMaskAttr% was equal to &HFF, the top bit of InRegs.cx would change and BASIC would generate an overflow error. Instead, we have to (tediously) set the top bit of InRegs.cx ourselves and then add the rest of the bits in.

First, we check to see if the top bit of SMaskAttr% (the bit that might cause a problem) is set. If it is, we set up an integer called TempS%, with only its top bit set:

```
     DIM InRegs AS RegType, OutRegs AS RegType

     REM Watch out for overflow as we load the attribute into the high byte

→    IF SMaskAttr% AND 2^7 THEN
            TempS% = -1 XOR &H7FFF     'Set top bit
     ELSE
            TempS% = 0
     END IF
                :
                :
```

The number -1 is stored in INTEGER format as &HFFFF (again, see Chapter 11 to find out why). To leave just the top bit set, we XOR that with &H7FFF. Then we do the same for InRegs.dx and CMaskAttr%, producing TempC% for the cursor mask like this:

```
     DIM InRegs AS RegType, OutRegs AS RegType

     REM Watch out for overflow as we load the attribute into the high byte

     IF SMaskAttr% AND 2^7 THEN TempS% = -1 XOR &H7FFF 'Set top bit
     ELSE
            TempS% = 0
     END IF

→    IF CMaskAttr% AND 2^7 THEN
```

```
          TempC% = -1 XOR &H7FFF 'Set top bit
ELSE
          TempC% = 0
END IF
:
:
```

Finally, we can load the masks into their registers like this:

```
DIM InRegs AS RegType, OutRegs AS RegType

REM Watch out for overflow as we load the attribute into the high byte

IF SMaskAttr% AND 2^7 THEN
        TempS% = -1 XOR &H7FFF'Set top bit
ELSE
        TempS% = 0
END IF

IF CMaskAttr% AND 2^7 THEN
        TempC% = -1 XOR &H7FFF 'Set top bit
ELSE
        TempC% = 0
END IF

        InRegs.bx = 0
→       InRegs.cx = TempS% OR (2^8 * (SMaskAttr% AND &H7F) + SMaskChar%)
        InRegs.dx = TempC% OR (2^8 * (CMaskAttr% AND &H7F) + CMaskChar%)
        InRegs.ax = &HA
        CALL INTERRUPT(&H33, InRegs, OutRegs)
```

Notice that we've gotten rid of the potentially troubling top bit in both SMaskAttr% and CMaskAttr% by ANDing them with &H7F before boosting what's left up into the top byte (which we do by multiplying by 2^8). Then we add the lower byte, SMaskChar% or CMaskChar%, and use the result to make up the lower 15 bits of InRegs.cx or InRegs.dx respectively. After these registers are loaded, we call interrupt &H33 service &HA to set the mouse cursor, and we're done.

Listing 3-11 shows the whole subprogram.

Listing 3-11.   MouseSetCursor ( ) Subprogram.   1 of 2

```
DECLARE SUB MouseSetCursor (SMaskChar%, SMaskAttr%, CMaskChar%, CMaskAttr%)
TYPE RegType
        ax      AS INTEGER
        bx      AS INTEGER
        cx      AS INTEGER
```

Listing 3-11. MouseSetCursor ( ) Subprogram.   2 of 2

```
        dx    AS INTEGER
        bp    AS INTEGER
        si    AS INTEGER
        di    AS INTEGER
        flags AS INTEGER
END TYPE

DECLARE SUB INTERRUPT (IntNo AS INTEGER, InRegs AS RegType, OutRegs AS RegType)

SUB MouseSetCursor (SMaskChar%, SMaskAttr%, CMaskChar%, CMaskAttr%)

        DIM InRegs AS RegType, OutRegs AS RegType

        REM Watch out for overflow as we load the attribute into the high byte

        IF SMaskAttr% AND 2^7 THEN
                TempS% = -1 XOR &H7FFF           'Set top bit
        ELSE
                TempS% = 0
        END IF

IF CMaskAttr% AND 2^7 THEN
        TempC% = -1 XOR &H7FFF                   'Set top bit
ELSE
                TempC% = 0
END IF

InRegs.bx = 0
InRegs.cx = TempS% OR (256 * (SMaskAttr% AND &H7F) + SMaskChar%)
InRegs.dx = TempC% OR (256 * (CMaskAttr% AND &H7F) + CMaskChar%)
InRegs.ax = &HA
CALL INTERRUPT(&H33, InRegs, OutRegs)
END SUB
```

And now we can use it to set the mouse cursor in text mode.

Making the Mouse Cursor into a Dot

Here's what MouseSetCursor( ) looks like in action:

```
REM MouseSetCursor example (ScMaskChar%, ScMaskAtr%, CurMaskChar%, CurMaskAtr%)

  DECLARE FUNCTION MouseInitialize% ( )
  DECLARE SUB MouseShowCursor ( )
  DECLARE SUB MouseSetCursor (ScMaskChar%, ScMaskAtr%, CurMaskChar%, CurMaskAtr%)

  Check% = MouseInitialize%

  LOCATE 1, 1
```

```
IF Check% = 0 THEN
    PRINT "Mouse driver not installed."
ELSE
    PRINT "Mouse Initialized."
    CALL MouseShowCursor

    REM Change mouse cursor to a single dot (ASCII 250)

    CALL MouseSetCursor(0, 0, 250, 7)
END IF
```

This program just changes the mouse cursor to a single dot (i.e., CHR$(250)) in the middle of the character position with a normal attribute (i.e., white on black) of 7.

TIP: You might want to use one of the ASCII characters that look like an arrow instead for your mouse cursor:

ASCII Number	Character
24	Up arrow
25	Down arrow
26	Right arrow
27	Left arrow

Keep in mind that you can only use MouseSetCursor( ) in text mode, and you are restricted to using one of the ASCII characters. For a complete set of the ASCII characters, see your BASIC documentation.

That completes our mouse support. We've set the mouse system up, displayed the mouse cursor, hidden it, and read button information. Now it's time to take a look at the BASIC PDS' Mouse support.

The Mouse in the BASIC PDS

The support for the mouse in the Professional Development System is not very strong — in fact, it's considerably weaker than what we've already developed.

To start, you must call MouseInit( ) to initalize the mouse (as we do above with MouseInitialize( )). Next, you can restrict the mouse cursor range to a specific area of the screen by calling MouseBorder(row1%, col1%, row2%, col2%), where the limiting box is described by (row1%, col1%) and (row2%, col2%):

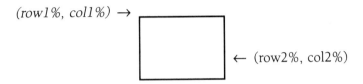

Figure 3-1

Then you can display the mouse cursor with MouseShow( ) and hide it again with MouseHide( ).

To read actual mouse events, however, you're limited to polling (i.e., calling repeatedly) the subprogram MousePoll( ). MousePoll( ) works like our subprogram MouseInformation( ) above, which means that you have to catch mouse actions as they occur. After MousePoll( ), there's only one last mouse subprogram — MouseDriver( ), which lets you pass arguments directly on to interrupt &H33 (and therefore access the other DOS mouse services directly). Since we can do that as easily with INTERRUPT( ), MouseDriver( ) doesn't add much utility.

Let's develop a program to report mouse position using the PDS mouse tools. If you're using QBX.EXE, you'll have to use the /L switch when loading. First, we initialize the mouse:

```
DECLARE SUB MouseInit ( )

        CALL MouseInit
        :
```

Then we show the mouse cursor:

```
DECLARE SUB MouseInit ()
DECLARE SUB MouseShow ()
        CALL MouseInit
        CALL MouseShow
        :
```

Now we can use MousePoll( ) to wait until you press the right mouse button. The variables it fills are: row%, col%, lButton%, and rButton%. Here, lButton% and rButton% return values of either TRUE or FALSE depending on whether or not the button is pushed, and the screen position is returned in text-mode coordinates:

```
      DECLARE SUB MouseInit ( )
      DECLARE SUB MousePoll (row%, col%, lButton%, rButton%)
      DECLARE SUB MouseShow ( )

              CALL MouseInit
              CALL MouseShow

              PRINT "This program waits for you to press the right mouse button..."
→  DO
      CALL MousePoll(row%, col%, lButton%, rButton%)
      LOOP WHILE rButton% = FALSE
      :
```

After the button is pressed, we can report the position of the mouse cursor like this:

```
      DECLARE SUB MouseInit ( )
      DECLARE SUB MousePoll (row%, col%, lButton%, rButton%)
      DECLARE SUB MouseShow ( )

              CALL MouseInit

              CALL MouseShow

              PRINT "This program waits for you to press the right mouse button..."

              DO
              CALL MousePoll(row%, col%, lButton%, rButton%)
              LOOP WHILE rButton% = FALSE

→ PRINT "The mouse cursor was at: ("; row%; ","; col%; ")"
```

And that's all there is to it — we've set up the mouse and used it in the PDS. Unlike the menu and window functions, the mouse functions in the BASIC ToolBox are quite simple.

Conclusion

That's it for the specific mouse subprograms and functions. Now, however, we're going to put them to work immediately in our pull-down menu system, coming up next in Chapter 4.

Pull-down Menus

IN THIS CHAPTER, we're actually going to write a complete, fully functional menu system, ready for use. You'll be able to pull down menus from a menubar and make selections with either the keyboard or the mouse. This is going to take some time and effort on our part, but we have already developed much of the programming technology needed when we covered windows and the mouse; all that remains now is to combine the two into a functional whole.

NOTE:	This is an example of modular programming.

We'll do that in this chapter (as well as taking a look at the PDS menu tools at the end). Our first step, as it should always be with programs of any size, is to get a clear picture of what we want.

Designing Our Menu System

We first have to consider what we want our menu system to look like on the screen. The menubar, with the screen attribute we've chosen for it, should appear at the top of the screen. If the user has a mouse, he or she should be able to simply click (left mouse button, as is usual for menus) on a menu name in the menu bar. That menu then pops open beneath it, with the screen attribute we've chosen for it (we should be able to pick a different attribute for each menu and the menubar). On the screen, opening menu 1 might look like Figure 4-1.

MenuBar ⌐

Menu 1	Menu 2	Menu 3	Menu 4
Choice 1			
Choice 2			
Choice 3	← Menu 1		
Choice 4			
Choice 5			
Choice 6			

Figure 4-1

The user then moves the mouse cursor to a specific line in the menu and releases the mouse button, and our program should then be informed which menu — and which choice in that menu — was chosen.

In addition, the menus should function in either text or graphics mode — and with or without a mouse. If there's no mouse, they should default back to keyboard-only use automatically. For example, we should be able to press Alt-M, where M stands for the first letter of the menu we wish to open. That menu pops open, and the user can then make a choice by pressing Alt-C, where C stands for the first letter of the menu choice he or she wishes to make.

We might, however, want to close the menu without making a choice. In that case, we could press Esc to close the open menu (this is standard for menu systems), or we could press Alt-A, where A is the first letter of another menu, or we could press Alt-M once again to toggle the menu closed.

Special Menu Considerations

Now let's think about writing the code. From a programming standpoint, we want to get our menus running with the minimum amount of trouble. We should have an initialization program — MenuInitialize( ) — to set up the labels in the menubar and menus themselves.

To show the menubar, we could have another subprogram, which we can call Menu-Show( ). To hide it again (we may not always want the menu system to be on), we can add MenuHide( ).

Now comes the tricky part: How do we get information about what menu selections were made? It would be best if the menu system could somehow run independently of our program and interrupt us when a menu choice was made. Unfortunately, that's beyond BASIC's capabilities. You can't have two program groups working at once under DOS BASIC.

A practical solution would be to have the menu system provide *all* the input for our program. In other words, whenever we needed any input, we could call a function named, say, MenuGetEvent$( ). This could act like INKEY$, MouseTimesPressed( ), MouseTimesReleased( ) and a menu input program all at once. If any keyboard, mouse, or menu event were pending, MenuGetEvent$( ) would let us know what it was (which means that we should check it frequently).

We can set it up like this: if MenuGetEvent$( ) returns a string that is one or two characters long, a character was typed, and we should treat the string just as you would a string from INKEY$. If there was a mouse event, the string will be either mouseup or mousedown, indicating that a mouse button was either pushed or released, and Menu-GetEvent$( ) reports the screen coordinates of that event. On the other hand, if the string is menuchoice, then one of the selections in a menu was chosen; MenuGetEvent$( ) reports the menu the choice was made from, and indicates which choice it was.

In this way, MenuGetEvent$( ) will be our primary input routine. The process, as we've designed it so far, goes like this:

1. Call MenuInitialize%( ) to initialize the menu system with the names of the menus and the names of the choices inside each menu.

2. To display the menu, use MenuShow( ). (MenuHide( ) will hide it again.)

3. Now use MenuGetEvent$( ) as the primary input to our program; treating it as a combination of INKEY$, a mouse monitor, and a menu monitor.

That's all there is to it. We've wrapped all keyboard, mouse, and menu input to your program into MenuGetEvent$( ). Now the only thing left is to write these routines.

Initializing Our Menus

Using MenuInitialize%( ) is the necessary first step towards using menus. We want our menu system to look like Figure 4-2.

MenuBar ⌐↓

Menu 1	Menu 2	Menu 3	Menu 4

Choice 1		
Choice 2		
Choice 3	← Menu 1	
Choice 4		
Choice 5		
Choice 6		

Figure 4-2

So we'll have to initialize all the menu names (the names that appear in the menubar), the menu choices (the names that appear in a given menu), the screen attribute of the menubar, and the screen attribute of each menu.

Let's design MenuInitialize%( ) now. To start, we have to pass the names of the menus themselves as they are to appear in the menubar. To pass those names we can use a one-dimensional array of type STRING named MenuNames( ). For example, if we set Menu-Names(1) to this:

```
MenuNames(1) = "Fruits"
```

then the first entry in the menubar would be Fruits (see Figure 4-3).

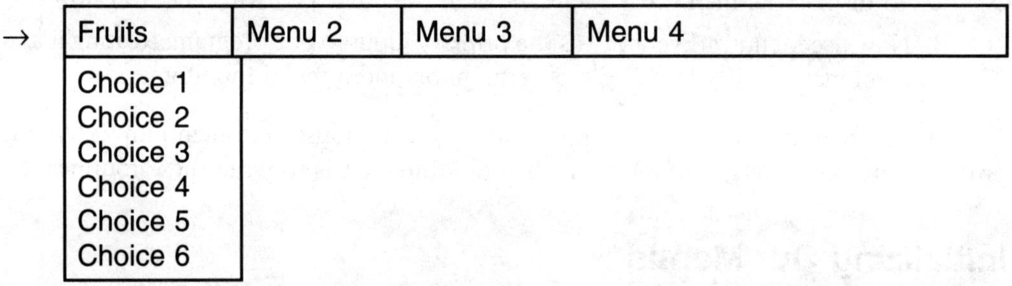

→
Fruits	Menu 2	Menu 3	Menu 4
Choice 1			
Choice 2			
Choice 3			
Choice 4			
Choice 5			
Choice 6			

Figure 4-3

The next menu name comes from MenuNames(2) and so on. The limits on the number of entries in MenuNames( ) and the size of each entry are set by the screen width and the menu width. A maximum of eight characters for each menu name, and a maximum of seven menus turns out to be a good compromise. Here's the call to MenuInitialize( ) so far:

```
CALL MenuInitialize%(MenuNames( )...)
```

Next, we have to pass the names of the individual choices in the menus that we've just named. We should be able to pass them as a two-dimensional array called, say, Menu-Choices( ), also of type STRING. For example, MenuChoices(1, 1) would be the first choice in menu 1, MenuChoices(1, 2) holds menu 1, choice 2, MenuChoices(2, 5) would represent menu 2, choice 5, and so on. For example, to put five choices in menu 1, we might do this:

```
MenuChoices(1, 1) = "Apples"
MenuChoices(1, 2) = "Bananas"
MenuChoices(1, 3) = "Grapes"
MenuChoices(1, 4) = "Peaches"
MenuChoices(1, 5) = "Oranges"
```

This would make menu 1 look like Figure 4-4.

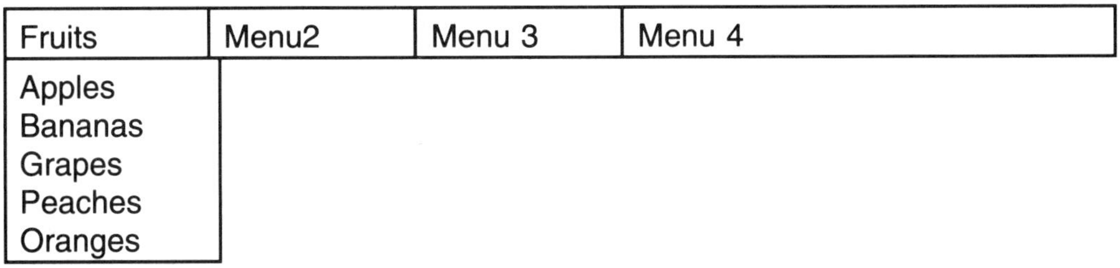

Fruits	Menu2	Menu 3	Menu 4
Apples Bananas Grapes Peaches Oranges			

Figure 4-4

Not all menus have to have the same number of entries, of course, and we must allow for that. We will only put in the number of entries for each menu that it should have (which leaves the unfilled entries as null strings). For example, we might set up menu 2 like this, with only three entries:

```
MenuChoices(2, 1) = "Peas"
MenuChoices(2, 2) = "Corn"
MenuChoices(2, 3) = "Broccoli"
```

This would make it look like Figure 4-5.

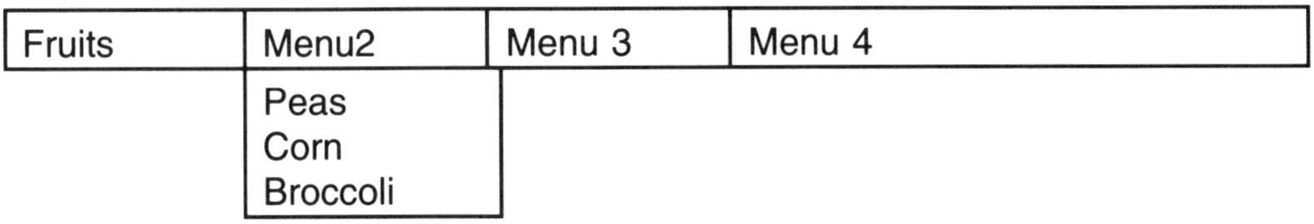

Fruits	Menu2	Menu 3	Menu 4
	Peas Corn Broccoli		

Figure 4-5

We also have to establish limits here on both string size and the number of menu choices; a maximum of 15 characters in a menu choice, and a maximum of 24 choices (or else the menu wouldn't fit on the screen), works pretty well.

This is how the call looks so far:

```
CALL MenuInitialize%(MenuNames( ), MenuChoices( )...)
```

The only items that are left are the screen attributes we want to use for the menubar and the menus themselves. Passing an attribute for the menubar is easy — we can just pass an INTEGER named BarAttrb%. This is the screen attribute you want the menubar to have:

```
CALL MenuInitialize%(MenuNames( ), MenuChoices( ), BarAttrb%...)
```

Finally, we can pass a different screen attribute for each of the menus using a one-dimensional array of INTEGERs named MenuAttrbs( ), menu attributes. For example, load MenuAttrbs(3) with the screen attribute you want menu 3 to have when it pops open. And we're done designing the call to MenuInitialize%( ):

```
CALL MenuInitialize%(MenuNames( ), MenuChoices( ), BarAttrb%, MenuAttrbs( ))
```

TIP: We may want a given menu choice to open a whole new set of menus and thus display a whole new menubar. For example, one menu choice could be File System. Once selected, we might want the menubar to change so that the menus now correspond to, say, Read, Write, Open, Close. To change menubars and menu choices, we can use MenuInitialize%( ) again, on the fly. We can call MenuInitialize%( ) to set up the new menus, MenuHide( ) to hide the current one, and then MenuShow( ) to display the new one (and then Menu-GetEvent$( ) to receive input).

Now let's write MenuInitialize%( ).

MenuInitialize%( )

Here are the inputs we've worked out for MenuInitialize%( ):

MenuNames( )	STRING	A one-dimensional array of menu name strings. For example, MenuNames(1) might equal File, so the first entry in the menubar will read File. Each string can be a maximum of eight characters long, and there is a maximum of seven strings (and hence seven menus).
MenuChoices( )	STRING	A two-dimensional array of menu choice strings. For example, if MenuChoices(1,1) is Open File..., then the first choice in the first menu will be Open File.... Each choice can be a maximum of 15 characters long. There is a maximum of 24 choices per menu (otherwise the menu won't fit on the screen).
BarAttrb%	INTEGER	The screen attribute of the menubar.
MenuAttrbs( )	INTEGER	A one-dimensional array of screen attributes for the menus themselves. For example, MenuAttrbs(1) is the screen attribute the menu system is to use with the first menu.

MenuInitialize%( ) should return 1 if the menus were successfully set up, and 0 otherwise. Like the window system, it will take some work to set things up.

First, let's put together the COMMONs we'll be using. We can begin with the dimensions of each menu. To make things easier for ourselves, we can treat each menu like a window, and adapt some of our window code to display it. Thinking of the set of menus as a set of windows, then, we start off like this:

```
COMMON SHARED /MenuA/ Rows( ) AS INTEGER, Cols( ) AS INTEGER, _
          TopRow( ) AS INTEGER, TopCol( ) AS INTEGER, _
          BotRow( ) AS INTEGER, BotCol( ) AS INTEGER
              :
              :
```

Next, still treating each menu as a window, we have to store the normal window arrays for each one. Text( ) will hold the contents of the window; i.e., the menu choices, row by row. OldText( ) will hold the text that was on the screen before the menu appeared, and OldAttrb( ) the attributes of each screen position that we overwrite. Finally, we need an array to hold the menu's attributes, Attribute( ):

```
    COMMON SHARED /MenuA/ Rows( ) AS INTEGER, Cols( ) AS INTEGER, _
                  TopRow( ) AS INTEGER, TopCol( ) AS INTEGER, _
                  BotRow( ) AS INTEGER, BotCol( ) AS INTEGER
→ COMMON SHARED /MenuB/ Attribute( ) AS INTEGER, Text( ) AS STRING, _
                  OldText( ) AS STRING, OldAttrb( ) AS STRING
                        :
                        :
```

What we've done for the menus/windows, we must now do for the menubar itself. We can store the text in the bar as a simple string named Bar$. We'll also need the bar's screen attribute, BarAttrb, the text that was on the screen before the menubar appeared, OldBar$, and the screen attributes at *each* character position we're going to overwrite, which we can store in a string named OldBarAttrb$.

There are two last, important menu variables here. First, we'll need the number of menus, and we can store that in a variable named NumMenus%. In addition, we have to know whether or not the menubar is on the screen, and therefore whether or not the menu system is active. We can keep track of that with a variable named MenusOnFlag%:

```
    COMMON SHARED /MenuA/ Rows( ) AS INTEGER, Cols( ) AS INTEGER, _
                  TopRow( ) AS INTEGER, TopCol( ) AS INTEGER, _
                  BotRow( ) AS INTEGER, BotCol( ) AS INTEGER
    COMMON SHARED /MenuB/ Attribute( ) AS INTEGER, Text( ) AS STRING, _
                  OldText( ) AS STRING, OldAttrb( ) AS STRING
→ COMMON SHARED /MenuC/ Bar$, BarAttrb, MenusOnFlag%, NumMenus%, OldBar$, _
                  OldBarAttrb$
```

That's it for the COMMONs; we can start MenuInitialize%( ) itself with a few preliminary boundary checks on the incoming arrays, then clear the necessary memory locations:

```
FUNCTION MenuInitialize% (MenuNames( ) AS STRING, MenuChoices( ) AS STRING, _
                 BarAttrb%, MenuAttrbs( ) AS INTEGER)

    NumMenus% = UBOUND(MenuNames, 1)
    IF NumMenus% > 7 THEN EXIT FUNCTION
    IF UBOUND(MenuChoices, 2) > 24 THEN EXIT FUNCTION

    ERASE Rows
    ERASE Cols
    ERASE TopRow
    ERASE TopCol
    ERASE BotRow
    ERASE BotCol
    ERASE Attribute
    ERASE OnFlag
    ERASE Text
    ERASE OldText
```

```
            ERASE OldAttrb
            Bar$ = ""
            MenusOnFlag% = 0
```

Now it's just a matter of filling them again. We start off by looping over each menus (there are NumMenus% of them), and assembling the menubar:

```
FUNCTION MenuInitialize% (MenuNames( ) AS STRING, MenuChoices( ) AS STRING, _
                BarAttrb%, MenuAttrbs( ) AS INTEGER)

        NumMenus% = UBOUND(MenuNames, 1)
        IF NumMenus% > 7 THEN EXIT FUNCTION
        IF UBOUND(MenuChoices, 2) > 24 THEN EXIT FUNCTION

        ERASE Rows
        ERASE Cols
        ERASE TopRow
        ERASE TopCol
        ERASE BotRow
        ERASE BotCol
        ERASE Attribute
        ERASE OnFlag
        ERASE Text
        ERASE OldText
        ERASE OldAttrb
        Bar$ = ""
        MenusOnFlag% = 0

→       BarAttrb = BarAttrb%
:
        FOR i = 1 TO NumMenus%
         Bar$ = Bar$+" "+ MenuNames(i)+ SPACES(8-LEN(MenuNames(i))) + CHR$(179)
                    :
                    :
        NEXT i
```

We place each menu name from MenuNames( ) into the bar and separate them with the vertical bar character, CHR$(179). While we're looping over all menus, we can fill each one with the correct choices from MenuChoices( ). These choices make up the text for each menu, so we'll store this information in the array Text( ), as we did for our windows. For a given menu, we have to loop over the number of choices MenuChoices( ), treating each choice as a row in the menu (and padding it with spaces):

```
FUNCTION MenuInitialize% (MenuNames( ) AS STRING, MenuChoices( ) AS STRING, _
                BarAttrb%, MenuAttrbs( ) AS INTEGER)

        NumMenus% = UBOUND(MenuNames, 1)
        IF NumMenus% > 7 THEN EXIT FUNCTION
```

```
       IF UBOUND(MenuChoices, 2) > 24 THEN EXIT FUNCTION

       ERASE Rows
       ERASE Rows
       ERASE Cols
       ERASE TopRow
       ERASE TopCol
       ERASE BotRow
       ERASE BotCol
       ERASE Attribute
       ERASE OnFlag
       ERASE Text
       ERASE OldText
       ERASE OldAttrb
       Bar$ = ""
       MenusOnFlag% = 0

       BarAttrb = BarAttrb%

       FOR i = 1 TO NumMenus%
         Bar$ = Bar$+" "+ MenuNames(i)+ SPACE$(8 - LEN(MenuNames(i))) + CHR$(179)
         FOR j = 1 TO UBOUND(MenuChoices, 2)
             Temp$ = MenuChoices(i, j)
             IF Temp$ <> "" THEN
                 IF LEN(Temp$) > 15 THEN EXIT FUNCTION
                 Rows(i) = Rows(i) + 1            'Number of rows in menu i
→                Text(i, j) = " " + Temp$ + SPACE$(15 - LEN(Temp$))
             END IF
         NEXT j
               :
               :
       NEXT i
```

Finally, there are a few more variables to be set each time we loop through for a given menu. We have to record, among other things, its top and bottom rows on the screen (recall that we're treating each menu as a window, and, therefore, the top row is row 2 — right under the menubar — for each menu); the left and right columns of the menu; and the attribute of the menu. After this, we round out the menubar so it's a full 80 characters long — the width of the screen.

```
FUNCTION MenuInitialize% (MenuNames( ) AS STRING, MenuChoices( ) AS STRING, _
                BarAttrb%, MenuAttrbs( ) AS INTEGER)

       NumMenus% = UBOUND(MenuNames, 1)
       IF NumMenus% > 7 THEN EXIT FUNCTION
       IF UBOUND(MenuChoices, 2) > 24 THEN EXIT FUNCTION

       ERASE Rows
       ERASE Cols
       ERASE TopRow
       ERASE TopCol
       ERASE BotRow
       ERASE BotCol
       ERASE Attribute
       ERASE OnFlag
       ERASE Text
```

```
                ERASE OldText
                ERASE OldAttrb
                Bar$ = ""
                MenusOnFlag% = 0

                BarAttrb = BarAttrb%

                FOR i = 1 TO NumMenus%
                 Bar$ = Bar$+" "+ MenuNames(i)+ SPACE$(8-LEN(MenuNames(i))) + CHR$(179)
                  FOR j = 1 TO UBOUND(MenuChoices, 2)
                      Temp$ = MenuChoices(i, j)
                      IF Temp$ <> "" THEN
                          IF LEN(Temp$) > 15 THEN EXIT FUNCTION
                          Rows(i) = Rows(i) + 1
                          Text(i, j) = " " + Temp$ + SPACE$(15 - LEN(Temp$))
                      END IF
                  NEXT j
→                 Cols(i) = 16
:                 TopRow(i) = 2
:                 TopCol(i) = 1 + 10 * (i - 1)
                  BotRow(i) = 1 + Rows(i)
                  BotCol(i) = TopCol(i) + 16
                  Attribute(i) = MenuAttrbs(i)
                NEXT i

                Bar$ = Bar$ + SPACE$(80 - LEN(Bar$))

                MenuInitialize% = 1
```

That's it for MenuInitialize%( ). Listing 4-1 shows the whole function.

Listing 4-1.   Menu Initialize% Function — Initializes Menu System.   1 of 2

```
DECLARE FUNCTION MenuInitialize% (MenuNames( ) AS STRING, MenuChoices( ) AS _
             STRING, BarAttrb%, MenuAttrbs( ) AS INTEGER)

        CONST MaxMenus = 7
        DIM Rows(1 TO MaxMenus) AS INTEGER
        DIM Cols(1 TO MaxMenus) AS INTEGER
        DIM TopRow(1 TO MaxMenus) AS INTEGER
        DIM TopCol(1 TO MaxMenus) AS INTEGER
        DIM BotRow(1 TO MaxMenus) AS INTEGER
        DIM BotCol(1 TO MaxMenus) AS INTEGER
        DIM Attribute(1 TO MaxMenus) AS INTEGER
        DIM Text(1 TO MaxMenus, 25) AS STRING
        DIM OldText(1 TO MaxMenus, 25) AS STRING
        DIM OldAttrb(1 TO MaxMenus, 25) AS STRING
        COMMON SHARED /MenuA/ Rows( ) AS INTEGER, Cols( ) AS INTEGER, _
                   TopCol( ) AS INTEGER, TopCol( ) AS INTEGER, _
                   BotRow( ) AS INTEGER, BotCol( ) AS INTEGER
        COMMON SHARED /MenuB/ Attribute( ) AS INTEGER, Text( ) AS STRING, _
                   OldText( ) AS STRING, OldAttrb( ) AS STRING
        COMMON SHARED /MenuC/ Bar$, BarAttrb, MenusOnFlag%, NumMenus%, OldBar$,_
                   OldBarAttrb$
```

Listing 4-1.   Menu Initialize% Function — Initializes Menu System.   2 of 2

```
FUNCTION MenuInitialize% (MenuNames( ) AS STRING, MenuChoices( ) AS STRING, _
             BarAttrb%, MenuAttrbs( ) AS INTEGER)

        MenuInitialize% = 0

        NumMenus% = UBOUND(MenuNames, 1)
        IF NumMenus% > 7 THEN EXIT FUNCTION
        IF UBOUND(MenuChoices, 2) > 24 THEN EXIT FUNCTION

        ERASE Rows
        ERASE Cols
        ERASE TopRow
        ERASE TopCol
        ERASE BotRow
        ERASE BotCol
        ERASE Attribute
        ERASE OnFlag
        ERASE Text
        ERASE OldText
        ERASE OldAttrb
        Bar$ = ""
        MenusOnFlag% = 0

        BarAttrb = BarAttrb%

        FOR i = 1 TO NumMenus%
         Bar$ = Bar$+" "+ MenuNames(i)+ SPACE$(8 - LEN(MenuNames(i))) + CHR$(179)
          FOR j = 1 TO UBOUND(MenuChoices, 2)
                Temp$ = MenuChoices(i, j)
                IF Temp$ <> "" THEN
                    IF LEN(Temp$) > 15 THEN EXIT FUNCTION
                    Rows(i) = Rows(i) + 1
                    Text(i, j) = " " + Temp$ + SPACE$(15 - LEN(Temp$))
                END IF
            NEXT j
            Cols(i) = 16
            TopRow(i) = 2
            TopCol(i) = 1 + 10 * (i - 1)
            BotRow(i) = 1 + Rows(i)
            BotCol(i) = TopCol(i) + 16
            Attribute(i) = MenuAttrbs(i)
        NEXT i

        Bar$ = Bar$ + SPACE$(80 - LEN(Bar$))

        MenuInitialize% = 1

END FUNCTION
```

At this point, all the menu COMMONs are filled and ready to roll. Keep in mind that to display the menubar on the screen, we'll have to call MenuShow( ) later.

Initializing a Test Menubar

Here's an example showing how to set up a menubar as we've designed it with three menu names in it:

```
DECLARE FUNCTION MenuInitialize% (MenuNames( ) AS STRING, MenuChoices( ) AS _
                STRING, BarAttrb%, MenuAttrbs( ) AS INTEGER)

DIM MenuNames(1 TO 3) AS STRING
DIM MenuChoices(1 TO 3, 1 TO 5) AS STRING
DIM MenuAttrbs(1 TO 3) AS INTEGER

        MenuNames(1) = "Fruits"
        MenuChoices(1, 1) = "Apples"
        MenuChoices(1, 2) = "Bananas"
        MenuChoices(1, 3) = "Grapes"
        MenuChoices(1, 4) = "Peaches"
        MenuChoices(1, 5) = "Oranges"

        MenuNames(2) = "Veggies"
        MenuChoices(2, 1) = "Peas"
        MenuChoices(2, 2) = "Corn"
        MenuChoices(2, 3) = "Broccoli"

        MenuNames(3) = "Meats"
        MenuChoices(3, 1) = "Chicken"
        MenuChoices(3, 2) = "Pork"
        MenuChoices(3, 3) = "Beef"
        MenuChoices(3, 4) = "Fish"

        FOR i = 1 TO 3
            MenuAttrbs(i) = &H61
        NEXT i
        BarAttrb% = &H24

        Check% = MenuInitialize%(MenuNames( ), MenuChoices( ), BarAttrb%, _
            MenuAttrbs( ))
        IF Check% = 0 THEN
            PRINT "Error."
        ELSE
            PRINT "Menu is set up."
        END IF
```

You can see how we load each of the arrays before calling MenuInitialize%( ). Once we do, however, we're all set; we can use MenuShow( ) — coming up next — to display the menubar.

Displaying the Menubar

Now we're ready to write MenuShow( ) and display the menubar across the top of the screen. In addition, this subprogram clears any mouse events that were waiting in the mouse queue (so that when you get menu input, you'll be responding to what occurred after the menubar appeared). Note that to make the menubar active after you've displayed it, you have to call MenuGetEvent$( ) and then wait for input.

Before we do anything, we have to take the mouse cursor off the screen (we'll restore it later). This is to avoid overwriting the mouse cursor with the menubar; as mentioned last chapter, if you overwrite the mouse cursor and then move the mouse, the mouse driver will restore the *original* (i.e., before the mouse cursor got there) character there, leaving a hole in the menubar:

```
SUB MenuShow

        DIM InRegs AS RegType, OutRegs AS RegType

        CurRow% = CSRLIN
        CurCol% = POS(0)

        REM Turn off mouse cursor

→       InRegs.ax = 2
        CALL INTERRUPT(&H33, InRegs, OutRegs)
        :
        :
```

NOTE: If there is no mouse or the mouse system was never initialized, then when your program turns the mouse cursor "back" on, there is no effect.

There are three steps to the body of MenuShow( ). First, we save the region of the screen we're about to overwrite — that is, the top row — with the BASIC SCREEN function (SCREEN allows us to pick up both characters and attributes):

```
SUB MenuShow

        DIM InRegs AS RegType, OutRegs AS RegType

        CurRow% = CSRLIN
        CurCol% = POS(0)

→       REM Save the old top bar
:
:               temp1$ = ""
                temp2$ = ""
                FOR j = 1 TO 80
                        temp1$ = temp1$ + CHR$(SCREEN(1, j))
                        temp2$ = temp2$ + CHR$(SCREEN(1, j, 1))
                NEXT j
                OldBar$ = temp1$
                OldBarAttrb$ = temp2$
                        :
                        :
```

Next, we display the new menubar on the screen, using interrupt &H10 service 9 exactly as we did in WindowShow( ):

```
DIM InRegs AS RegType, OutRegs AS RegType

CurRow% = CSRLIN
CurCol% = POS(0)

REM Save the old top bar

        temp1$ = ""
        temp2$ = ""
        FOR j = 1 TO 80
                temp1$ = temp1$ + CHR$(SCREEN(1, j))
                temp2$ = temp2$ + CHR$(SCREEN(1, j, 1))
        NEXT j
        OldBar$ = temp1$
        OldBarAttrb$ = temp2$

REM Now print the menu bar

InRegs.cx = 1

    FOR j = 1 TO 80
        LOCATE 1, j
        InRegs.ax = &H900 + ASC(MID$(Bar$, j, 1))
        InRegs.bx = BarAttrb
        CALL INTERRUPT(&H10, InRegs, OutRegs)
    NEXT j
        :
        :
```

Finally, we have to clear the way for the rest of the menu system. We do that by turning the mouse cursor back on, indicating that the menubar is on — and therefore that the menu system is active (by setting MenusOnFlag% to 1) — resetting the cursor to its original position, and clearing the mouse queue:

```
DIM InRegs AS RegType, OutRegs AS RegType

CurRow% = CSRLIN
CurCol% = POS(0)

REM Save the old top bar

        temp1$ = ""
        temp2$ = ""
        FOR j = 1 TO 80
                temp1$ = temp1$ + CHR$(SCREEN(1, j))
                temp2$ = temp2$ + CHR$(SCREEN(1, j, 1))
        NEXT j
        OldBar$ = temp1$
```

```
                OldBarAttrb$ = temp2$

        REM Now print the menu bar

        InRegs.cx = 1

            FOR j = 1 TO 80
                LOCATE 1, j
                InRegs.ax = &H900 + ASC(MID$(Bar$, j, 1))
                InRegs.bx = BarAttrb
                CALL INTERRUPT(&H10, InRegs, OutRegs)
            NEXT j

→       REM Turn mouse cursor back on
:
:       InRegs.ax = 1
        CALL INTERRUPT(&H33, InRegs, OutRegs)

        REM Show menu bar is on.

        MenusOnFlag% = 1

        LOCATE CurRow%, CurCol%

        REM Clear the mouse queue

        InRegs.bx = 0
        InRegs.ax = 5
        CALL INTERRUPT(&H33, InRegs, OutRegs)
        InRegs.bx = 1
        InRegs.ax = 5
        CALL INTERRUPT(&H33, InRegs, OutRegs)
        InRegs.bx = 0
        InRegs.ax = 6
        CALL INTERRUPT(&H33, InRegs, OutRegs)
        InRegs.bx = 1
        InRegs.ax = 6
        CALL INTERRUPT(&H33, InRegs, OutRegs)
```

And the menubar is now on, across the top of the screen. Listing 4-2 shows the whole subprogram.

Listing 4-2.   MenuShow ( ) Subprogram—Displays the Menubar.   1 of 3

```
DECLARE SUB MenuShow ( )

TYPE RegType
        ax      AS INTEGER
        bx      AS INTEGER
        cx      AS INTEGER
        dx      AS INTEGER
        bp      AS INTEGER
        si      AS INTEGER
        di      AS INTEGER
        flags   AS INTEGER
END TYPE
```

Listing 4-2. MenuShow ( ) Subprogram—Displays the Menubar.   2 of 3

```
DECLARE SUB INTERRUPT (IntNo AS INTEGER, InRegs AS RegType, OutRegs AS RegType)

        CONST MaxMenus = 7
        DIM Rows(1 TO MaxMenus) AS INTEGER
        DIM Cols(1 TO MaxMenus) AS INTEGER
        DIM TopRow(1 TO MaxMenus) AS INTEGER
        DIM TopCol(1 TO MaxMenus) AS INTEGER
        DIM BotRow(1 TO MaxMenus) AS INTEGER
        DIM BotCol(1 TO MaxMenus) AS INTEGER
        DIM Attribute(1 TO MaxMenus) AS INTEGER
        DIM Text(1 TO MaxMenus, 25) AS STRING
        DIM OldText(1 TO MaxMenus, 25) AS STRING
        DIM OldAttrb(1 TO MaxMenus, 25) AS STRING
        COMMON SHARED /MenuA/ Rows( ) AS INTEGER, Cols( ) AS INTEGER, _
                      TopRow( ) AS INTEGER, TopCol( ) AS INTEGER, _
                      BotRow( ) AS INTEGER, BotCol( ) AS INTEGER
        COMMON SHARED /MenuB/ Attribute( ) AS INTEGER, Text( ) AS STRING, _
                      OldText( ) AS STRING, OldAttrb( ) AS STRING
        COMMON SHARED /MenuC/ Bar$, BarAttrb, MenusOnFlag%, NumMenus%, _
                      OldBar$, OldBarAttrb$

SUB MenuShow

        DIM InRegs AS RegType, OutRegs AS RegType

        CurRow% = CSRLIN
        CurCol% = POS(0)

        REM Turn off mouse cursor

        InRegs.ax = 2
        CALL INTERRUPT(&H33, InRegs, OutRegs)

        REM Save the old top bar

                temp1$ = ""
                temp2$ = ""
                FOR j = 1 TO 80
                        temp1$ = temp1$ + CHR$(SCREEN(1, j))
                        temp2$ = temp2$ + CHR$(SCREEN(1, j, 1))
                NEXT j
                OldBar$ = temp1$
                OldBarAttrb$ = temp2$

        REM Now print the menu bar

        InRegs.cx = 1

            FOR j = 1 TO 80
                LOCATE 1, j
                InRegs.ax = &H900 + ASC(MID$(Bar$, j, 1))
                InRegs.bx = BarAttrb
                CALL INTERRUPT(&H10, InRegs, OutRegs)
            NEXT j

        REM Turn mouse cursor back on
```

Listing 4-2. MenuShow ( ) Subprogram—Displays the Menubar.   **3 of 3**

```
        InRegs.ax = 1
        CALL INTERRUPT(&H33, InRegs, OutRegs)

        REM Show menu bar is on.

        MenusOnFlag% = 1

        LOCATE CurRow%, CurCol%

        REM Clear the mouse queue

        InRegs.bx = 0
        InRegs.ax = 5
        CALL INTERRUPT(&H33, InRegs, OutRegs)
        InRegs.bx = 1
        InRegs.ax = 5
        CALL INTERRUPT(&H33, InRegs, OutRegs)
        InRegs.bx = 0
        InRegs.ax = 6
        CALL INTERRUPT(&H33, InRegs, OutRegs)
        InRegs.bx = 1
        InRegs.ax = 6
        CALL INTERRUPT(&H33, InRegs, OutRegs)

END SUB
```

Now let's see MenuShow( ) in action!

Showing Our Test Menubar

We can augment our MenuInitialize%( ) example so that the menubar is made to appear by calling MenuShow( ) at the very end:

```
DECLARE FUNCTION MenuInitialize% (MenuNames( ) AS STRING, MenuChoices( ) AS _
                STRING, Attrib%, MenuAttrbs( ) AS INTEGER)
DECLARE SUB MenuShow( )

DIM MenuNames(1 TO 3) AS STRING
DIM MenuChoices(1 TO 3, 1 TO 5) AS STRING
DIM MenuAttrbs(1 TO 3) AS INTEGER

        MenuNames(1) = "Fruits"
        MenuChoices(1, 1) = "Apples"
        MenuChoices(1, 2) = "Bananas"
        MenuChoices(1, 3) = "Grapes"
        MenuChoices(1, 4) = "Peaches"
        MenuChoices(1, 5) = "Oranges"

        MenuNames(2) = "Veggies"
        MenuChoices(2, 1) = "Peas"
        MenuChoices(2, 2) = "Corn"
```

```
MenuChoices(2, 3) = "Broccoli"

MenuNames(3) = "Meats"
MenuChoices(3, 1) = "Chicken"
MenuChoices(3, 2) = "Pork"
MenuChoices(3, 3) = "Beef"
MenuChoices(3, 4) = "Fish"

FOR i = 1 TO 3
    MenuAttrbs(i) = &H61
NEXT i
BarAttrb% = &H24

Check% = MenuInitialize%(MenuNames( ), MenuChoices( ), BarAttrb%,
        MenuAttrbs( ))

IF Check% = 0 THEN
    PRINT "Error."
ELSE
    PRINT "Menu is set up."
END IF

CALL MenuShow
```

Now the menubar appears on the screen (but is inactive). Note that one significant limitation of displaying the menubar is that you have to be very careful when scrolling the screen — you can scroll the menubar right off the top. If you do, of course, you can just call MenuShow( ) again without harm, but that gives the menubar a flickering appearance. Usually, programs that use menus carefully manage the screen anyway, and often don't scroll at all, so in practice this is not such a severe limitation.

TIP: You can actually control BASIC's attempts to scroll the screen in assembly language, although it is complicated. You need to write a terminate-and-stay-resident program to intercept calls to BIOS interrupt & H10, services 6 and 7— this is how BASIC scrolls the screen. For more details, see the appendix.

At this point, we've got the menubar on the screen, so the next natural step is to take it off.

Hiding the Menubar

This next subprogram, MenuHide( ), accompanies MenuShow( ). There are times when you'll want to remove the menubar from the top of the screen, and MenuHide( ) lets you do it.

TIP: One place you should definitely use MenuHide( ) is at the end of your program, to restore the screen.

All this subprogram does is to read the original top row of the screen from the menu COMMONs and replace it on the screen (after handling the mouse cursor as in MenuShow( )). It doesn't have to store the menubar first, of course, because that is already in memory (in the string Bar$).

First, we save the position of the cursor on the screen and turn off the mouse cursor:

```
SUB MenuHide

        DIM InRegs AS RegType, OutRegs AS RegType

        REM Turn off mouse cursor

        InRegs.ax = 2
        CALL INTERRUPT(&H33, InRegs, OutRegs)

        CurRow% = CSRLIN
        CurCol% = POS(0)
        :
        :
```

Next, we replace the old text:

```
SUB MenuHide

        DIM InRegs AS RegType, OutRegs AS RegType

        REM Turn off mouse cursor

        InRegs.ax = 2
        CALL INTERRUPT(&H33, InRegs, OutRegs)

        CurRow% = CSRLIN
        CurCol% = POS(0)

        REM Print the old text

        InRegs.cx = 1

→       FOR j = 1 TO 80
            LOCATE 1, j
            InRegs.ax = &H900 + ASC(MID$(OldBar$, j, 1))
            InRegs.bx = ASC(MID$(OldBarAttrb$, j, 1))
            CALL INTERRUPT(&H10, InRegs, OutRegs)
        NEXT j
            :
            :
```

At the end, we indicate that the menubar is off (and hence that the menu system is inactive and should simply pass input through to the calling program) by setting Menus-OnFlag% to 0. We also restore the mouse cursor, and move the screen cursor back to the position it had when MenuHide( ) was called:

```
SUB MenuHide

        DIM InRegs AS RegType, OutRegs AS RegType

        REM Turn off mouse cursor

        InRegs.ax = 2
        CALL INTERRUPT(&H33, InRegs, OutRegs)

        CurRow% = CSRLIN
        CurCol% = POS(0)

        REM Print the old text

        InRegs.cx = 1

            FOR j = 1 TO 80
                LOCATE 1, j
                InRegs.ax = &H900 + ASC(MID$(OldBar$, j, 1))
                InRegs.bx = ASC(MID$(OldBarAttrb$, j, 1))
                CALL INTERRUPT(&H10, InRegs, OutRegs)
            NEXT j

        REM Turn mouse cursor back on

        InRegs.ax = 1
        CALL INTERRUPT(&H33, InRegs, OutRegs)

        REM Show menu bar is off

        MenusOnFlag% = 0

        LOCATE CurRow%, CurCol%
```

And we're done. Listing 4-3 shows the whole subprogram.

Listing 4-3. MenuHide( ) Subprogram — Hides the Menubar.   **1 of 2**

```
DECLARE SUB MenuHide( )

TYPE RegType
            ax          AS INTEGER
            bx          AS INTEGER
            cx          AS INTEGER
            dx          AS INTEGER
            bp          AS INTEGER
```

Listing 4-3.   MenuHide( ) Subprogram — Hides the Menubar.   2 of 2

```
        si      AS INTEGER
        di      AS INTEGER
        flags   AS INTEGER
END TYPE

DECLARE SUB INTERRUPT (IntNo AS INTEGER, InRegs AS RegType, OutRegs AS RegType)

        CONST MaxMenus = 7
        DIM Rows(1 TO MaxMenus) AS INTEGER
        DIM Cols(1 TO MaxMenus) AS INTEGER
        DIM TopRow(1 TO MaxMenus) AS INTEGER
        DIM TopCol(1 TO MaxMenus) AS INTEGER
        DIM BotRow(1 TO MaxMenus) AS INTEGER
        DIM BotCol(1 TO MaxMenus) AS INTEGER
        DIM Attribute(1 TO MaxMenus) AS INTEGER
        DIM Text(1 TO MaxMenus, 25) AS STRING
        DIM OldText(1 TO MaxMenus, 25) AS STRING
        DIM OldAttrb(1 TO MaxMenus, 25) AS STRING
        COMMON SHARED /MenuA/ Rows( ) AS INTEGER, Cols( ) AS INTEGER, _
                      TopRow( ) AS INTEGER, TopCol( ) AS INTEGER, _
                      BotRow( ) AS INTEGER, BotCol( ) AS INTEGER
        COMMON SHARED /MenuB/ Attribute( ) AS INTEGER, Text( ) AS STRING, _
                      OldText( ) AS STRING, OldAttrb( ) AS STRING
        COMMON SHARED /MenuC/ Bar$, BarAttrb, MenusOnFlag%, NumMenus%, _
                      OldBar$, OldBarAttrb$

SUB MenuHide
        DIM InRegs AS RegType, OutRegs AS RegType

        CurRow% = CSRLIN
        CurCol% = POS(0)

        REM Turn off mouse cursor

        InRegs.ax = 2
        CALL INTERRUPT(&H33, InRegs, OutRegs)

        REM Print the old text

        InRegs.cx = 1

            FOR j = 1 TO 80
                LOCATE 1, j
                InRegs.ax = &H900 + ASC(MID$(OldBar$, j, 1))
                InRegs.bx = ASC(MID$(OldBarAttrb$, j, 1))
                CALL INTERRUPT(&H10, InRegs, OutRegs)
            NEXT j

        REM Turn mouse cursor back on

        InRegs.ax = 1
        CALL INTERRUPT(&H33, InRegs, OutRegs)

        REM Show menu bar is off

        MenusOnFlag% = 0

        LOCATE CurRow%, CurCol%

END SUB
```

Now let's put this new subprogram to work.

Hiding Our Test Menubar

This example just displays the menubar and then hides it when you press a key:

```
DECLARE FUNCTION MenuInitialize% (MenuNames() AS STRING, MenuChoices() AS _
        STRING, BarAttrb%, MenuAttrbs() AS INTEGER)
DECLARE SUB MenuShow()
DECLARE SUB MenuHide()

DIM MenuNames(1 TO 3) AS STRING
DIM MenuChoices(1 TO 3, 1 TO 5) AS STRING
DIM MenuAttrbs(1 TO 3) AS INTEGER

        MenuNames(1) = "Fruits"
        MenuChoices(1, 1) = "Apples"
        MenuChoices(1, 2) = "Bananas"
        MenuChoices(1, 3) = "Grapes"
        MenuChoices(1, 4) = "Peaches"
        MenuChoices(1, 5) = "Oranges"

        MenuNames(2) = "Veggies"
        MenuChoices(2, 1) = "Peas"
        MenuChoices(2, 2) = "Corn"
        MenuChoices(2, 3) = "Broccoli"

        MenuNames(3) = "Meats"
        MenuChoices(3, 1) = "Chicken"
        MenuChoices(3, 2) = "Pork"
        MenuChoices(3, 3) = "Beef"
        MenuChoices(3, 4) = "Fish"

        FOR i = 1 TO 3
            MenuAttrbs(i) = &H61
        NEXT i
        BarAttrb% = &H24

        Check% = MenuInitialize%(MenuNames(), MenuChoices(), BarAttrb%, _
            MenuAttrbs())

        IF Check% = 0 THEN
            PRINT "Error."
        ELSE
            PRINT "Menu is set up."
        END IF

        CALL MenuShow

        PRINT "Press any key to remove the menu bar."
        DO
        LOOP WHILE INKEY$ = ""

  →     CALL MenuHide
```

Now we're set. We've initialized the menubar and each of the menus. We've been able to place the menubar on the screen and take it off again. The next step is to receive input with MenuGetEvent$( ).

Calling MenuGetEvent$( ) is what makes the menubar active. You call it and then wait for input. MenuGetEvent$( ) is the heart of the menu system. This function has to handle many different types of input, however, and it's going to be a giant.

Reading Menu Input

At this point, we have to get program input (keyboard, mouse, and menu). After we've initialized the menu system and the menubar is displayed, we'll call MenuGetEvent$( ) to receive that input. This function will wait until a key is pressed, a mouse button is pushed or released, or a menu choice is made; then it will return and indicate what happened.

> **NOTE:** If you don't want to wait for input, we'll also write another function, Menu-CheckEvent$( ), the INKEY$ of our menu system. If there's a keyboard, mouse, or menu event waiting, it will report it. Otherwise, it returns immediately with a value of " ", as INKEY$ would.

Because we want MenuGetEvent$( ) to monitor the menus, the mouse, and the keyboard, we can design it to be used like this:

```
InString$ = MenuGetEvent$ (MenuNo%, ChoiceNo%, Button%, ScRow%, ScCol%)
```

Note the variables that we pass to MenuGetEvent$( ) here; they should be filled like this, depending on the string that was returned:

InString$	Means
STRING of LEN 1	Single character typed. Read as you would from INKEY$.
STRING of LEN 2	Character typed with an extended ASCII code. Read as you would from INKEY$.

"mousedown"	Mouse button was pressed: Button% = 0 for left button; Button% = 1 for right button. Screen coordinates: (ScRow%, ScCol%), using text-mode ranges (1-25 and 1-80)
"mouseup"	Mouse button was released: Button% = 0 for left button; Button% = 1 for right button. Screen coordinates: (ScRow%, ScCol%), using text-mode ranges (1-25 and 1-80).
"menuopen"	User opened a menu. Menu number in MenuNo%.
"menuclose"	User closed a menu. Menu number in MenuNo%.
"menuchoice"	A menu selection was made. MenuNo% = Menu number; ChoiceNo% = the number of the choice in that menu. Menu number and choice number correspond to the array indices of the arrays you passed to Menu-Initialize%( ).

If you're not interested in the mouseup, mousedown, menuopen, or menuclose events, just call MenuGetEvent$( ) again until you read a key or the it returns a string of menuchoice.

In that case, we can get the number of the menu chosen from MenuNo%, and number of the choice made in that menu from ChoiceNo%:

```
                          ↓               ↓
"menuchoice" = MenuGetEvent$ (MenuNo%, ChoiceNo%, Button%, ScRow%, ScCol%)
```

These numbers correspond to the indices in the arrays we've passed to MenuInitialize%( ). For example, if we've initialized menu 1 like this:

```
MenuChoices(1, 1) = "Apples"
MenuChoices(1, 2) = "Bananas"
MenuChoices(1, 3) = "Grapes"
MenuChoices(1, 4) = "Peaches"
MenuChoices(1, 5) = "Oranges"
```

and MenuGetEvent$( ) returns values of MenuNo% = 1 and ChoiceNo% = 4, then the choice made was MenuChoices(1, 4), or Peaches. In general, the choice made was Menu-Choices(MenuNo%, ChoiceNo%).

We can use the Button%, ScRow%, and ScCol% variables to report mouse events:

```
                                           ↓        ↓        ↓
"mousedown" = MenuGetEvent$ (MenuNo%, ChoiceNo%, Button%, ScRow%, ScCol%)
```

And, if a key was struck, MenuGetEvent$( ) will act just like INKEY$( ). In this way, we'll be able to report each type of input event.

We've already specified how the menu system should work in the beginning of the chapter — let's translate that into an outline for MenuGetEvent$( ):

```
DO
:          IF (a key was pressed) THEN
:                    MenuGetEvent$ = key that was pressed
:                    IF (menu system is on) THEN
:                            IF (Esc was pressed) THEN
:                                    IF (menu was open) THEN
:                                            [close menu and EXIT]
:                                    ELSE
:                                            EXIT FUNCTION
:                                    END IF
:                            END IF
:                            IF (Alt key matched a menu or choice name) THEN
:                                    [set menu arguments and EXIT]
:                            ELSE
:                                    EXIT FUNCTION
:                            END IF
:                    END IF
:                    EXIT FUNCTION
:          END IF
:
:          IF (a mouse button was used) THEN
:                    IF (it was the left mouse button) THEN
:                            IF (it was in a menu) THEN
:                                    [set menu arguments and EXIT]
:                            ELSE
:                                    [set mouse arguments and EXIT]
:                            END IF
:                    ELSE    'It was the right button
:                            [set mouse arguments and EXIT]
:                    END IF
:                    EXIT FUNCTION
:          END IF
:
LOOP WHILE 1
```

Even in outline, it's a lengthy listing. There are two primary parts to the code: the first checks to see if a key was typed and tries to interpret that key; and the second checks the mouse queue and tries to interpret mouse events. Let's start by taking a look at the key reading part. First, we start off by assigning a null string, " ", to MenuGetEvent$, and set up a DO...LOOP WHILE 1 loop that will continually wait for input:

```
FUNCTION MenuGetEvent$ (MenuNo%, ChoiceNo%, Button%, ScRow%, ScCol%) STATIC

        DIM InRegs AS RegType, OutRegs AS RegType
        MenuGetEvent$ = ""

        DO
        :
        :
        LOOP WHILE 1
```

Now we try to read in a key. If one is waiting, and the menubar is off (i.e., MenusOnFlag% = 0), we return with that value:

```
FUNCTION MenuGetEvent$ (MenuNo%, ChoiceNo%, Button%, ScRow%, ScCol%) STATIC

        DIM InRegs AS RegType, OutRegs AS RegType
        MenuGetEvent$ = ""

        DO
        InChar$ = INKEY$

        IF InChar$ <> "" THEN
           MenuGetEvent$ = InChar$
           IF MenusOnFlag% = 0 THEN EXIT FUNCTION    'Menu system on?
                   :
                   :
        END IF  'Check key
```

Next, we check to see if it was an Esc key, which closes a menu if it's open. If it was an Esc key and no menu is open, we pass the Esc on to the calling program.

On the other hand, if a menu *was* open and Esc was pushed, this is a "menuclose" event, and we close the menu, set the return value MenuNo% to inform the calling program which menu was closed and exit.

How will we know whether or not a menu is open? This is an important point: We have a flag, MenusOnFlag%, to indicate that the menubar is displayed — but no way to keep track of which menu might actually be open. For that reason, let's introduce a new variable named MenuNowOpen%. This important variable, which will appear frequently in MenuGetEvent$( ), holds the number of the menu now open; if no menu is open, it will hold 0 (we'll set the value in MenuNowOpen% whenever we open or close a menu). To check whether any menu is now open, therefore, we only have to check the value in MenuNowOpen%:

```
FUNCTION MenuGetEvent$ (MenuNo%, ChoiceNo%, Button%, ScRow%, ScCol%) STATIC

        DIM InRegs AS RegType, OutRegs AS RegType
        MenuGetEvent$ = ""

        DO
        InChar$ = INKEY$

        IF InChar$ <> "" THEN
          MenuGetEvent$ = InChar$
          IF MenusOnFlag% = 0 THEN EXIT FUNCTION       'Menu system on?
          IF ASC(InChar$) = 27 THEN   'Escape key
→         IF MenuNowOpen% = 0 THEN
:             EXIT FUNCTION
:
```

NOTE: We don't have to put MenuNowOpen% into the menu commons since it's entirely local to MenuGetEvent$( ), unlike MenusOnFlag%, which is also used by MenuShow( ) and MenuHide( ).

If there is a menu open, on the other hand, we'll have to close it, since Esc was pushed. Since we'll be opening and closing menus frequently, let's set up two subprograms named TurnOnMenu( ) and TurnOffMenu( ) that display and hide individual menus. These two routines are simple adaptations of our WindowShow( ) and WindowHide( ) subprograms, respectively. To close the currently open menu, for example, all we have to do is to CALL TurnOffMenu(MenuNowOpen%):

```
FUNCTION MenuGetEvent$ (MenuNo%, ChoiceNo%, Button%, ScRow%, ScCol%) STATIC

        DIM InRegs AS RegType, OutRegs AS RegType
        MenuGetEvent$ = ""

        DO
        InChar$ = INKEY$

        IF InChar$ <> "" THEN
          MenuGetEvent$ = InChar$
          IF MenusOnFlag% = 0 THEN EXIT FUNCTION    'Menu system on?
```

```
                IF ASC(InChar$) = 27 THEN  'Escape key
                   IF MenuNowOpen% = 0 THEN
                      EXIT FUNCTION
   →            ELSE
   :                  CALL TurnOffMenu(MenuNowOpen%)
   :                  MenuNo% = MenuNowOpen%
                      MenuNowOpen% = 0
                      MenuGetEvent$ = "menuclose"
                      EXIT FUNCTION
                   END IF
                END IF            'Escape key
                      :
                      :
             END IF  'Check key
```

If it wasn't an escape key but the length of the string INKEY$ returned was 1, then it's a normal key with no significance for us — we return it to the calling program. Otherwise, we check to see if it's an Alt key by examining the scan code (the second character in the string INKEY$ returned, which we've named InChar$). If it's not an Alt key, this key is not for us and we pass it to the calling program:

```
FUNCTION MenuGetEvent$ (MenuNo%, ChoiceNo%, Button%, ScRow%, ScCol%) STATIC

       DIM InRegs AS RegType, OutRegs AS RegType
       MenuGetEvent$ = ""

       DO
       InChar$ = INKEY$

       IF InChar$ <> "" THEN
          MenuGetEvent$ = InChar$
          IF MenusOnFlag% = 0 THEN EXIT FUNCTION     'Menu system on?
          IF ASC(InChar$) = 27 THEN  'Escape key
             IF MenuNowOpen% = 0 THEN
                EXIT FUNCTION
             ELSE
                CALL TurnOffMenu(MenuNowOpen%)
                MenuNo% = MenuNowOpen%
                MenuNowOpen% = 0
                MenuGetEvent$ = "menuclose"
                EXIT FUNCTION
             END IF
          END IF            'Escape key
   →      IF LEN(InChar$) = 1 THEN
   :         EXIT FUNCTION
   :      ELSE
             ScanCode = ASC(RIGHT$(InChar$,1))
             AltKey$ = ""
             IF ScanCode >=16 AND ScanCode <=25 THEN AltKey$=MID$("QWERTYUIOP",_
                                               ScanCode - 15,1)
             IF ScanCode >=30 AND ScanCode <=38 THEN AltKey$=MID$("ASDFGHJKL",_
                                               ScanCode - 29,1)
```

```
IF ScanCode >=44 AND ScanCode <=50 THEN AltKey$=MID$("ZXCVBNM", _
                                        ScanCode - 43,1)
IF AltKey$ = "" THEN EXIT FUNCTION
    :
    :
```

At this point, if we're still in the function, we've identified the key as an Alt key, and placed it in AltKey$. We have to check if it matches the first letter of a choice in the currently open menu (if one *is* currently open; see Figure 4-6). If it does, this is a menuchoice event; a choice was made in that menu. We have to set the values MenuNo% and ChoiceNo% appropriately for use by the calling program, close the menu, and exit:

Fruits	Menu2	Menu 3	Menu 4
Apples			
Bananas			
Grapes			
Peaches			
Oranges			

Figure 4-6

```
FUNCTION MenuGetEvent$ (MenuNo%, ChoiceNo%, Button%, ScRow%, ScCol%) STATIC

    DIM InRegs AS RegType, OutRegs AS RegType
    MenuGetEvent$ = ""


    DO
    InChar$ = INKEY$

    IF InChar$ <> "" THEN
      MenuGetEvent$ = InChar$
      IF MenusOnFlag% = 0 THEN EXIT FUNCTION    'Menu system on?
      IF ASC(InChar$) = 27 THEN    'Escape key
        IF MenuNowOpen% = 0 THEN
            EXIT FUNCTION
        ELSE
            CALL TurnOffMenu(MenuNowOpen%)
            MenuNo% = MenuNowOpen%
            MenuNowOpen% = 0
            MenuGetEvent$ = "menuclose"
            EXIT FUNCTION
        END IF
      END IF        'Escape key
      IF LEN(InChar$) = 1 THEN
        EXIT FUNCTION
      ELSE
        ScanCode = ASC(RIGHT$(InChar$,1))
```

```
        AltKey$ = ""
        IF ScanCode >=16 AND ScanCode <25= THEN AltKey$=MID$("QWERTYUIOP",_
                                                ScanCode - 15,1)
        IF ScanCode <=30 AND ScanCode >38= THEN AltKey$=MID$("ASDFGHJKL",_
                                                ScanCode - 29,1)
        IF ScanCode <=44 AND ScanCode >50= THEN AltKey$=MID$("ZXCVBNM",_
                                                ScanCode - 43,1)

        IF AltKey$ = "" THEN EXIT FUNCTION

→       IF MenuNowOpen% <> 0 THEN
:          FOR i = 1 TO Rows(MenuNowOpen%)
:              IF AltKey$ = UCASE$(MID$(Text(MenuNowOpen%,i),2,1)) THEN
                    MenuNo% = MenuNowOpen%
                    ChoiceNo% = i
                    CALL TurnOffMenu(MenuNowOpen%)
                    MenuNowOpen% = 0
                    MenuGetEvent$ = "menuchoice"
                    EXIT FUNCTION
               END IF
           NEXT i
        END IF
           :
           :
```

If we haven't exited the function at this point, then the Alt key hasn't matched a choice in a menu that's currently open (if any). In that case, we have to check and see if we're supposed to close that menu (i.e., referencing a menu with the same Alt key toggles it on and off); in that case, this is a menuclose event.

Otherwise, we must check if this Alt key matches another menu name in the menubar. If it does, this is a menuopen event; we open that menu (after first closing any open menu). Finally, if *nothing* matches, the Alt key wasn't for us and we pass it on to the calling program (keep in mind that NumMenus% is the number of menus in the menubar):

```
FUNCTION MenuGetEvent$ (MenuNo%, ChoiceNo%, Button%, ScRow%, ScCol%) STATIC

     DIM InRegs AS RegType, OutRegs AS RegType
     MenuGetEvent$ = ""

     DO
     InChar$ = INKEY$

     IF InChar$ <> "" THEN
        MenuGetEvent$ = InChar$
        IF MenusOnFlag% = 0 THEN EXIT FUNCTION     'Menu system on?
        IF ASC(InChar$) = 27 THEN    'Escape key
           IF MenuNowOpen% = 0 THEN
              EXIT FUNCTION
           ELSE
              CALL TurnOffMenu(MenuNowOpen%)
              MenuNo% = MenuNowOpen%
              MenuNowOpen% = 0
```

```
                    MenuGetEvent$ = "menuclose"
                    EXIT FUNCTION
               END IF
        END IF          'Escape key
        IF LEN(InChar$) = 1 THEN
          EXIT FUNCTION
        ELSE
          ScanCode = ASC(RIGHT$(InChar$,1))
          AltKey$ = ""
          IF ScanCode >=16 AND ScanCode <=25 THEN AltKey$=MID$("QWERTYUIOP",_
                                        ScanCode - 15,1)
          IF ScanCode >=30 AND ScanCode <=38 THEN AltKey$=MID$("ASDFGHJKL",_
                                        ScanCode - 29,1)
          IF ScanCode >=44 AND ScanCode <=50 THEN AltKey$=MID$("ZXCVBNM",_
                                        ScanCode - 43,1)
          IF AltKey$ = "" THEN EXIT FUNCTION

          IF MenuNowOpen% <> 0 THEN
             FOR i = 1 TO Rows(MenuNowOpen%)
                 IF Altkey$ = UCASE$(MID$(Text(MenuNowOpen%,i),2,1)) THEN
                    MenuNo% = MenuNowOpen%
                    ChoiceNo% = i
                    CALL TurnOffMenu(MenuNowOpen%)
                    MenuNowOpen% = 0
                    MenuGetEvent$ = "menuchoice"
                    EXIT FUNCTION
                 END IF
             NEXT i
          END IF

          FOR i = 1 TO NumMenus%
                 IF AltKey$ = UCASE$(MID$(Bar$,10*(i-1)+2,1)) THEN
                    IF MenuNowOpen% = i THEN     'This menu toggled off
                       MenuNo% = i
                       CALL TurnOffMenu(i)
                       MenuNowOpen% = 0
                       MenuGetEvent$ = "menuclose"
                       EXIT FUNCTION
                    END IF
                    IF MenuNowOpen% 0 THEN CALL TurnOffMenu(MenuNowOpen%)
                    MenuNo% = i          'Another menu turned on
                    ChoiceNo% = 0
                    MenuNowOpen% = i
                    CALL TurnOnMenu(i)
                    MenuGetEvent$ = "menuopen"
                 END IF
             NEXT i   'For i = 1 TO NumMenus%
          END IF          'Check char length
             EXIT FUNCTION
        END IF  'Check key
```

That's it for the key reading part of MenuGetEvent$( ). So far, we've covered half the function MenuGetEvent$( ). Let's turn to the mouse monitoring part.

Here, let's only work through the part of the code that deals with the left mouse button, the one that works the menu system. The part of MenuGetEvent$( ) that handles the right mouse button is pretty straightforward, and we'll put it into the full listing later; there's no use taking up pages covering it.

The left mouse button part itself can be broken up into two parts — was the left mouse button pressed or released? First we can check if it's been pressed. If it has been, we place the mouse cursor's screen row and screen column into the variables ScRow% and ScCol% in preparation for returning them to the calling program (and because we'll use those variables ourselves). To do that, we simply take the values returned in dx and cx, integer divide by 8, and add 1.

Note that if ScRow% was 1 and the menubar was on (MenusOnFlag% = 1), then this is a menuopen event (if the mouse cursor was lying on a menu name). In that case, we set the return value in MenuNo%, open the menu on the screen and then exit. Otherwise, we still have to report a mousedown event, and do so like this, where NumberTimes% is the number of times the left button was pressed:

```
REM *** Check for left mouse button pressed

Button% = 0
InRegs.bx = 0
InRegs.ax = 5
CALL INTERRUPT(&H33, InRegs, OutRegs)

NumberTimes% = OutRegs.bx          'Number of times left button pressed
ScRow% = OutRegs.dx \ 8 + 1
ScCol% = OutRegs.cx \ 8 + 1

IF NumberTimes% \ 0 THEN
        IF MenusOnFlag% AND (ScRow% = 1) THEN
                MenubarCandidate% = ScCol% \ 10 + 1
                IF MenubarCandidate% <= NumMenus% THEN
                        MenuNo% = MenubarCandidate%
                        ChoiceNo% = 0
                        MenuNowOpen% = MenubarCandidate%
                        CALL TurnOnMenu(MenubarCandidate%)
                        MenuGetEvent$ = "menuopen"
                        EXIT FUNCTION
                END IF
        ELSE
                MenuGetEvent$ = "mousedown"
                EXIT FUNCTION
        END IF
END IF
```

That's all there is to handling left button presses (it's only when you release the left button that you make a menu choice). Let's look at the left button released section of MenuGetEvent$( ) next. Again, if the button has been released, we load ScRow% and ScCol%.

Now it gets a little complex. If the menu bar is on (MenusOnFlag% = 1) and a menu is open (MenuNowOpen% is not 0), then we have to check if a menu event took place. Otherwise, we just exit and report a mouseup event because the left button was released. Here's the left button released part of the code:

```
REM *** Check for left mouse button released

InRegs.bx = 0
InRegs.ax = 6
CALL INTERRUPT(&H33, InRegs, OutRegs)

NumberTimes% = OutRegs.bx
ScRow% = OutRegs.dx \ 8 + 1
ScCol% = OutRegs.cx \ 8 + 1

IF NumberTimes% <> 0 THEN
   IF MenusOnFlag% AND (MenuNowOpen% <> 0) THEN
            :
      [Check for menu event]
            :
   ELSE
         MenuGetEvent$ = "mouseup"
         EXIT FUNCTION
   END IF 'Menu open
END IF 'NumberTimes% <> 0
```

To check for a menu event, we have to see if the mouse cursor was inside the menu that was open when the left button was released. If it was out of range (in either rows or columns), then the menu is supposed to close, and this is a menuclose event. Here's how that looks:

```
      REM *** Check for left mouse button released

      InRegs.bx = 0
      InRegs.ax = 6
      CALL INTERRUPT(&H33, InRegs, OutRegs)

      NumberTimes% = OutRegs.bx
      ScRow% = OutRegs.dx \ 8 + 1
      ScCol% = OutRegs.cx \ 8 + 1

      IF NumberTimes% <> 0 THEN
         IF MenusOnFlag% AND (MenuNowOpen% <> 0) THEN
→           IF ScRow% => 2 AND ScRow% <= 2 + Rows(MenuNowOpen%) THEN
:              IF ScCol% >= 1 + 10 * (MenuNowOpen%-1) AND ScCol% <=_
:                 10*(MenuNowOpen%) THEN

                  [Mouse cursor was in an open menu when
                   left button released -- get menu choice]
                     :
```

```
            ELSE
                MenuNo% = MenuNowOpen%
                CALL TurnOffMenu(MenuNowOpen%)
                MenuNowOpen% = 0
                MenuGetEvent$ = "menuclose"
                EXIT FUNCTION
            END IF
        ELSE
                MenuNo% = MenuNowOpen%
                CALL TurnOffMenu(MenuNowOpen%)
                MenuNowOpen% = 0
                MenuGetEvent$ = "menuclose"
                EXIT FUNCTION
        END IF
    ELSE
            MenuGetEvent$ = "mouseup"
            EXIT FUNCTION
    END IF 'Menu open
END IF 'NumberTimes% <> 0
```

This is the heart of the mouse part right here — the left button was released when the
mouse cursor was inside an open menu. Now we have to find out which choice was
made. That turns out to be easy; because the top row of each menu is 2, the choice that
was made, ChoiceNo%, is just ScRow% - 1 (see Figure 4-7). We report that choice and
close the menu:

```
REM *** Check for left mouse button released

InRegs.bx = 0
InRegs.ax = 6
CALL INTERRUPT(&H33, InRegs, OutRegs)

NumberTimes% = OutRegs.bx
ScRow% = OutRegs.dx \ 8 + 1
ScCol% = OutRegs.cx \ 8 + 1

IF NumberTimes% <> 0 THEN
  IF MenusOnFlag% AND (MenuNowOpen% <> 0) THEN
    IF ScRow% >= 2 AND ScRow% <= 2 + Rows(MenuNowOpen%) THEN
      IF ScCol% >= 1 + 10 * (MenuNowOpen%-1) AND ScCol% <= _
          10*(MenuNowOpen%) THEN
 →        ChoiceNo% = ScRow% - 1
          CALL TurnOffMenu(MenuNowOpen%)
          MenuNo% = MenuNowOpen%
          MenuNowOpen% = 0
          MenuGetEvent$ = "menuchoice"
          EXIT FUNCTION
      ELSE
          MenuNo% = MenuNowOpen%
          CALL TurnOffMenu(MenuNowOpen%)
          MenuNowOpen% = 0
          MenuGetEvent$ = "menuclose"
          EXIT FUNCTION
```

```
            END IF
    ELSE
                MenuNo% = MenuNowOpen%
                CALL TurnOffMenu(MenuNowOpen%)
                MenuNowOpen% = 0
                MenuGetEvent$ = "menuclose"
                EXIT FUNCTION
        END IF
  ELSE
            MenuGetEvent$ = "mouseup"
            EXIT FUNCTION
    END IF 'Menu open
END IF 'NumberTimes% <> 0
```

ScRow% = 1	Fruits	Menu2	Menu 3	Menu 4
ScRow% = 2	Apples		ChoiceNo% = 1	
ScRow% = 3	Bananas		ChoiceNo% = 2	
ScRow% = 4	Grapes		ChoiceNo% = 3	
	Peaches		:	
	Oranges			

Figure 4-7

This concludes the mouse part of MenuGetEvent$( ) — for the left mouse button. The right mouse button is much easier to handle since it can only generate mousedown and mouseup events. We'll leave that part up to the interested programmer. Listing 4-4 shows the whole giant function.

Listing 4-4. MenuGetEvent$ Function — Reads Menu Events.   1 of 6

```
DECLARE FUNCTION MenuGetEvent$ (MenuNo%, ChoiceNo%, Button%, ScRow%, ScCol%)
DECLARE SUB TurnOnMenu (MNumber%)
DECLARE SUB TurnOffMenu (MNumber%)

TYPE RegType
        ax      AS INTEGER
        bx      AS INTEGER
        cx      AS INTEGER
        dx      AS INTEGER
        bp      AS INTEGER
        si      AS INTEGER
        di      AS INTEGER
        flags   AS INTEGER
END TYPE

DECLARE SUB INTERRUPT (IntNo AS INTEGER, InRegs AS RegType, OutRegs AS RegType)

        CONST MaxMenus = 7
```

Listing 4-4. MenuGetEvent$ Function — Reads Menu Events.   2 of 6

```
      DIM Rows(1 TO MaxMenus) AS INTEGER
      DIM Cols(1 TO MaxMenus) AS INTEGER
      DIM TopRow(1 TO MaxMenus) AS INTEGER
      DIM TopCol(1 TO MaxMenus) AS INTEGER
      DIM BotRow(1 TO MaxMenus) AS INTEGER
      DIM BotCol(1 TO MaxMenus) AS INTEGER
      DIM Attribute(1 TO MaxMenus) AS INTEGER
      DIM Text(1 TO MaxMenus, 25) AS STRING
      DIM OldText(1 TO MaxMenus, 25) AS STRING
      DIM OldAttrb(1 TO MaxMenus, 25) AS STRING
      COMMON SHARED /MenuA/ Rows() AS INTEGER, Cols() AS INTEGER, _
                    TopRow() AS INTEGER, TopCol() AS INTEGER, _
                    BotRow() AS INTEGER, BotCol() AS INTEGER
      COMMON SHARED /MenuB/ Attribute() AS INTEGER, Text() AS STRING, _
                    OldText() AS STRING, OldAttrb() AS STRING
      COMMON SHARED /MenuC/ Bar$, BarAttrb, MenusOnFlag%, NumMenus%, OldBar$,_
                    OldBarAttrb$

FUNCTION MenuGetEvent$ (MenuNo%, ChoiceNo%, Button%, ScRow%, ScCol%) STATIC

      DIM InRegs AS RegType, OutRegs AS RegType

      MenuGetEvent$ = ""

      DO

      InChar$ = INKEY$

      IF InChar$ <> "" THEN
        MenuGetEvent$ = InChar$
        IF MenusOnFlag% = 0 THEN EXIT FUNCTION     'Menu system on?
        IF ASC(InChar$) = 27 THEN   'Escape key
           IF MenuNowOpen% = 0 THEN
              EXIT FUNCTION
           ELSE
              CALL TurnOffMenu(MenuNowOpen%)
              MenuNo% = MenuNowOpen%
              MenuNowOpen% = 0
              MenuGetEvent$ = "menuclose"
              EXIT FUNCTION
           END IF
        END IF          'Escape key
        IF LEN(InChar$) = 1 THEN
          EXIT FUNCTION
        ELSE
          SC = ASC(RIGHT$(InChar$,1))
          AltKey$ = ""
          IF SC >= 16 AND SC <= 25 THEN AltKey$ = MID$("QWERTYUIOP",
                                                    SC - 15,1)
          IF SC >= 30 AND SC <= 38 THEN AltKey$ = MID$("ASDFGHJKL",
                                                    SC - 29,1)
          IF SC >= 44 AND SC <= 50 THEN AltKey$ = MID$("ZXCVBNM",
                                                    SC - 43,1)

          IF AltKey$ = "" THEN EXIT FUNCTION

          IF MenuNowOpen% <> 0 THEN
             FOR i% = 1 TO Rows(MenuNowOpen%)
```

Listing 4-4. MenuGetEvent$ Function — Reads Menu Events. 3 of 6

```
                    IF AltKey$ = UCASE$(MID$(Text(MenuNowOpen%,i%),2,1)) THEN
                        MenuNo% = MenuNowOpen%
                        ChoiceNo% = i%
                        CALL TurnOffMenu(MenuNowOpen%)
                        MenuNowOpen% = 0
                        MenuGetEvent$ = "menuchoice"
                        EXIT FUNCTION
                    END IF
                NEXT i%
        END IF

        FOR i% = 1 TO NumMenus%
            IF AltKey$ = UCASE$(MID$(Bar$,10*(i%-1)+2,1)) THEN
                IF MenuNowOpen% = i% THEN
                    MenuNo% = i%
                    CALL TurnOffMenu(i%)
                    MenuNowOpen% = 0
                    MenuGetEvent$ = "menuclose"
                    EXIT FUNCTION
                END IF
                IF MenuNowOpen% <> 0 THEN CALL TurnOffMenu(MenuNowOpen%)
                MenuNo% = i%
                ChoiceNo% = 0
                MenuNowOpen% = i%
                CALL TurnOnMenu(i%)
                MenuGetEvent$ = "menuopen"
            END IF
        NEXT i%   'For i% = 1 TO NumMenus%
    END IF        'Check char length
        EXIT FUNCTION
END IF   'Check key

REM *** Check for left mouse button pressed

Button% = 0
InRegs.bx = 0
InRegs.ax = 5
CALL INTERRUPT(&H33, InRegs, OutRegs)

NumberTimes% = OutRegs.bx
ScRow% = OutRegs.dx \ 8 + 1
ScCol% = OutRegs.cx \ 8 + 1

IF NumberTimes% <> 0 THEN
        IF MenusOnFlag% AND (ScRow% = 1) THEN
                MenubarCandidate% = ScCol% \ 10 + 1
                IF MenubarCandidate% <= NumMenus% THEN
                    MenuNo% = MenubarCandidate%
                    ChoiceNo% = 0
                    MenuNowOpen% = MenubarCandidate%
                    CALL TurnOnMenu(MenubarCandidate%)
                    MenuGetEvent$ = "menuopen"
                    EXIT FUNCTION
                END IF
        ELSE
                MenuGetEvent$ = "mousedown"
                EXIT FUNCTION
```

Listing 4-4.   MenuGetEvent$ Function — Reads Menu Events.   4 of 6

```
            END IF
      END IF

      REM *** Check for left mouse button released

      InRegs.bx = 0
      InRegs.ax = 6
      CALL INTERRUPT(&H33, InRegs, OutRegs)

      NumberTimes% = OutRegs.bx
      ScRow% = OutRegs.dx \ 8 + 1
      ScCol% = OutRegs.cx \ 8 + 1

      IF NumberTimes% <> 0 THEN
        IF MenusOnFlag% AND (MenuNowOpen% <> 0) THEN
          IF ScRow% >= 2 AND ScRow% <= 2 + Rows(MenuNowOpen%) THEN
            IF ScCol% >= 1 + 10 * (MenuNowOpen%-1) AND ScCol% <= _
               10*(MenuNowOpen%) THEN
               ChoiceNo% = ScRow% - 1
               CALL TurnOffMenu(MenuNowOpen%)
               MenuNo% = MenuNowOpen%
               MenuNowOpen% = 0
               MenuGetEvent$ = "menuchoice"
               EXIT FUNCTION
            ELSE
               MenuNo% = MenuNowOpen%
               CALL TurnOffMenu(MenuNowOpen%)
               MenuNowOpen% = 0
               MenuGetEvent$ = "menuclose"
               EXIT FUNCTION
            END IF
          ELSE
               MenuNo% = MenuNowOpen%
               CALL TurnOffMenu(MenuNowOpen%)
               MenuNowOpen% = 0
               MenuGetEvent$ = "menuclose"
               EXIT FUNCTION
          END IF
        ELSE
             MenuGetEvent$ = "mouseup"
             EXIT FUNCTION
        END IF 'Menu open
      END IF 'NumberTimes% <> 0

      REM *** Check for right mouse button pressed

      Button% = 1
      InRegs.bx = 1
      InRegs.ax = 5
      CALL INTERRUPT(&H33, InRegs, OutRegs)

      NumberTimes% = OutRegs.bx
      ScRow% = OutRegs.dx \ 8 + 1
      ScCol% = OutRegs.cx \ 8 + 1

      IF NumberTimes% \ 0 THEN
             MenuGetEvent$ = "mousedown"
```

Listing 4-4.   MenuGetEvent$ Function — Reads Menu Events.   5 of 6

```
                EXIT FUNCTION
        END IF

        REM *** Check for right mouse button released

        InRegs.bx = 1
        InRegs.ax = 6
        CALL INTERRUPT(&H33, InRegs, OutRegs)

        NumberTimes% = OutRegs.bx
        ScRow% = OutRegs.dx \ 8 + 1
        ScCol% = OutRegs.cx \ 8 + 1

        IF NumberTimes% <> 0 THEN
                MenuGetEvent$ = "mousedown"
                EXIT FUNCTION
        END IF

        LOOP WHILE 1

END FUNCTION

SUB TurnOnMenu (MNumber%)

        DIM InRegs AS RegType, OutRegs AS RegType

        CurRow% = CSRLIN
        CurCol% = POS(0)

        InRegs.ax = 2
        CALL INTERRUPT(&H33, InRegs, OutRegs)

        REM Save the old section of screen

        rr = TopRow(MNumber%)
        cc = TopCol(MNumber%)
        rt = Rows(MNumber%)
        ct = Cols(MNumber%)

        FOR i = 1 TO rt
                temp1$ = ""
                temp2$ = ""
                FOR j = 1 TO ct
                        temp1$ = temp1$ + CHR$(SCREEN(rr + i - 1, cc + j - 1))
                        temp2$ = temp2$ + CHR$(SCREEN(rr + i - 1, cc + j - 1, 1))
                NEXT j
                OldText(MNumber%, i) = temp1$
                OldAttrb(MNumber%, i) = temp2$
        NEXT i

        REM Now print the new text

        TR = TopRow(MNumber%)
        TC = TopCol(MNumber%)
        LOCATE TR, TC
        InRegs.cx = 1
```

Listing 4-4. MenuGetEvent$ Function — Reads Menu Events. 6 of 6

```
            FOR i = 1 TO Rows(MNumber%)
                OR$ = Text(MNumber%, i)
                FOR j = 1 TO Cols(MNumber%)
                    InRegs.ax = &H900 + ASC(MID$(OR$, j, 1))
                    InRegs.bx = Attribute(MNumber%)
                    CALL INTERRUPT(&H10, InRegs, OutRegs)
                    LOCATE TR + i - 1, TC + j
                NEXT j
                    LOCATE TR + i, TC
            NEXT i

            InRegs.ax = 1
            CALL INTERRUPT(&H33, InRegs, OutRegs)

            LOCATE CurRow%, CurCol%

END SUB

SUB TurnOffMenu (MNumber%)

            CurRow% = CSRLIN
            CurCol% = POS(0)

            DIM InRegs AS RegType, OutRegs AS RegType

            InRegs.ax = 2
            CALL INTERRUPT(&H33, InRegs, OutRegs)

            REM Print the old text

            TR = TopRow(MNumber%)
            TC = TopCol(MNumber%)
            LOCATE TR, TC
            InRegs.cx = 1

            FOR i = 1 TO Rows(MNumber%)
                OR$ = OldText(MNumber%, i)
                OC$ = OldAttrb(MNumber%, i)
                FOR j = 1 TO Cols(MNumber%)
                    InRegs.ax = &H900 + ASC(MID$(OR$, j, 1))
                    InRegs.bx = ASC(MID$(OC$, j, 1))
                    CALL INTERRUPT(&H10, InRegs, OutRegs)
                    LOCATE TR + i - 1, TC + j
                NEXT j
                    LOCATE TR + i, TC
            NEXT i

            InRegs.ax = 1
            CALL INTERRUPT(&H33, InRegs, OutRegs)

            LOCATE CurRow%, CurCol%

END SUB
```

You can see that this is a monster. It even has its own two subprograms, TurnOn-Menu( ) and TurnOffMenu( ). Let's put this to work, making our menu system active and receiving menu input.

Waiting for Input from Our Test Menus

Here's how to use MenuGetEvent$( ) to read keyboard/mouse/menu input:

```
DECLARE FUNCTION MenuInitialize% (MenuNames() AS STRING, MenuChoices() AS _
                 STRING, Attrib%, MenuAttrbs() AS INTEGER)
DECLARE SUB MenuShow()
DECLARE FUNCTION MouseInitialize% ()
DECLARE SUB MouseShowCursor ()
DECLARE FUNCTION MenuGetEvent$(MenuNo%, ChoiceNo%, Button%, Row%, Col%)

DIM MenuNames(1 TO 3) AS STRING
DIM MenuChoices(1 TO 3, 1 TO 5) AS STRING
DIM MenuAttrbs(1 TO 3) AS INTEGER

        MenuNames(1) = "Fruits"
        MenuChoices(1, 1) = "Apples"
        MenuChoices(1, 2) = "Bananas"
        MenuChoices(1, 3) = "Grapes"
        MenuChoices(1, 4) = "Peaches"
        MenuChoices(1, 5) = "Oranges"

        MenuNames(2) = "Veggies"
        MenuChoices(2, 1) = "Peas"
        MenuChoices(2, 2) = "Corn"
        MenuChoices(2, 3) = "Broccoli"

        MenuNames(3) = "Meats"
        MenuChoices(3, 1) = "Chicken"
        MenuChoices(3, 2) = "Pork"
        MenuChoices(3, 3) = "Beef"
        MenuChoices(3, 4) = "Fish"

        FOR i = 1 TO 3
            MenuAttrbs(i) = &H61
        NEXT i
        BarAttrb% = &H24

        Check% = MenuInitialize%(MenuNames(), MenuChoices(), BarAttrb%, _
                 MenuAttrbs())

        IF Check% = 0 THEN
            PRINT "Error."
        ELSE
            PRINT "Menu is set up."
        END IF

        CALL MenuShow
```

```
Check% = MouseInitialize%

IF Check% = 0 THEN PRINT "Cannot open mouse."

CALL MouseShowCursor

PRINT "Make a menu selection."

DO
Check$ = MenuGetEvent$(MenuNo%, ChoiceNo%, Button%, Row%, Col%)
LOOP UNTIL Check$ = "menuchoice"

PRINT "That selection was ",MenuChoices(MenuNo%, ChoiceNo%)
```

This example program takes a little explaining. We're familiar with the way to set up menus using MenuInitialize%( ) and how to call MenuShow( ) directly after that. However, you should notice that the menu system does *not* turn the mouse cursor on automatically (because you may not want to use a mouse at all). Instead, we're responsible for doing that ourselves with MouseInitialize%( ) and MouseShowCursor( ). After we do, we're free to use the mouse with our menus:

```
     :
     :
  CALL MenuShow

→ Check% = MouseInitialize%

  IF Check% = 0 THEN PRINT "Cannot open mouse."

  CALL MouseShowCursor
```

The whole example program sets things up except for the meat of the last few lines:

```
     :
     :
  CALL MenuShow

  Check% = MouseInitialize%

  IF Check% = 0 THEN PRINT "Cannot open mouse."

  CALL MouseShowCursor

  PRINT "Make a menu selection."

→ DO
  Check$ = MenuGetEvent$(MenuNo%, ChoiceNo%, Button%, Row%, Col%)
  LOOP UNTIL Check$ = "menuchoice"

  PRINT "That selection was ", MenuChoices(MenuNo%, ChoiceNo%)
```

Here we call MenuGetEvent$( ) and keep calling it until it returns a menuchoice event. In that case, we know that the selection made was choice ChoiceNo% of menu Menu-No%. And we know what that was because we've initialized the menu system ourselves. That choice corresponds to MenuChoices(MenuNo%, ChoiceNo%).

When you run this program, then, a menubar appears and it prompts you to make a menu selection. When you do, using either the mouse or the keyboard, it prints out the exact selection you've made (Peaches, Apples, or whatever).

Congratulations, you're now using your own pull-down menus.

The second input function we'll work out is MenuCheckEvent$( ), which differs from MenuGetEvent$( ) only in that it doesn't wait for input.

Reading Menu Input without Waiting

This is the INKEY$ of our menu system. It's just like MenuGetEvent$( ), except that it doesn't wait for something to happen; if there are no keys, menu events, or mouse events waiting, MenuCheckEvent$ is set to " " and the function returns at once.

On the other hand, if there's something in the mouse queue or there's a key waiting, MenuCheckEvent$( ) handles them exactly as MenuGetEvent$( ) would. The only differences in the values they return is that MenuCheckEvent$( ) can return a null string, " ", but MenuGetEvent$( ) never can. Here's how to use it:

```
InString$ = MenuGetEvent$ (MenuNo%, ChoiceNo%, Button%, ScRow%, ScCol%)
```

After this line, InString$ will be set to one of the following values:

InString$	Means
" " (null string)	No key, mouse event, or menu event was pending.
STRING of LEN 1	Single character typed. Read as you would from INKEY$.
STRING of LEN 2	Character typed with an extended ASCII code. Read as you would from INKEY$.

"mousedown"	Mouse button was pressed: Button% = 0 for left button; Button% = 1 for right button. Screen coordinates: (ScRow%, ScCol%), using text-mode ranges (1-25 and 1-80)
"mouseup"	Mouse button was released: Button% = 0 for left button; Button% = 1 for right button. Screen coordinates: (ScRow%, ScCol%), using text-mode ranges (1-25 and 1-80).
"menuopen"	User opened a menu. Menu number in MenuNo%.
"menuclose"	User closed a menu. Menu number in MenuNo%.
"menuchoice"	A menu selection was made: MenuNo% = Menu number; ChoiceNo% = the number of the choice in that menu. Menu number and choice number correspond to the array indices of the arrays you passed to MenuInitialize%( ).

This function is almost exactly identical to MenuGetEvent$( ), which we've already covered. There are only two differences. First, the DO...LOOP WHILE 1 loop in MenuGetEvent$( ) has been removed. If you recall, that looked like this in the outline of MenuGetEvent$( ):

```
DO
:          IF (a key was pressed) THEN
:                  MenuGetEvent$ = key that was pressed
:                  IF (menu system is on) THEN
:                          IF (Esc was pressed) THEN
:                                  IF (menu was open) THEN
:                                          [close menu and EXIT]
:                                  ELSE
:                                          EXIT FUNCTION
:                                  END IF
:                          END IF
:                          IF (Alt key matched a menu or choice name) THEN
:                                  [set menu arguments and EXIT]
:                          ELSE
:                                  EXIT FUNCTION
:                          END IF
:                  END IF
:                  EXIT FUNCTION
:          END IF
:
:          IF (a mouse button was used) THEN
:                  IF (it was the left mouse button) THEN
:                          IF (it was in a menu) THEN
:                                  [set menu arguments and EXIT]
```

```
:                       ELSE
:                                 [set mouse arguments and EXIT]
:                       END IF
:               ELSE     'It was the right button
:                       [set mouse arguments and EXIT]
:               END IF
:               EXIT FUNCTION
:       END IF
LOOP WHILE 1
```

Without this loop, we will no longer wait for input. The only other change is that every occurrence of MenuGetEvent in this listing has been replaced with MenuCheckEvent. That's all there is to it. See Listing 4-5 for reference.

Listing 4-5.   MenuCheckEvent$—Reads Events without Waiting.   1 of 6

```
DECLARE FUNCTION MenuCheckEvent$ (MenuNo%, ChoiceNo%, Button%, ScRow%, ScCol%)
DECLARE SUB TurnOnMenu (MNumber%)
DECLARE SUB TurnOffMenu (MNumber%)

TYPE RegType
        ax      AS INTEGER
        bx      AS INTEGER
        cx      AS INTEGER
        dx      AS INTEGER
        bp      AS INTEGER
        si      AS INTEGER
        di      AS INTEGER
        flags   AS INTEGER
END TYPE

DECLARE SUB INTERRUPT (IntNo AS INTEGER, InRegs AS RegType, OutRegs AS RegType)

        CONST MaxMenus = 7
        DIM Rows(1 TO MaxMenus) AS INTEGER
        DIM Cols(1 TO MaxMenus) AS INTEGER
        DIM TopRow(1 TO MaxMenus) AS INTEGER
        DIM TopCol(1 TO MaxMenus) AS INTEGER
        DIM BotRow(1 TO MaxMenus) AS INTEGER
        DIM BotCol(1 TO MaxMenus) AS INTEGER
        DIM Attribute(1 TO MaxMenus) AS INTEGER
        DIM Text(1 TO MaxMenus, 25) AS STRING
        DIM OldText(1 TO MaxMenus, 25) AS STRING
        DIM OldAttrb(1 TO MaxMenus, 25) AS STRING
        COMMON SHARED /MenuA/ Rows() AS INTEGER, Cols() AS INTEGER,_
                TopRow() AS INTEGER, TopCol() AS INTEGER,_
                BotRow() AS INTEGER, BotCol() AS INTEGER
        COMMON SHARED /MenuB/ Attribute() AS INTEGER, Text() AS STRING,_
                OldText() AS STRING, OldAttrb() AS STRING
        COMMON SHARED /MenuC/ Bar$, BarAttrb, MenusOnFlag%, NumMenus%, OldBar$,_
                OldBarAttrb$
```

Listing 4-5.   MenuCheckEvent$—Reads Events without Waiting.   2 of 6

```
FUNCTION MenuCheckEvent$ (MenuNo%, ChoiceNo%, Button%, ScRow%, ScCol%) STATIC

        DIM InRegs AS RegType, OutRegs AS RegType

        MenuCheckEvent$ = ""

        InChar$ = INKEY$

        IF InChar$ <> "" THEN
           MenuCheckEvent$ = InChar$
           IF MenusOnFlag% = 0 THEN EXIT FUNCTION 'Menu system on?
           IF ASC(InChar$) = 27 THEN 'Escape key
              IF MenuNowOpen% = 0 THEN
                 EXIT FUNCTION
              ELSE
                 CALL TurnOffMenu(MenuNowOpen%)
                 MenuNo% = MenuNowOpen%
                 MenuNowOpen% = 0
                 MenuCheckEvent$ = "menuclose"
                 EXIT FUNCTION
              END IF
           END IF        'Escape key
           IF LEN(InChar$) = 1 THEN
              EXIT FUNCTION
           ELSE
              SC = ASC(RIGHT$(InChar$,1))
              AltKey$ = ""
              IF SC >= 16 AND SC <= 25 THEN AltKey$ = MID$("QWERTYUIOP", _
                                                          SC - 15,1)
              IF SC <= 30 AND SC <= 38 THEN AltKey$ = MID$("ASDFGHJKL", _
                                                          SC - 29,1)
              IF SC <= 44 AND SC <= 50 THEN AltKey$ = MID$("ZXCVBNM", _
                                                          SC - 43,1)
              IF AltKey$ = "" THEN EXIT FUNCTION

              IF MenuNowOpen% <> 0 THEN
                 FOR i% = 1 TO Rows(MenuNowOpen%)
                     IF AltKey$ = UCASE$(MID$(Text(MenuNowOpen%,i%),2,1)) THEN
                        MenuNo% = MenuNowOpen%
                        ChoiceNo% = i%
                        CALL TurnOffMenu(MenuNowOpen%)
                        MenuNowOpen% = 0
                        MenuCheckEvent$ = "menuchoice"
                        EXIT FUNCTION
                     END IF
                 NEXT i%
              END IF

              FOR i% = 1 TO NumMenus%
                  IF AltKey$ = UCASE$(MID$(Bar$,10*(i%-1)+2,1)) THEN
                     IF MenuNowOpen% = i% THEN
                        MenuNo% = i%
                        CALL TurnOffMenu(i%)
                        MenuNowOpen% = 0
                        MenuCheckEvent$ = "menuclose"
                        EXIT FUNCTION
```

Listing 4-5.   MenuCheckEvent$—Reads Events without Waiting.   3 of 6

```
                      END IF
                      IF MenuNowOpen% <> 0 THEN CALL TurnOffMenu(MenuNowOpen%)
                      MenuNo% = i%
                      ChoiceNo% = 0
                      MenuNowOpen% = i%
                      CALL TurnOnMenu(i%)
                      MenuCheckEvent$ = "menuopen"
                  END IF
              NEXT i% 'For i% = 1 TO NumMenus%
      END IF        'Check char length
          EXIT FUNCTION
END IF  'Check key

REM *** Check for left mouse button pressed

Button% = 0
InRegs.bx = 0
InRegs.ax = 5
CALL INTERRUPT(&H33, InRegs, OutRegs)

NumberTimes% = OutRegs.bx
ScRow% = OutRegs.dx \ 8 + 1
ScCol% = OutRegs.cx \ 8 + 1

IF NumberTimes% <> 0 THEN
        IF MenusOnFlag% AND (ScRow% = 1) THEN
                MenubarCandidate% = ScCol% \ 10 + 1
                IF MenubarCandidate% NumMenus% THEN
                    MenuNo% = MenubarCandidate%
                    ChoiceNo% = 0
                    MenuNowOpen% = MenubarCandidate%
                    CALL TurnOnMenu(MenubarCandidate%)
                    MenuCheckEvent$ = "menuopen"
                    EXIT FUNCTION
                END IF
        ELSE
                MenuCheckEvent$ = "mousedown"
                EXIT FUNCTION
        END IF
END IF

REM *** Check for left mouse button released

InRegs.bx = 0
InRegs.ax = 6
CALL INTERRUPT(&H33, InRegs, OutRegs)

NumberTimes% = OutRegs.bx
ScRow% = OutRegs.dx \ 8 + 1
ScCol% = OutRegs.cx \ 8 + 1

IF NumberTimes% <> 0 THEN
  IF MenusOnFlag% AND (MenuNowOpen% <> 0) THEN
      IF ScRow% >= 2 AND ScRow% <=2 + Rows(MenuNowOpen%) THEN
          IF ScCol% >= 1 + 10 * (MenuNowOpen%-1) AND ScCol%<= _
             10*(MenuNowOpen%) THEN
```

Listing 4-5.   MenuCheckEvent$—Reads Events without Waiting.   4 of 6

```
                              ChoiceNo% = ScRow% - 1
                              CALL TurnOffMenu(MenuNowOpen%)
                              MenuNo% = MenuNowOpen%
                              MenuNowOpen% = 0
                              MenuCheckEvent$ = "menuchoice"
                              EXIT FUNCTION
                      ELSE
                              MenuNo% = MenuNowOpen%
                              CALL TurnOffMenu(MenuNowOpen%)
                              MenuNowOpen% = 0
                              MenuCheckEvent$ = "menuclose"
                              EXIT FUNCTION
                      END IF
              ELSE
                              MenuNo% = MenuNowOpen%
                              CALL TurnOffMenu(MenuNowOpen%)
                              MenuNowOpen% = 0
                              MenuCheckEvent$ = "menuclose"
                              EXIT FUNCTION
              END IF
      ELSE
                      MenuCheckEvent$ = "mouseup"
                      EXIT FUNCTION
      END IF 'Menu open
END IF 'NumberTimes% <> 0

REM *** Check for right mouse button pressed

Button% = 1
InRegs.bx = 1
InRegs.ax = 5
CALL INTERRUPT(&H33, InRegs, OutRegs)

NumberTimes% = OutRegs.bx
ScRow% = OutRegs.dx \ 8 + 1
ScCol% = OutRegs.cx \ 8 + 1

IF NumberTimes% <> 0 THEN
        MenuCheckEvent$ = "mousedown"
        EXIT FUNCTION
END IF

REM *** Check for right mouse button released

InRegs.bx = 1
InRegs.ax = 6
CALL INTERRUPT(&H33, InRegs, OutRegs)

NumberTimes% = OutRegs.bx
ScRow% = OutRegs.dx \ 8 + 1
ScCol% = OutRegs.cx \ 8 + 1

IF NumberTimes% <> 0 THEN
        MenuCheckEvent$ = "mousedown"
        EXIT FUNCTION
END IF
```

Listing 4-5.   MenuCheckEvent$—Reads Events without Waiting.   5 of 6

```
END FUNCTION

SUB TurnOnMenu (MNumber%)

        DIM InRegs AS RegType, OutRegs AS RegType

        CurRow% = CSRLIN
        CurCol% = POS(0)

        InRegs.ax = 2
        CALL INTERRUPT(&H33, InRegs, OutRegs)

        REM Save the old section of screen

        rr = TopRow(MNumber%)
        cc = TopCol(MNumber%)
        rt = Rows(MNumber%)
        ct = Cols(MNumber%)

        FOR i = 1 TO rt
                temp1$ = ""
                temp2$ = ""
                FOR j = 1 TO ct
                        temp1$ = temp1$ + CHR$(SCREEN(rr + i - 1, cc + j - 1))
                        temp2$ = temp2$ + CHR$(SCREEN(rr + i - 1, cc + j - 1, 1))
                NEXT j
                OldText(MNumber%, i) = temp1$
                OldAttrb(MNumber%, i) = temp2$
        NEXT i

        REM Now print the new text

        TR = TopRow(MNumber%)
        TC = TopCol(MNumber%)
        LOCATE TR, TC
        InRegs.cx = 1

        FOR i = 1 TO Rows(MNumber%)
            OR$ = Text(MNumber%, i)
            FOR j = 1 TO Cols(MNumber%)
                InRegs.ax = &H900 + ASC(MID$(OR$, j, 1))
                InRegs.bx = Attribute(MNumber%)
                CALL INTERRUPT(&H10, InRegs, OutRegs)
                LOCATE TR + i - 1, TC + j
            NEXT j
                LOCATE TR + i, TC
        NEXT i

        InRegs.ax = 1
        CALL INTERRUPT(&H33, InRegs, OutRegs)

        LOCATE CurRow%, CurCol%

END SUB

SUB TurnOffMenu (MNumber%)
```

Listing 4-5. MenuCheckEvent$—Reads Events without Waiting.   **6 of 6**

```
        CurRow% = CSRLIN
        CurCol% = POS(0)

        DIM InRegs AS RegType, OutRegs AS RegType

        InRegs.ax = 2
        CALL INTERRUPT(&H33, InRegs, OutRegs)

        REM Print the old text

        TR = TopRow(MNumber%)
        TC = TopCol(MNumber%)
        LOCATE TR, TC
        InRegs.cx = 1

        FOR i = 1 TO Rows(MNumber%)
            OR$ = OldText(MNumber%, i)
            OC$ = OldAttrb(MNumber%, i)
            FOR j = 1 TO Cols(MNumber%)
                InRegs.ax = &H900 + ASC(MID$(OR$, j, 1))
                InRegs.bx = ASC(MID$(OC$, j, 1))
                CALL INTERRUPT(&H10, InRegs, OutRegs)
                LOCATE TR + i - 1, TC + j
            NEXT j
                LOCATE TR + i, TC
        NEXT i

        InRegs.ax = 1
        CALL INTERRUPT(&H33, InRegs, OutRegs)

        LOCATE CurRow%, CurCol%

END SUB
```

That's it. Let's see how to use MenuCheckEvent$( ) with an example.

Getting Input from Our Test Menus

Here's how to use MenuCheckEvent$( ):

```
DECLARE FUNCTION MenuInitialize% (MenuNames( ) AS STRING, MenuChoices( ) AS _
              STRING, Attrib%, MenuAttrbs( ) AS INTEGER)
DECLARE SUB MenuShow( )
DECLARE FUNCTION MouseInitialize% ( )
DECLARE SUB MouseShowCursor ( )
DECLARE FUNCTION MenuCheckEvent$(MenuNo%, ChoiceNo%, Button%, Row%, Col%)

DIM MenuNames(1 TO 3) AS STRING
DIM MenuChoices(1 TO 3, 1 TO 5) AS STRING
DIM MenuAttrbs(1 TO 3) AS INTEGER
```

```
MenuNames(1) = "Fruits"
MenuChoices(1, 1) = "Apples"
MenuChoices(1, 2) = "Bananas"
MenuChoices(1, 3) = "Grapes"
MenuChoices(1, 4) = "Peaches"
MenuChoices(1, 5) = "Oranges"

MenuNames(2) = "Veggies"
MenuChoices(2, 1) = "Peas"
MenuChoices(2, 2) = "Corn"
MenuChoices(2, 3) = "Broccoli"

MenuNames(3) = "Meats"
MenuChoices(3, 1) = "Chicken"
MenuChoices(3, 2) = "Pork"
MenuChoices(3, 3) = "Beef"
MenuChoices(3, 4) = "Fish"

FOR i = 1 TO 3
    MenuAttrbs(i) = &H61
NEXT i
BarAttrb% = &H24

Check% = MenuInitialize%(MenuNames( ), MenuChoices( ), BarAttrb%, _
        MenuAttrbs( ))

IF Check% = 0 THEN
    PRINT "Error."
ELSE
    PRINT "Menu is set up."
END IF

CALL MenuShow

Check% = MouseInitialize%

IF Check% = 0 THEN PRINT "Cannot open mouse."

CALL MouseShowCursor

DO
Check$ = MenuCheckEvent$(MenuNo%, ChoiceNo%, Button%, Row%, Col%)
LOOP UNTIL Check$ = "menuchoice"

PRINT "That selection was ",MenuChoices(MenuNo%, ChoiceNo%)
```

In this case, this example program is almost identical to the example program for MenuGetEvent$( ). We just loop over MenuCheckEvent$( ) here until we get an menuchoice event, and then print it out.

There are a few more things we should do to make our menu system more complete. For example, some some menu choices may be "toggle" items. For example, one menu choice in a word processor might be Spellchecking; if this is toggled on, then the automatic spelling of words is enabled. Let's add this capability to our set of menu tools.

Marking a Menu Selection

We can develop a subprogram to mark menu choices with a check mark; let's call this subprogram MenuMarkChoice( ). With it, you can show that a choice is toggled on — this subprogram will place a checkmark in front of the choice in the menu. (The next time the menu is opened, the user will see the checkmark.) For example, if Spellchecking is the entry in menu 6, choice 4, calling MenuMark(6, 4) will place a check in front of it. In general, we will be able to use MenuMarkChoice( ) like this:

```
CALL MenuMarkChoice (MenuNumber%, ChoiceNumber%)
```

These are the input parameters:

> MenuNumber%   The menu number of the choice to mark.
> ChoiceNumber%   The choice number to mark in that menu.

This subprogram is simplicity itself compared to MenuGetEvent$( ) or MenuCheckEvent$( ). All it does is to make a checkmark (CHR$(251)) the first character in the menu row holding that choice. Since the rows of the menus are stored as strings in Text(i, j), where i is the menu number and j is the choice number, that looks like this:

```
MID$(Text(MenuNumber%, ChoiceNumber%),1,1) = CHR$(251)
```

TIP: Since this code is so short, you might want to include it directly in your code instead of linking it in.

And that's it. Listing 4-6 shows the whole subprogram. Note that we still had to include the menu COMMONs (but only one line of code!)

Listing 4-6.   MenuMarkChoice Subprogram—Marks Menu Choice.   1 of 2

```
DECLARE SUB MenuMarkChoice (MenuNumber%, ChoiceNumber%)

        CONST MaxMenus = 7
        DIM Rows(1 TO MaxMenus) AS INTEGER
        DIM Cols(1 TO MaxMenus) AS INTEGER
        DIM TopRow(1 TO MaxMenus) AS INTEGER
        DIM TopCol(1 TO MaxMenus) AS INTEGER
        DIM BotRow(1 TO MaxMenus) AS INTEGER
```

Listing 4-6. MenuMarkChoice Subprogram—Marks Menu Choice. 2 of 2

```
        DIM BotCol(1 TO MaxMenus) AS INTEGER
        DIM Attribute(1 TO MaxMenus) AS INTEGER
        DIM Text(1 TO MaxMenus, 25) AS STRING
        DIM OldText(1 TO MaxMenus, 25) AS STRING
        DIM OldAttrb(1 TO MaxMenus, 25) AS STRING
        COMMON SHARED /MenuA/ Rows( ) AS INTEGER, Cols( ) AS INTEGER, _
                 TopRow( ) AS INTEGER, TopCol( ) AS INTEGER, _
                 BotRow( ) AS INTEGER, BotCol( ) AS INTEGER
        COMMON SHARED /MenuB/ Attribute( ) AS INTEGER, Text( ) AS STRING, _
                 OldText( ) AS STRING, OldAttrb( ) AS STRING
        COMMON SHARED /MenuC/ Bar$, BarAttrb, MenusOnFlag%, NumMenus%, OldBar$,_
                 OldBarAttrb$
    SUB MenuMarkChoice (MenuNumber%, ChoiceNumber%)

    →    MID$(Text(MenuNumber%, ChoiceNumber%),1,1) = CHR$(251)

    END SUB
```

Notice also that the choice is not immediately displayed on the screen as checked; that is, MenuMarkChoice( ) does not display the menu with the new checkmark in it. That is because toggling a choice on or off is itself a menuchoice event — when you toggle, say, Spellchecking on, the menu closes, as it should. To see that it is actually toggled on, you have to pull down that menu again. Now let's see how to use MenuMarkChoice( ).

Marking Items in Our Test Menus

In this example, we can toggle any of the menu choices on. (However, we have no way of toggling them off yet.)

```
DECLARE SUB MenuMarkChoice (MenuNumber%, ChoiceNumber%)

DECLARE FUNCTION MenuInitialize% (MenuNames( ) AS STRING, MenuChoices( ) AS _
                STRING, Attrib%, MenuAttrbs( ) AS INTEGER)
DECLARE SUB MenuShow ( )
DECLARE FUNCTION MouseInitialize% ( )
DECLARE SUB MouseShowCursor ( )
DECLARE FUNCTION MenuGetEvent$ (MenuNo%, ChoiceNo%, Button%, Row%, Col%)

DIM MenuNames(1 TO 3) AS STRING
DIM MenuChoices(1 TO 3, 1 TO 5) AS STRING
DIM MenuAttrbs(1 TO 3) AS INTEGER

        MenuNames(1) = "Fruits"
        MenuChoices(1, 1) = "Apples"
        MenuChoices(1, 2) = "Bananas"
        MenuChoices(1, 3) = "Grapes"
        MenuChoices(1, 4) = "Peaches"
```

```
        MenuChoices(1, 5) = "Oranges"

        MenuNames(2) = "Veggies"
        MenuChoices(2, 1) = "Peas"
        MenuChoices(2, 2) = "Corn"
        MenuChoices(2, 3) = "Broccoli"

        MenuNames(3) = "Meats"
        MenuChoices(3, 1) = "Chicken"
        MenuChoices(3, 2) = "Pork"
        MenuChoices(3, 3) = "Beef"
        MenuChoices(3, 4) = "Fish"

        FOR i = 1 TO 3
            MenuAttrbs(i) = &H61
        NEXT i
        BarAttrb% = &H24

        Check% = MenuInitialize%(MenuNames( ), MenuChoices( ), BarAttrb%, _
            MenuAttrbs( ))

        IF Check% = 0 THEN
            PRINT "Error."
        ELSE
            PRINT "Menu is set up."
        END IF

        CALL MenuShow

        Check% = MouseInitialize%

        IF Check% = 0 THEN PRINT "Cannot open mouse."

        CALL MouseShowCursor

        PRINT "Select menu choices to be marked. Type q to quit."

        DO
        Check$ = MenuGetEvent$(MenuNo%, ChoiceNo%, Button%, Row%, Col%)
        IF Check$ = "menuchoice" THEN CALL MenuMarkChoice(MenuNo%, ChoiceNo%)
        LOOP UNTIL UCASE$(Check$) = "Q"
```

All we do here is to ask the user to select menu choices to toggle:

```
PRINT "Select menu choices to be marked. Type q to quit."
:
```

Then we loop until a menu choice is made, and toggle that choice on with Menu-MarkChoice( ) (until q or Q is pressed, to indicate that we should quit):

```
PRINT "Select menu choices to be marked. Type q to quit."
```

```
DO
Check$ = MenuGetEvent$(MenuNo%, ChoiceNo%, Button%, Row%, Col%)
IF Check$ = "menuchoice" THEN CALL MenuMarkChoice(MenuNo%, ChoiceNo%)
LOOP UNTIL UCASE$(Check$) = "Q"
```

Since we now have a way of toggling menu choices on, the natural next step is to toggle them off.

Unmarking a Menu Selection

This subprogram just "unmarks" a choice in a menu. That is, if the choice is checked, MenuUnMarkChoice( ) removes the checkmark, showing that that choice is now toggled off. We can use it like this:

```
CALL MenuUnMarkChoice (MenuNumber%, ChoiceNumber%)
```

These are the inputs:

      MenuNumber%   The menu number of the choice to unmark.
      ChoiceNumber%   The choice number to unmark in that menu.

Like MenuMarkChoice( ), the listing here is very simple. The whole thing is contained in just this line:

```
MID$(Text(MenuNumber%, ChoiceNumber%),1,1) = ""
```

And all it does is make the first character in the line holding the indicated menu choice a space, " ". Listing 4-7 shows the whole subprogram.

```
Listing 4-7.   MenuUnMarkChoice—Unmarks a Menu Choice.          1 of 2

DECLARE SUB MenuUnMarkChoice (MenuNumber%, ChoiceNumber%)

        CONST MaxMenus = 7
        DIM Rows(1 TO MaxMenus) AS INTEGER
        DIM Cols(1 TO MaxMenus) AS INTEGER
        DIM TopRow(1 TO MaxMenus) AS INTEGER
        DIM TopCol(1 TO MaxMenus) AS INTEGER
        DIM BotRow(1 TO MaxMenus) AS INTEGER
        DIM BotCol(1 TO MaxMenus) AS INTEGER
        DIM Attribute(1 TO MaxMenus) AS INTEGER
```

Listing 4-7. MenuUnMarkChoice—Unmarks a Menu Choice.   2 of 2

```
        DIM Text(1 TO MaxMenus, 25) AS STRING
        DIM OldText(1 TO MaxMenus, 25) AS STRING
        DIM OldAttrb(1 TO MaxMenus, 25) AS STRING
        COMMON SHARED /MenuA/ Rows( ) AS INTEGER, Cols( ) AS INTEGER, _
                     TopRow( ) AS INTEGER, TopCol( ) AS INTEGER, _
                     BotRow( ) AS INTEGER, BotCol( ) AS INTEGER
        COMMON SHARED /MenuB/ Attribute( ) AS INTEGER, Text( ) AS STRING, _
                     OldText( ) AS STRING, OldAttrb( ) AS STRING
        COMMON SHARED /MenuC/ Bar$, BarAttrb, MenusOnFlag%, NumMenus%, OldBar$,_
                     OldBarAttrb$

SUB MenuUnMarkChoice (MenuNumber%, ChoiceNumber%)

        MID$(Text(MenuNumber%, ChoiceNumber%),1,1) = " "

END SUB
```

That's it. Let's look at an example.

Unmarking Items in Our Test Menus

Here's how to use both MenuMarkChoice( ) and MenuUnMarkChoice( ):

```
DECLARE FUNCTION MenuInitialize% (MenuNames( ) AS STRING, MenuChoices( ) AS _
               STRING, Attrib%, MenuAttrbs( ) AS INTEGER)
DECLARE SUB MenuShow ( )
DECLARE FUNCTION MouseInitialize% ( )
DECLARE SUB MouseShowCursor ( )
DECLARE FUNCTION MenuGetEvent$ (MenuNo%, ChoiceNo%, Button%, Row%, Col%)
DECLARE SUB MenuMarkChoice (MenuNumber%, ChoiceNumber%)
DECLARE SUB MenuUnMarkChoice(MenuNo%, ChoiceNo%)

DIM MenuNames(1 TO 3) AS STRING
DIM MenuChoices(1 TO 3, 1 TO 5) AS STRING
DIM MenuAttrbs(1 TO 3) AS INTEGER

        MenuNames(1) = "Fruits"
        MenuChoices(1, 1) = "Apples"
        MenuChoices(1, 2) = "Bananas"
        MenuChoices(1, 3) = "Grapes"
        MenuChoices(1, 4) = "Peaches"
        MenuChoices(1, 5) = "Oranges"

        MenuNames(2) = "Veggies"
        MenuChoices(2, 1) = "Peas"
        MenuChoices(2, 2) = "Corn"
        MenuChoices(2, 3) = "Broccoli"

        MenuNames(3) = "Meats"
        MenuChoices(3, 1) = "Chicken"
        MenuChoices(3, 2) = "Pork"
```

```
        MenuChoices(3, 3) = "Beef"
        MenuChoices(3, 4) = "Fish"

        FOR i = 1 TO 3
            MenuAttrbs(i) = &H61
        NEXT i
        BarAttrb% = &H24

        Check% = MenuInitialize%(MenuNames( ), MenuChoices( ), BarAttrb%, _
                MenuAttrbs( ))

        IF Check% = 0 THEN
            PRINT "Error."
        ELSE
            PRINT "Menu is set up."
        END IF

        CALL MenuShow

        Check% = MouseInitialize%

        IF Check% = 0 THEN PRINT "Cannot open mouse."

        CALL MouseShowCursor

        PRINT "Select menu choices to be marked. Type q to quit."

        DO
        Check$ = MenuGetEvent$(MenuNo%, ChoiceNo%, Button%, Row%, Col%)
        IF Check$ = "menuchoice" THEN CALL MenuMarkChoice(MenuNo%, ChoiceNo%)
        LOOP UNTIL UCASE$(Check$) = "Q"

        PRINT "Now select menu choices to be UNmarked. Type q to quit."

        DO
        Check$ = MenuGetEvent$(MenuNo%, ChoiceNo%, Button%, Row%, Col%)
        IF Check$ = "menuchoice" THEN CALL MenuUnMarkChoice(MenuNo%, ChoiceNo%)
        LOOP UNTIL UCASE$(Check$) = "Q"
```

This example program asks you to mark a few choices, as we've done in the previous
example program:

```
PRINT "Select menu choices to be marked. Type q to quit."

DO
Check$ = MenuGetEvent$(MenuNo%, ChoiceNo%, Button%, Row%, Col%)
IF Check$ = "menuchoice" THEN CALL MenuMarkChoice(MenuNo%, ChoiceNo%)
LOOP UNTIL UCASE$(Check$) = "Q"
  :
  :
```

Then you press "q" or "Q" and are given the opportunity to unmark them if you wish:

```
PRINT "Select menu choices to be marked. Type q to quit."

DO
Check$ = MenuGetEvent$(MenuNo%, ChoiceNo%, Button%, Row%, Col%)
IF Check$ = "menuchoice" THEN CALL MenuMarkChoice(MenuNo%, ChoiceNo%)
LOOP UNTIL UCASE$(Check$) = "Q"
→ PRINT "Now select menu choices to be UNmarked. Type q to quit."
:
: DO
Check$ = MenuGetEvent$(MenuNo%, ChoiceNo%, Button%, Row%, Col%)
IF Check$ = "menuchoice" THEN CALL MenuUnMarkChoice(MenuNo%, ChoiceNo%)
LOOP UNTIL UCASE$(Check$) = "Q"
```

Again, you type q or Q to quit.

There's only one more menu routine that we should develop; if you're using Menu-GetEvent$( ) or MenuCheckEvent$( ), you'll get menu input in the variables MenuNo% and ChoiceNo%:

```
InString$ = MenuGetEvent$ (MenuNo%, ChoiceNo%, Button%, ScRow%, ScCol%)
```

But you may not have kept the original arrays with the menu and choice names around. In that case, we should be able to interrogate our menu system to find out just what, say, Menu 5, Choice 3 is. For that reason, our last menu function is named Menu-ReadChoice$( ).

Checking Up on a Menu

If you want to see what a single menu choice was, e.g., the choice corresponding to MenuNo% and ChoiceNo% returned by MenuGetEvent%( ), you can call Menu-ReadChoice$(MenuNo%, ChoiceNo%).

Let's add another feature to this function: if we pass a menu number of 0, we can make MenuReadChoice%( ) return menu names from the menubar. For example, Menu-ReadChoice$(0, 2) should return the name of the second menu in the menubar (see Figure 4-8).

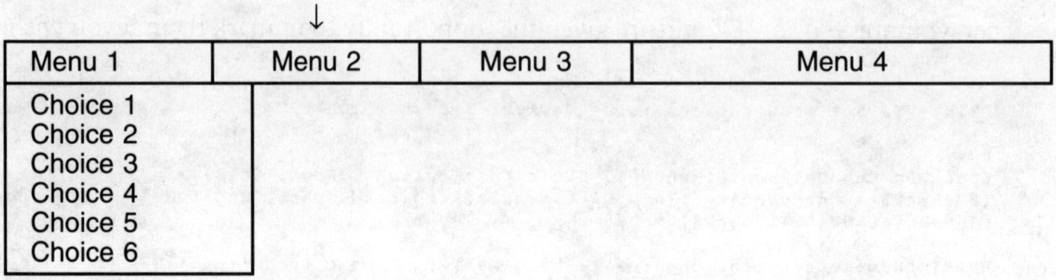

↓

Menu 1	Menu 2	Menu 3	Menu 4
Choice 1			
Choice 2			
Choice 3			
Choice 4			
Choice 5			
Choice 6			

Figure 4-8

Here's how we might use MenuReadChoice$( ):

```
ReadString$ = MenuReadChoice$ (MenuNo%, ChoiceNo%)
```

Here are the inputs that we can supply:

MenuNo%	The menu number (as passed to MenuInitialize%( )) of the choice you're interested in.
ChoiceNo%	The choice number of the choice in the menu you're interested in.

And here's what we want back:

MenuReadChoice$	MenuNo% = 0	MenuReadChoice$ = Menu name n from the menu bar (where n is the number passed in ChoiceNo%).
	MenuNo% = 1	MenuReadChoice$ = Choice name n in menu m (where n is the number passed in ChoiceNo% and m is the number passed in ChoiceNo%).

The programming here is straightforward; all we do is check whether we have to return a choice name or a menu name, and then do so. For a menu name, that looks like this:

```
IF MenuNo% = 0 THEN
      MenuReadChoice$ = RTRIM$(MID$(Bar$, (ChoiceNo%-1)*10 + 2, 8))
     :
     :
```

We use the BASIC function RTRIM$( ) to trim off trailing spaces. Otherwise, we have to report the name of a choice in a particular menu. Using both LTRIM$( ) and RTRIM$( ), that looks like this:

```
    IF MenuNo% = 0 THEN
            MenuReadChoice$ = RTRIM$(MID$(Bar$, (ChoiceNo%-1)*10 + 2, 8))
    ELSE
→           MenuReadChoice$ = RTRIM$(LTRIM$(Text(MenuNo%, ChoiceNo%)))
    END IF
```

Listing 4-8 shows the whole function.

Listing 4-8. MenuReadChoice$ Function.

```
DECLARE FUNCTION MenuReadChoice$ (MenuNo%, ChoiceNo%)

        CONST MaxMenus = 7
        DIM Rows(1 TO MaxMenus) AS INTEGER
        DIM Cols(1 TO MaxMenus) AS INTEGER
        DIM TopRow(1 TO MaxMenus) AS INTEGER
        DIM TopCol(1 TO MaxMenus) AS INTEGER
        DIM BotRow(1 TO MaxMenus) AS INTEGER
        DIM BotCol(1 TO MaxMenus) AS INTEGER
        DIM Attribute(1 TO MaxMenus) AS INTEGER
        DIM Text(1 TO MaxMenus, 25) AS STRING
        DIM OldText(1 TO MaxMenus, 25) AS STRING
        DIM OldAttrb(1 TO MaxMenus, 25) AS STRING
        COMMON SHARED /MenuA/ Rows( ) AS INTEGER, Cols( ) AS INTEGER, _
                      TopRow( ) AS INTEGER, TopCol( ) AS INTEGER, _
                      BotRow( ) AS INTEGER, BotCol( ) AS INTEGER
        COMMON SHARED /MenuB/ Attribute( ) AS INTEGER, Text( ) AS STRING, _
                      OldText( ) AS STRING, OldAttrb( ) AS STRING
        COMMON SHARED /MenuC/ Bar$, BarAttrb, MenusOnFlag%, NumMenus%, OldBar$,_
                      OldBarAttrb$

FUNCTION MenuReadChoice$ (MenuNo%, ChoiceNo%)

        IF MenuNo% = 0 THEN
                MenuReadChoice$ = RTRIM$(MID$(Bar$, (ChoiceNo%-1)*10 + 2, 8))
        ELSE
                MenuReadChoice$ = RTRIM$(LTRIM$(Text(MenuNo%, ChoiceNo%)))
        END IF

END FUNCTION
```

Now let's see MenuReadChoice$( ) at work.

Reading Items from Our Test Menus

The example program looks like this:

```
DECLARE FUNCTION MenuInitialize% (MenuNames( ) AS STRING, MenuChoices( ) AS _
       STRING, BarAttrb%, MenuAttrbs( ) AS INTEGER)
DECLARE FUNCTION MenuReadChoice$ (MenuNo%, ChoiceNo%)

DIM MenuNames(1 TO 3) AS STRING
DIM MenuChoices(1 TO 3, 1 TO 5) AS STRING, A(1 TO 3, 1 TO 5) AS STRING
DIM MenuAttrbs(1 TO 3) AS INTEGER, B(1 TO 3) AS INTEGER

        MenuNames(1) = "Fruits"
        MenuChoices(1, 1) = "Apples"
        MenuChoices(1, 2) = "Bananas"
        MenuChoices(1, 3) = "Grapes"
        MenuChoices(1, 4) = "Peaches"
        MenuChoices(1, 5) = "Oranges"

        MenuNames(2) = "Veggies"
        MenuChoices(2, 1) = "Peas"
        MenuChoices(2, 2) = "Corn"
        MenuChoices(2, 3) = "Broccoli"

        MenuNames(3) = "Meats"
        MenuChoices(3, 1) = "Chicken"
        MenuChoices(3, 2) = "Pork"
        MenuChoices(3, 3) = "Beef"
        MenuChoices(3, 4) = "Fish"

        FOR i = 1 TO 3
            MenuAttrbs(i) = &H61
        NEXT i
        BarAttrb% = &H24

        Check% = MenuInitialize%(MenuNames( ), MenuChoices( ), BarAttrb%, _
            MenuAttrbs( ))

        IF Check% = 0 THEN
            PRINT "Error."
        ELSE
            PRINT "Menu is set up."
        END IF

        PRINT "Choice 1 of menu 1 is: ", MenuReadChoice(1, 1)
        PRINT "Menu Number 1 is: ", MenuReadChoice(0, 1)
```

All this does is to set up a menu, tell you what menu 1, choice 1, is and what the name of menu 1 is.

And that's it for our menu system. We've been able to set our menus up, show or hide the menubar, read menu/keyboard/mouse input, toggle menu items on or off, and now interrogate the menu system for particular choice names. We've done a lot of work.

If you have the BASIC PDS, however, you might want to use the built-in menu system there. Let's take a look at what it has to offer.

Menus in the BASIC PDS

The BASIC PDS Toolbox also has a set of menu functions, and they're similar to what we've developed above. If you have the PDS, it's worth taking a look at how these functions work. Let's put together a sample program of the type we developed for Menu-GetEvent$( ) one that will place a menu on the screen and report which menu selection you've made.

NOTE: Even if you don't have the PDS, it's worth reading this section to see what's available.

Note that if you're using QBX.EXE, you'll have to load the Quick library we made in Chapter 2, UIASM.QLB. If we were to call our demo program MENUTEST.BAS, for example, we'd start QBX.EXE like this:

```
QBX MENUTEST \L UIASM
```

In addition, you have to load MENU.BAS, WINDOW.BAS, MOUSE.BAS, and GEN-ERAL.BAS, since the PDS menu system uses code in all of these.

TIP: QuickBASIC (QB or QBX) gives you the ability to load a number of files at once using .MAK files. To produce a .MAK file, load all the appropriate modules and select the save option in the file menu. The next time you load the main module, all the others will be loaded automatically.

On the other hand, if you're using BC.EXE, you'll have to include the library we made, UIASM.LIB, in your list of libraries to link.

Now let's see how the PDS menu system works. In the beginning of our program, we have to include the correct .BI files:

```
' $INCLUDE: 'C:\BC7\GENERAL.BI'
' $INCLUDE: 'C:\BC7\MOUSE.BI'
' $INCLUDE: 'C:\BC7\MENU.BI'
' $INCLUDE: 'C:\BC7\WINDOW.BI'
          :
          :
```

Next, we have to set up these COMMONs and dimension these arrays:

```
' $INCLUDE: 'C:\BC7\GENERAL.BI'
' $INCLUDE: 'C:\BC7\MOUSE.BI'
' $INCLUDE: 'C:\BC7\MENU.BI'
' $INCLUDE: 'C:\BC7\WINDOW.BI'

COMMON SHARED /uitools/ GloMenu           AS MenuMiscType       ←
COMMON SHARED /uitools/ GloTitle( )        AS MenuTitleType      :
COMMON SHARED /uitools/ GloItem( )          AS MenuItemType
DIM GloTitle(MAXMENU)           AS MenuTitleType
DIM GloItem(MAXMENU, MAXITEM)   AS MenuItemType
          :
          :
```

To make our example correspond to the one we've already developed for our function MenuGetEvent$( ), we can dimension the menu and choice name arrays like this:

```
' $INCLUDE: 'C:\BC7\GENERAL.BI'
' $INCLUDE: 'C:\BC7\MOUSE.BI'
' $INCLUDE: 'C:\BC7\MENU.BI'
' $INCLUDE: 'C:\BC7\WINDOW.BI'

COMMON SHARED /uitools/ GloMenu           AS MenuMiscType
COMMON SHARED /uitools/ GloTitle( )        AS MenuTitleType
COMMON SHARED /uitools/ GloItem( )          AS MenuItemType

DIM GloTitle(MAXMENU)           AS MenuTitleType
DIM GloItem(MAXMENU, MAXITEM)   AS MenuItemType

DIM MenuNames(1 TO 3) AS STRING                    ←
DIM MenuChoices(1 TO 3, 1 TO 5) AS STRING          :
DIM MenuAttrbs(1 TO 3) AS INTEGER                  :
          :
          :
```

And, we can fill them as we have before:

```
' $INCLUDE: 'C:\BC7\GENERAL.BI'
' $INCLUDE: 'C:\BC7\MOUSE.BI'
' $INCLUDE: 'C:\BC7\MENU.BI'
' $INCLUDE: 'C:\BC7\WINDOW.BI'

COMMON SHARED /uitools/ GloMenu              AS MenuMiscType
COMMON SHARED /uitools/ GloTitle( )          AS MenuTitleType
COMMON SHARED /uitools/ GloItem( )           AS MenuItemType

DIM GloTitle(MAXMENU)           AS MenuTitleType
DIM GloItem(MAXMENU, MAXITEM)   AS MenuItemType

DIM MenuNames(1 TO 3) AS STRING
DIM MenuChoices(1 TO 3, 1 TO 5) AS STRING
DIM MenuAttrbs(1 TO 3) AS INTEGER

        MenuNames(1) = "Fruits"                    ←
        MenuChoices(1, 1) = "Apples"               :
        MenuChoices(1, 2) = "Bananas"              :
        MenuChoices(1, 3) = "Grapes"
        MenuChoices(1, 4) = "Peaches"
        MenuChoices(1, 5) = "Oranges"

        MenuNames(2) = "Veggies"
        MenuChoices(2, 1) = "Peas"
        MenuChoices(2, 2) = "Corn"
        MenuChoices(2, 3) = "Broccoli"

        MenuNames(3) = "Meats"
        MenuChoices(3, 1) = "Chicken"
        MenuChoices(3, 2) = "Pork"
        MenuChoices(3, 3) = "Beef"
        MenuChoices(3, 4) = "Fish"

        FOR i = 1 TO 3
            MenuAttrbs(i) = &H61
        NEXT i
        BarAttrb% = &H24
        :
        :
```

Now we're ready to use the PDS menu system. We start by initializing that system with a call to the PDS subprogram MenuInit( ), and then we can load the menu and choice names with MenuSet( ).

You use MenuSet( ) like this:

```
CALL MenuSet(Menu%, Item%, State%, Text$, Accesskey%)
```

These are the inputs:

Menu%	Menu number.
Item%	Choice number in that menu (0 = menu name).

State%	0 = Choice is "disabled" — i.e., not a valid choice; 1 = Choice is "enabled" — this is the usual state; 2 = Choice is "enabled" and toggled with a checkmark.
Text$	The menu or choice name itself.
Accesskey%	The character position in Text$ of the letter to treat as standing for this choice. This letter is highlighted in the menu.

This means that we'll have to loop over MenuSet( ), calling it once for each menu choice. Here, then, is how we can load the data from our arrays into the PDS menu commons:

```
' $INCLUDE: 'C:\BC7\GEERAL.BI'
' $INCLUDE: 'C:\BC7\MOUSE.BI'
' $INCLUDE: 'C:\BC7\MENU.BI'
' $INCLUDE: 'C:\BC7\WINDOW.BI'

COMMON SHARED /uitools/ GloMenu          AS MenuMiscType
COMMON SHARED /uitools/ GloTitle( )      AS MenuTitleType
COMMON SHARED /uitools/ GloItem( )       AS MenuItemType

DIM GloTitle(MAXMENU)          AS MenuTitleType
DIM GloItem(MAXMENU, MAXITEM)  AS MenuItemType

DIM MenuNames(1 TO 3) AS STRING
DIM MenuChoices(1 TO 3, 1 TO 5) AS STRING
DIM MenuAttrbs(1 TO 3) AS INTEGER

        MenuNames(1) = "Fruits"
        MenuChoices(1, 1) = "Apples"
        MenuChoices(1, 2) = "Bananas"
        MenuChoices(1, 3) = "Grapes"
        MenuChoices(1, 4) = "Peaches"
        MenuChoices(1, 5) = "Oranges"

        MenuNames(2) = "Veggies"
        MenuChoices(2, 1) = "Peas"
        MenuChoices(2, 2) = "Corn"
        MenuChoices(2, 3) = "Broccoli"

        MenuNames(3) = "Meats"
        MenuChoices(3, 1) = "Chicken"
        MenuChoices(3, 2) = "Pork"
        MenuChoices(3, 3) = "Beef"
        MenuChoices(3, 4) = "Fish"
```

```
        FOR i = 1 TO 3
            MenuAttrbs(i) = &H61
        NEXT i
        BarAttrb% = &H24

→       CALL MenuInit
:
:       FOR i% = 1 TO 3
            CALL MenuSet(i%, 0, 1, MenuNames(i%), 1)
            FOR j% = 1 TO 5
                IF MenuChoices(i%, j%) <> "" THEN
                    CALL MenuSet(i%, j%, 1, MenuChoices(i%, j%), 1)
                END IF
            NEXT j%
        NEXT i%
        :
        :
```

Then we can call the PDS subprogram MenuColor( ) to set the color scheme, like this:

```
CALL MenuColor(Fore%, Back%, High%, Disab%, Curfore%, Curback%, CurHi%)
```

These are the inputs (see the discussion of attributes in Chapter 2 for more information about which colors are associated with which values):

Fore%	Menu foreground color (0-15)
Back%	Menu background color (0-7)
High%	Highlight color of the access key (0-15)
Disab%	Text color of disabled choices (0-15)
Curfore%	Menu cursor foreground color (0-15)
Curback%	Menu cursor background color (0-7)
CurHi%	Menu cursor color when over the access key (0-15)

After MenuColor( ), the next step is to call MenuPreProcess( ) to build the internal PDS indices needed to run the menus:

```
' $INCLUDE: 'C:\BC7\GENERAL.BI'
' $INCLUDE: 'C:\BC7\MOUSE.BI'
' $INCLUDE: 'C:\BC7\MENU.BI'
' $INCLUDE: 'C:\BC7\WINDOW.BI'

COMMON SHARED /uitools/ GloMenu         AS MenuMiscType
COMMON SHARED /uitools/ GloTitle()      AS MenuTitleType
COMMON SHARED /uitools/ GloItem()       AS MenuItemType
```

```
DIM GloTitle(MAXMENU)          AS MenuTitleType
DIM GloItem(MAXMENU, MAXITEM)  AS MenuItemType

DIM MenuNames(1 TO 3) AS STRING
DIM MenuChoices(1 TO 3, 1 TO 5) AS STRING
DIM MenuAttrbs(1 TO 3) AS INTEGER

        MenuNames(1) = "Fruits"
        MenuChoices(1, 1) = "Apples"
        MenuChoices(1, 2) = "Bananas"
        MenuChoices(1, 3) = "Grapes"
        MenuChoices(1, 4) = "Peaches"
        MenuChoices(1, 5) = "Oranges"

        MenuNames(2) = "Veggies"
        MenuChoices(2, 1) = "Peas"
        MenuChoices(2, 2) = "Corn"
        MenuChoices(2, 3) = "Broccoli"

        MenuNames(3) = "Meats"
        MenuChoices(3, 1) = "Chicken"
        MenuChoices(3, 2) = "Pork"
        MenuChoices(3, 3) = "Beef"
        MenuChoices(3, 4) = "Fish"

        FOR i = 1 TO 3
            MenuAttrbs(i) = &H61
        NEXT i
        BarAttrb% = &H24

        CALL MenuInit

        FOR i% = 1 TO 3
            CALL MenuSet(i%, 0, 1, MenuNames(i%), 1)
            FOR j% = 1 TO 5
                IF MenuChoices(i%, j%) <> "" THEN
                    CALL MenuSet(i%, j%, 1, MenuChoices(i%, j%), 1)
                END IF
            NEXT j%
        NEXT i%

        CALL MenuColor(14, 1, 12, 8, 14, 3, 12)

→       CALL MenuPreProcess
        :
```

Now it's time to actually display the menubar. We can use MenuShow( ) to do that, MouseShow( ) to display the mouse cursor, and then print out the prompt "Make a menu selection:"

```
' $INCLUDE: 'C:\BC7\GENERAL.BI'
' $INCLUDE: 'C:\BC7\MOUSE.BI'
' $INCLUDE: 'C:\BC7\MENU.BI'
' $INCLUDE: 'C:\BC7\WINDOW.BI'
```

```
COMMON SHARED /uitools/ GloMenu           AS MenuMiscType
COMMON SHARED /uitools/ GloTitle()        AS MenuTitleType
COMMON SHARED /uitools/ GloItem()         AS MenuItemType

DIM GloTitle(MAXMENU)           AS MenuTitleType
DIM GloItem(MAXMENU, MAXITEM)   AS MenuItemType

DIM MenuNames(1 TO 3) AS STRING
DIM MenuChoices(1 TO 3, 1 TO 5) AS STRING
DIM MenuAttrbs(1 TO 3) AS INTEGER

        MenuNames(1) = "Fruits"
        MenuChoices(1, 1) = "Apples"
        MenuChoices(1, 2) = "Bananas"
        MenuChoices(1, 3) = "Grapes"
        MenuChoices(1, 4) = "Peaches"
        MenuChoices(1, 5) = "Oranges"

        MenuNames(2) = "Veggies"
        MenuChoices(2, 1) = "Peas"
        MenuChoices(2, 2) = "Corn"
        MenuChoices(2, 3) = "Broccoli"

        MenuNames(3) = "Meats"
        MenuChoices(3, 1) = "Chicken"
        MenuChoices(3, 2) = "Pork"
        MenuChoices(3, 3) = "Beef"
        MenuChoices(3, 4) = "Fish"

        FOR i = 1 TO 3
            MenuAttrbs(i) = &H61
        NEXT i
        BarAttrb% = &H24

        CALL MenuInit

        FOR i% = 1 TO 3
            CALL MenuSet(i%, 0, 1, MenuNames(i%), 1)
            FOR j% = 1 TO 5
                IF MenuChoices(i%, j%) <> "" THEN
                    CALL MenuSet(i%, j%, 1, MenuChoices(i%, j%), 1)
                END IF
            NEXT j%
        NEXT i%

        CALL MenuColor(14, 1, 12, 8, 14, 3, 12)

        CALL MenuPreProcess

→       CALL MenuShow
:
        CALL MouseShow

        LOCATE 2, 1
        PRINT "Make a menu selection."
        :
        :
```

Now the menubar is on the screen; we're ready to receive input. The BASIC PDS system uses a method similar to the one we've used for our menu system to read input: there is a function named MenuInkey$( ) that operates much like our MenuCheck-Event$( ). To get menu or keyboard (but not mouse) input, we loop over MenuInkey$( ) until it returns a menu string. Then we have to interrogate the menu system to find out what choice was actually made:

```
' $INCLUDE: 'C:\BC7\GENERAL.BI'
' $INCLUDE: 'C:\BC7\MOUSE.BI'
' $INCLUDE: 'C:\BC7\MENU.BI'
' $INCLUDE: 'C:\BC7\WINDOW.BI'

COMMON SHARED /uitools/ GloMenu          AS MenuMiscType
COMMON SHARED /uitools/ GloTitle()       AS MenuTitleType
COMMON SHARED /uitools/ GloItem()        AS MenuItemType

DIM GloTitle(MAXMENU)          AS MenuTitleType
DIM GloItem(MAXMENU, MAXITEM)  AS MenuItemType

DIM MenuNames(1 TO 3) AS STRING
DIM MenuChoices(1 TO 3, 1 TO 5) AS STRING
DIM MenuAttrbs(1 TO 3) AS INTEGER

        MenuNames(1) = "Fruits"
        MenuChoices(1, 1) = "Apples"
        MenuChoices(1, 2) = "Bananas"
        MenuChoices(1, 3) = "Grapes"
        MenuChoices(1, 4) = "Peaches"
        MenuChoices(1, 5) = "Oranges"

        MenuNames(2) = "Veggies"
        MenuChoices(2, 1) = "Peas"
        MenuChoices(2, 2) = "Corn"
        MenuChoices(2, 3) = "Broccoli"

        MenuNames(3) = "Meats"
        MenuChoices(3, 1) = "Chicken"
        MenuChoices(3, 2) = "Pork"
        MenuChoices(3, 3) = "Beef"
        MenuChoices(3, 4) = "Fish"

        FOR i = 1 TO 3
            MenuAttrbs(i) = &H61
        NEXT i
        BarAttrb% = &H24

        CALL MenuInit

        FOR i% = 1 TO 3
            CALL MenuSet(i%, 0, 1, MenuNames(i%), 1)
            FOR j% = 1 TO 5
                IF MenuChoices(i%, j%) <> "" THEN
                    CALL MenuSet(i%, j%, 1, MenuChoices(i%, j%), 1)
```

```
              END IF
          NEXT j%
      NEXT i%

      CALL MenuColor(14, 1, 12, 8, 14, 3, 12)

      CALL MenuPreProcess

      CALL MenuShow

      CALL MouseShow

      LOCATE 2, 1
      PRINT "Make a menu selection."

→     DO
      Instring$ = MenuInkey$
      LOOP WHILE Instring$ <> "menu"
      :
```

When we leave this loop, a menu selection has been made; the PDS function Menu-Check(0) will return the number of the menu that the selection was made in, and Menu-Check(1) will return the choice number in that menu. This means that we'll be able to print out the selection made as shown in Listing 4-9.

Listing 4-9.   Using the BASIC PDS Menu System. 1 of 2

```
' $INCLUDE: 'C:\BC7\GENERAL.BI'
' $INCLUDE: 'C:\BC7\MOUSE.BI'
' $INCLUDE: 'C:\BC7\MENU.BI'
' $INCLUDE: 'C:\BC7\WINDOW.BI'

COMMON SHARED /uitools/ GloMenu          AS MenuMiscType
COMMON SHARED /uitools/ GloTitle()       AS MenuTitleType
COMMON SHARED /uitools/ GloItem()        AS MenuItemType

DIM GloTitle(MAXMENU)        AS MenuTitleType
DIM GloItem(MAXMENU, MAXITEM)  AS MenuItemType

DIM MenuNames(1 TO 3) AS STRING
DIM MenuChoices(1 TO 3, 1 TO 5) AS STRING
DIM MenuAttrbs(1 TO 3) AS INTEGER

      MenuNames(1) = "Fruits"
      MenuChoices(1, 1) = "Apples"
      MenuChoices(1, 2) = "Bananas"
      MenuChoices(1, 3) = "Grapes"
      MenuChoices(1, 4) = "Peaches"
      MenuChoices(1, 5) = "Oranges"

      MenuNames(2) = "Veggies"
      MenuChoices(2, 1) = "Peas"
      MenuChoices(2, 2) = "Corn"
```

Listing 4-9.   Using the BASIC PDS Menu System.   **2 of 2**

```
        MenuChoices(2, 3) = "Broccoli"

        MenuNames(3) = "Meats"
        MenuChoices(3, 1) = "Chicken"
        MenuChoices(3, 2) = "Pork"
        MenuChoices(3, 3) = "Beef"
        MenuChoices(3, 4) = "Fish"

        FOR i = 1 TO 3
            MenuAttrbs(i) = &H61
        NEXT i
        BarAttrb% = &H24

        CALL MenuInit

        FOR i% = 1 TO 3
            CALL MenuSet(i%, 0, 1, MenuNames(i%), 1)
            FOR j% = 1 TO 5
                IF MenuChoices(i%, j%) <> "" THEN
                    CALL MenuSet(i%, j%, 1, MenuChoices(i%, j%), 1)
                END IF
            NEXT j%
        NEXT i%

        CALL MenuColor(14, 1, 12, 8, 14, 3, 12)

        CALL MenuPreProcess

        CALL MenuShow

        CALL MouseShow

        LOCATE 2, 1
        PRINT "Make a menu selection."

        DO
        Instring$ = MenuInkey$
        LOOP WHILE Instring$ <> "menu"

    →   MenuNo% = MenuCheck(0)
    :   ChoiceNo% = MenuCheck(1)
    :
        LOCATE 3, 1
        PRINT "That selection was ", MenuChoices(MenuNo%, ChoiceNo%)
```

And that's it. At this point, we've made a menu selection, and our example program has deciphered what it was and reported it to us. You can see that, fundamentally, the PDS menu system is very similar to the one we've developed. The primary restriction is that you have to use it to read all input to your program. In practice, however, it usually works quite well.

Conclusion

That's the end of the menu system we'll develop, and the end of our survey of the PDS menu tools. With these systems, you can add a powerful set of pull-down menus to your programs with a few simple calls.

But we have much more power to add to your programs; as a case in point, let's turn to Chapter 5 right now and see what we can do with graphics.

Graphics

IN THIS CHAPTER we're going to examine the graphics resources in BASIC, and we'll see just how advanced we can get. As it turns out, BASIC is thoroughly stocked with graphics tools, enough for us to put together our own fully functional paint program (which is even going to save and load images to and from disk). We'll be able to draw circles, boxes, lines — even color them in. After the paint program, we'll spend a little time with the DRAW statement to produce some line graphics, and then we'll plunge into animation.

Animation is a hot graphics topic that is supported very well in BASIC. Computer animation revolves around the use of screen *sprites*, graphic images that you can move around and display rapidly on the screen. We'll design our own sprite — a small, colorful rocketship — and we'll also animate it, sending it blasting up the screen. After animation, we'll look into the PDS' Presentation Graphics tools, drawing pie, bar, and line charts with ease.

NOTE: If you do any business graphics, be sure to read about presentation graphics.

We'll end the chapter with a couple of low-level functions to determine what video card is in the computer you're working with, and what the current horizontal and vertical pixel ranges on the screen are. This exploration of the graphics environment can give your programs the power they need to make sure they're using the resources available fully.

Graphics is an exciting topic — and this is going to be an exciting chapter. Let's start with our paint program.

A Mouse-driven Paint Program

Our first graphics project is going to be a full power mouse-driven paint program. Even if you don't have a mouse, keep in mind that this program is really a vehicle to introduce the various BASIC graphics routines to us, so it's valuable to work through in any case.

Since we're going to use the mouse, we have to start by defining the TYPE RegType, as well as InRegs and OutRegs as before:

```
TYPE RegType
        ax      AS INTEGER
        bx      AS INTEGER
        cx      AS INTEGER
        dx      AS INTEGER
```

```
        bp    AS INTEGER
        si    AS INTEGER
        di    AS INTEGER
        flags AS INTEGER
END TYPE

        DIM InRegs AS RegType, OutRegs AS RegType
        :
        :
```

NOTE: Paint programs without mice are exercises in futility; there is no satisfactory way to use a paint program from the keyboard.

Our paint program has to handle many different types of actions: drawing pixels on the screen, drawing lines, boxes, circles, and even saving or loading images on disk. For that reason, organization is going to be important here, and we should make the main body of the program as simple as we can, breaking the rest of the code up into subroutines.

We choose the subroutine structure (i.e., GOSUB...RETURN) here so that all variables will be shared, and there's no advantage to using subprograms in this case. For example, we can start this way:

```
TYPE RegType
        ax    AS INTEGER
        bx    AS INTEGER
        cx    AS INTEGER
        dx    AS INTEGER
        bp    AS INTEGER
        si    AS INTEGER
        di    AS INTEGER
        flags AS INTEGER
END TYPE

        DIM InRegs AS RegType, OutRegs AS RegType

→       GOSUB Initialize
        :
```

TIP: In early versions of BASIC, all variables used to be shared (that is, global) and there were no functions or subprograms — only subroutines (which you use with GOSUB). Now, however, you can use functions and subprograms, making your variables private (that is, local). To share variables between them, you can use a SHARED COMMON.

In the Initialize subroutine, we can set the screen mode, print the menubar, and initialize the mouse. When the program actually starts, the first thing we'll do is to wait for the left mouse button to be pressed — you make all menu selections with the left mouse button, or begin drawing with the left mouse button. We can set up a perpetual loop, waiting for the left mouse button to be pressed:

```
TYPE RegType
        ax    AS INTEGER
        bx    AS INTEGER
        cx    AS INTEGER
        dx    AS INTEGER
        bp    AS INTEGER
        si    AS INTEGER
        di    AS INTEGER
        flags AS INTEGER
END TYPE

        DIM InRegs AS RegType, OutRegs AS RegType

        GOSUB Initialize

→       DO
            GOSUB GetLeftButtonPress
                    :
                    :
        LOOP WHILE 1

        END
```

We can set up the subroutine named GetLeftButtonPress to wait until the left button has been pressed. After that button has been pressed, we'll want to know is whether a menu selection was made; let's design GetLeftButtonPress to set a variable named MenuSelectionMade% to 1, if the mousedown occurred in the menubar, and 0, if otherwise. This will allow us to check for a menu selection this way:

```
TYPE RegType
        ax    AS INTEGER
        bx    AS INTEGER
        cx    AS INTEGER
        dx    AS INTEGER
        bp    AS INTEGER
        si    AS INTEGER
        di    AS INTEGER
        flags AS INTEGER
END TYPE

        DIM InRegs AS RegType, OutRegs AS RegType
```

```
        GOSUB Initialize

        DO
             GOSUB GetLeftButtonPress
→            IF MenuSelectionMade% THEN GOSUB MenuChoice
                  :
                  :
        LOOP WHILE 1

        END
```

If a menu selection *was* made, then we can handle it in a new subroutine we can name MenuChoice. There, we'll have to toggle internal flags to turn various drawing actions on or off. For example, if the user selected the Line option, then we can toggle a flag called LineFlag% to 1 in MenuChoice. With that option selected, we'll be ready to draw lines the next time the left mouse button goes down.

If the button *wasn't* pressed in row 1, MenuSelectionMade% will not be set — maybe we're supposed to start a drawing action, such as drawing lines or boxes. We can check what we're supposed to do (if anything) by checking the flags we set in MenuChoice, like this:

```
TYPE RegType
        ax    AS INTEGER
        bx    AS INTEGER
        cx    AS INTEGER
        dx    AS INTEGER
        bp    AS INTEGER
        si    AS INTEGER
        di    AS INTEGER
        flags AS INTEGER
END TYPE

        DIM InRegs AS RegType, OutRegs AS RegType
        DIM Storage(31266) AS INTEGER

        GOSUB Initialize

        DO
             GOSUB GetLeftButtonPress

             IF MenuSelectionMade% THEN
                  GOSUB MenuChoice
             ELSE
→                 IF DrawFlag% THEN GOSUB DrawPixel
                  IF LineFlag% THEN GOSUB DrawLine
                  IF BoxFlag% THEN GOSUB DrawBox
                  IF CircleFlag% THEN GOSUB DrawCircle
                  IF PaintFlag% THEN GOSUB DrawPaint
```

```
        END IF

    LOOP WHILE 1

    END
```

TIP: As you can see, the main procedure of PAINT.BAS has been made as modular as possible. The result is that it is easy to understand and easy to debug. Dividing the overall basics into components like that is called top-down programming, and most professional programmers work this way.

In other words, the action goes like this: the user can start drawing lines by selecting Line in the menubar. When a menu selection like that is made, we go to the subroutine MenuChoice and toggle the correct flag, LineFlag% to 1.

Then the user releases the mouse button. Internally, we return from MenuChoice, loop back to the top of our main loop, and wait for the next left button press in GetLeftButtonPress. The user moves the mouse to the drawing area below the menubar and presses the left mouse button. Internally, we return from GetLeftButtonPress with MenuSelectionMade% not set this time, so we check which flag is set (LineFlag%) and enter the correct subroutine (DrawLine). We stay in that subroutine, drawing the line, until the user releases the button.

From the user's point of view, the line appears with one end anchored where they've pressed the mouse button. The user can move the mouse cursor around the screen, pulling their end of the line as they require. When they release the button, the line becomes fixed (and we return from DrawLine to wait for the next left button press, which might be either a new line or a new menu selection).

That's all there is to it from a programming standpoint. The main procedure in our program is complete (note that we've added an array called Storage( ) above to hold the screen image for disk transfers). All that remains is to write the subroutines.

Subroutine Initialize

In the initialization subroutine, we have to set the screen mode and print the menubar. We can do that like this:

```
Initialize:
    SCREEN 8
    LOCATE 1, 1
    Fore% = 1
    Back% = 2
    COLOR Fore%, Back%
    PRINT "Exit    Color   Bkgrnd Draw    Line " + _
    "Box      Circle Paint   Save    Load";
    :
```

The menubar options in our full function paint program include:

Exit	Exit the program
Color	Set the drawing (foreground color)
Bkgrnd	Set the background color
Draw	Draw pixel by pixel
Line	Draw a line
Box	Draw a box
Circle	Draw a circle
Paint	Fill a shape in with solid color
Save	Save image to disk
Load	Load image from disk

We also have to initialize the mouse and show the mouse cursor:

```
Initialize:
    SCREEN 8
    LOCATE 1, 1
    Fore% = 1
    Back% = 2
    COLOR Fore%, Back%
    PRINT "Exit    Color   Bkgrnd Draw    Line " + _
    "Box      Circle Paint   Save    Load";

→   InRegs.ax = 0     'Initialize mouse
    CALL INTERRUPT(&H33, InRegs, OutRegs)

    InRegs.ax = 1     'Show mouse cursor
    CALL INTERRUPT(&H33, InRegs, OutRegs)
    :
    :
```

Finally, we can set all our drawing flags to 0, and we're done:

```
Initialize:
    SCREEN 8
    LOCATE 1, 1
    Fore% = 1
    Back% = 2
    COLOR Fore%, Back%
    PRINT "Exit    Color   Bkgrnd  Draw    Line    " + _
    "Box     Circle  Paint   Save    Load";

    InRegs.ax = 0    'Initialize mouse
    CALL INTERRUPT(&H33, InRegs, OutRegs)

    InRegs.ax = 1    'Show mouse cursor
    CALL INTERRUPT(&H33, InRegs, OutRegs)
→   DrawFlag% = 0
:   LineFlag% = 0
:   BoxFlag% = 0
    CircleFlag% = 0
    PaintFlag% = 0
    RETURN
```

Now we're ready for GetLeftButtonPress.

Subroutine GetLeftButtonPress

This subroutine is easy: All we have to do is to wait for the left mouse button to be pressed, which we can check with interrupt &H33 service 5 like this:

```
GetLeftButtonPress:

        DO
            InRegs.bx = 0            'Wait for left button press
            InRegs.ax = 5
            CALL INTERRUPT(&H33, InRegs, OutRegs)
        LOOP WHILE OutRegs.bx = 0
            :
```

We have to set the variable MenuSelectionMade% to report whether or not this was a menubar event. We can do that by simply checking whether the mouse cursor was in row 1, the menubar row:

```
GetLeftButtonPress:

        DO
            InRegs.bx = 0            'Wait for left button press
            InRegs.ax = 5
            CALL INTERRUPT(&H33, InRegs, OutRegs)
```

```
              LOOP WHILE OutRegs.bx = 0
    →         Row% = OutRegs.dx \ 8 + 1
    :         IF Row% = 1 THEN
    :             MenuSelectionMade% = 1
              ELSE
                  MenuSelectionMade% = 0
              END IF
              RETURN
```

That's it. Now we're ready to start handling menu selections.

Subroutine MenuChoice

In the MenuChoice subroutine, we can keep track of what menu choice or drawing option was selected. The menubar looks like Figure 5-1.

Exit	Color	Bkgrnd	Draw	Line	Box	Circle	Paint	Save	Load

Figure 5-1

Let's work through the options one by one. First, we have to reset all the drawing flags and figure out what choice was made; we can do that like this (each menu choice takes up eight screen columns, and each column is eight pixels wide):

```
MenuChoice:
          DrawFlag% = 0
          LineFlag% = 0
          BoxFlag% = 0
          CircleFlag% = 0
          PaintFlag% = 0
          Choice% = OutRegs.cx \ 64 + 1
              :
```

Next, we can do what is required by the menu choice made with a SELECT CASE statement. For example, for choice 1, Exit, we just end the program:

```
MenuChoice:
          DrawFlag% = 0
          LineFlag% = 0
          BoxFlag% = 0
          CircleFlag% = 0
          PaintFlag% = 0
          Choice% = OutRegs.cx \ 64 + 1
    →     SELECT CASE Choice%
              CASE 1
                      END
                  :
```

Choice 2 lets us set the foreground color; each time the user clicks on this selection, we should increment the foreground color through the 16 options available in this mode. We can indicate those colors by reprinting the word Color (which the user is clicking on) in the new foreground color. Note that we turn the mouse cursor off and on before working with the screen:

```
MenuChoice:
          DrawFlag% = 0
          LineFlag% = 0
          BoxFlag% = 0
          CircleFlag% = 0
          PaintFlag% = 0
          Choice% = OutRegs.cx \ 64 + 1
          SELECT CASE Choice%
                CASE 1
                        END
→         CASE 2
:                       Fore% = Fore% + 1
:                       IF Fore% > 15 THEN Fore% = 0
                        COLOR Fore%, Back%
                        InRegs.ax = 2  'Hide mouse cursor
                        CALL INTERRUPT(&H33, InRegs, OutRegs)
                        LOCATE 1, 9
                        PRINT "Color  ";
                        InRegs.ax = 1  'Show mouse cursor
                        CALL INTERRUPT(&H33, InRegs, OutRegs)
                        :
```

The next option changes the background color, which we can do with the BASIC COLOR statement. Each time we change the background color, the background of the whole screen changes, so the user can easily make a selection:

```
MenuChoice:
          DrawFlag% = 0
          LineFlag% = 0
          BoxFlag% = 0
          CircleFlag% = 0
          PaintFlag% = 0
          Choice% = OutRegs.cx \ 64 + 1
          SELECT CASE Choice%
                CASE 1
                        END
                CASE 2
                        Fore% = Fore% + 1
                        IF Fore% > 15 THEN Fore% = 0
                        COLOR Fore%, Back%
                        InRegs.ax = 2 'Hide mouse cursor
```

```
                    CALL INTERRUPT(&H33, InRegs, OutRegs)
                    LOCATE 1, 9
                    PRINT "Color ";
                    InRegs.ax = 1 'Show mouse cursor
                    CALL INTERRUPT(&H33, InRegs, OutRegs)
          CASE 3

                    Back% = Back% + 1
                    IF Back% > 7 THEN Back% = 0
                    COLOR Fore%, Back%
                    :
```

Now we come to the drawing options in the menubar (see Figure 5-2). Each of these options are going to be handled in their own subroutines, but we have to toggle the appropriate flags here. That looks like this:

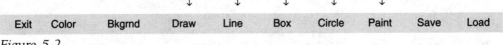

| | ↓ | | ↓ | | ↓ | | ↓ | | ↓ | | |
| Exit | Color | Bkgrnd | Draw | Line | Box | Circle | Paint | Save | Load |

Figure 5-2

```
MenuChoice:
          DrawFlag% = 0
          LineFlag% = 0
          BoxFlag% = 0
          CircleFlag% = 0
          PaintFlag% = 0
          Choice% = OutRegs.cx \ 64 + 1
          SELECT CASE Choice%
              CASE 1
                        END
              CASE 2
                        Fore% = Fore% + 1
                        IF Fore% > 15 THEN Fore% = 0
                        COLOR Fore%, Back%
                        InRegs.ax = 2 'Hide mouse cursor
                        CALL INTERRUPT(&H33, InRegs, OutRegs)
                        LOCATE 1, 9
                        PRINT "Color ";
                        InRegs.ax = 1 'Show mouse cursor
                        CALL INTERRUPT(&H33, InRegs, OutRegs)
              CASE 3
                        Back% = Back% + 1
                        IF Back% > 7 THEN Back% = 0
                        COLOR Fore%, Back%
              CASE 4
  →                     DrawFlag% = 1
              CASE 5
                        LineFlag% = 1
              CASE 6
                        BoxFlag% = 1
              CASE 7
                        CircleFlag% = 1
              CASE 8
                        PaintFlag% = 1
                        :
```

The following option, Save, lets us save the image to the disk. In particular, we can save it as a file named PAINT.DAT. Since we should save the file when the option is selected, we should handle this option here in MenuChoice.

NOTE: It would be more professional to allow the user to select the name of the disk file.

To save the screen image, we can use the BASIC GET statement to load it into an array. We'll need to set up an array, and we can use an array of integers named, say, Storage( ). We want to save the drawing area of the screen, whose top left corner will be $(X1, Y1) = (0, 8)$ (omitting the menubar) and whose bottom left corner is $(X2, Y2) = (639, 199)$. The number of bytes needed to store this image is given by the formula:

$$\text{Bytes} = 4 + \text{INT}(((X2-X1+1)*(\text{Bits/pixel/plane})+7)/8)*\text{planes}*((Y2-Y1)+1)$$

where Bits/pixel/plane is the number of bits per pixel per plane and planes is the number of planes in the present screen mode. To determine these values for a specific screen mode, see the BASIC documentation (or look at our subroutine SaveSprite coming up later). For mode 8 and the size of the image we want to save, we'll need 62,532 bytes, or 31,266 integers.

At this point, all we need to do is to use GET like this:

```
GET (0, 8)-(639, 199), Storage
```

This will load the screen image into the array Storage( ). (Note that we should turn the mouse cursor off first to avoid saving it too.)

Next, we can dump the array Storage( ) directly to a file on disk using BSAVE, BASIC's binary save routine. To do that, we have to give BSAVE the address of the data we want to save, and the number of bytes to save.

TIP: BASIC's BSAVE statement is extraordinary powerful; it is the quickest way of loading data to and from the disk that BASIC supports. Although we are using it here to save a screen image, it is more commonly used to save blocks of data quickly, especially arrays.

As you may already know, addresses in memory are made up of two words, a *segment* address and an *offset* address. Briefly, a segment is a 64K section of memory, and an offset is the location of a particular byte in that segment, as measured from the beginning of the segment (see Figure 5-3).

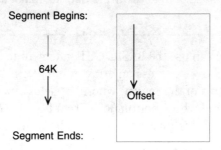

Figure 5-3

We will work with actual segment and offset values when we cover memory addressing thoroughly in Chapter 10. All we have to know now is that we have to supply BSAVE with both the segment and offset address of the array Storage( ). To get the segment address, BASIC provides the VARSEG( ) function. To get the offset in that segment, BASIC provides VARPTR( ).

We start by setting the segment address BASIC will use equal to the segment address of Storage( ) this way:

```
DEF SEG = VARSEG(Storage(1))
```

where Storage(1) is the first element in the array. Next, we just pass the name of the file we want to create on disk, PAINT.DAT, followed by the offset address of the first byte to write, which is VARPTR(Storage(1)), and the number of bytes to write, 62,532:

```
DEF SEG = VARSEG(Storage(1))
BSAVE "PAINT.DAT", VARPTR(Storage(1)), 62532
DEF SEG
```

At the end, we reset the segment address BASIC will use for data back to its original value with DEF SEG (no argument). Here's how it looks:

```
MenuChoice:
             DrawFlag% = 0
             LineFlag% = 0
             BoxFlag% = 0
             CircleFlag% = 0
             PaintFlag% = 0
             Choice% = OutRegs.cx \ 64 + 1
             SELECT CASE Choice%
                 CASE 1
                         END
                 CASE 2
                         Fore% = Fore% + 1
                         IF Fore% > 15 THEN Fore% = 0
                         COLOR Fore%, Back%
                         InRegs.ax = 2    'Hide mouse cursor
                         CALL INTERRUPT(&H33, InRegs, OutRegs)
                         LOCATE 1, 9
                         PRINT "Color ";
                         InRegs.ax = 1 'Show mouse cursor
                         CALL INTERRUPT(&H33, InRegs, OutRegs)
                 CASE 3
                         Back% = Back% + 1
                         IF Back% > 7 THEN Back% = 0
                         COLOR Fore%, Back%
                 CASE 4
                         DrawFlag% = 1
                 CASE 5
                         LineFlag% = 1
                 CASE 6
                         BoxFlag% = 1
                 CASE 7
                         CircleFlag% = 1
                 CASE 8
                         PaintFlag% = 1
                 CASE 9
                         InRegs.ax = 2 'Hide mouse cursor
                         CALL INTERRUPT(&H33, InRegs, OutRegs)
                         GET (0, 8)-(639, 199), Storage
                         DEF SEG = VARSEG(Storage(1))
   →                     BSAVE "PAINT.DAT", VARPTR(Storage(1)), 62532
                         DEF SEG
                         InRegs.ax = 1 'Show mouse cursor
                         CALL INTERRUPT(&H33, InRegs, OutRegs)
```

And that's it — we've been able to use BSAVE to save a graphics image on the disk.

The last option, Load, lets us read the image from the file and place it on the screen again. We can do that with BLOAD, BASIC's binary load routine, and PUT. Again, we have to supply BLOAD with the address of the beginning of Storage( ).

TIP: Just as BSAVE is BASIC's quickest way of saving data on disk, so BLOAD is
the fastest way of loading it.

We start by hiding the mouse cursor and loading PAINT.DAT back into memory like
this:

```
MenuChoice:
            DrawFlag% = 0
            LineFlag% = 0
            BoxFlag% = 0
            CircleFlag% = 0
            PaintFlag% = 0
            Choice% = OutRegs.cx \ 64 + 1
            SELECT CASE Choice%
                CASE 1
                            END
                CASE 2
                            Fore% = Fore% + 1
                            IF Fore% > 15 THEN Fore% = 0
                            COLOR Fore%, Back%
                            InRegs.ax = 2 'Hide mouse cursor
                            CALL INTERRUPT(&H33, InRegs, OutRegs)
                            LOCATE 1, 9
                            PRINT "Color ";
                            InRegs.ax = 1 'Show mouse cursor
                            CALL INTERRUPT(&H33, InRegs, OutRegs)
                CASE 3
                            Back% = Back% + 1
                            IF Back% > 7 THEN Back% = 0
                            COLOR Fore%, Back%
                CASE 4
                            DrawFlag% = 1
                CASE 5
                            LineFlag% = 1
                CASE 6
                            BoxFlag% = 1
                CASE 7
                            CircleFlag% = 1
                CASE 8
                            PaintFlag% = 1
                CASE 9
                            InRegs.ax = 2 'Hide mouse cursor
                            CALL INTERRUPT(&H33, InRegs, OutRegs)
                            GET (0, 8)-(639, 199), Storage
                            DEF SEG = VARSEG(Storage(1))
                            BSAVE "PAINT.DAT", VARPTR(Storage(1)), 62532
                            DEF SEG
                            InRegs.ax = 1 'Show mouse cursor
                            CALL INTERRUPT(&H33, InRegs, OutRegs)
                CASE 10
                            InRegs.ax = 2 'Hide mouse cursor
                            CALL INTERRUPT(&H33, InRegs, OutRegs)
                            DEF SEG = VARSEG(Storage(1))
           →                BLOAD "PAINT.DAT", VARPTR(Storage(1))
                            :
```

Next, we can place the image back on the screen, with the BASIC PUT statement, like this: PUT (0, 8), Storage, PSET. The GET and PUT statements transfer data to and from the screen rapidly, and both are cornerstones of graphics routines in BASIC. The PSET option here indicates that each bit that we're putting on the screen should overwrite what's already there. The default, if you do not specify any option such as PSET, is XOR — the image is XOR'd with whatever is already there. We'll use that option when working with screen sprites.

TIP: XOR has a special property: If you XOR A with B, and then XOR the result with B again, you'll get A back. This is why screen cursors are often XORed with screen characters — when you XOR the character with the cursor again, the original character reappears and the cursor can be moved elsewhere.

Finally, we just restore the mouse cursor, and we're done. Here's the whole subroutine MenuChoice:

```
MenuChoice:
            DrawFlag% = 0
            LineFlag% = 0
            BoxFlag% = 0
            CircleFlag% = 0
            PaintFlag% = 0
            Choice% = OutRegs.cx \ 64 + 1
            SELECT CASE Choice%
                CASE 1
                        END
                CASE 2
                        Fore% = Fore% + 1
                        IF Fore% > 15 THEN Fore% = 0
                        COLOR Fore%, Back%
                        InRegs.ax = 2 'Hide mouse cursor
                        CALL INTERRUPT(&H33, InRegs, OutRegs)
                        LOCATE 1, 9
                        PRINT "Color ";
                        InRegs.ax = 1 'Show mouse cursor
                        CALL INTERRUPT(&H33, InRegs, OutRegs)
                CASE 3
                        Back% = Back% + 1
                        IF Back% > 7 THEN Back% = 0
                        COLOR Fore%, Back%
```

```
                    CASE 4
                            DrawFlag% = 1
                    CASE 5
                            LineFlag% = 1
                    CASE 6
                            BoxFlag% = 1
                    CASE 7
                            CircleFlag% = 1
                    CASE 8
                            PaintFlag% = 1
                    CASE 9
                            InRegs.ax = 2 'Hide mouse cursor
                            CALL INTERRUPT(&H33, InRegs, OutRegs)
                            GET (0, 8)-(639, 199), Storage
                            DEF SEG = VARSEG(Storage(1))
                            BSAVE "PAINT.DAT", VARPTR(Storage(1)), 62532
                            DEF SEG
                            InRegs.ax = 1 'Show mouse cursor
                            CALL INTERRUPT(&H33, InRegs, OutRegs)
                    CASE 10
                            InRegs.ax = 2 'Hide mouse cursor
                            CALL INTERRUPT(&H33, InRegs, OutRegs)
                            DEF SEG = VARSEG(Storage(1))
                            BLOAD "PAINT.DAT", VARPTR(Storage(1))
                            DEF SEG
                            PUT (0, 8), Storage, PSET
            →               InRegs.ax = 1 'Show mouse cursor
                            CALL INTERRUPT(&H33, InRegs, OutRegs)
            END SELECT
RETURN
```

Subroutine DrawPixel

So far, we've handled everything but the drawing subroutines in our main procedure:

```
TYPE RegType
        ax      AS INTEGER
        bx      AS INTEGER
        cx      AS INTEGER
        dx      AS INTEGER
        bp      AS INTEGER
        si      AS INTEGER
        di      AS INTEGER
        flags   AS INTEGER
END TYPE

        DIM InRegs AS RegType, OutRegs AS RegType
        DIM Storage(31266) AS INTEGER

        GOSUB Initialize

        DO
            GOSUB GetLeftButtonPress

            IF MenuSelectionMade% THEN
```

```
                GOSUB MenuChoice
         ELSE
 →              IF DrawFlag% THEN GOSUB DrawPixel
                IF LineFlag% THEN GOSUB DrawLine
                IF BoxFlag% THEN GOSUB DrawBox
                IF CircleFlag% THEN GOSUB DrawCircle
                IF PaintFlag% THEN GOSUB DrawPaint
         END IF

    LOOP WHILE 1

    END
```

Let's handle them now. The first one is DrawPixel. When we enter this subroutine, we're supposed to keep setting the pixel at the current mouse cursor position until the mouse button is released. This way, the user will be able to draw by pressing the left mouse button and moving the mouse cursor around the screen.

We should start by clearing the mouse button release queue so we're not responding to a button release that occurred some time ago:

```
 DrawPixel:
             InRegs.bx = 0           'Get left button releases to clear queue
             InRegs.ax = 6
             CALL INTERRUPT(&H33, InRegs, OutRegs)
             :
```

Now we should keep looping until the mouse button is released (by checking interrupt &H33 service 6):

```
 DrawPixel:
             InRegs.bx = 0           'Get left button releases to clear queue
             InRegs.ax = 6
             CALL INTERRUPT(&H33, InRegs, OutRegs)

    →        DO
                   :
                 [Set current pixel]
                   :
                 InRegs.bx = 0              'Left Button Releases
                 InRegs.ax = 6
                 CALL INTERRUPT(&H33, InRegs, OutRegs)
             LOOP WHILE OutRegs.bx = 0

         RETURN
```

Every time through this loop while we're waiting for the mouse button to be released, we have to get the mouse cursor's current position and set the pixel there to the foreground color. We get the current position with interrupt &H33 service 3, hide the mouse cursor with service 2, set the pixel with a BASIC PSET( ) statement, and then show the mouse cursor again:

```
DrawPixel:
                InRegs.bx = 0                'Get left button releases to clear queue
                InRegs.ax = 6
                CALL INTERRUPT(&H33, InRegs, OutRegs)

                DO
        →           InRegs.ax = 3
        :           CALL INTERRUPT(&H33, InRegs, OutRegs)
                    X% = OutRegs.cx
                    Y% = OutRegs.dx
                    InRegs.ax = 2    'Hide mouse cursor
                    CALL INTERRUPT(&H33, InRegs, OutRegs)
                    PSET (X%, Y%)
                    InRegs.ax = 1    'Show mouse cursor
                    CALL INTERRUPT(&H33, InRegs, OutRegs)
                    InRegs.bx = 0                'Left Button Releases
                    InRegs.ax = 6
                    CALL INTERRUPT(&H33, InRegs, OutRegs)
                LOOP WHILE OutRegs.bx = 0

        RETURN
```

And that's all there is to it. The real work is done by PSET(X%, Y%), which sets the pixel at the current location to the foreground color. We've finished the first of the drawing subroutines.

Subroutine DrawLine

The next subroutine is DrawLine:

```
TYPE RegType
        ax       AS INTEGER
        bx       AS INTEGER
        cx       AS INTEGER
        dx       AS INTEGER
        bp       AS INTEGER
        si       AS INTEGER
        di       AS INTEGER
        flags    AS INTEGER
END TYPE

        DIM InRegs AS RegType, OutRegs AS RegType
        DIM Storage(31266) AS INTEGER

        GOSUB Initialize
```

```
DO
      GOSUB GetLeftButtonPress

      IF MenuSelectionMade% THEN
            GOSUB MenuChoice
      ELSE
            IF DrawFlag% THEN GOSUB DrawPixel
  →         IF LineFlag% THEN GOSUB DrawLine
            IF BoxFlag% THEN GOSUB DrawBox
            IF CircleFlag% THEN GOSUB DrawCircle
            IF PaintFlag% THEN GOSUB DrawPaint
      END IF

LOOP WHILE 1

END
```

We can handle this task with the BASIC LINE statement. You use it like this to draw a line from screen point (X1, Y1) to (X2, Y2):

```
LINE (X1, Y1) - (X2, Y2), Color%
```

Here, Color% is an optional argument that specifies the line's color. We'll make use of this argument to both draw and erase lines. When we arrive in DrawLine, the user has already clicked the mouse in the drawing area to establish the "anchor" point of one end of the line. Since all variables are global between subroutines, we can read that location from OutRegs.cx and OutRegs.dx, which are still with the location the user clicked at (in GetLeftButtonPress):

```
DrawLine:
      X% = OutRegs.cx
      Y% = OutRegs.dx
            :
```

This provides us with the anchor point of the line, (X%, Y%). When the user moves the mouse cursor to a new location (XNew%, YNew%), we'll draw a line from (X%, Y%) to (XNew%, YNew%); see Figure 5-4.

| X———————————— X |
| (X%, Y%)   (XNew%, YNew%) |

Figure 5-4

When the user moves to a new position after this, we'll set XNew% and YNew% to XOld% and YOld%, and erase that line by drawing over it in the background color (see Figure 5-5).

```
        X                              X
   (X%, Y%)                    (XOld%, YOld%)
```

Figure 5-5

And draw a new one to the new (XNew%, YNew%) (see Figure 5-6).

```
   X_____X
   (X%, Y%)                    (XNew%, YNew%)
```

Figure 5-6

In this way, one end of the line will always be anchored at the original click position, and the other will follow the mouse cursor around. When the user releases the left button, we'll make the line permanent. To do this, we first clear the left mouse button release queue, and loop, waiting for the left button to be released:

```
DrawLine:
        X% = OutRegs.cx
        Y% = OutRegs.dx
        XOld% = X%
        YOld% = Y%

→       InRegs.bx = 0              'Get left button releases to clear queue
:       InRegs.ax = 6
:       CALL INTERRUPT(&H33, InRegs, OutRegs)

        DO
            :
            InRegs.bx = 0          'Left Button Releases
            InRegs.ax = 6
            CALL INTERRUPT(&H33, InRegs, OutRegs)
        LOOP WHILE OutRegs.bx = 0
RETURN
```

Each time we loop, we have to check the new mouse cursor position, erasing the old line and drawing the new one (after hiding the mouse cursor). That looks like this:

```
DrawLine:
        X% = OutRegs.cx
        Y% = OutRegs.dx
        XOld% = X%
        YOld% = Y%
```

```
            InRegs.bx = 0              'Get left button releases to clear queue
            InRegs.ax = 6
            CALL INTERRUPT(&H33, InRegs, OutRegs)

            DO
→               InRegs.ax = 3
:               CALL INTERRUPT(&H33, InRegs, OutRegs)
                YNew% = OutRegs.dx
                XNew% = OutRegs.cx
                InRegs.ax = 2    'Hide mouse cursor
                CALL INTERRUPT(&H33, InRegs, OutRegs)
→               LINE (X%, Y%)-(XOld%, YOld%), Back%      'Erase old line
                LINE (X%, Y%)-(XNew%, YNew%), Fore%      'Draw new line
                XOld% = XNew%
                YOld% = YNew%
                InRegs.ax = 1    'Show mouse cursor
                CALL INTERRUPT(&H33, InRegs, OutRegs)
                InRegs.bx = 0              'Left Button Releases
                InRegs.ax = 6
                CALL INTERRUPT(&H33, InRegs, OutRegs)
            LOOP WHILE OutRegs.bx = 0
RETURN
```

And that's it. When the user releases the left mouse button, the line becomes final.

Subroutine DrawBox

The next subroutine is DrawBox. In fact, this subroutine is extremely simple, now that we've developed DrawLine. If we just add a "B" parameter to the end of the LINE statement in BASIC:

```
LINE (X1, Y1) - (X2, Y2), Color%, B ←
```

TIP: Adding the F option after the B option will make BASIC fill the box in with the same colors used to draw the sides.

Then we'll get a box with its upper left corner at (X1, Y1) and lower right corner at (X2, Y2). This is perfect for us: just copying over DrawLine and adding the B parameter means that the anchor point will now anchor one corner of the box, and the mouse cursor will drag the other corner around the screen. When the user releases the left mouse button, the box will become final:

```
DrawBox:
                    X% = OutRegs.cx
                    Y% = OutRegs.dx
                    XOld% = X%
                    YOld% = Y%

                    InRegs.bx = 0              'Get left button releases to clear queue
                    InRegs.ax = 6
                    CALL INTERRUPT(&H33, InRegs, OutRegs)

                    DO
                        InRegs.ax = 3
                        CALL INTERRUPT(&H33, InRegs, OutRegs)
                        YNew% = OutRegs.dx
                        XNew% = OutRegs.cx
                        InRegs.ax = 2    'Hide mouse cursor
                        CALL INTERRUPT(&H33, InRegs, OutRegs)
                        LINE (X%, Y%)-(XOld%, YOld%), Back%, B          ←
                        LINE (X%, Y%)-(XNew%, YNew%), Fore%, B
                        XOld% = XNew%
                        YOld% = YNew%
                        InRegs.ax = 1    'Show mouse cursor
                        CALL INTERRUPT(&H33, InRegs, OutRegs)
                        InRegs.bx = 0              'Left Button Releases
                        InRegs.ax = 6
                        CALL INTERRUPT(&H33, InRegs, OutRegs)
                    LOOP WHILE OutRegs.bx = 0
            RETURN
```

And that's all there is to it.

Subroutine DrawCircle

We can also draw circles in BASIC with the CIRCLE statement:

```
CIRCLE (X%, Y%), Radius!, Color%
```

TIP: You can even use the CIRCLE statement to draw arcs or ellipses in BASIC like this: CIRCLE (x, y), Radius%, Color%, START!, END!, ASPECT!
START! and END! indicate the starting and ending angles, respectively, for an arc (use radians). ASPECT! sets the aspect ratio for an ellipse.

Here we are drawing a circle centered at (X%, Y%), with radius Radius!, and with a color specified by the value in Color%. We can adapt DrawLine here too; we'll make the anchor point the center of the circle, and the mouse cursor location the edge of the circle (i.e., the radius will stretch from (X%, Y%) to (XNew%, YNew%)). We can do that by changing the LINE statements in DrawLine to CIRCLE statements like this:

```
DrawCircle:
            X% = OutRegs.cx
            Y% = OutRegs.dx
            XOld% = X%
            YOld% = Y%

            InRegs.bx = 0              'Get left button releases to clear queue
            InRegs.ax = 6
            CALL INTERRUPT(&H33, InRegs, OutRegs)

            DO
                InRegs.ax = 3
                CALL INTERRUPT(&H33, InRegs, OutRegs)
                YNew% = OutRegs.dx
                XNew% = OutRegs.cx
                InRegs.ax = 2    'Hide mouse cursor
                CALL INTERRUPT(&H33, InRegs, OutRegs)
        →       CIRCLE (X%, Y%), SQR((X% - XOld%) ^ 2 + (Y% - YOld%) ^ 2),_
        →           Back%
                CIRCLE (X%, Y%), SQR((X% - XNew%) ^ 2 + (Y% - YNew%) ^ 2)
                XOld% = XNew%
                YOld% = YNew%
                InRegs.ax = 1    'Show mouse cursor
                CALL INTERRUPT(&H33, InRegs, OutRegs)
                InRegs.bx = 0              'Left Button Releases
                InRegs.ax = 6
                CALL INTERRUPT(&H33, InRegs, OutRegs)
            LOOP WHILE OutRegs.bx = 0
        RETURN
```

And that's all there is to drawing circles.

Subroutine DrawPaint

The last subroutine we'll develop is DrawPaint. This subroutine will let us fill hollow figures with solid color. In this case, we can use the BASIC PAINT statement, like this:

```
PAINT (X%, Y%)
```

This statement fills an area in with the current foreground color. The problem is that this area must also be bounded by the current foreground color or by another color, which we can specify like this:

```
PAINT (X%, Y%), BorderColor%
```

This is a problem for us since our paint program is not sophisticated enough to figure out what the border color of the figure surrounding us at some given point is. Instead, we'll have to settle for painting in the current foreground color, which means that you can only paint figures that were drawn in the current foreground color (or you can set the foreground color to the color of the figure you want to fill in).

With that restriction, we can fill figures with color like this:

```
DrawPaint:
                X% = OutRegs.cx
                Y% = OutRegs.dx
                InRegs.ax = 2    'Hide mouse cursor
                CALL INTERRUPT(&H33, InRegs, OutRegs)
      →         PAINT (X%, Y%)
                InRegs.ax = 1    'Show mouse cursor
                CALL INTERRUPT(&H33, InRegs, OutRegs)
        RETURN
```

The Paint Program Listing

That's it for the paint program. Listing 5-1 shows the whole program, line by line.

Listing 5-1. A Mouse-driven Paint Program. 1 of 5

```
TYPE RegType
        ax      AS INTEGER
        bx      AS INTEGER
        cx      AS INTEGER
        dx      AS INTEGER
        bp      AS INTEGER
        si      AS INTEGER
        di      AS INTEGER
        flags   AS INTEGER
END TYPE

        DIM InRegs AS RegType, OutRegs AS RegType
        DIM Storage(31266) AS INTEGER

        GOSUB Initialize

        DO
            GOSUB GetLeftButtonPress

            IF MenuSelectionMade% THEN
```

Listing 5-1.   A Mouse-driven Paint Program.   2 of 5

```
                GOSUB MenuChoice
        ELSE
            IF DrawFlag% THEN GOSUB DrawPixel
            IF LineFlag% THEN GOSUB DrawLine
            IF BoxFlag% THEN GOSUB DrawBox
            IF CircleFlag% THEN GOSUB DrawCircle
            IF PaintFlag% THEN GOSUB DrawPaint
        END IF

    LOOP WHILE 1

    END

Initialize:
        SCREEN 8
        LOCATE 1, 1
        Fore% = 1
        Back% = 2
        COLOR Fore%, Back%
        PRINT "Exit    Color   Bkgrnd  Draw    Line     " + _
        "Box     Circle  Paint   Save     Load";

        InRegs.ax = 0    'Initialize mouse
        CALL INTERRUPT(&H33, InRegs, OutRegs)

        InRegs.ax = 1    'Show mouse cursor
        CALL INTERRUPT(&H33, InRegs, OutRegs)
        DrawFlag% = 0
        LineFlag% = 0
        BoxFlag% = 0
        CircleFlag% = 0
        PaintFlag% = 0
        RETURN

GetLeftButtonPress:

        DO
            InRegs.bx = 0            'Wait for left button press
            InRegs.ax = 5
            CALL INTERRUPT(&H33, InRegs, OutRegs)
        LOOP WHILE OutRegs.bx = 0
        Row% = OutRegs.dx \ 8  + 1
        IF Row% = 1 THEN
            MenuSelectionMade% = 1
        ELSE
            MenuSelectionMade% = 0
        END IF
        RETURN

MenuChoice:
        DrawFlag% = 0
        LineFlag% = 0
        BoxFlag% = 0
        CircleFlag% = 0
        PaintFlag% = 0
        Choice% = OutRegs.cx \ 64 4 + 1
```

Listing 5-1.   A Mouse-driven Paint Program.   3 of 5

```
            SELECT CASE Choice%
                CASE 1
                        END
                CASE 2
                        Fore% = Fore% + 1
                        IF Fore% > 15 THEN Fore% = 0
                        COLOR Fore%, Back%
                        InRegs.ax = 2    'Hide mouse cursor
                        CALL INTERRUPT(&H33, InRegs, OutRegs)
                        LOCATE 1, 9
                        PRINT "Color   ";
                        InRegs.ax = 1    'Show mouse cursor
                        CALL INTERRUPT(&H33, InRegs, OutRegs)
                CASE 3
                        Back% = Back% + 1
                        IF Back% > 7 THEN Back% = 0
                        COLOR Fore%, Back%
                CASE 4
                        DrawFlag% = 1
                CASE 5
                        LineFlag% = 1
                CASE 6
                        BoxFlag% = 1
                CASE 7
                        CircleFlag% = 1
                CASE 8
                        PaintFlag% = 1
                CASE 9
                        InRegs.ax = 2    'Hide mouse cursor
                        CALL INTERRUPT(&H33, InRegs, OutRegs)
                        GET (0, 8)-(639, 199), Storage
                        DEF SEG = VARSEG(Storage(1))
                        BSAVE "PAINT.DAT", VARPTR(Storage(1)), 62532
                        DEF SEG
                        InRegs.ax = 1    'Show mouse cursor
                        CALL INTERRUPT(&H33, InRegs, OutRegs)
                CASE 10
                        InRegs.ax = 2    'Hide mouse cursor
                        CALL INTERRUPT(&H33, InRegs, OutRegs)
                        DEF SEG = VARSEG(Storage(1))
                        BLOAD "PAINT.DAT", VARPTR(Storage(1))
                        DEF SEG
                        PUT (0, 8), Storage, PSET
                        InRegs.ax = 1    'Show mouse cursor
                        CALL INTERRUPT(&H33, InRegs, OutRegs)
            END SELECT
        RETURN

DrawPixel:
            InRegs.bx = 0               'Get left button releases to clear queue
            InRegs.ax = 6
            CALL INTERRUPT(&H33, InRegs, OutRegs)

            DO
                InRegs.ax = 3
                CALL INTERRUPT(&H33, InRegs, OutRegs)
```

Listing 5-1. A Mouse-driven Paint Program.   4 of 5

```
                    X% = OutRegs.cx
                    Y% = OutRegs.dx
                    InRegs.ax = 2    'Hide mouse cursor
                    CALL INTERRUPT(&H33, InRegs, OutRegs)
                    PSET (X%, Y%)
                    InRegs.ax = 1    'Show mouse cursor
                    CALL INTERRUPT(&H33, InRegs, OutRegs)
                    InRegs.bx = 0             'Left Button Releases
                    InRegs.ax = 6
                    CALL INTERRUPT(&H33, InRegs, OutRegs)
                LOOP WHILE OutRegs.bx = 0

        RETURN

DrawLine:
                X% = OutRegs.cx
                Y% = OutRegs.dx
                XOld% = X%
                YOld% = Y%

                InRegs.bx = 0             'Get left button releases to clear queue
                InRegs.ax = 6
                CALL INTERRUPT(&H33, InRegs, OutRegs)

                DO
                    InRegs.ax = 3
                    CALL INTERRUPT(&H33, InRegs, OutRegs)
                    YNew% = OutRegs.dx
                    XNew% = OutRegs.cx
                    InRegs.ax = 2    'Hide mouse cursor
                    CALL INTERRUPT(&H33, InRegs, OutRegs)
                    LINE (X%, Y%)-(XOld%, YOld%), Back%
                    LINE (X%, Y%)-(XNew%, YNew%), Fore%
                    XOld% = XNew%
                    YOld% = YNew%
                    InRegs.ax = 1    'Show mouse cursor
                    CALL INTERRUPT(&H33, InRegs, OutRegs)
                    InRegs.bx = 0             'Left Button Releases
                    InRegs.ax = 6
                    CALL INTERRUPT(&H33, InRegs, OutRegs)
                LOOP WHILE OutRegs.bx = 0
        RETURN

DrawBox:
                X% = OutRegs.cx
                Y% = OutRegs.dx
                XOld% = X%
                YOld% = Y%

                InRegs.bx = 0             'Get left button releases to clear queue
                InRegs.ax = 6
                CALL INTERRUPT(&H33, InRegs, OutRegs)

                DO
                    InRegs.ax = 3
                    CALL INTERRUPT(&H33, InRegs, OutRegs)
```

Listing 5-1. A Mouse-driven Paint Program. 5 of 5

```
                    YNew% = OutRegs.dx
                    XNew% = OutRegs.cx
                    InRegs.ax = 2    'Hide mouse cursor
                    CALL INTERRUPT(&H33, InRegs, OutRegs)
                    LINE (X%, Y%)-(XOld%, YOld%), Back%, B
                    LINE (X%, Y%)-(XNew%, YNew%), Fore%, B
                    XOld% = XNew%
                    YOld% = YNew%
                    InRegs.ax = 1    'Show mouse cursor
                    CALL INTERRUPT(&H33, InRegs, OutRegs)
                    InRegs.bx = 0            'Left Button Releases
                    InRegs.ax = 6
                    CALL INTERRUPT(&H33, InRegs, OutRegs)
                LOOP WHILE OutRegs.bx = 0
        RETURN

DrawCircle:
            X% = OutRegs.cx
            Y% = OutRegs.dx
            XOld% = X%
            YOld% = Y%

            InRegs.bx = 0            'Get left button releases to clear queue
            InRegs.ax = 6
            CALL INTERRUPT(&H33, InRegs, OutRegs)

            DO
                InRegs.ax = 3
                CALL INTERRUPT(&H33, InRegs, OutRegs)
                YNew% = OutRegs.dx
                XNew% = OutRegs.cx
                InRegs.ax = 2    'Hide mouse cursor
                CALL INTERRUPT(&H33, InRegs, OutRegs)
                CIRCLE (X%, Y%), SQR((X% - XOld%) ^ 2 + (Y% - YOld%) ^ 2),_
                    Back%
                CIRCLE (X%, Y%), SQR((X% - XNew%) ^ 2 + (Y% - YNew%) ^ 2)
                XOld% = XNew%
                YOld% = YNew%
                InRegs.ax = 1    'Show mouse cursor
                CALL INTERRUPT(&H33, InRegs, OutRegs)
                InRegs.bx = 0            'Left Button Releases
                InRegs.ax = 6
                CALL INTERRUPT(&H33, InRegs, OutRegs)
            LOOP WHILE OutRegs.bx = 0
        RETURN

DrawPaint:
            X% = OutRegs.cx
            Y% = OutRegs.dx
            InRegs.ax = 2    'Hide mouse cursor
            CALL INTERRUPT(&H33, InRegs, OutRegs)
            PAINT (X%, Y%)
            InRegs.ax = 1    'Show mouse cursor
            CALL INTERRUPT(&H33, InRegs, OutRegs)
        RETURN
```

Give it a try; it works well, and creating your own figures on the screen can be a lot of fun. Now, however, we're going to press on with our exploration of graphics, but before getting into sprites and animation, there's a popular way of drawing on the screen that we should look at: the DRAW statement.

Drawing a Clock

You can use DRAW to produce "vector" graphics — that is, line graphics — on the screen. DRAW takes a *string* as its argument. For example, this statement draws a hexagon on the screen:

```
DRAW "BU50 NL25 F12 D20 G12 L50 H12 U20 E12 R25 BD22"
```

TIP: The DRAW instruction is BASIC's most compact way to produce graphics.

Each letter is a directive to DRAW, and each number is a length in pixels. Here's what the letters mean:

U	Up
D	Down
L	Left
R	Right
E	Up and right
F	Down and right
G	Down and left
H	Up and left
B	Pen up (don't draw)
N	Pen down (draw)

This table allows us to decipher our DRAW statement. When we first use DRAW, its "pen" is at the center of the screen. Here, we pick up the pen (so we don't draw on the screen) and move up 50 pixels, then put the pen down and move to the left 25 pixels:

```
DRAW "BU50 NL25..."
```

Next, we move diagonally down and to the right by 12 pixels, and then straight down by 20:

```
DRAW "BU50 NL25 F12 D20..."
```

Then we move diagonally left and down by 12, to the left 20 units, and so on, until our hexagon is finished:

```
DRAW "BU50 NL25 F12 D20 G12 L50 H12 U20 E12 R25 BD22"
```

As it turns out, you can draw at angles other than just 0, 45, and 90 degrees. You can use the "TA=" (Tilt Angle) argument to *rotate* the drawing actions that follow. For example, this draws a line of 50 pixels straight up; that is, at 90 degrees:

```
DRAW "NU50"
```

However, we might want to draw this line at 95 degrees instead. To do that, we tilt our axes by 5 degrees counterclockwise:

```
ANG = 5
DRAW "TA="+VARPTR$(ANG)+" NU50"
```

This strange form, where we pass a string pointer to a variable holding the tilt angle, is required when you want to use the TA= argument. In this case, we tilt the vertical 5 degrees counterclockwise, so a line that was formerly straight up is now at 95 degrees. A negative angle would have tilted the axes clockwise. Keep in mind that the tilt remains in effect until you change it.

Let's put this to work by drawing a clock that displays the current time. We start by drawing our hexagon and then moving the pen back to it center:

```
SCREEN 8
DRAW "BU50 NL25 F12 D20 G12 L50 H12 U20 E12 R25 BD22"
:
```

Now we calculate the angle from vertical of both the minute and hour hands using the BASIC TIMER function (notice that we make the angles negative, since we want to treat them as clockwise angles):

```
      SCREEN 8
      DRAW "BU50 NL25 F12 D20 G12 L50 H12 U20 E12 R25 BD22"
      TimeMark! = TIMER
      Hours! = INT(TimeMark! / 3600)
      Remainder! = TimeMark! - 3600 * Hours!
      IF Hours! > 12 THEN Hours! = Hours! - 12
 →    HourAngle! = -Hours! / 12 * 360
      Minutes! = INT(Remainder! / 60)
      MinuteAngle! = -Minutes! / 60 * 360
      :
```

Finally, we can just draw the hour and minute hands like this:

```
      SCREEN 8
      DRAW "BU50 NL25 F12 D20 G12 L50 H12 U20 E12 R25 BD22"
      TimeMark! = TIMER
      Hours! = INT(TimeMark! / 3600)
      Remainder! = TimeMark! - 3600 * Hours!
      IF Hours! > 12 THEN Hours! = Hours! - 12
      HourAngle! = -Hours! / 12 * 360
      Minutes! = INT(Remainder! / 60)
      MinuteAngle! = -Minutes! / 60 * 360
 →    DRAW "TA=" + VARPTR$(HourAngle!) + " NU8"
      DRAW "TA=" + VARPTR$(MinuteAngle!) + " NU12"
```

If you prefer, you can revise this program so that it keeps updating the figure on the screen. As it stands, it only draws the clock once, reflecting the current time.

Now that we've gained some familiarity with the DRAW statement, let's move on to screen sprites and animation.

Sprites and Animation

A screen sprite is a small graphics image that you can put on the screen any place you like; for instance, in our example program, we design a small rocket ship, complete with fire coming out of the tail. After this image is designed and stored, you can place it anywhere you want on the screen, and we'll animate the image, sending it blasting up the screen.

Just as we did with our paint program, we can cut the task of designing and using screen sprites up into subroutines, which we call from the main body of the program.

Let's call this program SPRITE.BAS.

We begin by designing the sprite itself. To make that process easier, we can use an array of type STRING, and, since color values can range from 0 to 15, we use the appropriate hex digit to design the sprite pixel by pixel. For example, here's how we start SPRITE.BAS with the design of the rocket ship:

```
DIM SpriteArray(1 TO 16) AS STRING

        SpriteArray(1)  =  "0000000010000000"
        SpriteArray(2)  =  "0000000010000000"
        SpriteArray(3)  =  "0000000111000000"
        SpriteArray(4)  =  "0000001131100000"
        SpriteArray(5)  =  "0000001131100000"
        SpriteArray(6)  =  "0000011333110000"
        SpriteArray(7)  =  "0000011333110000"
        SpriteArray(8)  =  "0010011333110010"
        SpriteArray(9)  =  "0011001131100110"
        SpriteArray(10) =  "0011101131101110"
        SpriteArray(11) =  "0011111131111110"
        SpriteArray(12) =  "0011100131001110"
        SpriteArray(13) =  "0011001111100110"
        SpriteArray(14) =  "0010000222000010"
        SpriteArray(15) =  "0000000222000000"
        SpriteArray(16) =  "0000000020000000"
               :
```

NOTE: By restricting ourselves to color values ranging from 0 to 15 (that is, 0 to &HF), we are excluding the advanced VGA mode, which can take color values from 0 to &HFF.

Now we can place the screen into a graphics mode and use a subroutine to draw this sprite on the screen, converting string after string into pixels on the screen:

```
DIM SpriteArray(1 TO 16) AS STRING

        SpriteArray(1)  =  "0000000010000000"
        SpriteArray(2)  =  "0000000010000000"
        SpriteArray(3)  =  "0000000111000000"
        SpriteArray(4)  =  "0000001131100000"
        SpriteArray(5)  =  "0000001131100000"
        SpriteArray(6)  =  "0000011333110000"
        SpriteArray(7)  =  "0000011333110000"
        SpriteArray(8)  =  "0010011333110010"
        SpriteArray(9)  =  "0011001131100110"
        SpriteArray(10) =  "0011101131101110"
        SpriteArray(11) =  "0011111131111110"
        SpriteArray(12) =  "0011100131001110"
```

```
        SpriteArray(13) = "0011001111100110"
        SpriteArray(14) = "0010000222000010"
        SpriteArray(15) = "0000000222000000"
        SpriteArray(16) = "0000000020000000"

→       ScreenMode% = 1
        GOSUB DrawSprite
        :
```

Now that we've placed the sprite on the screen, we can store it in an array with a subroutine named GetSprite. To do that, we have to dimension an array to hold the sprite data, which we can call GetArray( ). Since we might want to change our sprite size as we design it, let's make this a *dynamic* array, which means that we'll be able to adjust it to the size we need with a REDIM statement in GetSprite:

```
' $DYNAMIC        ←

DIM SpriteArray(1 TO 16) AS STRING
DIM GetArray(1) AS INTEGER        ←

        SpriteArray(1)  = "0000000010000000"
        SpriteArray(2)  = "0000000010000000"
        SpriteArray(3)  = "0000000111000000"
        SpriteArray(4)  = "0000001131100000"
        SpriteArray(5)  = "0000001131100000"
        SpriteArray(6)  = "0000011333110000"
        SpriteArray(7)  = "0000011333110000"
        SpriteArray(8)  = "0010011333110010"
        SpriteArray(9)  = "0011001131100110"
        SpriteArray(10) = "0011101131101110"
        SpriteArray(11) = "0011111131111110"
        SpriteArray(12) = "0011100131001110"
        SpriteArray(13) = "0011001111100110"
        SpriteArray(14) = "0010000222000010"
        SpriteArray(15) = "0000000222000000"
        SpriteArray(16) = "0000000020000000"

        ScreenMode% = 1
        GOSUB DrawSprite

        GOSUB GetSprite          ←
        :
```

TIP: Redimensioning dynamic arrays with REDIM is a new and powerful capability in BASIC. You use REDIM primarily when memory space is at a premium — you can shrink or expand the sizes of your arrays to fit what's available. The BASIC Professional Development System goes even farther wtih its SET-MEM( ) function, giving you still more control over memory.

As in our paint program, we may want to store the sprite to disk and then retrieve it, so let's add two subroutines named SaveSprite and LoadSprite which will do that:

```
' $DYNAMIC

DIM SpriteArray(1 TO 16) AS STRING
DIM GetArray(1) AS INTEGER

        SpriteArray(1)  =  "0000000010000000"
        SpriteArray(2)  =  "0000000010000000"
        SpriteArray(3)  =  "0000000111000000"
        SpriteArray(4)  =  "0000001131100000"
        SpriteArray(5)  =  "0000001131100000"
        SpriteArray(6)  =  "0000011333110000"
        SpriteArray(7)  =  "0000011333110000"
        SpriteArray(8)  =  "0010011333110010"
        SpriteArray(9)  =  "0011001131100110"
        SpriteArray(10) =  "0011101131101110"
        SpriteArray(11) =  "0011111131111110"
        SpriteArray(12) =  "0011100131001110"
        SpriteArray(13) =  "0011001111100110"
        SpriteArray(14) =  "0010000222000010"
        SpriteArray(15) =  "0000000222000000"
        SpriteArray(16) =  "0000000020000000"

        ScreenMode% = 1
        GOSUB DrawSprite

        GOSUB GetSprite

        GOSUB SaveSprite

        GOSUB LoadSprite
        :
```

To make sure the sprite made it back from the disk intact, we can display it on the screen with the BASIC PUT statement, like this, which puts the sprite at location (50, 50):

```
' $DYNAMIC

DIM SpriteArray(1 TO 16) AS STRING
DIM GetArray(1) AS INTEGER

        SpriteArray(1)  =  "0000000010000000"
        SpriteArray(2)  =  "0000000010000000"
        SpriteArray(3)  =  "0000000111000000"
        SpriteArray(4)  =  "0000001131100000"
        SpriteArray(5)  =  "0000001131100000"
        SpriteArray(6)  =  "0000011333110000"
        SpriteArray(7)  =  "0000011333110000"
        SpriteArray(8)  =  "0010011333110010"
        SpriteArray(9)  =  "0011001131100110"
```

```
        SpriteArray(10) = "0011101131101110"
        SpriteArray(11) = "0011111131111110"
        SpriteArray(12) = "0011100131001110"
        SpriteArray(13) = "0011001111100110"
        SpriteArray(14) = "0010000222000010"
        SpriteArray(15) = "0000000222000000"
        SpriteArray(16) = "0000000020000000"

        ScreenMode% = 1
        GOSUB DrawSprite

        GOSUB GetSprite

        GOSUB SaveSprite

        GOSUB LoadSprite

   →    PUT (50, 50), GetArray
        :
```

Now we're ready for some animation. We can put together a loop, putting the sprite on the screen, erasing it, then moving it up a little and repeating the action so that it appears to be flying upwards. As mentioned earlier, PUT's default method is to XOR the bits in a screen image with what's already there. That means that when we PUT the same image in the same place for a second time, it disappears (any number XOR'd with itself is 0). Then we're free to draw the spaceship a little higher up the screen, erase it, and so on. At the very end, we have to draw the rocket ship one last time (since every previous image of it was erased). Listing 5-2 shows how the animation loop looks.

Listing 5-2. Sprite. BAS—Draw and Animate Screen Sprites.   1 of 2

```
' $DYNAMIC

DIM SpriteArray(1 TO 16) AS STRING
DIM GetArray(1) AS INTEGER

        SpriteArray(1)  =  "0000000010000000"
        SpriteArray(2)  =  "0000000010000000"
        SpriteArray(3)  =  "0000000111000000"
        SpriteArray(4)  =  "0000001131100000"
        SpriteArray(5)  =  "0000001131100000"
        SpriteArray(6)  =  "0000011333110000"
        SpriteArray(7)  =  "0000011333110000"
        SpriteArray(8)  =  "0010011333110010"
        SpriteArray(9)  =  "0011001131100110"
        SpriteArray(10) =  "0011101131101110"
        SpriteArray(11) =  "0011111131111110"
        SpriteArray(12) =  "0011100131001110"
        SpriteArray(13) =  "0011001111100110"
        SpriteArray(14) =  "0010000222000010"
        SpriteArray(15) =  "0000000222000000"
```

Listing 5-2. **Sprite. BAS—Draw and Animate Screen Sprites.** **2 of 2**

```
         SpriteArray(16) = "0000000020000000"

         ScreenMode% = 1
         GOSUB DrawSprite

         GOSUB GetSprite

         GOSUB SaveSprite
         GOSUB LoadSprite

         PUT (50, 50), GetArray

   →     FOR i = 1 TO 100
             PUT (100, 100 - i), GetArray
             PUT (100, 100 - i), GetArray
         NEXT i

         PUT (100, 0), GetArray

         END
```

And that's it, we've completed SPRITE.BAS, including animation. All that remains is to write the subroutines. Let's turn to those next.

Subroutine DrawSprite

We're supposed to decode the sprite as defined in the STRING array SpriteArray( ) in this subroutine. We can start by placing the screen into the graphics mode we've defined, ScreenMode%, and picking a location to display the sprite on the screen. Let's choose (10, 10):

```
DrawSprite:
         SCREEN ScreenMode%
         XStart = 10
         YStart = 10
         :
```

Then we decipher the strings in the array SpriteArray( ) and use the BASIC PSET statement to turn pixels on. We decode each pixel's color value by looping over each string in the array — and looping over each character in the string — to place the color value of the current pixel into the variable CurrentColor%:

```
DrawSprite:
        SCREEN ScreenMode%
        XStart = 10
        YStart = 10
        FOR i = 1 TO UBOUND(A, 1)
                FOR j = 1 TO LEN(SpriteArray(i))
    →                   CurrentColor% = ASC(UCASE$(MID$(SpriteArray(i), j, 1)))
                            :
                            :
                NEXT j
        NEXT i
        :
        :
```

Now that we have the character (a hex digit) in CurrentColor%, we have to decode it into a color value from 0 to 15. We do that this way, then use PSET( ) to turn the appropriate pixel on:

```
DrawSprite:
        SCREEN ScreenMode%
        XStart = 10
        YStart = 10
        FOR i = 1 TO UBOUND(A, 1)
                FOR j = 1 TO LEN(SpriteArray(i))
                        CurrentColor% = ASC(UCASE$(MID$(SpriteArray(i), j, 1)))
    →                   IF CurrentColor% <= ASC("9") THEN
                                CurrentColor% = CurrentColor% - ASC("0")
                        ELSE
                                CurrentColor% = CurrentColor% - ASC("A") + 10
                        END IF
                        PSET (XStart + j - 1, YStart + i - 1), CurrentColor%
                NEXT j
        NEXT i
        :
        :
```

At this point, the sprite is on the screen, and we're done. Listing 5-3 shows the whole subroutine.

Listing 5-3.   DrawSprite Subroutine.   1 of 2

```
DrawSprite:
        SCREEN ScreenMode%
        XStart = 10
        YStart = 10
        FOR i = 1 TO UBOUND(A, 1)
                FOR j = 1 TO LEN(SpriteArray(i))
                        CurrentColor% = ASC(UCASE$(MID$(SpriteArray(i), j, 1)))
                        IF CurrentColor% <= ASC("9") THEN
                                CurrentColor% = CurrentColor% - ASC("0")
```

Listing 5-3. DrawSprite Subroutine. 2 of 2

```
                       ELSE
                                  CurrentColor% = CurrentColor% - ASC("A") + 10
                       END IF
                       PSET (XStart + j - 1, YStart + i - 1), CurrentColor%
            NEXT j
      NEXT i
RETURN
```

The next job is loading the sprite into an array where we can work with it.

Subroutine GetSprite

This subroutine is supposed to read the sprite from the screen and store it in the array GetArray( ). There are, it turns out, standard formulas to determine the memory storage needed for a sprite of a given size, depending on screen mode. All we need is the dimension of the sprite in pixels, which we can get from the dimensions of the array SpriteArray( ), and the screen mode, which is already in the variable ScreenMode%. We determine the number of 16-bit words needed to store the sprite and place that value in SpriteSize, like this:

```
GetSprite:

      Cols = LEN(SpriteArray(1))
      Rows = UBOUND (SpriteArray, 1)

      SELECT CASE ScreenMode%
            CASE 1
                  SpriteSize = (4+INT(((Rows+1)*2+7)/8)*1*(Cols+1) + 1) \ 2:
            CASE 2, 11
                  SpriteSize = (4+INT(((Rows+1)*1+7)/8)*1*(Cols+1) + 1) \ 2:
            CASE 7, 8, 9, 12
                  SpriteSize = (4+INT(((Rows+1)*1+7)/8)*4*(Cols+1) + 1) \ 2:
            CASE 10
                  SpriteSize = (4+INT(((Rows+1)*1+7)/8)*2*(Cols+1) + 1) \ 2:
            CASE 13
                  SpriteSize = (4+INT(((Rows+1)*8+7)/8)*1*(Cols+1) + 1) \ 2:
            CASE ELSE
                  SpriteSize = 0
      END SELECT
            :
```

Now we've got to redimension GetArray( ) to match since we know how many 16-bit words — that is, INTEGERs — we'll need, we can use REDIM to redimension GetArray( ) on the fly (note that we have to use the directive ' $DYNAMIC at the beginning of SPRITE.BAS to make the arrays dynamic):

```
GetSprite:

        Cols = LEN(SpriteArray(1))
        Rows = UBOUND (SpriteArray, 1)

        SELECT CASE ScreenMode%
            CASE 1
                SpriteSize = (4+INT(((Rows+1)*2+7)/8)*1*(Cols+1) + 1) \ 2:
            CASE 2, 11
                SpriteSize = (4+INT(((Rows+1)*1+7)/8)*1*(Cols+1) + 1) \ 2:
            CASE 7, 8, 9, 12
                SpriteSize = (4+INT(((Rows+1)*1+7)/8)*4*(Cols+1) + 1) \ 2:
            CASE 10
                SpriteSize = (4+INT(((Rows+1)*1+7)/8)*2*(Cols+1) + 1) \ 2:
            CASE 13
                SpriteSize = (4+INT(((Rows+1)*8+7)/8)*1*(Cols+1) + 1) \ 2:
            CASE ELSE
                SpriteSize = 0
        END SELECT
   →    REDIM GetArray(1 TO SpriteSize) AS INTEGER
        :
```

Now we just have use GET to store the sprite, and we're done. Listing 5-4 shows the completed subroutine.

Listing 5-4. GetSprite Subroutine

```
GetSprite:

        Cols = LEN(SpriteArray(1))
        Rows = UBOUND (SpriteArray, 1)

        SELECT CASE ScreenMode%
            CASE 1
                SpriteSize = (4+INT(((Rows+1)*2+7)/8)*1*(Cols+1) + 1) \ 2:
            CASE 2, 11
                SpriteSize = (4+INT(((Rows+1)*1+7)/8)*1*(Cols+1) + 1) \ 2:
            CASE 7, 8, 9, 12
                SpriteSize = (4+INT(((Rows+1)*1+7)/8)*4*(Cols+1) + 1) \ 2:
            CASE 10
                SpriteSize = (4+INT(((Rows+1)*1+7)/8)*2*(Cols+1) + 1) \ 2:
            CASE 13
                SpriteSize = (4+INT(((Rows+1)*8+7)/8)*1*(Cols+1) + 1) \ 2:
            CASE ELSE
                SpriteSize = 0
        END SELECT
        REDIM GetArray(1 TO SpriteSize) AS INTEGER
   →    GET (10, 10)-(10 + Rows, 10 + Cols), GetArray
        RETURN
```

That's it. We've stored the sprite in GetArray( ). The next two subroutines let us store the sprite on disk, and load it back into memory.

Subroutine SaveSprite

We'll just use BSAVE to save the sprite to disk, as shown is Listing 5-5.

Listing 5-5.   SavesSprite( ) Subroutine.

```
SaveSprite:
        DEF SEG = VARSEG(GetArray(1))
  →     BSAVE "SPRITE.DAT", VARPTR(GetArray(1)), 2 * UBOUND(GetArray, 1)
        DEF SEG
        RETURN
```

And that's all there is to it: we have created a file named SPRITE.DAT and saved the sprite in it. Now we have to read it from the disk again.

Subroutine LoadSprite

This final sprite subroutine just loads the sprite back into GetArray( ) with BLOAD, much as we've already seen in our paint program. That process works as shown in Listing 5-6.

Listing 5-6.   LoadSprite Subroutine.

```
LoadSprite:

        DEF SEG = VARSEG(GetArray(1))
  →     BLOAD "SPRITE.DAT", VARPTR(GetArray(1))
        DEF SEG
        RETURN
```

That's all there is to it.

The SPRITE.BAS Listing

Listing 5-7 shows the whole program SPRITE.BAS, including the animation loop at the end of the main body of the program:

Listing 5-7.   SPRITE.BAS—Draw and Animate Screen Sprite.   1 of 2

```
' $DYNAMIC

DIM SpriteArray(1 TO 16) AS STRING
DIM GetArray(1) AS INTEGER

        SpriteArray(1)  =  "0000000010000000"
        SpriteArray(2)  =  "0000000010000000"
        SpriteArray(3)  =  "0000000111000000"
        SpriteArray(4)  =  "0000001131100000"
        SpriteArray(5)  =  "0000001131100000"
        SpriteArray(6)  =  "0000011333110000"
        SpriteArray(7)  =  "0000011333110000"
        SpriteArray(8)  =  "0010011333110010"
        SpriteArray(9)  =  "0011001131100110"
        SpriteArray(10) =  "0011101131101110"
        SpriteArray(11) =  "0011111131111110"
        SpriteArray(12) =  "0011100131001110"
        SpriteArray(13) =  "0011001111100110"
        SpriteArray(14) =  "0010000222000010"
        SpriteArray(15) =  "0000000222000000"
        SpriteArray(16) =  "0000000020000000"


        ScreenMode% = 1
        GOSUB DrawSprite

        GOSUB GetSprite

        GOSUB SaveSprite

        GOSUB LoadSprite

        PUT (50, 50), GetArray

        FOR i = 1 TO 100
            PUT (100, 100 - i), GetArray
            PUT (100, 100 - i), GetArray
        NEXT i

        PUT (100, 0), GetArray

        END

DrawSprite:
        SCREEN ScreenMode%
        XStart = 10
        YStart = 10
        FOR i = 1 TO UBOUND(SpriteArray, 1)
                FOR j = 1 TO LEN(SpriteArray(i))
                        CurrentColor% = ASC(UCASE$(MID$(SpriteArray(i), j, 1)))
                        IF CurrentColor% <= ASC("9") THEN
                                CurrentColor% = CurrentColor% - ASC("0")
                        ELSE
                                CurrentColor% = CurrentColor% - ASC("A") + 10
                        END IF
                        PSET (XStart + j - 1, YStart + i - 1), CurrentColor%
                NEXT j
```

Listing 5-7. SPRITE.BAS—Draw and Animate Screen Sprite.   2 of 2

```
        NEXT i
        RETURN

GetSprite:
        Cols = LEN(SpriteArray(1))
        Rows = UBOUND (SpriteArray, 1)

        SELECT CASE ScreenMode%
            CASE 1
                SpriteSize = (4+INT(((Rows+1)*2+7)/8)*1*(Cols+1) + 1) \ 2:
            CASE 2, 11
                SpriteSize = (4+INT(((Rows+1)*1+7)/8)*1*(Cols+1) + 1) \ 2:
            CASE 7, 8, 9, 12
                SpriteSize = (4+INT(((Rows+1)*1+7)/8)*4*(Cols+1) + 1) \ 2:
            CASE 10
                SpriteSize = (4+INT(((Rows+1)*1+7)/8)*2*(Cols+1) + 1) \ 2:
            CASE 13
                SpriteSize = (4+INT(((Rows+1)*8+7)/8)*1*(Cols+1) + 1) \ 2:
            CASE ELSE
                SpriteSize = 0
        END SELECT
        REDIM GetArray(1 TO SpriteSize) AS INTEGER
        GET (10, 10)-(10 + Rows, 10 + Cols), GetArray
        RETURN

SaveSprite:
        DEF SEG = VARSEG(GetArray(1))
        BSAVE "SPRITE.DAT", VARPTR(GetArray(1)), 2 * UBOUND(GetArray, 1)
        DEF SEG
        RETURN

LoadSprite:

        DEF SEG = VARSEG(GetArray(1))
        BLOAD "SPRITE.DAT", VARPTR(GetArray(1))
        DEF SEG
        RETURN
```

In this program, we first design and draw the sprite, then we load it into GetArray( ). Using SaveSprite, we're able to save it on disk, and LoadSprite loads it back in again. Finally, we've seen how to animate the rocketship by looping over PUT( ) statements. Give this program a try — it draws a credible rocket ship zooming up the screen. Now, however, we're ready to press on, and we can turn to the Presentation Graphics resources offered in the BASIC PDS.

Presentation Graphics in the BASIC PDS

If you have the BASIC PDS, there's another type of graphics you should be aware of, especially if you do any business programming, called Presentation Graphics. This package of routines can present data in a variety of chart formats. For example, let's say that we wanted to track peanut butter consumption by region, where these were our figures:

Region	Peanut Butter Consumption (tons)
North	219
East	19
South	119
West	319

Using the PDS Presentation Graphics packages, we could display our data in a pie chart, a bar chart, or a line chart — and we'll take a look at all three here.

Pie Charts

To start, we should note that if you're using QuickBasic, QBX.EXE, you'll need to load the special Presentation Graphics Quick library named CHRTBEFR.QLB like this (for a program name PIE.BAS):

```
QBX PIE /L CHRTBEFR
```

On the other hand, if you're using BC.EXE (version 7.0 or later), you would link to the library CHRTBEFR.LIB like this:

```
LINK PIE,,,CHRTBEFR;
```

Now let's develop our pie chart program, PIE.BAS. We have to include two .BI files that come with the PDS first:

```
' $INCLUDE: 'C:\BC7\FONTB.BI'
' $INCLUDE: 'C:\BC7\CHRTB.BI'
         :
```

Next, we'll need to load the name of each of our four regions into an array (which we'll name Regions( )), the peanut butter consumption in each region into another array (named Consumption( )), and create one last array named Exploded( ).

```
'  $INCLUDE: 'C:\BC7\FONTB.BI'
'  $INCLUDE: 'C:\BC7\CHRTB.BI'

        DIM Regions(4) AS STRING
        DIM Consumption(4) AS SINGLE
        DIM Exploded(4) AS INTEGER
            :
```

This final array is only necessary for pie charts. If the value in Exploded( ) corresponding to a particular section of the pie is nonzero, that section is treated as "exploded," meaning that it is drawn as though it were being separated from the rest of the pie. We'll leave the values in Exploded( ) at 0, meaning that none of our pie slices will be exploded from the rest of the pie. Let's fill the other arrays now:

```
'  $INCLUDE: 'C:\BC7\FONTB.BI'
'  $INCLUDE: 'C:\BC7\CHRTB.BI'

        DIM Regions(4) AS STRING
        DIM Consumption(4) AS SINGLE
        DIM Exploded(4) AS INTEGER

        Regions(1) = "North"
        Regions(2) = "East"
        Regions(3) = "South"
        Regions(4) = "West"

        Consumption(1) = 219
        Consumption(2) = 19
        Consumption(3) = 119
        Consumption(4) = 319
        :
        :
```

Now we have to select a graphics mode, but we can't just use SCREEN( ). Instead, we have to use the new PDS statement ChartScreen( ).

The argument we pass to ChartScreen( ) has to be a valid BASIC screen mode; in this case, let's use (VGA-only) mode 12:

```
'  $INCLUDE: 'C:\BC7\FONTB.BI'
'  $INCLUDE: 'C:\BC7\CHRTB.BI'

        DIM Regions(4) AS STRING
        DIM Consumption(4) AS SINGLE
        DIM Exploded(4) AS INTEGER

        Regions(1) = "North"
        Regions(2) = "East"
```

```
    Regions(3) = "South"
    Regions(4) = "West"

    Consumption(1) = 219
    Consumption(2) = 19
    Consumption(3) = 119
    Consumption(4) = 319

    CALL ChartScreen(12)    ←
    :
    :
```

Now we're ready to specify what type of graph we want. We do that by setting up a variable of type ChartEnvironment, which is defined like this in CHRTB.BI:

```
TYPE ChartEnvironment
    ChartType    AS INTEGER      ' 1=Bar, 2=Column, 3=Line, 4=Scatter, 5=Pie
    ChartStyle   AS INTEGER      ' Depends on type
    DataFont     AS INTEGER      ' Font to use for plot characters
    ChartWindow  AS RegionType   ' Overall chart window
    DataWindow   AS RegionType   ' Data portion of chart
    MainTitle    AS TitleType    ' Main title options
    SubTitle     AS TitleType    ' Second line title options
    XAxis        AS AxisType     ' X-axis options
    YAxis        AS AxisType     ' Y-axis options
    Legend       AS LegendType   ' Legend options
END TYPE
```

We have to pass a variable of this type to the PDS graphing tools, and setting the fields in this data structure allows us to specify the titles we want in our chart. Let's call our ChartEnvironment variable OurChart:

```
' $INCLUDE: 'C:\BC7\FONTB.BI'
' $INCLUDE: 'C:\BC7\CHRTB.BI'

        DIM OurChart AS ChartEnvironment     ←
        DIM Regions(4) AS STRING
        DIM Consumption(4) AS SINGLE
        DIM Exploded(4) AS INTEGER

        Regions(1) = "North"
        Regions(2) = "East"
        Regions(3) = "South"
        Regions(4) = "West"

        Consumption(1) = 219
        Consumption(2) = 19
        Consumption(3) = 119
        Consumption(4) = 319
```

```
      CALL ChartScreen(12)
      :
      :
```

Now we have to indicate the *type* and *style* of chart we want. We can use one of these (predefined) constants to indicate the type of chart we want — cBar, cColumn, cLine, cScatter, or cPie. We'll choose cPie to ask for a pie chart. We also have to select the style of the chart from these options for each type:

Type	Style
Bar	cPlain or cStacked
Column	cPlain or cStacked
Line	cLines or cNoLines
Scatter	cLines or cNoLines
Pie	cPercent or cNoPercent

For our example, let's choose the pie chart type (cPie) drawn in a style that marks each slice with the percentage it represents of the whole (cPercent). We use the PDS subprogram DefaultChart( ) to let the PDS Presentation Graphics package know what our selections are:

```
' $INCLUDE: 'C:\BC7\FONTB.BI'
' $INCLUDE: 'C:\BC7\CHRTB.BI'

      DIM OurChart AS ChartEnvironment
      DIM Regions(4) AS STRING
      DIM Consumption(4) AS SINGLE
      DIM Exploded(4) AS INTEGER

      Regions(1) = "North"
      Regions(2) = "East"
      Regions(3) = "South"
      Regions(4) = "West"

      Consumption(1) = 219
      Consumption(2) = 19
      Consumption(3) = 119
      Consumption(4) = 319

      CALL ChartScreen(12)

  →   CALL DefaultChart(OurChart, cPie, cPercent)
      :
      :
```

Finally, we fill the Title fields in the data structure OurChart, and we're ready to place the chart on the screen:

```
' $INCLUDE: 'C:\BC7\FONTB.BI'
' $INCLUDE: 'C:\BC7\CHRTB.BI'

        DIM OurChart AS ChartEnvironment
        DIM Regions(4) AS STRING
        DIM Consumption(4) AS SINGLE
        DIM Exploded(4) AS INTEGER

        Regions(1) = "North"
        Regions(2) = "East"
        Regions(3) = "South"
        Regions(4) = "West"

        Consumption(1) = 219
        Consumption(2) = 19
        Consumption(3) = 119
        Consumption(4) = 319

        CALL ChartScreen(12)

        CALL DefaultChart(OurChart, cPie, cPercent)

    →   OurChart.MainTitle.Title = "Peanut Butter Consumption"
    :   OurChart.MainTitle.TitleColor = 15
        OurChart.MainTitle.Justify = cCenter
        OurChart.SubTitle.Title = "Consumption (Tons)"
        OurChart.SubTitle.TitleColor = 11
        OurChart.SubTitle.Justify = cCenter
        OurChart.ChartWindow.Border = cYes
    :
```

To actually display it, we call ChartPie( ) with these arguments:

```
CALL ChartPie (OurChart, Regions( ), Consumption( ), Exploded( ), 4)
```

Here, OurChart is the ChartEnvironment variable we set up, Regions( ) holds the titles of each pie section; Consumption( ) holds the actual numerical data to plot; Exploded( ) indicates which pie slice(s) should be exploded; and the final integer, in this case 4, indicates how many data points there are. We can call ChartPie( ) and then finish up as shown in Listing 5-8.

Listing 5-8. A PDS Pie Chart.

```
' $INCLUDE: 'C:\BC7\FONTB.BI'
' $INCLUDE: 'C:\BC7\CHRTB.BI'

        DIM OurChart AS ChartEnvironment
        DIM Regions(4) AS STRING
        DIM Consumption(4) AS SINGLE
        DIM Exploded(4) AS INTEGER

        Regions(1) = "North"
        Regions(2) = "East"
        Regions(3) = "South"
        Regions(4) = "West"

        Consumption(1) = 219
        Consumption(2) = 19
        Consumption(3) = 119
        Consumption(4) = 319

        CALL ChartScreen(12)

        CALL DefaultChart(OurChart, cPie, cPercent)

        OurChart.MainTitle.Title = "Peanut Butter Consumption"
        OurChart.MainTitle.TitleColor = 15
        OurChart.MainTitle.Justify = cCenter
        OurChart.SubTitle.Title = "Consumption (Tons)"
        OurChart.SubTitle.TitleColor = 11
        OurChart.SubTitle.Justify = cCenter
        OurChart.ChartWindow.Border = cYes

   →    CALL ChartPie(OurChart, Regions( ), Consumption( ), Exploded( ), 4)
        SLEEP
```

Notice that we placed a BASIC SLEEP statement at the end of the code to hold the pie chart on the screen until we press a key.

TIP: The BASIC SLEEP statement replaces the older DO: LOOP WHILE INKEY$ = " ". If you use it with a number, like: sleep 5, BASIC will pause for five seconds.

All this may seem like a lot of work to display a simple graph, but now that we've got the skeleton of the program working, it will be easy to adapt for other chart types.

Bar Charts

For example, we can put together a bar chart example very easily from what we already have. We just need to omit the definition of Exploded( ), which has no use in a bar chart, and specify a plain style bar chart to DefaultChart( ):

```
' $INCLUDE: 'C:\BC7\FONTB.BI'
' $INCLUDE: 'C:\BC7\CHRTB.BI'

        DIM OurChart AS ChartEnvironment
        DIM Regions(4) AS STRING
        DIM Consumption(4) AS SINGLE

        Regions(1) = "North"
        Regions(2) = "East"
        Regions(3) = "South"
        Regions(4) = "West"

        Consumption(1) = 219
        Consumption(2) = 19
        Consumption(3) = 119
        Consumption(4) = 319

        CALL ChartScreen(12)

  →     CALL DefaultChart(OurChart, cBar, CPlain)
        :
        :
```

Next, we add titles for the X and Y axes (which had no meaning and, therefore, were not used when we drew a pie chart), and call Chart( ) — not ChartPie( ) — to display the bar graph. (See Listing 5-9.)

Listing 5-9. A PDS Bar Graph. 1 of 2

```
' $INCLUDE: 'C:\BC7\FONTB.BI'
' $INCLUDE: 'C:\BC7\CHRTB.BI'

        DIM OurChart AS ChartEnvironment
        DIM Regions(4) AS STRING
        DIM Consumption(4) AS SINGLE

        Regions(1) = "North"
        Regions(2) = "East"
        Regions(3) = "South"
        Regions(4) = "West"

        Consumption(1) = 219
        Consumption(2) = 19
        Consumption(3) = 119
        Consumption(4) = 319

        CALL ChartScreen(12)

        CALL DefaultChart(OurChart, cBar, CPlain)
```

Listing 5-9.   A PDS Bar Graph.   2 of 2

```
     OurChart.MainTitle.Title = "Peanut Butter Consumption"
     OurChart.MainTitle.TitleColor = 15
     OurChart.MainTitle.Justify = cCenter
     OurChart.SubTitle.Title = "Consumption (Tons)"
     OurChart.SubTitle.TitleColor = 11
     OurChart.SubTitle.Justify = cCenter
     OurChart.ChartWindow.Border = cYes

→    OurChart.XAxis.AxisTitle.Title = "Consumption"
     OurChart.YAxis.AxisTitle.Title = "Region"

     CALL Chart(OurChart, Regions( ), Consumption( ), 4)
     SLEEP
```

And that's it, the bar chart is now on the screen. Let's work through one more type of Presentation Graphics chart — line charts.

Line Charts

It's easy to adapt our example to produce a line chart where all the displayed points are connected by a line. We just specify what we want to DefaultChart( ):

```
' $INCLUDE: 'C:\BC7\FONTB.BI'
' $INCLUDE: 'C:\BC7\CHRTB.BI'

     DIM OurChart AS ChartEnvironment
     DIM Regions(4) AS STRING
     DIM Consumption(4) AS SINGLE

     Regions(1) = "North"
     Regions(2) = "East"
     Regions(3) = "South"
     Regions(4) = "West"

     Consumption(1) = 219
     Consumption(2) = 19
     Consumption(3) = 119
     Consumption(4) = 319

     CALL ChartScreen(12)

→    CALL DefaultChart(OurChart, cLine, cLine)
     :
     :
```

Then we call Chart( ) again (Chart( ) plots bar, column, and line charts depending on what you've asked for with DefaultChart( )). (See Listing 5-10.)

```
Listing 5-10.   A Line Chart.
' $INCLUDE: 'C:\BC7\FONTB.BI'
' $INCLUDE: 'C:\BC7\CHRTB.BI'

        DIM OurChart AS ChartEnvironment
        DIM Regions(4) AS STRING
        DIM Consumption(4) AS SINGLE

        Regions(1) = "North"
        Regions(2) = "East"
        Regions(3) = "South"
        Regions(4) = "West"

        Consumption(1) = 219
        Consumption(2) = 19
        Consumption(3) = 119
        Consumption(4) = 319

        CALL ChartScreen(12)

        CALL DefaultChart(OurChart, cLine, cLine)

        OurChart.MainTitle.Title = "Peanut Butter Consumption"
        OurChart.MainTitle.TitleColor = 15
        OurChart.MainTitle.Justify = cCenter
        OurChart.SubTitle.Title = "Consumption (Tons)"
        OurChart.SubTitle.TitleColor = 11
        OurChart.SubTitle.Justify = cCenter
        OurChart.ChartWindow.Border = cYes

        OurChart.XAxis.AxisTitle.Title = "Region"
        OurChart.YAxis.AxisTitle.Title = "Number"

→       CALL Chart(OurChart, Regions( ), Consumption( ), 4)
        SLEEP
```

And that's it: our line chart is on the screen.

Now we've worked through pie charts, bar charts, and line charts. As you can see, the PDS offers a good set of tools for presenting data.

Before we wrap up our tour of BASIC graphics, however, let's include two advanced functions to give us a little more power. The first one will tell us what video card is in the computer, and the second one will tell us what the current X and Y pixel ranges are on the screen.

What Video Card Do We Have?

It's appropriate to end the Graphics chapter with a function that lets you investigate what video adapter card is installed in the computer. This has always been a difficult thing to do, and after you take a look at the listing we're going to develop, you'll see why. However, knowing what video adapter card is available means that you know what screen modes you can use, an indispensible piece of information if your program uses graphics.

> **NOTE:** With this function, you won't need to ask the user about installed graphics equipment.

Let's call our function GetVideoCard$( ). To make this function useful, we can have it return these outputs (as STRINGs):

```
GetVideoCard$              "MDA" = monochrome adapter card
                           "CGA" = color graphics adapter card
                           "EGA" = enhanced graphics adapter card
                           "PGA" = professional grahics adapter card
                           "VGA" = variable graphics array card
```

> **NOTE:** The MDA is a specific type of monitor, a monochrome monitor, and does *not* refer to a screen that can display graphics but only in black and white. The MDA can only support BIOS mode 7.

This function is going to take a little work. We'll have to check if the machine's BIOS can support a VGA, then an EGA, then work down to CGAs or MDAs. For each new monitor type, a new level of BIOS was produced, so we interrogate the computer's BIOS directly to see how advanced the version we're working with is.

First, we check to see if the BIOS in the machine is advanced enough to support interrupt &H10 service &H1A, which would tell us exactly what video card is installed. If so, &H1A is returned in al, and a video code in bl. We can just check that code like this, with a SELECT CASE statement:

```
FUNCTION GetVideoCard$

    DIM InRegs AS RegType, OutRegs AS RegType
    InRegs.ax = &H1A00
    CALL INTERRUPT(&H10, InRegs, OutRegs)
    IF (OutRegs.ax AND &HFF) = &H1A THEN
         Code = OutRegs.bx AND &HFF
         SELECT CASE Code
             CASE 1
                  GetVideoCard$ = "MDA"
             CASE 2
```

```
                        GetVideoCard$ = "CGA"
            CASE 4 TO 5
                        GetVideoCard$ = "EGA"
            CASE 6
                        GetVideoCard$ = "PGA"
            CASE 7 TO 8
                        GetVideoCard$ = "VGA"
       END SELECT
       EXIT FUNCTION
              :
              :
```

However, only relatively recent BIOSes (those that can handle the VGA) support this service. If it is not supported, we have to continue by checking for an EGA with interrupt &H10 service &H12. If we call this service with bl = &H10, and, on return, bl is no longer equal to &H10, an EGA is installed. Note that, unlike service &H1A, this service only indicates the presence or absence of a single type of monitor, the EGA. If there is an EGA, we can exit:

```
    FUNCTION GetVideoCard$

        DIM InRegs AS RegType, OutRegs AS RegType
        InRegs.ax = &H1A00
        CALL INTERRUPT(&H10, InRegs, OutRegs)
        IF (OutRegs.ax AND &HFF) = &H1A THEN
            Code = OutRegs.bx AND &HFF
            SELECT CASE Code
                CASE 1
                        GetVideoCard$ = "MDA"
                CASE 2
                        GetVideoCard$ = "CGA"
                CASE 4 TO 5
                        GetVideoCard$ = "EGA"
                CASE 6
                        GetVideoCard$ = "PGA"
                CASE 7 TO 8
                        GetVideoCard$ = "VGA"
            END SELECT
            EXIT FUNCTION
        ELSE
→           InRegs.ax = &H1200
:           InRegs.bx = &H10
:           CALL INTERRUPT(&H10, InRegs, OutRegs)
            IF (OutRegs.bx AND &HFF) < > &H10 THEN
            GetVideoCard$ = "EGA"
                EXIT FUNCTION
                    :
                    :
```

Otherwise, there are only two options left, CGA and MDA. Since the MDA can only support BIOS video mode 7, we check the current video mode. If it's 7, we have an MDA. If not, a CGA:

```
FUNCTION GetVideoCard$

    DIM InRegs AS RegType, OutRegs AS RegType
    InRegs.ax = &H1A00
    CALL INTERRUPT(&H10, InRegs, OutRegs)
    IF (OutRegs.ax AND &HFF) = &H1A THEN
        Code = OutRegs.bx AND &HFF
        SELECT CASE Code
            CASE 1
                GetVideoCard$ = "MDA"
            CASE 2
                GetVideoCard$ = "CGA"
            CASE 4 TO 5
                GetVideoCard$ = "EGA"
            CASE 6
                GetVideoCard$ = "PGA"
            CASE 7 TO 8
                GetVideoCard$ = "VGA"
        END SELECT
        EXIT FUNCTION
    ELSE
        InRegs.ax = &H1200
        InRegs.bx = &H10
        CALL INTERRUPT(&H10, InRegs, OutRegs)
        IF (OutRegs.bx AND &HFF) < > &H10 THEN
            GetVideoCard$ = "EGA"
            EXIT FUNCTION
        ELSE
→           InRegs.ax = &HF00
:           CALL INTERRUPT(&H10, InRegs, OutRegs)
:           IF (OutRegs.ax AND &HFF) = 7 THEN
                GetVideoCard$ = "MDA"
                EXIT FUNCTION
            ELSE
                GetVideoCard$ = "CGA"
                EXIT FUNCTION
            END IF
        END IF
    END IF
END IF
```

And we're done. Listing 5-11 shows the whole function, GetVideoCard$( ).

Listing 5-11.   GetVideo Card$ Function.

```
DECLARE FUNCTION GetVideoCard$ ( )
TYPE RegType
        ax       AS INTEGER
        bx       AS INTEGER
        cx       AS INTEGER
        dx       AS INTEGER
        bp       AS INTEGER
        si       AS INTEGER
        di       AS INTEGER
        flags    AS INTEGER
END TYPE

DECLARE SUB INTERRUPT (IntNo AS INTEGER, InRegs AS RegType, OutRegs AS RegType)

FUNCTION GetVideoCard$

REM This function returns a 3-letter string: "MDA" (monochrome adapter card)
REM "CGA" (color graphics adapter), "EGA" (enhanced graphics adapter),
REM "PGA" (professional graphics adapter), "VGA" (variable graphics array)

    DIM InRegs AS RegType, OutRegs AS RegType
    InRegs.ax = &H1A00
    CALL INTERRUPT(&H10, InRegs, OutRegs)
    IF (OutRegs.ax AND &HFF) = &H1A THEN
        Code = OutRegs.bx AND &HFF
        SELECT CASE Code
            CASE 1
                GetVideoCard$ = "MDA"
            CASE 2
                GetVideoCard$ = "CGA"
            CASE 4 TO 5
                GetVideoCard$ = "EGA"
            CASE 6
                GetVideoCard$ = "PGA"
            CASE 7 TO 8
                GetVideoCard$ = "VGA"
        END SELECT
        EXIT FUNCTION
    ELSE
        InRegs.ax = &H1200
        InRegs.bx = &H10
        CALL INTERRUPT(&H10, InRegs, OutRegs)
        IF (OutRegs.bx AND &HFF) < > &H10 THEN
            GetVideoCard$ = "EGA"
            EXIT FUNCTION
        ELSE
            InRegs.ax = &HF00
            CALL INTERRUPT(&H10, InRegs, OutRegs)
            IF (OutRegs.ax AND &HFF) = 7 THEN
                GetVideoCard$ = "MDA"
                EXIT FUNCTION
            ELSE
                GetVideoCard$ = "CGA"
                EXIT FUNCTION
            END IF
        END IF
    END IF

END FUNCTION
```

And here's how to put GetVideoCard$( ) to work:

```
REM Example of GetVideoCard$()
DECLARE FUNCTION GetVideoCard$ ()
PRINT "The video card is: "; GetVideoCard$
```

This example program will tell you what the video card in your machine is. Let's go on to find another important piece of information about the graphics environment — the horizontal and vertical pixel ranges on the screen.

Finding the Screen's Pixel Ranges

Let's put together one last function to explore the graphics environment before finishing up. Here we're going to determine the number of pixels on the screen both horizontally and vertically in the current screen mode. Let's call this function GetXYRanges%(XRange%, YRange%). Here are the outputs we might want this function to produce:

XRange%	Number of pixels horizontally in the current screen mode
YRange%	Number of pixels vertically in the current screen mode
GetXYRanges%	INTEGER 0 = screen not in a graphics mode; INTEGER 1 = X (Y) range in XRange% (YRange%)

Note that we allow for the possibility that the screen is not in a graphics mode, in which case the pixel count is meaningless and GetXYRanges%( ) should return a 0.

The function shown in Listing 5-12 is just a single SELECT CASE statement, based on the BIOS screen mode.

Listing 5-12. GetXYRange% Function.

```
DECLARE FUNCTION GetXYRanges% (XRange%, YRange%)
REM This function returns the x and y pixel ranges for current graphics mode

TYPE RegType
        ax      AS INTEGER
        bx      AS INTEGER
        cx      AS INTEGER
        dx      AS INTEGER
        bp      AS INTEGER
        si      AS INTEGER
        di      AS INTEGER
        flags   AS INTEGER
END TYPE

DECLARE SUB INTERRUPT (IntNo AS INTEGER, InRegs AS RegType, OutRegs AS RegType)

FUNCTION GetXYRanges% (XRange%, YRange%)

    DIM InRegs AS RegType, OutRegs AS RegType
    InRegs.ax = &HF00
    CALL INTERRUPT(&H10, InRegs, OutRegs)
    Mode = (&HFF AND OutRegs.ax)

    GetXYRanges% = 1

    SELECT CASE Mode
        CASE 4, 5, 13, 19
                XRange% = 320
                YRange% = 200
        CASE 6, 10, 14
                XRange% = 640
                YRange% = 200
        CASE 8
                XRange% = 160
                YRange% = 200
        CASE 9
                XRange% = 320
                YRange% = 200
        CASE 15, 16
                XRange% = 640
                YRange% = 350
        CASE 17, 18
                XRange% = 640
                YRange% = 480
        CASE ELSE
                GetXYRanges% = 0
    END SELECT

END FUNCTION
```

There is no amazing programming going on here. Everything is already set up, depending on the BIOS screen mode. Here's how to use GetXYRanges%( ):

```
REM Example of GetXYRanges

DECLARE FUNCTION GetXYRanges%(Xrange%, Yrange%)

SCREEN 2
Check% = GetXYRanges%(XRange%, YRange%)

LOCATE 1, 1
IF Check% < > 0 THEN
    PRINT "X, Y Ranges are: ",XRange%, YRange%
END IF
```

Note that we check the value of GetXYRanges% — i.e., make sure that it is not 0 — to make sure XRange% and YRange% hold valid values.

Conclusion

And that's it for graphics. We've worked through a lot in this chapter: We've developed our own paint program, a screen clock, animated a small rocketship, plotted peanut butter consumption by geographical region, and finished up with some low-level information about the graphics environment. Try the paint program or design your own sprite — it can be a lot of fun. Graphics can add a very professional feel to a program if it's handled correctly.

Now we're ready to move on, however, so let's turn to a topic of interest to many programmers: database programming. We'll see what the PDS offers us here with ISAM database programming in Chapter 6.

Databasing

THIS CHAPTER IS an exploration of the Indexed Sequential Access Method (ISAM) system in the BASIC Professional Development System. If you don't have the PDS, you might still want to read along to get an idea of what's available, especially if you're interested in databases. The ISAM system provides an easy way to set up a database program from within BASIC (and the very fact that such a system is in the PDS shows the depth of Microsoft's commitment to BASIC). It's a serious system, set up for serious applications.

NOTE: The ISAM system is one of the major reasons programmers upgrade to the PDS.

So what is ISAM? Briefly, it's a method of quickly changing the apparent order of records in a file. For example, you may be a careful person who prefers to order your friends by height or age. Towards that end, you may have devised a new data TYPE to hold information about each friend:

```
TYPE Friend
        Name AS STRING * 50
        Age AS INTEGER
        Height AS INTEGER
        HomeTown AS STRING * 50
END TYPE
```

Each variable in this type is a *field* in database terminology, and, together, all these fields make up a *record*. After defining a data type, you can set up a variable of this type named MyFriend like this:

```
TYPE Friend
        Name AS STRING * 50
        Age AS INTEGER
        Height AS INTEGER
        HomeTown AS STRING * 50
    END TYPE

→ DIM MyFriend AS Friend
```

And then fill all the fields in this record with values like this:

```
TYPE Friend
        Name AS STRING * 50
        Age AS INTEGER
        Height AS INTEGER
        HomeTown AS STRING * 50
END TYPE

DIM MyFriend AS Friend

→ MyFriend.Name = "Doug"
  MyFriend.Age = 33
  MyFriend.Height = 70       'Inches
  MyFriend.HomeTown = "Redlands"
```

You can even make a file of such records, like the one shown in Figure 6-1. This file is a database. The records in it are in the order in which we inserted them into the file, one after the other, which is called *insertion order*.

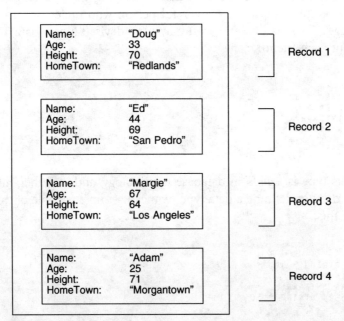

Figure 6-1

If we were to make this an ISAM file (which we would have to specify when we first create the file), the ISAM system would automatically begin the file with an index of the records, as shown in Figure 6-2.

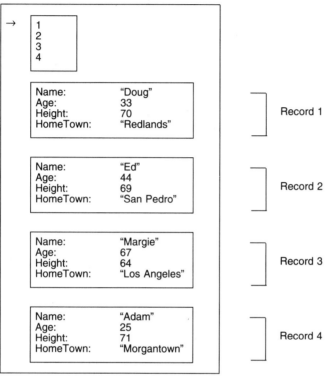

Figure 6-2

This index just lists the record numbers in the order in which they were inserted into the file, and, in the ISAM system, this index is referred to as the NULL index (see Figure 6-3). The NULL index is the default index of the records in the file, and it's always created when you open a file for ISAM output and put records into it.

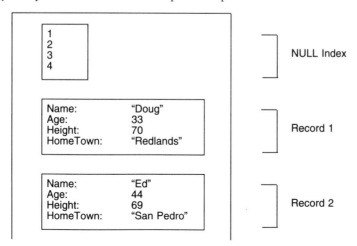

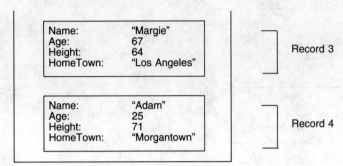

Figure 6-3

However, the crux of the ISAM system is that you can build other indices as well. For example, we can (and will) instruct the ISAM system to create an index of the records in your file by age. For easy reference, we can even give this index a name; e.g., Friends-ByAge (see Figure 6-4). Note that the order in this index is different from that in the NULL index. Here, the records are listed in terms of increasing age.

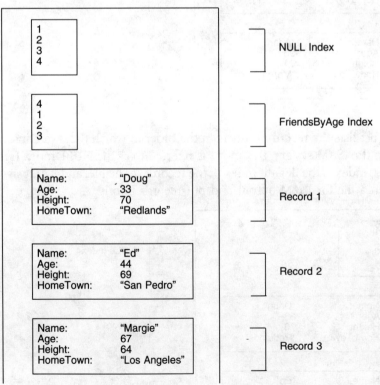

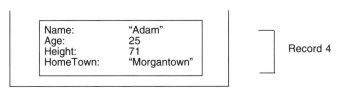

Figure 6-4

The way we'll create indices with ISAM is through the new BASIC statement, CREATE-INDEX. Similarly, we can create another index on the height of your friends, which we can call FriendsByHeight (see Figure 6-5).

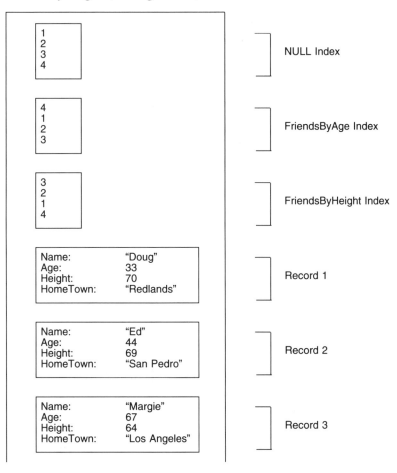

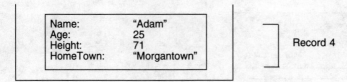

Figure 6-5

The Current Database Index

These indices themselves actually become part of the file (ISAM handles all this automatically when you create a new index). However, only one index at a time can be the *current index*. And whenever you make an index the current index, the apparent order of the records in the file is changed to match its ordering.

Before you've created any indices, the NULL index is the current index (see Figure 6-6). If you ask for the first record in this file, you'll get record 1; the next record will be record 2 and so forth, just mirroring the insertion order of the records.

Figure 6-6

On the other hand, you can select which index is the current index with the SET-INDEX statement. For example, you may make the FriendsByAge index the current index with SETINDEX (see Figure 6-7).

Figure 6-7

Now, when you ask for the first record from this file, you'll get the entry that's really record 4, not record 1 (Adam has the lowest age of all the friends). The next record after that will really be record 1, followed by record 2 and then 3. In other words, the file now appears to be sorted by age. (Note that the file has not really been resorted. The ISAM system uses pointers to point to each record, and it is these pointers that are actually sorted.)

TIP: Sorting a file by sorting pointers to each record, and not each record itself, saves ISAM the trouble of moving each record's data. It's a trick all professional database systems use, and the result is that ISAM can manage records considerably faster than any other method in BASIC.

Similarly, if you made FriendsByHeight the current index, the file would appear to be sorted by height. When you retrieve the first record from the file, it will be the record of the person with the lowest height. The next record will be that of the person with the next lowest height, and so on up to the tallest person.

Ordering records like this can be very useful. For example, if you wanted to exclude all people below the age of thirty, you'd order your file by age, giving you this ordering of ages, record by record:

> 25 (Adam)
> 33 (Doug)
> 44 (Ed)
> 67 (Margie)

You would then scan up the file for the first age above 30 (this can be done with the SEEK statement, as we'll see), which is Doug:

> 25 (Adam)
> →33 (Doug)
> 44 (Ed)
> 67 (Margie)

Since the records are ordered, you know that all records before this one are of people under thirty, and can be discarded. All records after this point can be preserved; handling data like this is the fundamental part of a database program.

Now let's put this all into code.

Our Database Program

Before actually writing any BASIC, we should mention that you'll need a little preparation before you can work with ISAM.

This time, you don't need to create or load new Quick libraries. Instead, you have to load a TSR (Terminate and Stay Resident) program that holds the ISAM code. This program is named PROISAMD.EXE; it contains all the code needed to run all database programs. Just run it once before using any ISAM routines and then start QBX as usual. If your database program is DB.BAS, you'd type QBX DB. If you're using BC.EXE (version 7.0 or later), just compile and link the program into DB.EXE, run PROISAMD.EXE, and then run DB.EXE.

TIP: There is a shorter program than PROISAMD.EXE named PROISAM.EXE, which is all you need to run *most* ISAM program. Although using PRO-ISAM.EXE lets you save RAM, it omits a few routines — including CREATEINDEX.

Now we're free to do some programming. Our database program will do some of the things we've been talking about, and we can even use the list of friends we've developed. We can start by structuring our data records with TYPE and creating a variable named MyFriend of that type:

```
TYPE Friend
        Name AS STRING * 50
        Age AS INTEGER
        Height AS INTEGER
        HomeTown AS STRING * 50
END TYPE

DIM MyFriend AS Friend
:
:
```

Now we can create our ISAM file. To do that, we simply say OPEN "FRIENDS.DAT" FOR ISAM (as opposed to opening it under other BASIC options such as APPEND), like this:

```
    TYPE Friend
            Name AS STRING * 50
            Age AS INTEGER
            Height AS INTEGER
            HomeTown AS STRING * 50
    END TYPE

    DIM MyFriend AS Friend
→   OPEN "FRIENDS.DAT" FOR ISAM Friend "Pals" AS #1
    :
    :
```

Let's take a look at this OPEN statement. We start with OPEN "FRIENDS.DAT" FOR ISAM, which is clear enough, since we want this file to be an ISAM file. The next keyword, Friend, indicates the TYPE of the records we'll be using so that ISAM can structure each record in the file. The following keyword, Pals, is the *table name*, and the number (#1) is the file number as is normal in BASIC.

All the records of a particular data type (such as TYPE Friend) make up a table in the database file. For example, when we've filled FRIENDS.DAT with all our friends, all the records will be in a single table, which we're naming Pals (see Figure 6-8).

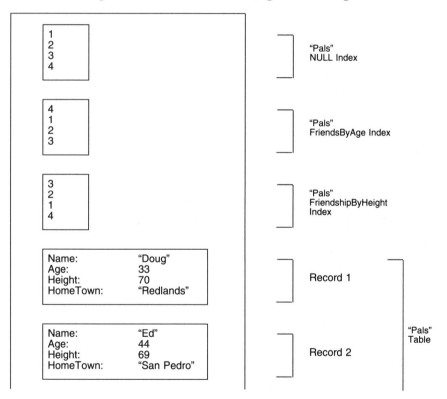

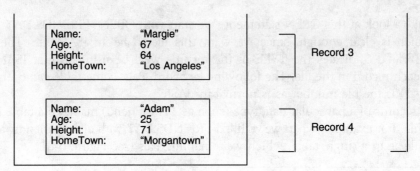

Figure 6-8

But we might also have another table with a different record type — say TYPE Enemy — in the same file, and this would make up a new table that we can call NotPals (see Figure 6-9).

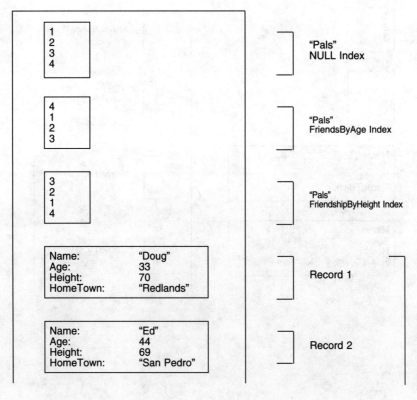

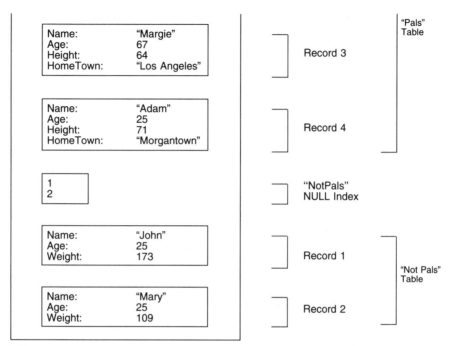

Figure 6-9

If we wanted to work with the NotPals table, we'd open up the *same* file again, but this time we'd specify a different record TYPE (Enemy), and a different file number:

```
OPEN "FRIENDS.DAT" FOR ISAM Friend "Pals" AS #1
OPEN "FRIENDS.DAT" FOR ISAM Enemy "NotPals" AS #2
```

What's referred to in the rest of BASIC as a file number (i.e., 1 and 2 as we've opened them so far) are really *table numbers* in ISAM. When you create indices, search for matches, or perform other operations in ISAM, you have to specify the table number as well.

TIP: The reason you can have multiple tables in ISAM is to avoid the need for relational databases, where you have to tie records from different files together. Here, you can put all your data, even data that would normally go into different files, into the same file. And ISAM files can be huge; the upper limit is 128 megabytes.

We're going to limit ourselves to one table (Pals) in this chapter. And our table number is going to be 1:

```
TYPE Friend
        Name AS STRING * 50
        Age AS INTEGER
        Height AS INTEGER
        HomeTown AS STRING * 50
END TYPE

DIM MyFriend AS Friend

→ OPEN "FRIENDS.DAT" FOR ISAM Friend "Pals" AS #1
        :
        :
```

Now we have to insert the data we want, record by record, into FRIENDS.DAT. We can do that with the INSERT statement, like this:

```
TYPE Friend
        Name AS STRING * 50
        Age AS INTEGER
        Height AS INTEGER
        HomeTown AS STRING * 50
END TYPE

DIM MyFriend AS Friend

OPEN "FRIENDS.DAT" FOR ISAM Friend "Pals" AS #1

MyFriend.Name = "Doug"
MyFriend.Age = 33
MyFriend.Height = 70      'Inches
MyFriend.HomeTown = "Redlands"
→ INSERT 1, MyFriend

MyFriend.Name = "Ed"
MyFriend.Age = 44
MyFriend.Height = 69       'Inches
MyFriend.HomeTown = "San Pedro"
→ INSERT 1, MyFriend

MyFriend.Name = "Margie"
MyFriend.Age = 67
MyFriend.Height = 64       'Inches
MyFriend.HomeTown = "Los Angeles"
→ INSERT 1, MyFriend

MyFriend.Name = "Adam"
MyFriend.Age = 25
MyFriend.Height = 71       'Inches
```

```
MyFriend.HomeTown = "Morgantown"
→ INSERT 1, MyFriend
  :
  :
```

It's an easy process; we just fill the fields in MyFriend with the data we want, and then INSERT MyFriend into the file FRIENDS.DAT (which we've opened as #1).

So far, then the database file FRIENDS.DAT has all four records loaded, and the NULL index has been automatically set up by ISAM (see Figure 6-10).

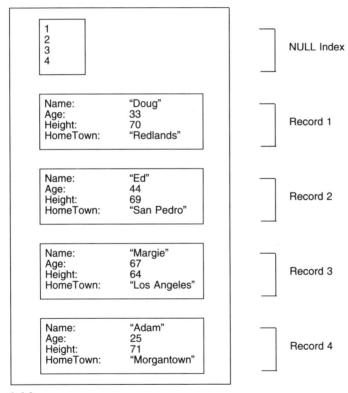

Figure 6-10

Now we can go on to create the other two indices, FriendsByAge and FriendsByHeight. To do that we use CREATEINDEX, passing it the file number, the name we want to give to this index, a parameter named *unique%*, and the name of the field we want to sort on (Age):

```
TYPE Friend
        Name AS STRING * 50
        Age AS INTEGER
        Height AS INTEGER
        HomeTown AS STRING * 50
END TYPE

DIM MyFriend AS Friend

OPEN "FRIENDS.DAT" FOR ISAM Friend "Pals" AS #1

MyFriend.Name = "Doug"
MyFriend.Age = 33
MyFriend.Height = 70      'Inches
MyFriend.HomeTown = "Redlands"
INSERT 1, MyFriend

MyFriend.Name = "Ed"
MyFriend.Age = 44
MyFriend.Height = 69      'Inches
MyFriend.HomeTown = "San Pedro"
INSERT 1, MyFriend

MyFriend.Name = "Margie"
MyFriend.Age = 67
MyFriend.Height = 64       'Inches
MyFriend.HomeTown = "Los Angeles"
INSERT 1, MyFriend

MyFriend.Name = "Adam"
MyFriend.Age = 25
MyFriend.Height = 71       'Inches
MyFriend.HomeTown = "Morgantown"
INSERT 1, MyFriend

PRINT "Sorting by age..."
→ CREATEINDEX 1, "FriendsByAge", 0, "Age"
:
:
```

The unique% field indicates whether or not ISAM will tolerate the insertion of records with the same value in this field as one that already exists in the database. For example, if we set unique% to 1, demanding unique entries only, and then tried to enter a record for Pete, whose age is 33 (the same as Doug's), a trapable error would be generated (i.e., use ON ERROR GOTO...). In this chapter we are not going to worry about the uniqueness of records, so we'll set this value to 0. Now the database file looks like this Figure 6-11.

NULL Index

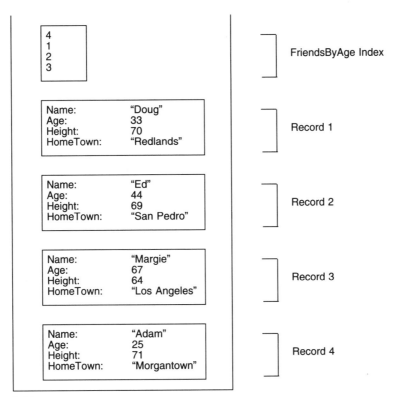

Figure 6-11

We know what order we've inserted the records into the file. Now we can sort them according to age by making the FriendsByAge index the current index and printing out each friend's name. We start off with SETINDEX:

```
TYPE Friend
        Name AS STRING * 50
        Age AS INTEGER
        Height AS INTEGER
        HomeTown AS STRING * 50
END TYPE

DIM MyFriend AS Friend

OPEN "FRIENDS.DAT" FOR ISAM Friend "Pals" AS #1

MyFriend.Name = "Doug"
MyFriend.Age = 33
MyFriend.Height = 70     'Inches
MyFriend.HomeTown = "Redlands"
INSERT 1, MyFriend

MyFriend.Name = "Ed"
```

```
    MyFriend.Age = 44
    MyFriend.Height = 69      'Inches
    MyFriend.HomeTown = "San Pedro"
    INSERT 1, MyFriend

    MyFriend.Name = "Margie"
    MyFriend.Age = 67
    MyFriend.Height = 64        'Inches
    MyFriend.HomeTown = "Los Angeles"
    INSERT 1, MyFriend

    MyFriend.Name = "Adam"
    MyFriend.Age = 25
    MyFriend.Height = 71        'Inches
    MyFriend.HomeTown = "Morgantown"
    INSERT 1, MyFriend

    PRINT "Sorting by age..."

    CREATEINDEX 1, "FriendsByAge", 0, "Age"

→   SETINDEX 1, "FriendsByAge"
    :
    :
```

This is easy enough — we're just making the FriendsByAge index the current index for file 1 (actually table 1). Now we can print the names out in this new order.

The ISAM system supports a number of statements for moving around in a database file. Here's a list of the ones we'll find useful:

```
MOVEFIRST FileNumber
MOVELAST FileNumber
MOVENEXT FileNumber
MOVEPREVIOUS FileNumber
EOF(FileNumber)
BOF(FileNumber)
```

Keep in mind that what's listed in the ISAM documentation as FileNumber, as above, is really the table number. In other words, confusing as it may be, you can actually have as many file numbers for a specific file as there are tables in that file.

The MOVE statements are self-explanatory. EOF(FileNumber) returns TRUE (i.e., all bits set: &HFFFF) if we're at the end of the table, and BOF(FileNumber) returns TRUE if we're at the beginning. Otherwise, they return FALSE (0).

With all this in mind, here's how we print out the new ordering of the records in FRIENDS.DAT, now sorted by age:

```
TYPE Friend
        Name AS STRING * 50
        Age AS INTEGER
        Height AS INTEGER
        HomeTown AS STRING * 50
END TYPE

DIM MyFriend AS Friend

OPEN "FRIENDS.DAT" FOR ISAM Friend "Pals" AS #1

MyFriend.Name = "Doug"
MyFriend.Age = 33
MyFriend.Height = 70     'Inches
MyFriend.HomeTown = "Redlands"
INSERT 1, MyFriend

MyFriend.Name = "Ed"
MyFriend.Age = 44
MyFriend.Height = 69     'Inches
MyFriend.HomeTown = "San Pedro"
INSERT 1, MyFriend

MyFriend.Name = "Margie"
MyFriend.Age = 67
MyFriend.Height = 64     'Inches
MyFriend.HomeTown = "Los Angeles"
INSERT 1, MyFriend

MyFriend.Name = "Adam"
MyFriend.Age = 25
MyFriend.Height = 71     'Inches
MyFriend.HomeTown = "Morgantown"
INSERT 1, MyFriend

PRINT "Sorting by age..."

CREATEINDEX 1, "FriendsByAge", 0, "Age"

SETINDEX 1, "FriendsByAge"

→ MOVEFIRST 1

DO
    RETRIEVE 1, MyFriend
    PRINT MyFriend.Name
    MOVENEXT 1
LOOP WHILE NOT EOF(1)
    :
    :
```

What we do is to move to the first record in the file:

```
MOVEFIRST 1
:
```

And then we enter a DO loop that loops over each record in the file by continually using MOVENEXT until EOF(1) becomes true:

```
MOVEFIRST 1

DO
      :
      :
    MOVENEXT 1
LOOP WHILE NOT EOF(1)
```

When we're at the beginning of the file, the first record in the current index is the *current record*. When we use MOVENEXT 1, the next record in that index becomes the current record. We can look at the current record by retrieving it, using RETRIEVE, into a variable of type Friend, such as MyFriend:

```
MOVEFIRST 1

DO
    RETRIEVE 1, MyFriend
      :
    MOVENEXT 1
LOOP WHILE NOT EOF(1)
```

RETRIEVE 1, MyFriend reads the current record from the databse file and places it into MyFriend. That means that we can print out the name of the person in the current record with PRINT like this:

```
    MOVEFIRST 1

    DO
        RETRIEVE 1, MyFriend
→       PRINT MyFriend.Name
        MOVENEXT 1
    LOOP WHILE NOT EOF(1)
```

And that's the way to loop over the ordered records of an ISAM file.

We can also create our second index, FriendsByHeight, like this:

```
TYPE Friend
        Name AS STRING * 50
        Age AS INTEGER
        Height AS INTEGER
        HomeTown AS STRING * 50
END TYPE

DIM MyFriend AS Friend

OPEN "FRIENDS.DAT" FOR ISAM Friend "Pals" AS #1

MyFriend.Name = "Doug"
MyFriend.Age = 33
MyFriend.Height = 70      'Inches
MyFriend.HomeTown = "Redlands"
INSERT 1, MyFriend

MyFriend.Name = "Ed"
MyFriend.Age = 44
MyFriend.Height = 69      'Inches
MyFriend.HomeTown = "San Pedro"
INSERT 1, MyFriend

MyFriend.Name = "Margie"
MyFriend.Age = 67
MyFriend.Height = 64      'Inches
MyFriend.HomeTown = "Los Angeles"
INSERT 1, MyFriend

MyFriend.Name = "Adam"
MyFriend.Age = 25
MyFriend.Height = 71      'Inches
MyFriend.HomeTown = "Morgantown"
INSERT 1, MyFriend

PRINT "Sorting by age..."

CREATEINDEX 1, "FriendsByAge", 0, "Age"

SETINDEX 1, "FriendsByAge"

MOVEFIRST 1

DO
RETRIEVE 1, MyFriend
PRINT MyFriend.Name
MOVENEXT 1
LOOP WHILE NOT EOF(1)

PRINT "Sorting by height..."

CREATEINDEX 1, "FriendsByHeight", 0, "Height"
    :
    :
```

The structure here is exactly parallel to the creation of FriendsByAge, except that now we sort on the Height field and give the index a different name. At this point, the database file looks like Figure 6-12.

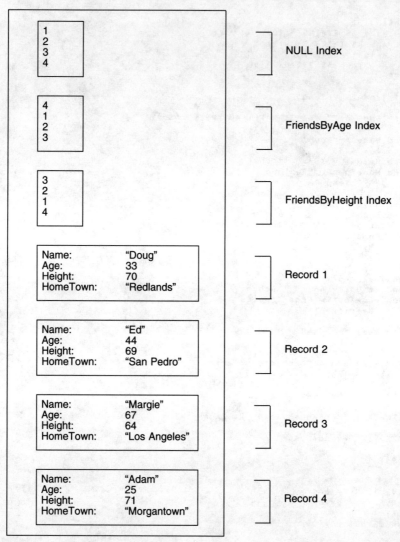

Figure 6-12

We can make FriendsByHeight the current index and print the records out in that order just as we did for FriendsByAge:

```
TYPE Friend
        Name AS STRING * 50
        Age AS INTEGER
        Height AS INTEGER
        HomeTown AS STRING * 50
END TYPE

DIM MyFriend AS Friend

OPEN "FRIENDS.DAT" FOR ISAM Friend "Pals" AS #1

MyFriend.Name = "Doug"
MyFriend.Age = 33
MyFriend.Height = 70      'Inches
MyFriend.HomeTown = "Redlands"
INSERT 1, MyFriend

MyFriend.Name = "Ed"
MyFriend.Age = 44
MyFriend.Height = 69      'Inches
MyFriend.HomeTown = "San Pedro"
INSERT 1, MyFriend

MyFriend.Name = "Margie"
MyFriend.Age = 67
MyFriend.Height = 64      'Inches
MyFriend.HomeTown = "Los Angeles"
INSERT 1, MyFriend

MyFriend.Name = "Adam"
MyFriend.Age = 25
MyFriend.Height = 71      'Inches
MyFriend.HomeTown = "Morgantown"
INSERT 1, MyFriend

PRINT "Sorting by age..."

CREATEINDEX 1, "FriendsByAge", 0, "Age"

SETINDEX 1, "FriendsByAge"

MOVEFIRST 1

DO
    RETRIEVE 1, MyFriend
    PRINT MyFriend.Name
    MOVENEXT 1
LOOP WHILE NOT EOF(1)

PRINT "Sorting by height..."

CREATEINDEX 1, "FriendsByHeight", 0, "Height"

→ SETINDEX 1, "FriendsByHeight"
:
```

```
: MOVEFIRST 1

  DO
        RETRIEVE 1, MyFriend
        PRINT MyFriend.Name
        MOVENEXT 1
  LOOP WHILE NOT EOF(1)
  :
  :
```

That's it for reordering the whole file. Now let's start searching through our database for specific values.

Seeking Records

A big part of working with a database is being able to find records that meet a certain criterion quickly. For example, we may want to search for a person that is 33 years old.

To perform this and other operations, ISAM provides the SEEK statements: SEEKGT, SEEKGE, and SEEKEQ. Using them is simple. If you wanted to find a person with age 33 in our table, table 1, you would make FriendsByAge the current index (so ISAM knows what field you're interested in examining), and then use the statement SEEKEQ 1, 33. In code, that looks like this:

```
TYPE Friend
        Name AS STRING * 50
        Age AS INTEGER
        Height AS INTEGER
        HomeTown AS STRING * 50
END TYPE

DIM MyFriend AS Friend

OPEN "FRIENDS.DAT" FOR ISAM Friend "Pals" AS #1

MyFriend.Name = "Doug"
MyFriend.Age = 33
MyFriend.Height = 70     'Inches
MyFriend.HomeTown = "Redlands"
INSERT 1, MyFriend

MyFriend.Name = "Ed"
MyFriend.Age = 44
MyFriend.Height = 69     'Inches
MyFriend.HomeTown = "San Pedro"
```

```
INSERT 1, MyFriend

MyFriend.Name = "Margie"
MyFriend.Age = 67
MyFriend.Height = 64     'Inches
MyFriend.HomeTown = "Los Angeles"
INSERT 1, MyFriend

MyFriend.Name = "Adam"
MyFriend.Age = 25
MyFriend.Height = 71     'Inches
MyFriend.HomeTown = "Morgantown"
INSERT 1, MyFriend

PRINT "Sorting by age..."

CREATEINDEX 1, "FriendsByAge", 0, "Age"

SETINDEX 1, "FriendsByAge"

MOVEFIRST 1

DO
    RETRIEVE 1, MyFriend
    PRINT MyFriend.Name
    MOVENEXT 1
LOOP WHILE NOT EOF(1)

PRINT "Sorting by height..."

CREATEINDEX 1, "FriendsByHeight", 0, "Height"

SETINDEX 1, "FriendsByHeight"

MOVEFIRST 1

DO
    RETRIEVE 1, MyFriend
    PRINT MyFriend.Name
    MOVENEXT 1
LOOP WHILE NOT EOF(1)

PRINT "Seeking a person with age of 33..."

SETINDEX 1, "FriendsByAge"

MOVEFIRST 1

SEEKEQ 1, 33
    :
    :
```

TIP: You can make your own ISAM masters from MOVE, SEEK, and EOF.

If there is no match, EOF(1) will be set true. If EOF(1) is not true, however, there was a match and it will be the current record, which we can print out with RETRIEVE:

```
TYPE Friend
        Name AS STRING * 50
        Age AS INTEGER
        Height AS INTEGER
        HomeTown AS STRING * 50
END TYPE

DIM MyFriend AS Friend

OPEN "FRIENDS.DAT" FOR ISAM Friend "Pals" AS #1

MyFriend.Name = "Doug"
MyFriend.Age = 33
MyFriend.Height = 70     'Inches
MyFriend.HomeTown = "Redlands"
INSERT 1, MyFriend

MyFriend.Name = "Ed"
MyFriend.Age = 44
MyFriend.Height = 69     'Inches
MyFriend.HomeTown = "San Pedro"
INSERT 1, MyFriend

MyFriend.Name = "Margie"
MyFriend.Age = 67
MyFriend.Height = 64     'Inches
MyFriend.HomeTown = "Los Angeles"
INSERT 1, MyFriend

MyFriend.Name = "Adam"
MyFriend.Age = 25
MyFriend.Height = 71     'Inches
MyFriend.HomeTown = "Morgantown"
INSERT 1, MyFriend

PRINT "Sorting by age..."

CREATEINDEX 1, "FriendsByAge", 0, "Age"

SETINDEX 1, "FriendsByAge"

MOVEFIRST 1

DO
    RETRIEVE 1, MyFriend
    PRINT MyFriend.Name
    MOVENEXT 1
LOOP WHILE NOT EOF(1)

PRINT "Sorting by height..."
```

```
    CREATEINDEX 1, "FriendsByHeight", 0, "Height"

    SETINDEX 1, "FriendsByHeight"

    MOVEFIRST 1

    DO
        RETRIEVE 1, MyFriend
        PRINT MyFriend.Name
        MOVENEXT 1
    LOOP WHILE NOT EOF(1)

    PRINT "Seeking a person with age of 33..."

    SETINDEX 1, "FriendsByAge"

    MOVEFIRST 1

    SEEKEQ 1, 33

→   IF EOF(1) THEN
            PRINT "No Match."
    ELSE
        RETRIEVE 1, MyFriend
        PRINT MyFriend.Name
    END IF
    :
    :
```

In a similar way, we can search for a person with a height over seven feet (that is, 84 inches) with SEEKGT:

```
    TYPE Friend
            Name AS STRING * 50
            Age AS INTEGER
            Height AS INTEGER
            HomeTown AS STRING * 50
    END TYPE

    DIM MyFriend AS Friend

    OPEN "FRIENDS.DAT" FOR ISAM Friend "Pals" AS #1

    MyFriend.Name = "Doug"
    MyFriend.Age = 33
    MyFriend.Height = 70      'Inches
    MyFriend.HomeTown = "Redlands"
    INSERT 1, MyFriend

    MyFriend.Name = "Ed"
    MyFriend.Age = 44
    MyFriend.Height = 69      'Inches
    MyFriend.HomeTown = "San Pedro"
    INSERT 1, MyFriend
```

```
    MyFriend.Name = "Margie"
    MyFriend.Age = 67
    MyFriend.Height = 64     'Inches
    MyFriend.HomeTown = "Los Angeles"
    INSERT 1, MyFriend

    MyFriend.Name = "Adam"
    MyFriend.Age = 25
    MyFriend.Height = 71      'Inches
    MyFriend.HomeTown = "Morgantown"
    INSERT 1, MyFriend

    PRINT "Sorting by age..."

    CREATEINDEX 1, "FriendsByAge", 0, "Age"

    SETINDEX 1, "FriendsByAge"

    MOVEFIRST 1

    DO
        RETRIEVE 1, MyFriend
        PRINT MyFriend.Name
        MOVENEXT 1
    LOOP WHILE NOT EOF(1)

    PRINT "Sorting by height..."

    CREATEINDEX 1, "FriendsByHeight", 0, "Height"

    SETINDEX 1, "FriendsByHeight"

    MOVEFIRST 1

    DO
        RETRIEVE 1, MyFriend
        PRINT MyFriend.Name
        MOVENEXT 1
    LOOP WHILE NOT EOF(1)

    PRINT "Seeking a person with age of 33..."

    SETINDEX 1, "FriendsByAge"

    MOVEFIRST 1

    SEEKEQ 1, 33

    IF EOF(1) THEN
            PRINT "No Match."
    ELSE
        RETRIEVE 1, MyFriend
        PRINT MyFriend.Name
    END IF
→  PRINT "Seeking people with height over seven feet..."

    SETINDEX 1, "FriendsByHeight"
```

```
MOVEFIRST 1

SEEKGT 1, 84

IF EOF(1) THEN
        PRINT "No Match."
ELSE
    RETRIEVE 1, MyFriend
    PRINT MyFriend.Name
END IF
:
:
```

Since there is no match, EOF(1) is true, and "No Match." is printed out.

ISAM provides other ways of managing records besides inserting them as we've seen. You can also delete them or change the values in them. Let's start by deleting some records.

Deleting Records

Let's say that we wanted to delete all records of friends whose age was over 40. We could seek these records out by making FriendsByAge the current index (with SET-INDEX), and then using a SEEKGT 1, 40 statement.

If we find any matches (i.e., EOF(1) is FALSE), we can simply delete them with the statement DELETE 1, which deletes the current record in table 1. After removing all records meeting this criterion, we can print the remainder out:

```
TYPE Friend
        Name AS STRING * 50
        Age AS INTEGER
        Height AS INTEGER
        HomeTown AS STRING * 50
END TYPE

DIM MyFriend AS Friend

OPEN "FRIENDS.DAT" FOR ISAM Friend "Pals" AS #1

MyFriend.Name = "Doug"
MyFriend.Age = 33
MyFriend.Height = 70     'Inches
MyFriend.HomeTown = "Redlands"
INSERT 1, MyFriend

MyFriend.Name = "Ed"
MyFriend.Age = 44
MyFriend.Height = 69     'Inches
```

```
MyFriend.HomeTown = "San Pedro"
INSERT 1, MyFriend

MyFriend.Name = "Margie"
MyFriend.Age = 67
MyFriend.Height = 64      'Inches
MyFriend.HomeTown = "Los Angeles"
INSERT 1, MyFriend

MyFriend.Name = "Adam"
MyFriend.Age = 25
MyFriend.Height = 71      'Inches
MyFriend.HomeTown = "Morgantown"
INSERT 1, MyFriend

PRINT "Sorting by age..."

CREATEINDEX 1, "FriendsByAge", 0, "Age"

SETINDEX 1, "FriendsByAge"

MOVEFIRST 1

DO
    RETRIEVE 1, MyFriend
    PRINT MyFriend.Name
    MOVENEXT 1
LOOP WHILE NOT EOF(1)

PRINT "Sorting by height..."

CREATEINDEX 1, "FriendsByHeight", 0, "Height"

SETINDEX 1, "FriendsByHeight"

MOVEFIRST 1

DO
    RETRIEVE 1, MyFriend
    PRINT MyFriend.Name
    MOVENEXT 1
LOOP WHILE NOT EOF(1)

PRINT "Seeking a person with age of 33..."

SETINDEX 1, "FriendsByAge"

MOVEFIRST 1

SEEKEQ 1, 33

IF EOF(1) THEN
        PRINT "No Match."
ELSE
    RETRIEVE 1, MyFriend
    PRINT MyFriend.Name
END IF
```

```
PRINT "Seeking people with height over seven feet..."

SETINDEX 1, "FriendsByHeight"

MOVEFIRST 1

SEEKGT 1, 84

IF EOF(1) THEN
        PRINT "No Match."
ELSE
    RETRIEVE 1, MyFriend
    PRINT MyFriend.Name
END IF

→ PRINT "Deleting everyone over 40..."
:
: SETINDEX 1, "FriendsByAge"

DO
    SEEKGT 1, 40

    IF NOT EOF(1) THEN
        RETRIEVE 1, MyFriend
        DELETE 1
    END IF

LOOP UNTIL EOF(1)

PRINT "Here's who's left..."

MOVEFIRST 1

DO
    RETRIEVE 1, MyFriend
    PRINT MyFriend.Name
    MOVENEXT 1
LOOP WHILE NOT EOF(1)
:
:
```

As you can see, deleting records is easy, but be careful, since it's impossible to get them back. Also, you shouldn't expect your ISAM file (in this case, FRIENDS.DAT) to get any smaller when you delete records. In the first place, the minimum size of an ISAM file is 64K, which includes 32K of overhead and 32K of space for records.

When the data space is used up, the ISAM system adds more space in 32K chunks (it does this because its internal searching algorithms work better with data chunks of this size). When you delete a record, the file is not compacted; instead, that record's space is just made available. A new record may be written there in the future.

TIP: If you have deleted many records and really want to compact an ISAM file, use the utility program ISAMPACK, but keep in mind that it works in 32K chunks, and, therefore, can only compact a file if more than 32K has been deleted.

Besides deleting records, we can change the individual fields inside them, as you'd expect. You do that with UPDATE.

Updating ISAM Files

Let's say that Doug has a birthday, and his age changes from 33 to 34; we could delete his record in FRIENDS.DAT and then INSERT a new one to correct his record, but the ISAM system provides a far easier method.

To update records, we can use the UPDATE statement. In this case, all we have to do is to make Doug's record the current record, read it into a variable of TYPE Friend — such as MyFriend — with RETRIEVE, change the Age field to 34, and then use the statement UPDATE 1, MyFriend to update FRIENDS.DAT. This statement updates the current record in file 1 using the values in MyFriend. The entire process looks like this:

```
TYPE Friend
        Name AS STRING * 50
        Age AS INTEGER
        Height AS INTEGER
        HomeTown AS STRING * 50
END TYPE

DIM MyFriend AS Friend

OPEN "FRIENDS.DAT" FOR ISAM Friend "Pals" AS #1

MyFriend.Name = "Doug"
MyFriend.Age = 33
MyFriend.Height = 70     'Inches
MyFriend.HomeTown = "Redlands"
INSERT 1, MyFriend

MyFriend.Name = "Ed"
MyFriend.Age = 44
MyFriend.Height = 69      'Inches
MyFriend.HomeTown = "San Pedro"
INSERT 1, MyFriend

MyFriend.Name = "Margie"
MyFriend.Age = 67
MyFriend.Height = 64     'Inches
MyFriend.HomeTown = "Los Angeles"
INSERT 1, MyFriend
```

```
MyFriend.Name = "Adam"
MyFriend.Age = 25
MyFriend.Height = 71      'Inches
MyFriend.HomeTown = "Morgantown"
INSERT 1, MyFriend

PRINT "Sorting by age..."

CREATEINDEX 1, "FriendsByAge", 0, "Age"

SETINDEX 1, "FriendsByAge"

MOVEFIRST 1

DO
    RETRIEVE 1, MyFriend
    PRINT MyFriend.Name
    MOVENEXT 1
LOOP WHILE NOT EOF(1)

PRINT "Sorting by height..."

CREATEINDEX 1, "FriendsByHeight", 0, "Height"

SETINDEX 1, "FriendsByHeight"

MOVEFIRST 1

DO
    RETRIEVE 1, MyFriend
    PRINT MyFriend.Name
    MOVENEXT 1
LOOP WHILE NOT EOF(1)

PRINT "Seeking a person with age of 33..."

SETINDEX 1, "FriendsByAge"

MOVEFIRST 1

SEEKEQ 1, 33

IF EOF(1) THEN
        PRINT "No Match."
ELSE
    RETRIEVE 1, MyFriend
    PRINT MyFriend.Name
END IF

PRINT "Seeking people with height over seven feet..."

SETINDEX 1, "FriendsByHeight"

MOVEFIRST 1

SEEKGT 1, 84
```

```
    IF EOF(1) THEN
            PRINT "No Match."
    ELSE
        RETRIEVE 1, MyFriend
        PRINT MyFriend.Name
    END IF

    PRINT "Deleting everyone over 40..."

    SETINDEX 1, "FriendsByAge"

    DO
    SEEKGT 1, 40

    IF NOT EOF(1) THEN
        RETRIEVE 1, MyFriend
        DELETE 1
    END IF

    LOOP UNTIL EOF(1)

    PRINT "Here's who's left..."

    MOVEFIRST 1

    DO
        RETRIEVE 1, MyFriend
        PRINT MyFriend.Name
        MOVENEXT 1
    LOOP WHILE NOT EOF(1)
→   PRINT "Changing Doug's age to 34..."
    :
    : CREATEINDEX 1, "FriendsByName", 0, "Name"

    SETINDEX 1, "FriendsByName"

    SEEKEQ 1, "Doug"

    RETRIEVE 1, MyFriend
    MyFriend.Age = 34

    UPDATE 1, MyFriend
    :
    :
```

Then we can print everyone's name and ages out to make sure the change was effective. Here's the final program.

Listing 6-1. Database Program Using ISAM. 1 of 3

```
TYPE Friend
        Name AS STRING * 50
        Age AS INTEGER
        Height AS INTEGER
        HomeTown AS STRING * 50
END TYPE

DIM MyFriend AS Friend

OPEN "FRIENDS.DAT" FOR ISAM Friend "Pals" AS #1

MyFriend.Name = "Doug"
MyFriend.Age = 33
MyFriend.Height = 70     'Inches
MyFriend.HomeTown = "Redlands"
INSERT 1, MyFriend

MyFriend.Name = "Ed"
MyFriend.Age = 44
MyFriend.Height = 69     'Inches
MyFriend.HomeTown = "San Pedro"
INSERT 1, MyFriend

MyFriend.Name = "Margie"
MyFriend.Age = 67
MyFriend.Height = 64     'Inches
MyFriend.HomeTown = "Los Angeles"
INSERT 1, MyFriend

MyFriend.Name = "Adam"
MyFriend.Age = 25
MyFriend.Height = 71     'Inches
MyFriend.HomeTown = "Morgantown"
INSERT 1, MyFriend

PRINT "Sorting by age..."

CREATEINDEX 1, "FriendsByAge", 0, "Age"

SETINDEX 1, "FriendsByAge"

MOVEFIRST 1

DO
    RETRIEVE 1, MyFriend
    PRINT MyFriend.Name
    MOVENEXT 1
LOOP WHILE NOT EOF(1)

PRINT "Sorting by height..."

CREATEINDEX 1, "FriendsByHeight", 0, "Height"

SETINDEX 1, "FriendsByHeight"

MOVEFIRST 1

DO
    RETRIEVE 1, MyFriend
```

Listing 6-1. Database Program Using ISAM.   2 of 3

```
    PRINT MyFriend.Name
    MOVENEXT 1
LOOP WHILE NOT EOF(1)

PRINT "Seeking a person with age of 33..."

SETINDEX 1, "FriendsByAge"

MOVEFIRST 1

SEEKEQ 1, 33

IF EOF(1) THEN
        PRINT "No Match."
ELSE
    RETRIEVE 1, MyFriend
    PRINT MyFriend.Name
END IF

PRINT "Seeking people with height over seven feet..."

SETINDEX 1, "FriendsByHeight"

MOVEFIRST 1

SEEKGT 1, 84

IF EOF(1) THEN
        PRINT "No Match."
ELSE
    RETRIEVE 1, MyFriend
    PRINT MyFriend.Name
END IF

PRINT "Deleting everyone over 40..."

SETINDEX 1, "FriendsByAge"

DO
SEEKGT 1, 40

IF NOT EOF(1) THEN
    RETRIEVE 1, MyFriend
    DELETE 1
END IF

LOOP UNTIL EOF(1)

PRINT "Here's who's left..."

MOVEFIRST 1

DO
    RETRIEVE 1, MyFriend
    PRINT MyFriend.Name
    MOVENEXT 1
```

Listing 6-1.   Database Program Using ISAM.   3 of 3

```
LOOP WHILE NOT EOF(1)

PRINT "Changing Doug's age to 34..."

CREATEINDEX 1, "FriendsByName", 0, "Name"

SETINDEX 1, "FriendsByName"

SEEKEQ 1, "Doug"

RETRIEVE 1, MyFriend
MyFriend.Age = 34

UPDATE 1, MyFriend

SetIndex 1, "FriendsByAge"

DO
    RETRIEVE 1, MyFriend
    PRINT MyFriend.Name;"'s age is: ";MyFriend.Age
    MOVENEXT 1
LOOP WHILE NOT EOF(1)

CLOSE #1
```

At the end, note that we close this table (and therefore the file, since there's only one table in it) with CLOSE 1.

That's it for our database: it's not exactly a general purpose database (because it has no user interface) but it has let us explore the ISAM system. Now, however, it's time to move on and take a look at the other ways we have of handling data in BASIC.

Advanced Data
Handling and Sorting

IN THIS CHAPTER we'll work through just about all the ways there are of organizing data in BASIC (and then we'll add a few of our own). Organizing your data for easy access can be crucial in program development for speed in both program coding and execution. In fact, organizing your data at the beginning may win you more than half the battle of writing a program.

We'll work through the most helpful methods of arranging data, including arrays, data structures, linked lists, circular buffers, and binary trees. Programmers — especially advanced programmers — should be familiar with these common methods of organizing data and not have to continually reinvent the wheel. And, at the end of the chapter, we'll examine two fast sorting methods to get the most out of our data, as well as a fast searching algorithm to search through sorted arrays.

BASIC Variables

The most elementary method of organizing data is by storing it in simple variables. Here are the standard types used in BASIC:

Type	Symbol	Bytes	Range
INTEGER	%	2	-32,768 to 32,767
LONG	&	4	-2,147,483,648 to 2,147,483,647
SINGLE	!	4	-3.402823E38 to -1.40129E-45
DOUBLE	#	8	-1.79769313486232D308 to -2.2250738585072D-308
CURRENCY	@	8	-$922337203685477.5808 to $922337203685477.5807
STRING	$	32K	Strings can range up to 32K characters (bytes)

We're familiar with all of these, except perhaps the new CURRENCY type available in the BASIC PDS. You use that type to store amounts of money. Here's an example (results are printed out to the nearest cent):

```
Savings@ = 6000.00
Rent@ = 775.00
Food@ = 124.50
Bills@ = 513.72

Savings@ = Savings@ - Rent@
```

```
Savings@ = Savings@ - Food@
Savings@ = Savings@ - Bills@

PRINT "Money left: $"; Savings@
```

This example prints out how much of your savings are left after paying rent and the bills. For most purposes, you can think of a CURRENCY variable as a very long integer with four decimal places added on to it as well (although the last two decimal places are for internal accuracy only). We'll see more of the CURRENCY type in Chapter 11.

NOTE: Note that the currency type can hold numbers over 400,000 times as large as LONG integers with complete integer accuracy. This has led some programmers to supplant the LONG type with the CURRENCY type.

The DATA Statement

The next step up in data handling is the DATA statement. Most BASIC programmers are already familiar with DATA. Here's an example in which we calculate the sum and product of the numbers 1-10, stored in a DATA statement:

```
    Sum& = 0
    Product& = 1

    FOR i = 1 TO 10
→        READ Number&
         Sum& = Sum& + Number&
    NEXT i

    PRINT "The sum of your data is:"; Sum&

    RESTORE      'Start data over

    FOR i = 1 TO 10
         READ Number&
         Product& = Product& * Number&
    NEXT i

    PRINT "The product of your data is:"; Product&

    DATA 1, 2, 3, 4, 5, 6, 7, 8, 9, 10
```

In this case, we define our data with the DATA statement:

```
DATA 1, 2, 3, 4, 5, 6, 7, 8, 9, 10
```

Read it with READ (which reads a number from the DATA statement and moves on to the next number for the next READ operation):

```
    FOR i = 1 TO 10
→           READ Number&
            Sum& = Sum& + Number&
    NEXT i
```

And then we can start the whole data list over again with RESTORE:

```
→ RESTORE       'Start data over

  FOR i = 1 TO 10
          READ Number&
          Product& = Product& * Number&
  NEXT i
```

This is one way of handling data. Of course, one of the purposes of putting numeric data into a computer is to organize it, and the most common way of doing that is with the next step towards higher data organization — arrays.

Arrays

We're all familiar with arrays, such as the one in this Listing 7.1.

Listing 7-1. Array Example.   1 of 2

```
DIM Array(10, 2) AS CURRENCY  ←

REM Fill Array(n,1) with today's sales:

Array(1, 1) = 10.00
Array(2, 1) = 53.00
Array(3, 1) = 7.17
Array(4, 1) = 9.67
Array(5, 1) = 87.99
Array(6, 1) = 14.00
Array(7, 1) = 91.19
Array(8, 1) = 12.73
Array(9, 1) = 1.03
Array(10, 1) = 5.04

REM Fill Array(n,2) with yesterday's sales:

Array(1, 2) = 9.67
```

Listing 7-1. Array Example.   2 of 2

```
Array(2, 2) = 3.5
Array(3, 2) = 8.97
Array(4, 2) = 10.00
Array(5, 2) = 78.33
Array(6, 2) = 17.00
Array(7, 2) = 91.36
Array(8, 2) = 12.73
Array(9, 2) = 16.12
Array(10, 2) = 7.98

PRINT "     SALES (in $)"
PRINT "Yesterday     Today"
PRINT "---------     -----"
FOR i = 1 TO 10
        PRINT Array(i, 1), Array(i, 2)
NEXT i
PRINT "---------     -----"

Sum1@ = 0
Sum2@ = 0
FOR i = 1 TO 10
    Sum1@ = Sum1@ + Array(i, 1)
    Sum2@ = Sum2@ + Array(i, 2)
NEXT i

PRINT Sum1@, Sum2@; " = Total"
```

In this program, we're setting up an array of 10 rows and 2 columns to hold sales values for the last two days:

```
DIM Array(10, 2) AS CURRENCY

REM Fill Array(n,1) with today's sales:

Array(1, 1) = 10.00
Array(2, 1) = 53.00
Array(3, 1) = 7.17
Array(4, 1) = 9.67
Array(5, 1) = 87.99
Array(6, 1) = 14.00
Array(7, 1) = 91.19
Array(8, 1) = 12.73
Array(9, 1) = 1.03
Array(10, 1) = 5.04

REM Fill Array(n,2) with yesterday's sales:

Array(1, 2) = 9.67
Array(2, 2) = 3.5
Array(3, 2) = 8.97
Array(4, 2) = 10.00
Array(5, 2) = 78.33
Array(6, 2) = 17.00
```

```
Array(7, 2) = 91.36
Array(8, 2) = 12.73
Array(9, 2) = 16.12
Array(10, 2) = 7.98
        :
        :
```

Figure 7-1 shows the array produced:

Col 1	Col 2	
10.00	9.67	← Row 1
53.00	3.5	← Row 2
7.17	8.97	
9.67	10.00	
87.99	78.33	
14.00	17.00	
91.19	91.36	
12.73	12.73	
1.03	16.12	
5.04	7.98	

Figure 7-1

Now we can reach each day's column of sales just by incrementing the column index. In this format, we can perform parallel operations on parallel sets of data, like adding the columns of sales to produce sums as in our example program:

```
DIM Array(10, 2) AS CURRENCY

REM Fill Array(n,1) with today's sales:

Array(1, 1) = 10.00
Array(2, 1) = 53.00
Array(3, 1) = 7.17
Array(4, 1) = 9.67
Array(5, 1) = 87.99
Array(6, 1) = 14.00
Array(7, 1) = 91.19
Array(8, 1) = 12.73
Array(9, 1) = 1.03
Array(10, 1) = 5.04

REM Fill Array(n,2) with yesterday's sales:

Array(1, 2) = 9.67
Array(2, 2) = 3.5
Array(3, 2) = 8.97
Array(4, 2) = 10.00
Array(5, 2) = 78.33
```

```
Array(6, 2) = 17.00
Array(7, 2) = 91.36
Array(8, 2) = 12.73
Array(9, 2) = 16.12
Array(10, 2) = 7.98

PRINT "     SALES (in $)"
PRINT "Yesterday       Today"
PRINT "---------       -----"
FOR i = 1 TO 10
       PRINT Array(i, 1), Array(i, 2)
NEXT i
PRINT "---------       -----"

Sum1@ = 0
Sum2@ = 0
FOR i = 1 TO 10                                ←
    Sum1@ = Sum1@ + Array(i, 1)
    Sum2@ = Sum2@ + Array(i, 2)
NEXT i

PRINT Sum1@, Sum2@; " = Total"
```

Arrays don't get very complex in BASIC, unlike in C, where array names are just pointers (and two-dimensional array names are just pointers to pointers). There you can really go wild, saving both time and memory by converting all array references to pointer references — and making your code extremely hard to read at the same time.

As it is, we've gotten about as complex as arrays get in BASIC, so let's move on to the next most advanced way of organizing data after arrays: data structures.

Data Structures

We can group the standard data types together and come up with a whole new type of our own. In fact, we've already used TYPE frequently throughout the book to define our data structures InRegs and OutRegs which we use with INTERRUPT( ) or INTER-RUPTX( ). We've also defined data records with TYPE in Chapter 6 on ISAM databases. To define a TYPE named Person, we can do this:

```
TYPE Person
FirstName AS STRING * 20
LastName AS STRING * 20
END TYPE
:
```

This data structure just stores a person's first and last names. We can set up a variable of this type, or, even more powerfully, an array of variables of this type:

```
TYPE Person
FirstName AS STRING * 20
LastName AS STRING * 20
END TYPE

→ DIM People(10) AS Person
:

And then we reference them like this:

TYPE Person
FirstName AS STRING * 20
LastName AS STRING * 20
END TYPE

DIM People(10) AS Person

People(1).FirstName = "Al"
People(1).LastName = "Einstein"

People(2).FirstName = "Frank"
People(2).LastName = "Roosevelt"

People(2).FirstName = "Charlie"
People(2).LastName = "DeGaulle"

PRINT People(1).FirstName
:
```

TIP: One of the most common uses for TYPE in BASIC is to create structured records that can be written to or read from a sequential access file (using write # or input #). Giving all the variables in each record one uniform TYPE name makes them much easier to handle (as we did in the previous chapter) and you can reach each field with . operator.

But that's not the end to working with data structures. If there is some connection between the elements of our array, we can connect them into a *linked list.*

Linked Lists

Linked lists are good for organizing data items into sequential chains, especially if you have a number of such chains to manage and want to use space efficiently.

They work this way: For each data item, there is also a pointer pointing to the next data item. The last pointer in the chain is a null pointer with a value of 0 (so you know the list is done when you reach it). (See Figure 7-2.)

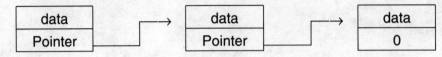

Figure 7-2

We find the next item in the list by referring to the pointer in the present item. At any time, you can add another data item to the list, as long as you update the current pointer to point to the new data item.

A prominent example of a linked list in your computer is the File Allocation Table (FAT) on disks. This is a list of the clusters allocated to files for storage. Files are stored cluster by cluster, and for each cluster on the disk, there is one entry in the FAT.

NOTE: A cluster is the minimum size of disk storage allocation; on diskettes, clusters are two sectors — 1,024 bytes — long. This means, incidentally, that the amount of free diskette space is always reported in units of 1,024 bytes.

To see what clusters a file is stored in, you get its first cluster number from the internal data in its directory entry — let's say that number is 2. That means that the first section of the file is stored in cluster 2 on the disk. This number is also the key to theFAT for us. We can find the *next* cluster occupied by the file by looking in cluster 2's entry in the FAT (see Figure 7-3).

FAT   ↓

Entry #	2	3	4	5	6	7	8	9	10	11	12	13
	3	4	6	32	7	END	29	10	END	0	0	0

Figure 7-3

That cluster's entry in the FAT holds 3, which is the number of the next cluster that the file occupies on the disk. To find the cluster after 3, check the entry in the File Allocation Table for that cluster (See Figure 7-4).

FAT   ↓

Entry #	2	3	4	5	6	7	8	9	10	11	12	13
	3	4	6	32	7	END	29	10	END	0	0	0
		↑										

Figure 7-4

That holds 4, so the next section of the file is in cluster 4. To continue from there, check the number in the FAT entry for cluster 4 (Figure 7-5).

Figure 7-5

That number is 6, and you continue on until you come to the end-of-file mark in the FAT (Figure 7-6).

FAT
Entry #

2	3	4	5	6	7	8	9	10	11	12	13
3	4	6	32	7	END	29	10	END	0	0	0

Figure 7-6

In other words, this file is stored in clusters 2, 3, 4, 6, and 7. Notice that 5 was already taken by another file, which is also weaving its own thread of clusters through the FAT at the same time.

TIP: Linked lists are used when you want to use memory or disk space efficiently and have to keep track of a number of sequential chains of data.

When this file is deleted, its entries in the FAT can be written over, and those clusters can be taken by another file.

Let's see an example of a linked list in BASIC. For example, we might have the two distinct career paths shown in Figure 7-7 to keep track of:

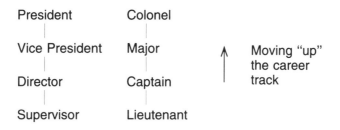

Figure 7-7

We can connect the various levels with a linked list. We start by setting up a variable of type Person as follows:

```
    REM Linked List Example

→  TYPE Person
    Rank AS STRING * 20
    SuperiorPointer AS INTEGER
    END TYPE

    DIM People(10) AS Person
    :
```

Now we fill the Rank fields — we can fill them in any order; the pointers will keep them straight:

```
    REM Linked List Example

    TYPE Person
    Rank AS STRING * 20
    SuperiorPointer AS INTEGER
    END TYPE

    DIM People(10) AS Person

→  People(1).Rank = "Supervisor"
    People(2).Rank = "Major"
    People(3).Rank = "Director"
    People(4).Rank = "President"
    People(5).Rank = "Captain"
    People(6).Rank = "Vice President"
    People(7).Rank = "Colonel"
    People(8).Rank = "Lieutenant"
    :
```

For each entry in People( ), there's also a superior position. For example, the superior of the entry in People(1), Supervisor, is in People(3), Director. To link the entries in each of the two chains, we have to point to the superior rank by filling the pointers Person( ).SuperiorPointer:

```
    REM Linked List Example

    TYPE Person
    Rank AS STRING * 20
    SuperiorPointer AS INTEGER
    END TYPE

    DIM People(10) AS Person
```

```
   People(1).Rank = "Supervisor"
   People(2).Rank = "Major"
   People(3).Rank = "Director"
   People(4).Rank = "President"
   People(5).Rank = "Captain"
   People(6).Rank = "Vice President"
   People(7).Rank = "Colonel"
   People(8).Rank = "Lieutenant"

→ People(1).SuperiorPointer = 3
: People(2).SuperiorPointer = 7
: People(3).SuperiorPointer = 6
   People(4).SuperiorPointer = 0
   People(5).SuperiorPointer = 2
   People(6).SuperiorPointer = 4
   People(7).SuperiorPointer = 0
   People(8).SuperiorPointer = 5
   :
```

Now that all the items in the two lists are linked, we can accept a number, 1 or 2, and work our way through the first or second linked list, printing out the various Rank names as we go. (See Listing 7-2.)

Listing 7-2. A Linked List Example.   **1 of 2**

```
REM Linked List Example

TYPE Person
Rank AS STRING * 20
SuperiorPointer AS INTEGER
END TYPE

DIM People(10) AS Person

People(1).Rank = "Supervisor"
People(2).Rank = "Major"
People(3).Rank = "Director"
People(4).Rank = "President"
People(5).Rank = "Captain"
People(6).Rank = "Vice President"
People(7).Rank = "Colonel"
People(8).Rank = "Lieutenant"

People(1).SuperiorPointer = 3
People(2).SuperiorPointer = 7
People(3).SuperiorPointer = 6
People(4).SuperiorPointer = 0
People(5).SuperiorPointer = 2
People(6).SuperiorPointer = 4
People(7).SuperiorPointer = 0
People(8).SuperiorPointer = 5

PRINT "Choose a life track, 1 or 2: ";
DO
```

Listing 7-2.   A Linked List Example.   **2 of 2**

```
        InString$ = INKEY$
   LOOP WHILE InString$ = ""
   PRINT

   SELECT CASE InString$      'Get pointer to first record.
       CASE "1"
            Index = 1
       CASE "2"
            Index = 8
   END SELECT

→ DO
        PRINT People(Index).Rank      'Print out results.
        Index = People(Index).SuperiorPointer
   LOOP WHILE Index <> 0
```

For example, asking this program to print out life track 1 results in this list:

> Supervisor
> Director
> Vice President
> President

Note that we must know in advance that chain 1 starts with entry 1 and chain 2 with entry 8. We always need the first entry to use as a key to the first position in the linked list. After that we can work our way up either chain of command; as we do so, we print out the current Rank and get a pointer to (that is, the array index number of) the next Rank at the same time.

Circular Buffers

There is another type of linked list that programmers often use — a list where the last item points to the first one so the whole thing forms a circle. This is called a circular buffer. The most well-known circular buffer in your computer is the keyboard buffer.

What happens there is that while one part of the operating system is putting key codes into the keyboard buffer, another part of the operating system is taking them out. The location in the buffer where the next key code will be placed is called the *tail*, and the location where the next key code is to be read from is called the *head*.

When keys are typed in, the tail advances. When they are read, the head does. As you write to and read from the keyboard buffer, the head and tail march around (each data location can be either the head or the tail). When the buffer is filled, the tail comes up behind the head, and the buffer-full warning beeps.

TIP: You use circular buffers when some part of your program is writing data and some other part is reading it, but at different rates. Store the location of the head and tail positions, and, after you put data into the buffer, advance the tail. When you take data out, advance the head. This way, you can use the same memory space for both reading and writing.

The primary problem with linked lists, however, is that all access to their data is sequential access. To find the last entry in a linked list, for example, you have to start at the very first one and work your way back. That's ok for files tracked through the FAT (where you need every FAT entry before you can read the whole file), but it's a terrible method if you're only looking for a specific record. A better way is to make what's called a *binary tree*.

Binary Trees

Binary trees differ from linked lists in that, for the first time, we're going to start to order our data. We can start with a linked list as shown in Figure 7-8. And then make it a *doubly linked list* as shown in Figure 7-9.

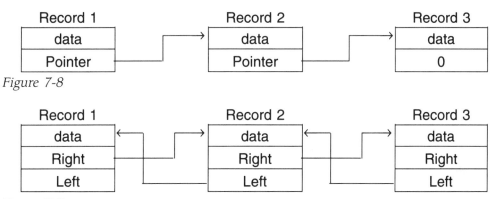

Figure 7-8

Figure 7-9

Now there are two pointers in each record: one scans up the chain, the other down. Doubly linked lists have many uses in themselves, but this is still not a binary tree. Instead, let's put in some values for the data fields, -5, 0, and 2 (see Figure 7-10).

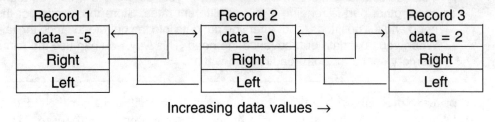

Figure 7-10

Notice that we've constructed a hierarchy based on data values here, arranging them from left to right in increasing order (-5, 0, 2). The record with the data value closest to the median data value becomes the *root* of our binary tree (see Figure 7-11).

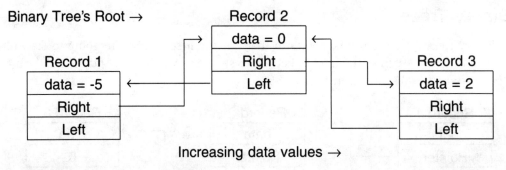

Figure 7-11

Because it has the data value closest to the middle of all three records, record 2 is the root of our binary tree. If we wanted to find a record with a data value of, say, -5, we'd start at the root, record 2, whose data value is 0. Since -5 is less than 0, we would next search the record to its left (since data values decrease to the left). This record is record 1, with a data value of -5, which means that we've found our target value.

This might seem like a small gain here, but imagine having a list like this:

First name = "Denise"
  Age = 23

First name = "Ed"
  Age = 46

First name = "Nick"
  Age = 47

First name = "Dennis"
  Age = 42

First name = "Doug"
  Age = 33

First name = "Margo"
  Age = 27

First name = "John"
  Age = 41

First name = "Cheryl"
  Age = 28

Let's say that it is your job to coordinate this list and find a person with a specified age. To construct a binary tree, you'd pick the person with an age as close to the median as possible (Doug), and put the tree together like Figure 7-12.

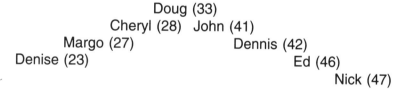

Figure 7-12

Now you can start with Doug and just keep working until you find the age you require. For example, to find the person who is 46 years old, start at Doug, who is 33. Since 46 is greater than 33, continue moving to the right through John and Dennis to Ed, who is the person we're searching for.

> **TIP:** Binary trees are good for so-called "expert systems," where each node corresponds to a question and the two branches correspond to the answers yes and no.

We should note that this is an extremely simple binary tree since, with the exception of Doug, each node only has one way to go. In general, each node can go both ways. Let's put this example into code. We start off by defining a new Person TYPE which has two pointers, one to the next older person, and one to the next younger:

```
    REM Binary Tree example.

→   TYPE Person
    FirstName AS STRING * 20
    Age AS INTEGER
    NextYoungerPerson AS INTEGER
    NextOlderPerson AS INTEGER
    END TYPE

    DIM People(10) AS Person
    :
    :
```

Then we fill each record:

```
    REM Binary Tree example.

    TYPE Person
    FirstName AS STRING * 20
    Age AS INTEGER
    NextYoungerPerson AS INTEGER
    NextOlderPerson AS INTEGER
    END TYPE

    DIM People(10) AS Person

→   People(1).FirstName = "Denise"
:   People(1).Age = 23
:   People(1).NextYoungerPerson = 0
    People(1).NextOlderPerson = 6

    People(2).FirstName = "Ed"
    People(2).Age = 46
    People(2).NextYoungerPerson = 4
    People(2).NextOlderPerson = 3

    People(3).FirstName = "Nick"
    People(3).Age = 47
    People(3).NextYoungerPerson = 2
```

```
People(3).NextOlderPerson = 0

People(4).FirstName = "Dennis"
People(4).Age = 42
People(4).NextYoungerPerson = 7
People(4).NextOlderPerson = 2

People(5).FirstName = "Doug"
People(5).Age = 33
People(5).NextYoungerPerson = 8
People(5).NextOlderPerson = 7

People(6).FirstName = "Margo"
People(6).Age = 27
People(6).NextYoungerPerson = 1
People(6).NextOlderPerson = 8

People(7).FirstName = "John"
People(7).Age = 41
People(7).NextYoungerPerson = 5
People(7).NextOlderPerson = 4

People(8).FirstName = "Cheryl"
People(8).Age = 28
People(8).NextYoungerPerson = 6
People(8).NextOlderPerson = 5
    :
    :
```

Now we can search for the first person who is 46 years old. First, we start off at the root:

```
REM Binary Tree example.

TYPE Person
FirstName AS STRING * 20
Age AS INTEGER
NextYoungerPerson AS INTEGER
NextOlderPerson AS INTEGER
END TYPE

DIM People(10) AS Person

People(1).FirstName = "Denise"
People(1).Age = 23
People(1).NextYoungerPerson = 0
People(1).NextOlderPerson = 6

People(2).FirstName = "Ed"
People(2).Age = 46
People(2).NextYoungerPerson = 4
People(2).NextOlderPerson = 3

People(3).FirstName = "Nick"
People(3).Age = 47
```

```
    People(3).NextYoungerPerson = 2
    People(3).NextOlderPerson = 0

    People(4).FirstName = "Dennis"
    People(4).Age = 42
    People(4).NextYoungerPerson = 7
    People(4).NextOlderPerson = 2

    People(5).FirstName = "Doug"
    People(5).Age = 33
    People(5).NextYoungerPerson = 8
    People(5).NextOlderPerson = 7

    People(6).FirstName = "Margo"
    People(6).Age = 27
    People(6).NextYoungerPerson = 1
    People(6).NextOlderPerson = 8

    People(7).FirstName = "John"
    People(7).Age = 41
    People(7).NextYoungerPerson = 5
    People(7).NextOlderPerson = 4

    People(8).FirstName = "Cheryl"
    People(8).Age = 28
    People(8).NextYoungerPerson = 6
    People(8).NextOlderPerson = 5

→  BinaryTreeRoot% = 5        'Doug has about the median age

    PRINT "Searching for a person 46 years old..."

    CurrentRecord% = BinaryTreeRoot%
    :
    :
```

Then we check to see if that person is 46 years old:

```
    REM Binary Tree example.

    TYPE Person
    FirstName AS STRING * 20
    Age AS INTEGER
    NextYoungerPerson AS INTEGER
    NextOlderPerson AS INTEGER
    END TYPE

    DIM People(10) AS Person

    People(1).FirstName = "Denise"
    People(1).Age = 23
    People(1).NextYoungerPerson = 0
    People(1).NextOlderPerson = 6

    People(2).FirstName = "Ed"
    People(2).Age = 46
```

```
People(2).NextYoungerPerson = 4
People(2).NextOlderPerson = 3

People(3).FirstName = "Nick"
People(3).Age = 47
People(3).NextYoungerPerson = 2
People(3).NextOlderPerson = 0

People(4).FirstName = "Dennis"
People(4).Age = 42
People(4).NextYoungerPerson = 7
People(4).NextOlderPerson = 2

People(5).FirstName = "Doug"
People(5).Age = 33
People(5).NextYoungerPerson = 8
People(5).NextOlderPerson = 7

People(6).FirstName = "Margo"
People(6).Age = 27
People(6).NextYoungerPerson = 1
People(6).NextOlderPerson = 8

People(7).FirstName = "John"
People(7).Age = 41
People(7).NextYoungerPerson = 5
People(7).NextOlderPerson = 4

People(8).FirstName = "Cheryl"
People(8).Age = 28
People(8).NextYoungerPerson = 6
People(8).NextOlderPerson = 5

BinaryTreeRoot% = 5     'Doug has about the median age

PRINT "Searching for a person 46 years old..."

CurrentRecord% = BinaryTreeRoot%

DO
:     IF People(CurrentRecord%).Age = 46 THEN
:         PRINT "That person is: "; People(CurrentRecord%).FirstName
          EXIT DO
      END IF
      :
      :
```

If not, then we have to compare the current person's age to 46. If it's less, then we want the NextOlderPerson. If greater, then we want the NextYoungerPerson. That looks like this:

```
REM Binary Tree example.

TYPE Person
FirstName AS STRING * 20
Age AS INTEGER
NextYoungerPerson AS INTEGER
NextOlderPerson AS INTEGER
END TYPE

DIM People(10) AS Person

People(1).FirstName = "Denise"
People(1).Age = 23
People(1).NextYoungerPerson = 0
People(1).NextOlderPerson = 6

People(2).FirstName = "Ed"
People(2).Age = 46
People(2).NextYoungerPerson = 4
People(2).NextOlderPerson = 3

People(3).FirstName = "Nick"
People(3).Age = 47
People(3).NextYoungerPerson = 2
People(3).NextOlderPerson = 0

People(4).FirstName = "Dennis"
People(4).Age = 42
People(4).NextYoungerPerson = 7
People(4).NextOlderPerson = 2

People(5).FirstName = "Doug"
People(5).Age = 33
People(5).NextYoungerPerson = 8
People(5).NextOlderPerson = 7

People(6).FirstName = "Margo"
People(6).Age = 27
People(6).NextYoungerPerson = 1
People(6).NextOlderPerson = 8

People(7).FirstName = "John"
People(7).Age = 41
People(7).NextYoungerPerson = 5
People(7).NextOlderPerson = 4

People(8).FirstName = "Cheryl"
People(8).Age = 28
People(8).NextYoungerPerson = 6
People(8).NextOlderPerson = 5

BinaryTreeRoot% = 5      'Doug has about the median age

PRINT "Searching for a person 46 years old..."

CurrentRecord% = BinaryTreeRoot%   DO
    IF People(CurrentRecord%).Age = 46 THEN
        PRINT "That person is: "; People(CurrentRecord%).FirstName
        EXIT DO
    END IF
    IF People(CurrentRecord%).Age > 46 THEN
        CurrentRecord% = People(CurrentRecord%).NextYoungerPerson
```

```
:          ELSE
                CurrentRecord% = People(CurrentRecord%).NextOlderPerson
           END IF
     LOOP WHILE CurrentRecord% <> 0
```

And that's how to search through a binary tree — we just keep going until we find what we're looking for (or we run out of branches).

With binary trees, we've started ordering our data. That is, we've established the relative position of a record with respect to its two neighbors. But what if we wanted to sort all the data? Sorting data is, of course, a very common thing to do; it's the next, more advanced step in organizing our data. And, because it's so common, we should explore it in some detail. To do that, we'll work through two of the fastest algorithms available, shell sorts and the Quicksort. And we'll put them to work.

TIP: It's hard to know which sorting routine will work best for your application before you see it in action. For that reason, you should test both of the following methods on your data.

Shell Sorts

The standard shell sort is always popular among programmers. It works like this: say you had a one-dimensional array with these values in it:

    8 7 6 5 4 3 2 1

To sort this list into ascending order, divide it into two partitions as shown in Figure 7-13.

            8 7 6 5   4 3 2 1
            |_____| |_____|

Figure 7-13

Then compare the first element of the first partition with the first element of the second (see Figure 7-14).

            ↓   ↓
            8 7 6 5   4 3 2 1
            |_____| |_____|

Figure 7-14

In this case, 8 is greater than 4, so we switch the elements, and go on to compare the next pair (Figure 7-15).

↓   ↓

4 7 6 5   8 3 2 1

Figure 7-15

Again, 7 is greater than 3, so we switch and go on (Figure 7-16).

↓   ↓

4 3 6 5   8 7 2 1

Figure 7-16

We also switch 6 and 2 and then look at the last pair as shown in (Figure 7-17).

↓   ↓

4 3 2 5   8 7 6 1

Figure 7-17

After we switch them too, we get this as the new list:

4 3 2 1 8 7 6 5

While this is somewhat better than before, we're still not done. The next step is to divide each partition itself into two partitions, and repeat the process, comparing 4 with 2 and 8 with 6 (see Figure 7-18).

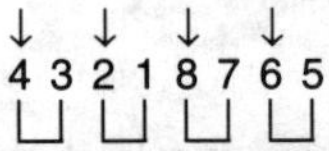

↓ ↓ ↓ ↓

4 3 2 1 8 7 6 5

Figure 7-18

We switch both pairs and go on, comparing 3 with 1 and 7 with 5 (Figure 7-19).

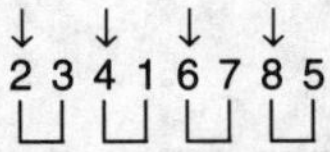

↓ ↓ ↓ ↓

2 3 4 1 6 7 8 5

Figure 7-19

Again, we switch the second set of two pairs, leaving us with this:

2 1 4 3 6 5 8 7

This looks even closer. Now the partition size is down to one element, which means that this is the last time we'll need to sort the list. We need to compare the first, and only, element in each partition with the first, and only, element in the next partition. Here that means that we compare elements 2, 4, 6, and 8 with elements 1, 3, 5, and 7. When we swap them all, we get:

1 2 3 4 5 6 7 8

And that is how the standard shell sort works — at least if there's an even number of items to sort (in which case breaking them up into balanced partitions is easy). The case where we have an odd number of elements is slightly more difficult. For example, if we had a list of nine elements to sort, we would start by breaking them up into two partitions as shown in Figure 7-20 (note that there is no last element in the second partition).

9 8 7 6 5   4 3 2 1 x

Figure 7-20

Now we'd compare as before, switching as necessary, until we try to compare a value in the first partition to a value in the second partition that isn't there (see Figure 7-21).

4 3 2 1 5   9 8 7 6 x

Figure 7-21

In this case, we just don't perform any comparison (i.e., there is no value in the x position that might have to be placed earlier in the array). Instead, we just continue on to the next smaller partition size. We keep going as before, working until the partition size becomes 1, perform the final switches, and then we're done.

Now let's see this in code. We start off by dimensioning an array and filling it with values (which are as out of order as they can be):

```
DIM Array(9) AS INTEGER  ←

Array(1) = 9
Array(2) = 8
Array(3) = 7
Array(4) = 6
Array(5) = 5
Array(6) = 4
Array(7) = 3
Array(8) = 2
Array(9) = 1
   :
   :
```

We can also print those values out so they can be compared with the sorted list later:

```
DIM Array(9) AS INTEGER

Array(1) = 9
Array(2) = 8
Array(3) = 7
Array(4) = 6
Array(5) = 5
Array(6) = 4
Array(7) = 3
Array(8) = 2
Array(9) = 1

PRINT " i            Array(i)"    ←
PRINT "---          --------"    :
FOR i = 1 TO 9                    :
        PRINT i, Array(i)
NEXT i
PRINT
PRINT "Sorting..."
        :
        :
```

Now we have to implement our shell sort. In this type of sorting routine, we loop over partition size (PartitionSize% below), so let's set that loop up first:

```
DIM Array(9) AS INTEGER

Array(1) = 9
Array(2) = 8
Array(3) = 7
Array(4) = 6
Array(5) = 5
Array(6) = 4
Array(7) = 3
Array(8) = 2
Array(9) = 1

PRINT " i            Array(i)"
PRINT "---          --------"
FOR i = 1 TO 9
        PRINT i, Array(i)
NEXT i
PRINT
PRINT "Sorting..."

        NumItems% = UBOUND(Array, 1)
        PartitionSize% = INT((NumItems% + 1) / 2)
```

```
→        DO
         :
         :
→        LOOP WHILE PartitionSize% > 0
         :
         :
```

In this loop, we loop over partition size, cutting it in half each time through (see Figure 7-22).

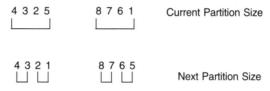

Figure 7-22

For every partition size, however, the list is broken up into a different number of partitions, and we have to loop over those partitions so we can compare elements in the current partition to the elements of the next one (Figure 7-23).

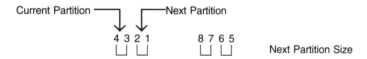

Figure 7-23

The loop over partitions looks like this (note that when we're done with each partition, we cut the partition size in half):

```
DIM Array(9) AS INTEGER

Array(1) = 9
Array(2) = 8
Array(3) = 7
Array(4) = 6
Array(5) = 5
Array(6) = 4
Array(7) = 3
Array(8) = 2
Array(9) = 1
PRINT " i          Array(i)"
PRINT "---         --------"
FOR i = 1 TO 9
        PRINT i, Array(i)
```

```
NEXT i
PRINT
PRINT "Sorting..."

        NumItems% = UBOUND(Array, 1)
        PartitionSize% = INT((NumItems% + 1) / 2)

        DO
→           NumPartitions% = (NumItems% + 1) / PartitionSize%
            Low% = 1
            FOR i = 1 TO NumPartitions% - 1
                  :
                  :
            NEXT i
            PartitionSize% = PartitionSize% \ 2
        LOOP WHILE PartitionSize% > 0
        :
        :
```

Finally, we have to loop over each element in the current partition, comparing it to the corresponding element in the next partition (see Figure 7-24).

Figure 7-24

This is the element-by-element comparison. We'll go from Array(Low%) to Array(High%) in the current partition, where Low% is the array index at the beginning of this partition and High% is the index of the element at the end, comparing each element to the corresponding one in the next partition:

```
DIM Array(9) AS INTEGER

Array(1) = 9
Array(2) = 8
Array(3) = 7
Array(4) = 6
Array(5) = 5
Array(6) = 4
Array(7) = 3
Array(8) = 2
Array(9) = 1

PRINT " i          Array(i)"
PRINT "---         --------"
```

```
FOR i = 1 TO 9
        PRINT i, Array(i)
NEXT i
PRINT
PRINT "Sorting..."

        NumItems% = UBOUND(Array, 1)
        PartitionSize% = INT((NumItems% + 1) / 2)

        DO
            NumPartitions% = (NumItems% + 1) / PartitionSize%
            Low% = 1
            FOR i = 1 TO NumPartitions% - 1
                High% = Low% + PartitionSize% - 1
                IF High% > NumItems% - PartitionSize% THEN High% = _
                    NumItems% - PartitionSize%
    →           FOR j = Low% TO High%
                    IF Array(j) > Array(j + PartitionSize%) THEN
                            :
                            :
    →               END IF
                NEXT j
                Low% = Low% + PartitionSize%
            NEXT i
            PartitionSize% = PartitionSize% \ 2
        LOOP WHILE PartitionSize% > 0
        :
        :
```

If it turns out that the element in the later partition is smaller than the element in the current one, we have to swap them, which we can do handily with the BASIC SWAP statement:

```
DIM Array(9) AS INTEGER

Array(1) = 9
Array(2) = 8
Array(3) = 7
Array(4) = 6
Array(5) = 5
Array(6) = 4
Array(7) = 3
Array(8) = 2
Array(9) = 1

PRINT " i          Array(i)"
PRINT "---         --------"
FOR i = 1 TO 9
        PRINT i, Array(i)
NEXT i
PRINT
PRINT "Sorting..."
```

```
        NumItems% = UBOUND(Array, 1)
        PartitionSize% = INT((NumItems% + 1) / 2)

        DO
            NumPartitions% = (NumItems% + 1) / PartitionSize%
            Low% = 1
            FOR i = 1 TO NumPartitions% - 1
               High% = Low% + PartitionSize% - 1
               IF High% > NumItems% - PartitionSize% THEN High% = _
                   NumItems% - PartitionSize%
               FOR j = Low% TO High%
                   IF Array(j) > Array(j + PartitionSize%) THEN
                       SWAP Array(j), Array(j + PartitionSize%)
                   END IF
               NEXT j
               Low% = Low% + PartitionSize%
            NEXT i
            PartitionSize% = PartitionSize% \ 2
        LOOP WHILE PartitionSize% > 0
        :
        :
```

And that's it. We loop over partition sizes, over each partition, and over each element in the current partition, swapping it with its counterpart in the next partition if necessary. At the end, we can print out the newly sorted array. Listing 7-3 shows the whole program.

Listing 7-3. Shell Sort Program.

```
DIM Array(9) AS INTEGER

Array(1) = 9
Array(2) = 8
Array(3) = 7
Array(4) = 6
Array(5) = 5
Array(6) = 4
Array(7) = 3
Array(8) = 2
Array(9) = 1

PRINT " i           Array(i)"
PRINT "---          --------"
FOR i = 1 TO 9
        PRINT i, Array(i)
NEXT i
PRINT
PRINT "Sorting..."

        NumItems% = UBOUND(Array, 1)
        PartitionSize% = INT((NumItems% + 1) / 2)
```

Listing 7-3.   Shell Sort Program.   2 of 2

```
        DO
            NumPartitions% = (NumItems% + 1) / PartitionSize%
            Low% = 1
            FOR i = 1 TO NumPartitions% - 1
                High% = Low% + PartitionSize% - 1
                IF High% > NumItems% - PartitionSize% THEN High% = _
                    NumItems% - PartitionSize%
                FOR j = Low% TO High%
                    IF Array(j) > Array(j + PartitionSize%) THEN
                        SWAP Array(j), Array(j + PartitionSize%)
                    END IF
                NEXT j
                Low% = Low% + PartitionSize%
            NEXT i
            PartitionSize% = PartitionSize%  2
        LOOP WHILE PartitionSize% > 0

PRINT
PRINT " i           Array(i)"
PRINT "---          --------"
FOR i = 1 TO 9
        PRINT i, Array(i)
NEXT i
```

We can even do the same thing for two-dimensional arrays. In that case, we simply sort the array on one of its columns. For example, we can adapt the above program to handle a two-dimensional array by adding a column index (Col%) to Array( ) (see Listing 7-4).

Listing 7-4.   Two-dimensional Shell Sort Program.   1 of 2

```
DIM Array(9, 4) AS INTEGER

Array(1, 1) = 9
Array(2, 1) = 8
Array(3, 1) = 7
Array(4, 1) = 6
Array(5, 1) = 5
Array(6, 1) = 4
Array(7, 1) = 3
Array(8, 1) = 2
Array(9, 1) = 1

PRINT " i           Array(i,1)"
PRINT "---          ----------"
FOR i = 1 TO 9
        PRINT i, Array(i, 1)
NEXT i
PRINT
```

Listing 7-4. Two-dimensional Shell Sort Program   2 of 2

```
PRINT "Sorting..."

        NumItems% = UBOUND(Array, 1)
        PartitionSize% = INT((NumItems% + 1) / 2)→
        DO
            NumPartitions% = (NumItems% + 1) / PartitionSize%
            Low% = 1
            FOR i = 1 TO NumPartitions% - 1
                High% = Low% + PartitionSize% - 1
                IF High% > NumItems% - PartitionSize% THEN High% = _
                    NumItems% - PartitionSize%
                FOR j = Low% TO High%
→                   IF Array(j, Col%)  Array(j + PartitionSize%, Col%) THEN
                        SWAP Array(j, Col%) > Array(j + PartitionSize%, Col%)
                    END IF
                NEXT j
                Low% = Low% + PartitionSize%
            NEXT i
            PartitionSize% = PartitionSize% \ 2
        LOOP WHILE PartitionSize% > 0

PRINT
PRINT " i          Array(i,1)"
PRINT "---          ----------"
FOR i = 1 TO 9
        PRINT i, Array(i, 1)
NEXT i
```

And now we're able to sort two-dimensional arrays on a specified column.

That concludes our tour of shell sorts. Let's turn to QuickSorts next.

Quicksorts

Besides shell sorts, another popular sorting algorithm is the Quicksort. That sorting routine works like this: first we find a key, or test, value to compare values to. The best value here would be the median value of the elements of the array, but in practice a random entry is usually chosen. Here, we'll choose a value from the center of the array.

Then we divide the array into two partitions: those less than the test value, and those greater. We move upwards in the array until we come to the first value that is greater than the test value, and down the array (starting from the end) until we find a number less than the test value. Then we swap them. We keep going until all the numbers in the first partition are less than the test value, and all the numbers in the second partition are greater.

Next, we do the same thing to each partition: we select a new test value from each partition and break that partition into two *new* partitions. One of those new partitions holds the numbers less than that test value, while the other holds those ugreater. We keep going in that way, splitting partitions continuously until there are just two numbers in a partition, at which point we compare and switch them if necessary.

You may have noticed that each subsequent step is itself a QuickSort. That is, to start, we divide the array into two partitions less than and greater than the test value, then take each partition and break *it* into two partitions depending on a new test value, and so on. In this way, QuickSorts lend themselves easily to recursion, and that's the way they're usually coded. And the QuickSort we'll develop here is no exception.

If the term *recursion* is new to you, you should know that it just refers to a routine that calls itself. If a programming task can be divided into a number of identical levels, it can be dealt with recursively. Each time the routine calls itself, it deals with a deeper level. After the final level is reached, control returns through each successive level back to the beginning. Let's see how this looks in code.

TIP: Recursion is one of the most powerful programming techniques. Its virtues include making code compact and easier to debug. On the other hand, you should know that the overhead involved in the successive calls can make it more inefficient in memory usage and speed.

Since this routine is recursive, we will set up a subprogram called SortQuick( ) to call from the main program (this subprogram will call itself repeatedly):

```
CALL SortQuick(Array( ), SortFrom%, SortTo%)
```

We just pass the array name to sort, the index to start sorting from (SortFrom%) and the index to sort to (SortTo%). Working this way will be useful when we have to sort a particular partition in the array.

In SortQuick( ), we first handle the final case; that is, a partition of only two elements:

```
SUB SortQuick (Array( ) AS INTEGER, SortFrom%, SortTo%)

    IF SortFrom% >= SortTo% THEN EXIT SUB
    IF SortFrom% + 1 = SortTo% THEN   'Final case of recursion
        IF Array(SortFrom%) > Array(SortTo%) THEN
            SWAP Array(SortFrom%), Array(SortTo%)
        END IF
    :
    :
```

In this case, we just compare each element to its neighbor (the only other element in this partition) and swap them if needed. That's all there is to the final case in the Quick-sort algorithm.

If the partition size is greater than two, however, we have to sort the values from Array(SortFrom%) to Array(SortTo%) according to a test value, dividing the elements into two new partitions, and then call SortQuick( ) again on each new partition. Let's see how that works. First, we pick a test value, then we divide the present partition into two partitions on the basis of it.

We start by moving up from the bottom of the partition, swapping any values that we find are greater than the test value:

```
SUB SortQuick (Array( ) AS INTEGER, SortFrom%, SortTo%)

        IF SortFrom% >= SortTo% THEN EXIT SUB
        IF SortFrom% + 1 = SortTo% THEN  'Final case of recursion
            IF Array(SortFrom%) > Array(SortTo%) THEN
                SWAP Array(SortFrom%), Array(SortTo%)
            END IF

→       ELSE    'Have to split problem and call again
            AtRandom = (SortFrom% + SortTo%) \ 2
            Test = Array(AtRandom)
            SWAP Array(AtRandom), Array(SortTo%)

→       DO
            REM Split into two partitions

→           FOR i = SortFrom% TO SortTo% - 1
                    IF Array(i) > Test THEN EXIT FOR
            NEXT i
                    :
                    :
→           IF i < j THEN SWAP Array(i), Array(j)
→       LOOP UNTIL i >= j
                    :
                    :
```

And we also scan from the top of the partition down in the same loop, looking for the first value that's smaller than the test value:

```
SUB SortQuick (Array( ) AS INTEGER, SortFrom%, SortTo%)

        IF SortFrom% >= SortTo% THEN EXIT SUB
        IF SortFrom% + 1 = SortTo% THEN  'Final case of recursion
            IF Array(SortFrom%) > Array(SortTo%) THEN
                SWAP Array(SortFrom%), Array(SortTo%)
            END IF
```

```
        ELSE    'Have to split problem and call again
            AtRandom = (SortFrom% + SortTo%) \ 2
            Test = Array(AtRandom)
            SWAP Array(AtRandom), Array(SortTo%)

            DO
                REM Split into two partitions

                FOR i = SortFrom% TO SortTo% - 1
                        IF Array(i) > Test THEN EXIT FOR
                NEXT i

→               FOR j = SortTo% TO i + 1 STEP -1
                        IF Array(j) < test THEN EXIT FOR
                NEXT j

                IF i < j THEN SWAP Array(i), Array(j)

            LOOP UNTIL i >= j
                :
                :
```

We keep going until i and j meet, at which time we've created our two new partitions. Next we can call SortQuick( ) again for each of the resulting partitions (which may be of unequal size):

```
SUB SortQuick (Array( ) AS INTEGER, SortFrom%, SortTo%)

     IF SortFrom% >= SortTo% THEN EXIT SUB
     IF SortFrom% + 1 = SortTo% THEN  'Final case of recursion
         IF Array(SortFrom%) > Array(SortTo%) THEN
             SWAP Array(SortFrom%), Array(SortTo%)
         END IF

     ELSE    'Have to split problem and call again
         AtRandom = (SortFrom% + SortTo%) \ 2
         Test = Array(AtRandom)
         SWAP Array(AtRandom), Array(SortTo%)

         DO

             FOR i = SortFrom% TO SortTo% - 1
                     IF Array(i) > Test THEN EXIT FOR
             NEXT i

             FOR j = SortTo% TO i + 1 STEP -1
                     IF Array(j) < Test THEN EXIT FOR
             NEXT j

             IF i < j THEN SWAP Array (i), Array(j)

         LOOP UNTIL i >= j

         SWAP Array(SortTo%), Array(i)
```

```
        REM Now work on two partitions

→       CALL SortQuick(Array( ), SortFrom%, i - 1)
        CALL SortQuick(Array( ), i + 1, SortTo%)
                 :
                 :
```

And that's all there is to it; the sort will continue recursively until we get down to the final case of a partition size of 1, the final swaps will be done if necessary, and then we're finished. Listing 7-5 shows the whole thing.

Listing 7-5. QuickSort Program.   1 of 2

```
DECLARE SUB SortQuick (Array( ) AS INTEGER, SortFrom%, SortTo%)

DIM Array(9) AS INTEGER

Array(1) = 9
Array(2) = 8
Array(3) = 7
Array(4) = 6
Array(5) = 5
Array(6) = 4
Array(7) = 3
Array(8) = 2
Array(9) = 1

PRINT " i          Array(i)"
PRINT "---        --------"
FOR i = 1 TO 9
        PRINT i, Array(i)
NEXT i

CALL SortQuick(Array( ), 1, UBOUND(Array, 1))

PRINT
PRINT "Sorting..."
PRINT
PRINT " i          Array(i)"
PRINT "---        --------"
FOR i = 1 TO 9
        PRINT i, Array(i)
NEXT i

SUB SortQuick (Array( ) AS INTEGER, SortFrom%, SortTo%)

        IF SortFrom% >= SortTo% THEN EXIT SUB
        IF SortFrom% + 1 = SortTo% THEN   'Final case
           IF Array(SortFrom%) > Array(SortTo%) THEN
                SWAP Array(SortFrom%), Array(SortTo%)
           END IF
```

Listing 7-5. QuickSort Program. 2 of 2

```
        ELSE        'Have to split problem
            AtRandom = (SortFrom% + SortTo%) \ 2
            Test = Array(AtRandom)
            SWAP Array(AtRandom), Array(SortTo%)

            DO

                FOR i = SortFrom% TO SortTo% - 1
                        IF Array(i) > Test THEN EXIT FOR
                NEXT i

                FOR j = SortTo% TO i + 1 STEP -1
                        IF Array(j) < Test THEN EXIT FOR
                NEXT j

                IF i < j THEN SWAP Array(i), Array(j)

            LOOP UNTIL i >= j

            SWAP Array(SortTo%), Array(i)

            CALL SortQuick(Array( ), SortFrom%, i - 1)
            CALL SortQuick(Array( ), i + 1, SortTo%)

        END IF

END SUB
```

Just as with out shell sort program, we can adapt the Quicksort program to work with a two-dimensional array, sorting on the values in one of its columns (the column number is given in Col%):

Listing 7-6. Two-dimensional QuickSort Program. 1 of 2

```
DECLARE SUB SortQuick (Array( ) AS INTEGER, SortFrom%, SortTo%, Col%)

DIM Array(9, 4) AS INTEGER

Array(1, 1) = 9
Array(2, 1) = 8
Array(3, 1) = 7
Array(4, 1) = 6
Array(5, 1) = 5
Array(6, 1) = 4
Array(7, 1) = 3
Array(8, 1) = 2
Array(9, 1) = 1

PRINT " i           Array(i,1)"
PRINT "---          ----------"
FOR i = 1 TO 9
```

Listing 7-6. Two-dimensional QuickSort Program. 2 of 2

```
        PRINT i, Array(i, 1)
NEXT iCol% = 1  ←
CALL SortQuick(Array( ), 1, UBOUND(Array, 1), Col%)  ←

PRINT
PRINT "Sorting..."
PRINT
PRINT " i          Array(i,1)"
PRINT "---         ----------"
FOR i = 1 TO 9
        PRINT i, Array(i, 1)
NEXT i

SUB SortQuick (Array( ) AS INTEGER, SortFrom%, SortTo%, Col%)

        IF SortFrom% >= SortTo% THEN EXIT SUB
        IF SortFrom% + 1 = SortTo% THEN  'Final case
            IF Array(SortFrom%, Col%) > Array(SortTo%, Col%) THEN
                SWAP Array(SortFrom%, Col%), Array(SortTo%, Col%)
            END IF

        ELSE    'Have to split problem
            AtRandom = (SortFrom% + SortTo%) \ 2
            Test = Array(AtRandom, Col%)
            SWAP Array(AtRandom, Col%), Array(SortTo%, Col%)

            DO

                FOR i = SortFrom% TO SortTo% - 1
                        IF Array(i, Col%) > Test THEN EXIT FOR
                NEXT i

                FOR j = SortTo% TO i + 1 STEP -1
                        IF Array(j, Col%) < Test THEN EXIT FOR
                NEXT j

                IF i < j THEN SWAP Array(i, Col%), Array(j, Col%)

            LOOP UNTIL i >= j

            SWAP Array(SortTo%, Col%), Array(i, Col%)

            CALL SortQuick(Array( ), SortFrom%, i - 1, Col%)
            CALL SortQuick(Array( ), i + 1, SortTo%, Col%)

        END IF

END SUB
```

That's it for sorting. Both the shell sort and the Quicksort are pretty fast. The one you should use will depend on your application. You might want to try them both and use the faster of the two.

Searching Your Data

Now that we've ordered our data, it becomes much easier to search through. If the data is unordered, we'd have no choice but to simply check one value after another until we found a match, as shown in Listing 7-7.

Listing 7-7.   Unordered Data Search.

```
REM Unordered Search

DIM Array(9) AS INTEGER

Array(1) = 9
Array(2) = 7
Array(3) = 8
Array(4) = 3
Array(5) = 5
Array(6) = 4
Array(7) = 6
Array(8) = 2
Array(9) = 1

PRINT "Searching the unordered list for the value 1."

FOR i = 1 TO UBOUND(Array,1)
        IF Array(i) = 1 THEN
                PRINT "Value of 1 in element";i
        END IF
NEXT i
```

We just keep scanning up the list of values until we find what we're looking for. On the other hand, we can be more intelligent when searching a sorted list. For example, if our sorted array had these values in it:

$$1 \ 2 \ 3 \ 4 \ 5 \ 6 \ 7 \ 8 \ 9 \ 10 \ 11 \ 12 \ 13 \ 14 \ 15$$

and we were searching for the entry with 10 in it, we could start off in the center of the list as shown in Figure 7-25.

Figure 7-25

Since 10 is greater than 8, we divide the *upper* half of the array in two and check the midpoint again (see Figure 7-26).

Figure 7-26

The value we're looking for, 10, is less than 12, so we move *down* and cut the remaining distance in half (Figure 7-27).

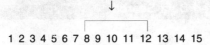

Figure 7-27

In this way, we've zeroed in on our number, cutting down the number of values we have to check. Let's see how this looks in a program.

First, we set up our array. In this example, let's search an array of 9 elements for the entry with 8 in it:

```
   REM Ordered Search

   DIM Array(9) AS INTEGER

   Array(1) = 1
   Array(2) = 2
   Array(3) = 3
   Array(4) = 4
   Array(5) = 5
   Array(6) = 6
   Array(7) = 7
   Array(8) = 8
   Array(9) = 9

→ SearchValue% = 8
   PRINT "Searching the ordered list for the value 8."
   :
   :
```

Now we cut the array into two partitions and check the test value that is right between them, at position TestIndex%:

```
   REM Ordered Search

   DIM Array(9) AS INTEGER

   Array(1) = 1
   Array(2) = 2
   Array(3) = 3
   Array(4) = 4
   Array(5) = 5
```

```
     Array(6) = 6
     Array(7) = 7
     Array(8) = 8
     Array(9) = 9

     SearchValue% = 8
     PRINT "Searching the ordered list for the value 8."

→ Partition% = (UBOUND(Array, 1) + 1) \ 2
     TestIndex% = Partition%
          :
          :
```

Then we need to start searching. We will keep looping over partition size: if the partition becomes 0 without any success, then the value we're looking for isn't in the array:

```
     REM Ordered Search

     DIM Array(9) AS INTEGER

     Array(1) = 1
     Array(2) = 2
     Array(3) = 3
     Array(4) = 4
     Array(5) = 5
     Array(6) = 6
     Array(7) = 7
     Array(8) = 8
     Array(9) = 9

     SearchValue% = 8
     PRINT "Searching the ordered list for the value 8."

     Partition% = (UBOUND(Array, 1) + 1) \ 2
     TestIndex% = Partition%
→ DO
        Partition% = Partition% \ 2
             :
        Search this partition
             :
→ LOOP WHILE Partition% > 0
     :
     :
```

Let's first check to see if we've found our value, and, if so, we can quit:

```
REM Ordered Search

DIM Array(9) AS INTEGER

Array(1) = 1
Array(2) = 2
Array(3) = 3
Array(4) = 4
Array(5) = 5
Array(6) = 6
Array(7) = 7
Array(8) = 8
Array(9) = 9

SearchValue% = 8
PRINT "Searching the ordered list for the value 8."

Partition% = (UBOUND(Array, 1) + 1) \ 2
TestIndex% = Partition%

DO
    Partition% = Partition%  2
    IF Array(TestIndex%) = SearchValue% THEN
        PRINT "Value of"; SearchValue%; "in element"; TestIndex%
        EXIT DO
    END IF
        :
        :
LOOP WHILE Partition% > 0
    :
    :
```

If we haven't found our value, we have to go on to the next iteration of the loop, setting TestIndex% to the middle of either the higher or lower partition, and then dividing that partition into two new partitions. If the search value is bigger than the value at our current location in the array, we want to move to the partition at higher values:

```
REM Ordered Search

DIM Array(9) AS INTEGER

Array(1) = 1
Array(2) = 2
Array(3) = 3
Array(4) = 4
Array(5) = 5
Array(6) = 6
Array(7) = 7
Array(8) = 8
Array(9) = 9

SearchValue% = 8
PRINT "Searching the ordered list for the value 8."
```

```
    Partition% = (UBOUND(Array, 1) + 1) \ 2
    TestIndex% = Partition%

    DO
        Partition% = Partition% \ 2
        IF Array(TestIndex%) = SearchValue% THEN
            PRINT "Value of"; SearchValue%; "in element"; TestIndex%
            EXIT DO
        END IF
→       IF Array(TestIndex%) < SearchValue% THEN
            TestIndex% = TestIndex% + Partition%
            :
            :
    LOOP WHILE Partition% > 0
    :
    :
```

But if the search value is smaller, on the other hand, we want to move to the lower partition (which holds lower values):

```
    REM Ordered Search

    DIM Array(9) AS INTEGER

    Array(1) = 1
    Array(2) = 2
    Array(3) = 3
    Array(4) = 4
    Array(5) = 5
    Array(6) = 6
    Array(7) = 7
    Array(8) = 8
    Array(9) = 9

    SearchValue% = 8
    PRINT "Searching the ordered list for the value 8."

    Partition% = (UBOUND(Array, 1) + 1) \ 2
    TestIndex% = Partition%

    DO
        Partition% = Partition% \ 2
        IF Array(TestIndex%) = SearchValue% THEN
            PRINT "Value of"; SearchValue%; "in element"; TestIndex%
            EXIT DO
        END IF
        IF Array(TestIndex%) < SearchValue% THEN
            TestIndex% = TestIndex% + Partition%
→       ELSE
            TestIndex% = TestIndex% - Partition%
        END IF
    LOOP WHILE Partition% > 0
    :
```

And that's almost all there is. We just keep going until we find what we're looking for, or the partition size becomes 0, in which case it's not there.

If we were unsuccessful, however, there are two last remaining tests that we should apply: we should check the value we're searching for against the very first and last entries in the array. That is, our algorithm demands that all numbers that it checks be straddled by two other values, and that's true of every element in the array except for the first and last ones. That means that if we didn't find what we were looking for, we have to check these last two values explicitly (see Listing 7-8).

Listing 7-8. An Ordered Search Program.

```
REM Ordered Search

DIM Array(9) AS INTEGER

Array(1) = 1
Array(2) = 2
Array(3) = 3
Array(4) = 4
Array(5) = 5
Array(6) = 6
Array(7) = 7
Array(8) = 8
Array(9) = 9

SearchValue% = 8
PRINT "Searching the ordered list for the value 8."

Partition% = (UBOUND(Array, 1) + 1) \ 2
TestIndex% = Partition%

DO
    Partition% = Partition% \ 2
    IF Array(TestIndex%) = SearchValue% THEN
        PRINT "Value of"; SearchValue%; "in element"; TestIndex%
        EXIT DO
    END IF
    IF Array(TestIndex%) < SearchValue% THEN
        TestIndex% = TestIndex% + Partition%
    ELSE
        TestIndex% = TestIndex% - Partition%
    END IF
LOOP WHILE Partition% > 0

REM Can only find straddled numbers, so add these tests:

    IF Array(1) = SearchValue% THEN
        PRINT "Value of"; SearchValue%; "in element 1"
    END IF

    IF Array(UBOUND(Array, 1)) = SearchValue% THEN
        PRINT "Value of"; SearchValue%; "in element"; UBOUND(Array, 1)
    END IF
```

And we're done with the ordered search.

Conclusion

That's it for data handling and sorting. We've seen most of the popular ways of handling numeric data in this chapter. When we're designing code, it's always important to organize our data correctly. As mentioned earlier, that can be half the battle of writing a program.

Soon we'll be ready to start our look at low-level programming and assembly language, but before we do, let's see how to debug our programs in the next chapter.

Debugging

BEFORE WE TACKLE assembly language, let's take a look at an important part of program development, one the advanced programmer should be familiar with, namely debugging. Bugs are an unfortunate fact of life, especially when long or complex programs are involved. But the tools that modern programmer has to find and fix bugs have never been better or more powerful.

We'll look at two debuggers in this chapter: the built-in debugger in QuickBASIC, and the stand-alone debugger named CodeView. Each of these are appropriate at different times. If you're using QuickBASIC primarily, it's natural to reach for the Debug window when you need it. If you're using the command-line compiler, you'll probably use CodeView to debug your programs. Let's start by getting the bugs out of a program under QuickBASIC.

TIP: For debugging the assembly language programs in the next chapter, a good choice is DEBUG.COM, which came free with DOS.

QuickBASIC Debugging

For the purposes of this chapter, let's set ourselves the task of alphabetizing 10 or so names, like these:

> John
> Tim
> Edward
> Samuel
> Frank
> Todd
> George
> Ralph
> Leonard
> Thomas

We can start by setting up an array to hold all the names:

```
DIM Names(10) AS STRING

Names(1) = "John"
Names(2) = "Tim"
Names(3) = "Edward"
Names(4) = "Samuel"
Names(5) = "Frank"
Names(6) = "Todd"
Names(7) = "George"
Names(8) = "Ralph"
Names(9) = "Leonard"
Names(10) = "Thomas"
:
```

Then we arrange them in alphabetical order with these BASIC instructions (this part of the code has two bugs in it):

```
    DIM Names(10) AS STRING

    Names(1) = "John"
    Names(2) = "Tim"
    Names(3) = "Edward"
    Names(4) = "Samuel"
    Names(5) = "Frank"
    Names(6) = "Todd"
    Names(7) = "George"
    Names(8) = "Ralph"
    Names(9) = "Leonard"
    Names(10) = "Thomas"

→   FOR i = i TO 10
 :          FOR j = i TO 10
 :                  IF Names(i) > Names(j) THEN
                         Temp$ = Names(i)
                         Names(j) = Names(j)
                         Names(j) = Temp$
                     END IF
            NEXT j
    NEXT i
    :
```

Finally, we can print out the result, name by name:

```
    DIM Names(10) AS STRING

    Names(1) = "John"
    Names(2) = "Tim"
    Names(3) = "Edward"
    Names(4) = "Samuel"
    Names(5) = "Frank"
    Names(6) = "Todd"
    Names(7) = "George"
    Names(8) = "Ralph"
    Names(9) = "Leonard"
    Names(10) = "Thomas"
```

```
   FOR i = i TO 10
         FOR j = i TO 10
               IF Names(i) > Names(j) THEN
                     Temp$ = Names(i)
                     Names(j) = Names(j)
                     Names(j) = Temp$
               END IF
         NEXT j
   NEXT i

→  FOR k = 1 TO 10
         PRINT Names(k)
   NEXT k
```

Unfortunately, this is the result of the program:

> John
> Tim
> Tim
> Tim
> Tim
> Todd
> Todd
> Todd
> Todd
> Todd

It's time to debug. If we were using QuickBASIC, that process is easy to start. Figure 8-1 shows what the QuickBASIC window looks like with our program (called, say, ALPHA.BAS) already loaded:

File	Edit	View	Search	Run	Debug	Calls	Options		Help

```
      Names(5) = "Frank"
      Names(6) = "Todd"
      Names(7) = "George"
      Names(8) = "Ralph"
      Names(9) = "Leonard"
      Names(10) = "Thomas"

      FOR i = i TO 10
            FOR j = i TO 10
                  IF Names(i) > Names(j) THEN
                        Temp$ = Names(i)
                        Names(j) = Names(j)
                        Names(j) = Temp$
                  END IF
```

```
              NEXT j
      NEXT i
------------------------------Immediate------------------------------


<Shift+F1=Help>  <F6=Window> <F2=Subs> <F5=Run> <F8=Step>    │ 00018:033
```

Figure 8-1

All we have to do is to move up to the menu bar at the top of the screen and select the Debug option. A menu like the one in Figure 8-2 opens.

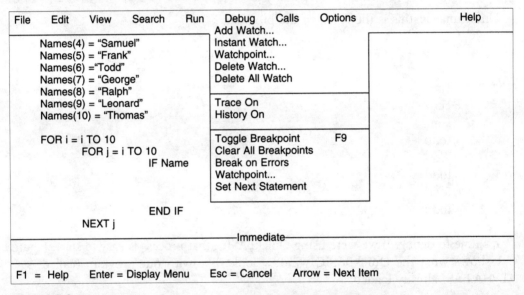

Figure 8-2

The obvious problem in our program is that the entries in the Names( ) array are being filled incorrectly. We can watch the array being filled with the Add Watch... option. We select that option and a window opens, asking for the expression to be watched (see Figure 8-3).

```
File    Edit    View    Search    Run    Debug    Calls    Options                    Help

       Names(5) = "Frank"
       Names(6) = "Todd"
       Names(7) = "George"
```

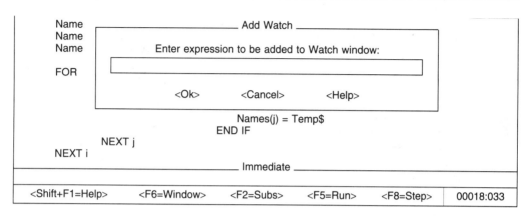

```
Name                              ___ Add Watch ___
Name
Name                  Enter expression to be added to Watch window:

FOR        ┌──────────────────────────────────────────┐
           └──────────────────────────────────────────┘

                  <Ok>          <Cancel>          <Help>

                           Names(j) = Temp$
                        END IF
              NEXT j
        NEXT i
                         ___ Immediate ___

 <Shift+F1=Help>    <F6=Window>    <F2=Subs>    <F5=Run>    <F8=Step>    00018:033
```

Figure 8-3

The two Names( ) references in our program are Names(i) and Names(j), and we can watch both of them. We just type "Names(i)" in the Add Watch dialog box to watch Names(i) and then repeat the process for Names(j). The display changes, as shown in Figure 8-4, with the current value of Names(i) and Names(j) in the top of the window.

```
 File    Edit    View    Search    Run    Debug    Calls    Options              Help
 ──────────────────────────────────────────────────────────────────────────────────
 ALPHA.BAS Names(i):        ←
 ALPHA.BAS Names(j):        ←
 ──────────────────────────────────────────────────────────────────────────────────
     Names(8) = "Ralph"
     Names(9) = "Leonard"
     Names(10) = "Thomas"

     FOR i = i TO 10
           FOR j = i TO 10
                 If Names(i) > Names(j) THEN
                     Temp$ = Names(i)
                     Names(j) = Names(j)
                     Names(j) = Temp$
                 END IF
           NEXT j
     NEXT i
                         ──Immediate ──

 <Shift+F1=Help>    <F6=Window>    <F2=Subs>    <F5=Run>    <F8=Step>    00018:033
```

Figure 8-4

Now we'll be able to track the values in Names(i) and Names(j) when we stop the program midway through its execution. And we can do that by setting *breakpoint.* A breakpoint halts program execution when it is reached. For example, we can set a breakpoint by moving the cursor on the screen down to the line that reads IF Names(i) > Names(j) THEN and pressing F9 (or selecting Toggle Breakpoint in the Debug menu). A line appears on the screen to indicate that a breakpoint has been set (see Figure 8-5).

TIP: A program is not limited to one breakpoint — you can put as many in as you like. For example, if you're having trouble with the value of some variable, one powerful technique is to break at *every* place that value is changed so you can see what's going on.

```
 File     Edit     View     Search    Run    Debug    Calls    Options                    Help
┌────────────────────────────────────────────────────────────────────────────────────────────┐
│ ALPHA.BAS Names(i):                                                                          │
│ ALPHA.BAS Names(j):                                                                          │
├──────────────────────────────────────────────────────────────────────────────────────────────┤
│      Names(8) = "Ralph"                                                                       │
│      Names(9) = "Leonard"                                                                     │
│      Names(10) = "Thomas"                                                                     │
│                                                                                              │
│      FOR i = i TO 10                                                                          │
│              FOR j = i TO 10                                                                  │
│ ─────────────────────── IF Names(i) > Names(j) THEN ───────────────────────                  │
│                      Temp$ = Names(i)                                                         │
│                      Names(j) = Names(j)                                                      │
│                      Names(j) = Temp$                                                         │
│                  END IF                                                                      │
│              NEXT j                                                                           │
│      NEXT i                                                                                   │
│ ─────────────────────────────Immediate ─────────────────────────────────                    │
├──────────────────────────────────────────────────────────────────────────────────────────────┤
│ <Shift+F1=Help>      <F6=Window>      <F2=Subs>      <F5=Run>      <F8=Step> │ 00018:033      │
└────────────────────────────────────────────────────────────────────────────────────────────┘
```

Figure 8-5

Now we run the program by selecting Start in the Run menu. Program execution continues until we reach the breakpoint and then stops. We look at the displayed values of Names(i) and Names(j), only to find that they are unchanged (in the Watch window at the top). (See Figure 8-6.)

```
 File    Edit    View    Search    Run    Debug    Calls    Options                    Help
┌──────────────────────────────────────────────────────────────────────────────────┐
│  ALPHA.BAS Names(i):       ←                                                       │
│  ALPHA.BAS Names(j):       ←                                                       │
│     Names(8) = "Ralph"                                                             │
│     Names(9) = "Leonard"                                                           │
│     Names(10) = "Thomas"                                                           │
│                                                                                    │
│     FOR i = i TO 10                                                                │
│           FOR j = i TO 10                                                          │
│  ────────────────────IF Names(i) > Names(j) THEN ──────────────────────           │
│                       Temp$ = Names(i)                                             │
│                       Names(j) = Names(j)                                          │
│                       Names(j) = Temp$                                             │
│                   END IF                                                           │
│            NEXT j                                                                  │
│        NEXT i                                                                      │
│  ─────────────────────────────Immediate ──────────────────────────────            │
├──────────────────────────────────────────────────────────────────────────────────┤
│ <Shift+F1=Help>    <F6=Window>    <F2=Subs>    <F5=Run>    <F8=Step>  │ 00018:033 │
└──────────────────────────────────────────────────────────────────────────────────┘
```

Figure 8-6

In other words, the line IF Names(i) > Names(j) THEN is comparing nothing. The values in Names(i) and Names(j) are not valid. At this point in the program, the beginning, both i and j are supposed to point to the first element in the array. That is, both i and j should be 1. We can check the value of i simply by placing the cursor on it and selecting the Instant Watch... option in the Debug menu (see Figure 8-7).

```
 File    Edit    View    Search    Run    Debug    Calls    Options                  Help
┌──────────────────────────────────────┬─────────────────────────┬──────────────────┐
│                                       │ Add Watch...            │                  │
│   ALPHA.BAS Names(i):                 │ Instant Watch...   ←    │                  │
│   ALPHA.BAS Names(j):                 │ Watchpoint...           │                  │
│  ─────────────────────────────────── │ Delete Watch...         │                  │
│     Names(7) = "George"               │ Delete All Watch        │                  │
│     Names(8) = "Ralph"                │─────────────────────────│                  │
│     Names(9) = "Leonard"              │ Trace On                │                  │
│     Names(10) = "Thomas"              │ History On              │                  │
│                                       │─────────────────────────│                  │
│     FOR i = i TO 10                   │ Toggle Breakpoint    F9 │                  │
│           FOR j = i TO 10             │ Clear All Breakpoints   │                  │
│  ─────────────────────IF Name         │ Break on Errors         │                  │
│                                       │ Watchpoint...           │                  │
│                                       │ Set Next Statement      │                  │
│                   END IF              └─────────────────────────┘                  │
│            NEXT j                                                                  │
│        NEXT i                                                                      │
│  ─────────────────────────────Immediate──────────────────────────────             │
├──────────────────────────────────────────────────────────────────────────────────┤
│ F1 = Help    Enter = Display Menu    Esc = Cancel    Arrow = Next Item             │
└──────────────────────────────────────────────────────────────────────────────────┘
```

Figure 8-7

And a window shown in Figure 8-8 appears, displaying the current value of i.

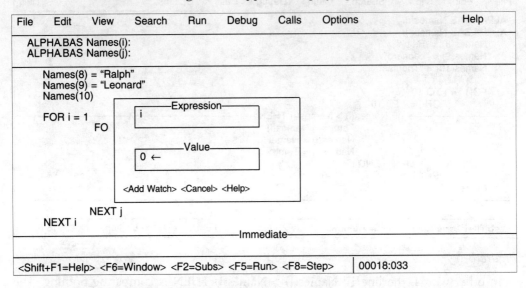

Figure 8-8

We see that i = 0, which is a problem. This line in the code must be changed to FOR i = 1 to 10 because we need to initialize i before using it:

```
DIM Names(10) AS STRING

Names(1) = "John"
Names(2) = "Tim"
Names(3) = "Edward"
Names(4) = "Samuel"
Names(5) = "Frank"
Names(6) = "Todd"
Names(7) = "George"
Names(8) = "Ralph"
Names(9) = "Leonard"
Names(10) = "Thomas"

→ FOR i = i TO 10
        FOR j = i TO 10
            IF Names(i) > Names(j) THEN
                Temp$ = Names(i)
                Names(j) = Names(j)
                Names(j) = Temp$
            END IF
        NEXT j
```

```
NEXT i

FOR k = 1 TO 10
        PRINT Names(k)
NEXT k
```

However, when we make the change and run the program, we still see:

John
Tim
Tim
Tim
Tim
Todd
Todd
Todd
Todd
Todd

Obviously there is still a problem. Let's examine the part of the program where the actual elements are switched, the only other part of the program. We can put a breakpoint in at the end of the element switching section as shown in Figure 8-9.

```
File    Edit    View    Search    Run    Debug    Calls    Options              Help
─────────────────────────────────────────────────────────────────────────────────
  ALPHA.BAS Names(i):
  ALPHA.BAS Names(j):
─────────────────────────────────────────────────────────────────────────────────
    Names(8) = "Ralph"
    Names(9) = "Leonard"
    Names(10) = "Thomas"

    FOR i = i TO 10
            FOR j = i TO 10
                    IF Names(i) > Names(j) THEN
                        Temp$ = Names(i)
                        Names(j) = Names(j)
                  ──────Names(j) =Temp$────────────────────────────────────────────
                        END IF
            NEXT j
    NEXT i
─────────────────────────────────────Immediate────────────────────────────────────


─────────────────────────────────────────────────────────────────────────────────
<Shift+F1=Help> <F6=Window> <F2=Subs> <F5=Run> <F8=Step>    │  00018:033
```

Figure 8-9

And then we run the program. Execution halts at the breakpoint, and we examine Names(i) and Names(j) (see Figure 8-10).

File	Edit	View	Search	Run	Debug	Calls	Options	Help

```
ALPHA.BAS Names(i): "John"    ←
ALPHA.BAS Names(j): "Edward"  ←

    Names(8) = "Ralph"
    Names(9) = "Leonard"
    Names(10) = "Thomas"

    FOR i = i TO 10
          FOR j = i TO 10
                IF Names(i)  >Names(j) THEN
                      Temp$ = Names(i)
                      Names(j) = Names(j)
                      Names(j) = Temp$
                END IF
          NEXT j
    NEXT i
                                    Immediate
```

| <Shift+F1=Help> <F6=Window> <F2=Subs> <F5=Run> <F8=Step> | 00018:033 |

Figure 8-10

The exchange of array elements is supposed to go like this: we take the value in Names(i) and place it in Temp$. Then we copy the element in Names(j) and place it into Names(i). The final step is to move Temp$ into Names(j). At this breakpoint, all but the final step has been taken: We are about to move the value in Temp$ into Names(j).

In other words, we'd expect Names(i) and Names(j) to hold the same value, but they do not. Names(i) holds John and Names(j) holds Edward. Something is wrong. If we look back one line in our code, we see this line:

```
DIM Names(10) AS STRING

Names(1) = "John"
Names(2) = "Tim"
Names(3) = "Edward"
Names(4) = "Samuel"
Names(5) = "Frank"
Names(6) = "Todd"
Names(7) = "George"
Names(8) = "Ralph"
Names(9) = "Leonard"
Names(10) = "Thomas"

FOR i = 1 TO 10
```

```
            FOR j = i TO 10
                    IF Names(i)  Names(j) THEN
                            Temp$ = Names(i)
        →                   Names(j) = Names(j)
                            Names(j) = Temp$
                    END IF
            NEXT j
    NEXT i

    FOR k = 1 TO 10
            PRINT Names(k)
    NEXT k
```

It is apparent that this line should be Names(i) = Names(j). We make the change, yielding the debugged program (shown in Listing 8-1).

Listing 8-1.   Debugged Alphabetizing Program.

```
DIM Names(10) AS STRING

Names(1) = "John"
Names(2) = "Tim"
Names(3) = "Edward"
Names(4) = "Samuel"
Names(5) = "Frank"
Names(6) = "Todd"
Names(7) = "George"
Names(8) = "Ralph"
Names(9) = "Leonard"
Names(10) = "Thomas"

FOR i = 1 TO 10
        FOR j = i TO 10
                IF Names(i) > Names(j) THEN
                        Temp$ = Names(i)
                        Names(i) = Names(j)
                        Names(j) = Temp$
                END IF
        NEXT j
NEXT i

FOR k = 1 TO 10
        PRINT Names(k)
NEXT k
```

And this is the final result when we run it:

        Edward
        Frank
        George
        John

Leonard

Ralph

Samuel

Thomas

Tim

Todd

The program has been debugged. Now let's take a look at the same process under CodeView.

CodeView

> **TIP:** CodeView can debug all Microsoft languages, not just BASIC. This can come in handy if you interface BASIC to assembly language, as we'll do later.

Once again, let's start with the same program (with the two bugs in it):

```
DIM Names(10) AS STRING

Names(1) = "John"
Names(2) = "Tim"
Names(3) = "Edward"
Names(4) = "Samuel"
Names(5) = "Frank"
Names(6) = "Todd"
Names(7) = "George"
Names(8) = "Ralph"
Names(9) = "Leonard"
Names(10) = "Thomas"

FOR i = i TO 10
        FOR j = i TO 10
                IF Names(i) > Names(j) THEN
                        Temp$ = Names(i)
                        Names(j) = Names(j)
                        Names(j) = Temp$
                END IF
        NEXT j
NEXT i

FOR k = 1 TO 10
        PRINT Names(k)
NEXT k
```

We cannot use the QB (or QBX) environment with CodeView, however. Instead, we must compile our program, ALPHA.BAS, like this with BC.EXE:

```
D:\>BC /Zi ALPHA;

Microsoft (R) QuickBASIC Compiler Version 4.50
(C) Copyright Microsoft Corporation 1982-1988.
All rights reserved.
Simultaneously published in the U.S. and Canada.

43997 Bytes Available
42104 Bytes Free

    0 Warning Error(s)
    0 Severe  Error(s)
```

The /Zi switch is a necessary step in preparing for CodeView; it instructs the compiler to retain the line number and symbol information that CodeView will need. Next we link, setting up for CodeView with the /Co switch to the linker like this:

```
D:\> LINK /Co ALPHA;

Microsoft (R) Overlay Linker  Version 3.69
Copyright (C) Microsoft Corp 1983-1988.  All rights reserved.
```

And that's it; ALPHA.EXE has been produced and we're ready to run our program. When we do, however, we get this result, as before:

John
Tim
Tim
Tim
Tim
Todd
Todd
Todd
Todd
Todd

Obviously, there is a problem. We can debug ALPHA.EXE with CodeView by typing CV ALPHA. The CodeView screen shown in Figure 8-11 appears:

TIP: CodeView can also be started in sequential mode (without windows) if you use the IT switch. In this mode, you can redirect its output to a file — which gives you a complete record of your debugging session for later reference.

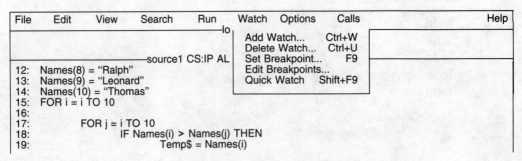

```
 File     Edit     View     Search     Run     Debug     Calls     Options                        Help
                                        ──local──
                     ──────source 1 CS:IP ALPHA.BAS (ACTIVE)──────
  1:   DIM Names(10) AS STRING
  2:
  3:
  4:
  5:   Names(1) = "John"
  6:   Names(2) = "Tim"
  7:   Names(3) = "Edward"
  8:   Names(4) = "Samuel"
  9:   Names(5) = "Frank"
 10:   Names(6) = "Todd"
 11:   Names(7) = "George"
 12:   Names(8) = "Ralph"
                                     ──Command──
 >


     <F8=Trace>          <F10=Step>          <F5=Go>     <F6=Window>  <F8=Display>
```

Figure 8-11

CodeView is the premier debugger for the PC; the abilities of this package are practically unlimited, but we'll only get a chance to scratch the surface in this chapter. We can start as we did with QuickBASIC, by watching both Names(i) and Names(j). We do that by pulling down the Watch menu and selecting Add Watch... (see Figure 8-12).

```
 File     Edit     View     Search     Run     Watch     Options     Calls                        Help
                                        ──lo──┌──────────────────────────┐
                                              │ Add Watch...      Ctrl+W │
                      ──────source1 CS:IP AL──│ Delete Watch...   Ctrl+U │
                                              │ Set Breakpoint...     F9 │
 12:   Names(8) = "Ralph"                     │ Edit Breakpoints...      │
 13:   Names(9) = "Leonard"                   │ Quick Watch    Shift+F9 │
 14:   Names(10) = "Thomas"                   └──────────────────────────┘
 15:   FOR i = i TO 10
 16:
 17:           FOR j = i TO 10
 18:                 IF Names(i) > Names(j) THEN
 19:                     Temp$ = Names(i)
```

```
| 20:                      Names(j) = Names(j)
| 21:                      Names(j) = Temp$
| 22:          END IF
| 23:      NEXT j
|                               ─────────Command─────────────────────
| >
|
| <F8=Trace>    <F10=Step>    <F5=Go>    <F6=Window>   <F3=Display>
```

Figure 8-12

The window shown in Figure 8-13 opens up, much like the window in QuickBASIC. We can type Names(i), and then repeat the process for Names(j):

```
File    Edit    View    Search    Run    Watch    Options    Calls              Help
                              ─────────local──────
                         ─────source1 CS:IP ALPHA.BAS (ACTIVE)────────────
  12:     Names(8) = "Ralph"
  13:     Names(9)          ─────────────Add Watch────────
  14:     Names(10         ┌──────────────────────────────────────┐
  15:                      │  Expression: [Names(i)  ←        ]   │
  16:     FOR i =          │                                      │
  17:                      │                                      │
  18:                      │       <Ok><CANCEL> <Help>            │
  19:                      └──────────────────────────────────────┘
  20:                      Names(j) = Names(j)
  21:                      Names(j) = Temp$
  22:              END IF
  23:       NEXT j
                               ─────────Command──────────────
  >

  <F8=Trace>  <F10=Step>  <F5=Go>  <F6=Window>  <F3=Display>
```

Figure 8-13

The top window splits in two, and a watch window appears. Figure 8-14 shows what the Watch window looks like:

```
File    Edit    View    Search    Run    Watch    Options    Calls              Help
                  ─────────local──────               │ Names(i)=" " ← ─watch─
                                                     │ Names(j)=" " ←
                          ─────source1 CS:IP ALPHA.BAS (ACTIVE)────────
  12:     Names(8) = "Ralph"
  13:     Names(9) = "Leonard"
  14:     Names(10) = "Thomas"
  15:
  16:     FOR i = i TO 10
  17:           FOR j = i TO 10
  18:                 IF Names(i) > Names(j) THEN
  19:                       Temp$ = Names(i)
```

```
20:                              Names(j) = Names(j)
21:                              Names(j) = Temp$
22:                    END IF
23:          NEXT j
                              ─────Command──────────────────────────
>
```

```
<F8=Trace>   <F10=Step>   <F5=Go>   <F6=Window>   <F3=Display>
```

Figure 8-14

NOTE: Every one of the CodeView windows may be independently scrolled, and, if an expression goes off the screen, we can always use the scroll bars to display it fully.

We can put a breakpoint in, just as we did with QuickBASIC, at the line IF Names(i) > Names(j) THEN with F9 (or by using Set Breakpoint in the Watch window). CodeView is a command-driven debugger; to execute the program up to the breakpoint, we can just type g for go (see Figure 8-15.)

```
File    Edit    View    Search    Run    Watch    Options    Calls              Help
                    ─────local─────                    ─────────watch─────
                                        │ Names(i)=" "
                                        │ Names(j)=" "
                              ─────source1 CS:IP ALPHA.BAS (ACTIVE)─────
12:      Names(8) = "Ralph"
13:      Names(9) = "Leonard"
14:      Names(10) = "Thomas"
15:
16:      FOR i = i TO 10
17:              FOR j = i TO 10
18:──────────────────────IF Names(i) > Names(j) THEN────────────────────
19:                      Temp$ = Names(i)
20:                      Names(j) = Names(j)
21:                      Names(j) = Temp$
22:              END IF
23:          NEXT j
                              ─────Command──────────────────────────
>g ←
```

```
<F8=Trace>   <F10=Step>   <F5=Go>   <F6=Window>   <F3=Display>
```

Figure 8-15

Execution continues until it hits our breakpoint. Then we can examine the watch window. As shown in Figure 8-16, Names(i) and Names(j) are still null strings, although they should have been assigned to character strings already.

```
 File    Edit    View    Search    Run    Watch    Options    Calls                   Help
 ───────────────────────local──────────────────────┌─────watch─────────────────
                                                    │ Names(i)="  "←
                                                    │ Names(j)="  "←
 ───────────────────────────source1 CS:IP ALPHA.BAS (ACTIVE)────────────────────
  12:      Names(8) = "Ralph"
  13:      Names(9) = "Leonard"
  14:      Names(10) = "Thomas"
  15:
  16:      FOR i = i TO 10
  17:           FOR j = i TO 10
  18: ───────────────────────IF Names(i) > Names(j) THEN─────────────────────────
  19:                     Temp$ = Names(i)
  20:                     Names(j) = Names(j)
  21:                     Names(j) = Temp$
  22:                END IF
  23:           NEXT j
 ──────────────────────────────────Command──────────────────────────────────────
 >g
 >
 ────────────────────────────────────────────────────────────────────────────────
 <F8=Trace>   <F10=Step>   <F5=Go>   <F6=Window>   <F3=Display>
```

Figure 8-16

We can check the value of the indices i and j with the ? command. In this case, the ?i command tells CodeView to display the current value of i (see Figure 8-17).

```
 File    Edit    View    Search    Run    Watch    Options    Calls                   Help
 ───────────────────────local──────────────────────┌─────watch─────────────────
                                                    │ Names(i)="  "
                                                    │ Names(j)="  "
 ───────────────────────────source1 CS:IP ALPHA.BAS (ACTIVE)────────────────────
  13:      Names(9) = "Leonard"
  14:      Names(10) = "Thomas"
  15:
  16:      FOR i = i TO 10
  17:           FOR j = i TO 10
  18: ───────────────────────IF Names(i) > Names(j) THEN─────────────────────────
  19:                     Temp$ = Names(i)
  20:                     Names(j) = Names(j)
  21:                     Names(j) = Temp$
  22:                END IF
  23:           NEXT j
 ──────────────────────────────────Command──────────────────────────────────────
 >?i ←
 0  ←
 >
 ────────────────────────────────────────────────────────────────────────────────
 <F8=Trace>   <F10=Step>   <F5=Go>   <F6=Window>   <F3=Display>
```

Figure 8-17

And we see that it is 0. Again, we see that this line in the program is causing problems:

```
    DIM Names(10) AS STRING

    Names(1) = "John"
    Names(2) = "Tim"
    Names(3) = "Edward"
    Names(4) = "Samuel"
    Names(5) = "Frank"
    Names(6) = "Todd"
    Names(7) = "George"
    Names(8) = "Ralph"
    Names(9) = "Leonard"
    Names(10) = "Thomas"

→  FOR i = i TO 10
          FOR j = i TO 10
                 IF Names(i) > Names(j) THEN
                        Temp$ = Names(i)
                        Names(j) = Names(j)
                        Names(j) = Temp$
                 END IF
          NEXT j
    NEXT i

    FOR k = 1 TO 10
          PRINT Names(k)
    NEXT k
```

TIP: CodeView can even evaluate BASIC expressions for you. For example, ?ASC ("A") + 5 will give you a result of 70. This is a good way of checking your code if you're unsure about the effect of some statements — and you can do it without leaving CodeView.

And we can change it to FOR i = 1 TO 10. Unfortunately, the partially debugged program still gives us the same output:

```
John
Tim
Tim
Tim
Tim
Todd
Todd
Todd
Todd
Todd
```

We can turn back to CodeView. This time, we put a breakpoint farther down in the code at the end of the section that switches the elements in the array (see Figure 8-18.)

```
 File     Edit     View     Search     Run     Watch     Options     Calls          Help
 ───────────────local──────────────────────────────watch──────
                                                │ Names(i)="  "
                                                │ Names(j)="  "
                                   ──────source1 CS:IP ALPHA.BAS (ACTIVE)──────
  12:      Names(8) = "Ralph"
  13:      Names(9) = "Leonard"
  14:      Names(10) = "Thomas"
  15:
  16:      FOR i = i TO 10
  17:           FOR j = i TO 10
  18:                IF Names(i) > Names(j) THEN
  19:                     Temp$ = Names(i)
  20:                     Names(j) = Names(j)
  21: ───────────────────────────────Names(j) = Temp$──────────
  22:           END IF
  23:      NEXT j
                                   ──────────Command──────────
  >
 ─────────────────────────────────────────────────────────────
 <F8=Trace>   <F10=Step>   <F5=Go>   <F6=Window>   <F3=Display>
```

Figure 8-18

Once again, we type g for go, and the program executes until it reaches the breakpoint. As before, the section of code that switches array elements works in three steps. First, it movesNames(i) into Temp$, then moves Names(j) into Names(i), and ends up by moving Temp$ into Names(j). At this breakpoint, all but the last step has been completed, which means that Names(i) and Names(j) should hold the same values. In fact, Names(i) = "John" and Names(j) = "Edward" (see Figure 8-19.)

```
 File     Edit     View     Search     Run     Watch     Options     Calls          Help
 ───────────────local──────────────────────────────watch──────
                                                │ Names(i)="John"      ←
                                                │ Names(j)="Edward"    ←
                                   ──────source1 CS:IP ALPHA.BAS (ACTIVE)──────
  12:      Names(8) = "Ralph"
  13:      Names(9) = "Leonard"
  14:      Names(10) = "Thomas"
  15:
  16:      FOR i = i TO 10
  17:           FOR j = i TO 10
  18:                IF Names(i) > Names(j) THEN
  19:                     Temp$ = Names(i)
  20:                     Names(j) = Names(j)
  21: ───────────────────────────────Names(j) = Temp$──────────
  22:                IF END
```

23:	NEXT j

————————————————Command————————————————————————

>g

<F8=Trace>   <F10=Step>   <F5=Go>   <F6=Window>   <F3=Display>

Figure 8-19

That indicates that there is a problem with the way the array elements are loaded during the switching process. We check the code and find that the line immediately before the breakpoint is in error:

```
DIM Names(10) AS STRING

Names(1) = "John"
Names(2) = "Tim"
Names(3) = "Edward"
Names(4) = "Samuel"
Names(5) = "Frank"
Names(6) = "Todd"
Names(7) = "George"
Names(8) = "Ralph"
Names(9) = "Leonard"
Names(10) = "Thomas"

FOR i = 1 TO 10
        FOR j = i TO 10
                IF Names(i) > Names(j) THEN
                        Temp$ = Names(i)
        →               Names(j) = Names(j)
                        Names(j) = Temp$
                END IF
        NEXT j
NEXT i

FOR k = 1 TO 10
        PRINT Names(k)
NEXT k
```

We switch this line to Names(i) = Names(j), yielding the debugged program (shown in Listing 8-2).

Listing 8-2.   Debugged Alphabetizing Program

```
DIM Names(10) AS STRING

Names(1)  =  "John"
Names(2)  =  "Tim"
Names(3)  =  "Edward"
Names(4)  =  "Samuel"
Names(5)  =  "Frank"
Names(6)  =  "Todd"
Names(7)  =  "George"
Names(8)  =  "Ralph"
Names(9)  =  "Leonard"
Names(10) =  "Thomas"


FOR i = 1 TO 10
        FOR j = i TO 10
                IF Names(i) > Names(j) THEN
                        Temp$ = Names(i)
                        Names(i) = Names(j)
                        Names(j) = Temp$
                END IF
        NEXT j
NEXT i

FOR k = 1 TO 10
        PRINT Names(k)
NEXT k
```

And the output is correct as well:

    Edward
    Frank
    George
    John
    Leonard
    Ralph
    Samuel
    Thomas
    Tim
    Todd

The program has been debugged. CodeView is a powerful debugger, and it provides many, many tools for the programmer. It is worth noticing that, besides breakpoints, CodeView also has *tracepoints* and *watchpoints*. A tracepoint is variable breakpoint that is taken when a specified value changes. The value can be either the value of a variable or the value of some expression. For example, when the value in a certain variable changes, the tracepoint is activated.

A watchpoint is a variable breakpoint that is taken when a specified expression becomes true (that is, nonzero). In other words, you can give CodeView a BASIC expression to test as it steps through a program; when that expression becomes true, the watchpoint is activated. All in all, we've just scratched the surface here; if you run into serious bugs, you'll often find assistance in CodeView.

NOTE: CodeView will not help you debug memory-resident files, however; nor can it retain symbolic information in programs that are made into .COM files.

That ends our discussion of debugging. For more information, see the QuickBASIC or the CodeView manuals. Now, however, it is time to start moving on to assembly language to add real speed and power to our BASIC code. We'll do that be beginning to see what the operating system has to offer us.

Chapter 9

A Tour of BIOS and DOS

ONE OF THE most powerful ways of augmenting BASIC is to use the resources available to us in BIOS (the Basic Input/Output System that is already in the computer's ROM) and DOS, and BASIC allows us to reach the computer's low-level resources directly with its INTERRUPT( ) and INTERRUPTX( ) routines.

TIP:	You can often do some things that BASIC does in a fraction of the time by interfacing to DOS and BIOS. The most common example is fast file manipulation.

In this chapter, we're going to make a tour of BIOS and DOS, and we'll examine all the services they provide (as listed in the appendix at the end of this book). These services are built into the operating system, which means they're available to us as BASIC programmers. We're not going to limit our exploration to just looking. We're going to put together some subprograms and functions that will let us make use of this added power.

For example, we'll write routines that can search for files matching a given file specification (including wildcards), one that can find the amount of free space left on a target disk, another one that can tell us what equipment is installed in the computer, and others. To develop these and more, let's get started with the BIOS interrupts immediately.

The BIOS Interrupts

The BIOS interrupts are are given numbers 0 through &H1F. Each of these interrupts corresponds to prewritten assembly language code that is already resident in memory, and that we can reach through INTERRUPT( ) or INTERRUPTX( ). The low-level BIOS interrupts, up to &H10, are not often used by programmers, however, with the exception of interrupt 9. This is the hardware interrupt that reads keys from the keyboard. Every time a key is struck, an interrupt 9 is executed. It's possible to *intercept* this interrupt, and handle these keystrokes yourself, which is the basis of many TSR pop-up programs. Here's what the interrupts 0 through &HF do:

Interrupt 0	Divide By 0 (Generated if a program divides by 0)
Interrupt 1	Single Step (Used by debuggers)
Interrupt 2	NonMaskable Hardware Interrupt (NMI)
Interrupt 3	Breakpoint (Used by debuggers)
Interrupt 4	Overflow
Interrupt 5	Print Screen

Interrupts 6 and 7	Reserved
Interrupt 8	Time of Day
Interrupt 9	Keyboard
Interrupt &HA	Reserved
Interrupts &HB-&HF	BIOS end interrupt routine, resets interrupt handler

In particular, you might notice interrupt 5, which is the interrupt called when you press the Print Screen key. If you execute an interrupt 5 with INTERRUPT( ), you'll print the screen out.

The first big BIOS interrupt is interrupt &H10, which handles the screen at the lowest level. Here are those services:

Interrupt &H10	Service 0	Set Screen Mode
Interrupt &H10	Service 1	Set Cursor Type
Interrupt &H10	Service 2	Set Cursor Position
Interrupt &H10	Service 3	Find Cursor Position
Interrupt &H10	Service 4	Read Light Pen Position
Interrupt &H10	Service 5	Set Active Display Page
Interrupt &H10	Service 6	Scroll Active Page Up
Interrupt &H10	Service 7	Scroll Active Page Down
Interrupt &H10	Service 8	Read Attribute/Character at Cursor Position
Interrupt &H10	Service 9	Write Attribute/Character at Cursor Position
Interrupt &H10	Service &HA	Write Character ONLY at Cursor Position
Interrupt &H10	Service &HB	Set Color Palette
Interrupt &H10	Service &HC	Write Dot (Set Pixel)
Interrupt &H10	Service &HD	Read Dot (Read pixel color)
Interrupt &H10	Service &HE	Teletype Write to Active Page
Interrupt &H10	Service &HF	Return Video State
Interrupt &H10	Service &H10	Set Palette Registers
Interrupt &H10	Service &H10	Function 0 Set Individual Palette Register

Interrupt &H10	Service &H10	Function 1 Set Overscan (Border) Register
Interrupt &H10	Service &H10	Function 2 Set All Palette Registers
Interrupt &H10	Service &H10	Function 7 Read Individual Palette Register
Interrupt &H10	Service &H10	Function 8 Read Overscan (Border) Register
Interrupt &H10	Service &H10 Function &H10	Set DAC Register
Interrupt &H10	Service &H10 Function &H12	Set DAC Registers
Interrupt &H10	Service &H10 Function &H13	Select Color Page Mode
Interrupt &H10	Service &H11	Character Generator
Interrupt &H10	Service &H12	Alternate Select

To select a service from an interrupt, load the service's number into the ah register. Some of these services are pretty complex, and it's not appropriate to spend too much time on them in our tour of the system's resources. However, it's often useful to know what the video mode is, so let's put together a small function to find the current BIOS screen mode.

The BIOS Screen Mode

If you know the current BIOS mode, you know the number of rows and columns (or pixels) available on the screen, and the number of colors you can display at once. Here is a list of BIOS modes and what they mean as far as video capability is concerned:

BIOS mode	Display lines	Number of colors	Adapter cards	Maximum pages allowed
0	40x25	B&W text	CGA, EGA, VGA	8
1	40x25	Color text	CGA, EGA, VGA	8
2	80x25	B&W text	CGA, EGA, VGA	4 (CGA) 8 (EGA, VGA)
3	80x25	Color text	CGA, EGA, VGA	4 (CGA) 8 (EGA, VGA)

4	320x200 4	CGA, EGA, VGA	1
5	320x200 B&W	CGA, EGA, VGA	1
6	640x200 2 (on or off)	CGA, EGA, VGA	1
7	80x25 Monochrome	MDA, EGA, VGA	1 (MDA) 8 (EGA, VGA)
8	160x200 16	PCjr	1
9	320x200 16	PCjr	1
A	640x200 1	PCjr	1
B	Reserved for future use.		
C	Reserved for future use.		
D	320x200 16	EGA, VGA	8
E	640x200 16	EGA, VGA	4
F	640x350 monochrome	EGA, VGA	2
10H	640x350 16	EGA, VGA	2
11H	640x480 2	VGA	1
12H	640x480 16	VGA	1
13H	320x200 256	VGA	1

To get the BIOS video mode, we can look in the appendix to see that interrupt &H10 service &HF is what we want. Let's write a function named VideoMode%( ) to return the video mode. We start off by loading ah with &HF and calling INTERRUPT( ):

```
   DIM InRegs AS RegType, OutRegs AS RegType
→  InRegs.ax = &HF00
   CALL INTERRUPT(&H10, InRegs, OutRegs)
      :
```

Checking the appendix, we see that the video mode is returned in al, the bottom eight bits of the ax register. To return that as the value of the function VideoMode%, we AND ax with &HFF:

```
   DIM InRegs AS RegType, OutRegs AS RegType
   InRegs.ax = &HF00
   CALL INTERRUPT(&H10, InRegs, OutRegs)
→  VideoMode% = &HFF AND OutRegs.ax
```

And that's all there is to it. Listing 9-1 shows the whole function.

Listing 9-1.   VideoMode% Function — Determines Video Mode.

```
DECLARE FUNCTION VideoMode% ( )

TYPE RegType
        ax       AS INTEGER
        bx       AS INTEGER
        cx       AS INTEGER
        dx       AS INTEGER
        bp       AS INTEGER
        si       AS INTEGER
        di       AS INTEGER
        flags    AS INTEGER
END TYPE

DECLARE SUB INTERRUPT (IntNo AS INTEGER, InRegs AS RegType, OutRegs AS RegType)

FUNCTION VideoMode%

  DIM InRegs AS RegType, OutRegs AS RegType
  InRegs.ax = &HF00
  CALL INTERRUPT(&H10, InRegs, OutRegs)
  VideoMode% = &HFF AND OutRegs.ax

END FUNCTION
```

And here's a short program that puts VideoMode%( ) to work:

```
REM Example of VideoMode

DECLARE FUNCTION VideoMode% ( )

Mode% = VideoMode%        ←

PRINT "Mode ="; Mode%
```

When you run it, it sets the variable Mode% to the value returned by the function VideoMode%( ) and prints it out.

The next BIOS interrupt is interrupt &H11, equipment determination: This interrupt tells us what kind of hardware is installed in the computer. Since this information is often useful to the BASIC programmer, let's take a closer look.

Determining Equipment Installed in Your Computer

There's a lot of power in interrupt &H11. For example, you can see whether a math coprocessor, an internal modem, printer, or a mouse is installed. This interrupt fills the ax register like this, bit by bit:

ax bits	Indicates
15,14	Number of printers installed
13	Internal modem installed? (1 = yes)
12	Not used
11,10,9	Number of RS-232 cards attached
8	Not used
7,6	Number of diskette drives: 00 = 1 drive; 01 = 2 drives
5,4	Video type: 01 = 40x25 color; 10 = 80x25 color; 11 = 80x25 mono
3	Not used
2	Mouse installed? (1 = yes)
1	Math coprocessor installed? (1 = yes)
0	Diskette drives installed? (1 = yes)

Let's develop a small function, GetEquipment%( ), to return this information to us. The actual code will be simplicity itself. We just make use of interrupt &H11, and, upon return, the ax register will be packed full of bits indicating the equipment status. We can set GetEquipment% to that value and return:

```
    DIM InRegs AS RegType, OutRegs AS RegType
    CALL INTERRUPT(&H11, InRegs, OutRegs)
  → GetEquipment% = OutRegs.ax
```

After we return this 16-bit word to the calling program, we can decode its bits as shown above (or you might want to adapt this function to do that for you). Listing 9-2 shows the whole function.

Listing 9-2. GetEquipment% — Returns Installed Equipment.	1 of 2

```
DECLARE FUNCTION GetEquipment% ( )

TYPE RegType
        ax      AS INTEGER
        bx      AS INTEGER
        cx      AS INTEGER
        dx      AS INTEGER
        bp      AS INTEGER
        si      AS INTEGER
        di      AS INTEGER
```

Listing 9-2.   GetEquipment% — Returns Installed Equipment.   **2 of 2**

```
        flags    AS INTEGER
END TYPE

DECLARE SUB INTERRUPT (IntNo AS INTEGER, InRegs AS RegType, OutRegs AS RegType)

FUNCTION GetEquipment%

REM Returns this word, bit by bit:
REM Bits      Means
REM ----      --------------------------------------------------------------
REM 15,14     Number of Printers installed
REM 13        Internal modem installed? (1 = yes)
REM 12        Not used
REM 11,10,9   Number of RS-232 cards attached
REM 8         Not used
REM 7,6       Number of diskette drives. 00 = 1 drive; 01 = 2 drives
REM 5,4       Video type. 01 = 40x25 color; 10 = 80x25 color; 11 = 80x25 mono
REM 3         Not used
REM 2         Mouse installed? (1 = yes)
REM 1         Math coprocessor installed? (1 = yes)
REM 0         Diskettes installed? (1 = yes)

    DIM InRegs AS RegType, OutRegs AS RegType
    CALL INTERRUPT(&H11, InRegs, OutRegs)
    GetEquipment% = OutRegs.ax

END FUNCTION
```

This example program, for example, checks whether or not a math coprocessor is installed:

```
REM Example of GetEquipment%

DECLARE FUNCTION GetEquipment% ()

Check% = GetEquipment%

IF (Check% AND 2) THEN
    PRINT "You have a math coprocessor."
ELSE
    PRINT "You do not have a math coprocessor."
END IF
```

As you can see, the BIOS and DOS interrupts have some real utility to offer BASIC programmers, and, through INTERRUPT( ) and INTERRUPTX( ), we can put them to work.

TIP:	Testing bit 2 of the return value from this service tells you whether or not a mouse is installed (1=yes). This is a good test for your program to make before using the mouse program we developed in Chapter 3.

Now let's continue our tour of BIOS and DOS. Interrupt &H12 was originally designed to determine the size of installed memory, but it only returns the amount of memory installed on the motherboard, not on add-in cards, which means that it's no longer reliable.

The next interrupt, &H13, is huge. This is the interrupt that handles the diskette and disk drives at the lowest level. Because of the sensitive nature of disk data, we're not going to make use of interrupt &H13 in this book, but it does pack a lot of power:

Interrupt &H13	Service 0	Reset Disk
Interrupt &H13	Service 1	Read Status of Last Operation
Interrupt &H13	Service 2	Read Sectors into Memory
Interrupt &H13	Service 3	Write Sectors to Disk
Interrupt &H13	Service 4	Verify Sectors
Interrupt &H13	Service 8	Return Drive Parameters
Interrupt &H13	Services &HA	and &HB Reserved
Interrupt &H13	Service &HC	Seek
Interrupt &H13	Service &HD	Alternate Disk Reset
Interrupt &H13	Services &HE and &HF	Reserved
Interrupt &H13	Service &H10	Test Drive Ready
Interrupt &H13	Service &H11	Recalibrate Hard Drive
Interrupt &H13	&H12 - &H14	Diagnostic Services
Interrupt &H13	Service &H19	Park Heads PS/2 Only

The next couple of interrupts have largely to do with I/O. For example, interrupt &H14 is the one that handles the serial port:

Interrupt &H14	AH=0	Initialize RS232 Port
Interrupt &H14	AH=1	Send Character Through Serial Port
Interrupt &H14	AH=2	Receive Character From Serial Port
Interrupt &H14	AH=3	Return Serial Port's Status

Interrupt &H15 handles the (now completely obsolete) cassette port that was installed on the original PC: Interrupt &H15 Cassette I/O.

Interrupt &H16 handles the keyboard data; this interrupt lets you read the keys that have been struck (while interrupt 9 is the low level interrupt that reads the bits directly from the keyboard and decodes them into characters):

Interrupt &H16	Service 0	Read Key from Keyboard
Interrupt &H16	Service 1	Check if Key Ready to be Read
Interrupt &H16	Service 2	Find Keyboard Status

Interrupt &H17 handles the printer:

Interrupt &H17	Service 0	Print character in al
Interrupt &H17	Service 1	Initialize Printer Port
Interrupt &H17	Service 2	Read Printer Status into ah

Interrupt &H18 is the resident ROM BASIC interrupt. Early PCs, including the original PC, had a small version of BASIC in ROM so that if you turned on the machine without a boot diskette, something still happened. In this case, this internal version of BASIC started. If you execute interrupt &H18 in these machines, ROM BASIC will start: Interrupt &H18 Resident BASIC.

Interrupt &H19 is the boot interrupt. When you turn your machine on, this is the interrupt that is executed. And, by calling this interrupt yourself, you can reboot your machine as well (a rather dramatic way of ending a program): Interrupt &H19 Bootstrap.

Interrupt &H1A handles the time of day (this is the interrupt the DOS commands TIME and DATE use):

| Interrupt &H1A | Service 0 | Read Time of Day |
| Interrupt &H1A | Service 1 | Set Time of Day |

The remainder of the BIOS interrupts, with the exception of interrupt &H1C, are not software routines at all. Instead, they hold various tables and addresses. For example, interrupt &H1B holds the address that control is transferred to when you press ^Break, and interrupt &H1D holds the current video parameters. Interrupt &H1E holds the address of the diskette parameters, and you can change these values if you know what you're doing (including the seek and reset times to speed things up). Interrupt &H1F can hold the address of graphics characters used on the screen:

Interrupt &H1B   Keyboard Break Address
Interrupt &H1C   Timer Tick Interrupt
Interrupt &H1D   Video Parameter Tables
Interrupt &H1E   Diskette Parameters
Interrupt &H1F   Graphics Character Definitions

Interrupt &H1C is the "timer tick" interrupt, and it's called whenever the internal timer increments its count (18.2 times a second). Many TSRs use this interrupt to take control of the machine temporarily.

NOTE: TSRs take control by changing the internal address of this interrupt to point to their own code in memory. That way, every time there is a timer tick, their code is run.

These are the last of the BIOS interrupts. Let's continue our tour by exploring DOS.

The DOS Interrupts

The DOS interrupts go from &H20 to &H3F. The first of these, interrupt &H20, is called at the assembly language level when a program is done and wants to return control to DOS. This is the interrupt that places the C:\> prompt back on the screen: Interrupt &H20 Program Terminate. With the introduction of other methods of ending programs, interrupt &H20 has become slightly obsolete. One other way of ending a program is interrupt &H21 service &H4C, which allows you to return an error code indicating success or failure.

Now we come to the monster interrupt, the biggest of them all, interrupt &H21. Almost all of DOS' capabilities — handling files, reading keys, printing on the screen — are wrapped up in the services of this interrupt. This is the interrupt that all the DOS commands (such as COPY, FORMAT, or DIR) use.

You may have noticed that we can print on the screen and read keys with some of the BIOS services as well, and that's true. However, the DOS services are more sophisticated than the low-level BIOS services; in fact, many of the DOS services call the BIOS services themselves for low-level control.

Unfortunately, there's no real plan or layout to the interrupt &H21 services. Roughly, however, the first ones deal with character input and output (except for service 0, which does exactly the same thing as interrupt &H20):

Interrupt &H21	Service 0	Program Terminate
Interrupt &H21	Service 1	Keyboard Input
Interrupt &H21	Service 2	Character Output on Screen
Interrupt &H21	Service 3	Standard Auxiliary Device Input
Interrupt &H21	Service 4	Standard Auxiliary Device Output
Interrupt &H21	Service 5	Printer Output
Interrupt &H21	Service 6	Console I/O
Interrupt &H21	Service 7	Console Input Without Echo
Interrupt &H21	Service 8	Console Input w/o Echo with ^C Check
Interrupt &H21	Service 9	Character String Print
Interrupt &H21	Service &HA	String Input
Interrupt &H21	Service &HB	Check Input Status
Interrupt &H21	Service &HC	Clear Keyboard Buffer and Invoke Service

We've already seen one or two of these services in action. The next two services let you reset a disk or change the default disk:

| Interrupt &H21 | Service &HD | Disk Reset |
| Interrupt &H21 | Service &HE | Select Disk |

In the BASIC PDS, you can use the CHDRIVE statement to set the default drive. CHDRIVE, however, is not available in QuickBASIC, so we can write a new function — SetDefaultDisk%( ) — for QuickBASIC users. Interrupt &H21 service &HE will let us change the default drive as we require.

Setting the Default Disk

We can set the default disk with the function we're going to write, SetDefaultDisk%( ). We should make this function return 0 if there's a problem (i.e., the target disk doesn't exist), and 1 for success. Here's how we could use SetDefaultDisk%( ):

```
   Drive$ = "A"
 → Check% = SetDefaultDisk% (Drive$)
   IF Check% = 0 THEN PRINT "Error."
```

We can use interrupt &H21 service &HE here. First, we can check the passed parameter Drive$ to make sure it is only one character long:

```
  SetDefaultDisk% = 0

→ IF LEN(Drive$) <> 1 THEN EXIT FUNCTION
    :
```

Service &HE expects the new default drive number — 0 for A, 1 for B, etc. — in the dl register, so we can proceed like this:

```
  SetDefaultDisk% = 0

→ IF LEN(Drive$) <> 1 THEN EXIT FUNCTION

  InRegs.ax = &HE00
  InRegs.dx = ASC(UCASE$(Drive$)) - ASC("A")
  CALL INTERRUPT(&H21, InRegs, OutRegs)
    :
```

Afterwards, we can check the new drive number (returned in al) against the drive number we requested (still in dl) to make sure the change was actually made:

```
  SetDefaultDisk% = 0

  IF LEN(Drive$) <> 1 THEN EXIT FUNCTION
  InRegs.ax = &HE00
  InRegs.dx = ASC(UCASE$(Drive$)) - ASC("A")
  CALL INTERRUPT(&H21, InRegs, OutRegs)
→ IF (InRegs.dx AND &HFF) <> (InRegs.ax AND &HFF) THEN EXIT FUNCTION

  SetDefaultDisk% = 1
```

If the present drive is not the same as the drive we requested, we exit, leaving SetDefaultDisk% equal to 0 and indicating failure. If it is the same, we set SetDefaultDrive% to 1 and exit. Listing 9-3 shows the entire function.

Listing 9-3.   Set DefaultDisk% (Drive$) Function.

```
DECLARE FUNCTION SetDefaultDisk% (Drive$)

FUNCTION SetDefaultDisk% (Drive$)

   DIM InRegs AS RegType, OutRegs AS RegType

   SetDefaultDisk% = 0

   IF LEN(Drive$) <> 1 THEN EXIT FUNCTION

   InRegs.ax = &HE00
   InRegs.dx = ASC(UCASE$(Drive$)) - ASC("A")
   CALL INTERRUPT(&H21, InRegs, OutRegs)
   IF (InRegs.dx AND &HFF) <> (InRegs.ax AND &HFF) THEN EXIT FUNCTION

   SetDefaultDisk% = 1

END FUNCTION
```

Let's press on with our tour of DOS. The following group of DOS services deals mostly with files. These services, however, are mostly obsolete, and should be avoided:

Interrupt &H21	Service &HF	Open Preexisting File
Interrupt &H21	Service &H10	Close File
Interrupt &H21	Service &H11	Search for First Matching File
Interrupt &H21	Service &H12	Search for Next Matching File
Interrupt &H21	Service &H13	Delete Files
Interrupt &H21	Service &H14	Sequential Read
Interrupt &H21	Service &H15	Sequential Write
Interrupt &H21	Service &H16	Create File
Interrupt &H21	Service &H17	Rename File

NOTE: These services work with *file control blocks*, which cannot handle pathnames (they were used primarily in the days before hard disks). The modern file services start with &H3C.

Then there are some more disk services:

Interrupt &H21	Service &H18	Internal to DOS
Interrupt &H21	Service &H19	Find Default Disk
Interrupt &H21	Service &H1A	Set the DTA Location
Interrupt &H21	Service &H1B	FAT Information for Default Drive
Interrupt &H21	Service &H1C	FAT Information for Specified Drive
Interrupt &H21	Services &H1D - &H20	Internal to DOS

Some of these services are quite useful. In fact, while we're here, we can make use of one of these services, service &H19, which returns the default disk.

Getting the Default Disk

We can write a function named GetDefaultDisk$( ) to return a one-character string indicating the current drive's letter:

```
DriveNow$ = GetDefaultDisk$ ( )
```

This function will make use of interrupt &H21 service &H19 to determine what the default disk is.

TIP: Interrupt &H21 service &H19 is useful if you've just been passed control in a subprogram and want to find out if you're dealing with a hard drive or a diskette drive.

To request service &H19, we simply load ah with &H19 and call interrupt &H21. The default disk number is returned in al. Here, 0 corresponds to drive A, 1 to B, and so on. We convert the number in al to a drive letter like this:

```
    DIM InRegs AS RegType, OutRegs AS RegType
    InRegs.ax = &H1900
    CALL INTERRUPT(&H21, InRegs, OutRegs)
→ GetDefaultDisk$ = CHR$((OutRegs.ax AND &HFF) + ASC("A"))
```

And that's all there is to it. Listing 9-4 shows the complete function.

Listing 9-4.   Get DefaultDisk$ ( ) Function.   1 of 2

```
DECLARE FUNCTION GetDefaultDisk$ ( )
TYPE RegType
          ax        AS INTEGER
          bx        AS INTEGER
          cx        AS INTEGER
          dx        AS INTEGER
          bp        AS INTEGER
          si        AS INTEGER
          di        AS INTEGER
```

Listing 9-4.   Get DefaultDisk$ ( ) Function.   2 of 2

```
        flags    AS INTEGER
END TYPE

DECLARE SUB INTERRUPT (IntNo AS INTEGER, InRegs AS RegType, OutRegs AS RegType)

FUNCTION GetDefaultDisk$

    DIM InRegs AS RegType, OutRegs AS RegType
    InRegs.ax = &H1900
    CALL INTERRUPT(&H21, InRegs, OutRegs)
    GetDefaultDisk$ = CHR$((OutRegs.ax AND &HFF) + ASC("A"))

END FUNCTION
```

And here's a short program that puts GetDefaultDisk$( ) to use:

```
REM Example of GetDefaultDisk$

DECLARE FUNCTION GetDefaultDisk$ ( )

PRINT "The Default disk is: "; GetDefaultDisk$
```

This is about as short and to the point as you could want. It simply prints out the default disk's drive letter, as returned by GetDefaultDisk$.

The next DOS services deal mostly with file I/O. These are part of the outmoded DOS file services that we should avoid. These are the file control block file I/O services.

Interrupt &H21	Service &H21	Random Read
Interrupt &H21	Service &H22	Random Write
Interrupt &H21	Service &H23	File Size.
Interrupt &H21	Service &H24	Set Random Record Field
Interrupt &H21	Service &H25	Set Interrupt Vector
Interrupt &H21	Service &H26	Create a New Program Segment (PSP)
Interrupt &H21	Service &H27	Random Block Read
Interrupt &H21	Service &H28	Random Block Write
Interrupt &H21	Service &H29	Parse Filename

Then, in typical interrupt &H21 fashion, there's a collection of services without anything in common:

Interrupt &H21	Service &H2A	Get Date
Interrupt &H21	Service &H2B	Set Date
Interrupt &H21	Service &H2C	Get Time
Interrupt &H21	Service &H2D	Set Time
Interrupt &H21	Service &H2E	Set or Reset Verify Switch
Interrupt &H21	Service &H2F	Get Current Disk Transfer Area
Interrupt &H21	Service &H30	Get DOS Version Number
Interrupt &H21	Service &H31	Terminate Process and Keep Resident
Interrupt &H21	Service &H32	Internal to DOS
Interrupt &H21	Service &H33	Control-Break Check
Interrupt &H21	Service &H34	Internal to DOS
Interrupt &H21	Service &H35	Get Interrupt Vector

The next group of services deal largely with disks again:

Interrupt &H21	Service &H36	Get Free Disk Space
Interrupt &H21	Service &H37	Internal to DOS
Interrupt &H21	Service &H38	Returns Country Dependent Information
Interrupt &H21	Service &H39	Create a Subdirectory
Interrupt &H21	Service &H3A	Delete a Subdirectory
Interrupt &H21	Service &H3B	Change Current Directory

One of these — interrupt &H21 service &H36, get free disk space — is particularly useful to the BASIC programmer. Let's develop a function around it.

Finding Free Disk Space

Here we'll put together a function that returns the space available (in bytes) on a disk drive of your choosing. We can call this function DiskFree&( ), and use it this way:

```
BytesLeft& = DiskFree& (Drive$)
```

TIP: DiskFree$( ) can be exceptionally useful if you have a large output file to generate and want to check the target disk first.

Here Drive$ is the letter corresponding to the drive you want to check (e.g., C). Since it's possible that the specified drive might not exist, we should make DiskFree& return a value of -1 if there's been an error.

To start, we have to load &H36 into ah:

```
DIM InRegs AS RegType, Outregs AS RegType

DiskFree& = -1
IF LEN(Drive$) <> 1 THEN EXIT FUNCTION

→ InRegs.ax = &H3600
     :
     :
```

We also have to place the drive number in dl, the low eight bits of the dx register. For this service (and unlike service &H19), the drive number is 1 for drive A, 2 for drive B, and so on. In other words, just ASC(UCASE$(Drive$)) - ASC("A") + 1. Then we call INTERRUPT( ):

```
DIM InRegs AS RegType, Outregs AS RegType

DiskFree& = -1
IF LEN(Drive$) <> 1 THEN EXIT FUNCTION

InRegs.ax = &H3600
→ InRegs.dx = ASC(UCASE$(Drive$)) - ASC("A") + 1
CALL INTERRUPT(&H21, InRegs, Outregs)
     :
     :
```

If this service places a -1 in ax, then the target drive doesn't exist or isn't responding. In that case, we have to return with DiskFree& set to -1:

```
DIM InRegs AS RegType, Outregs AS RegType

DiskFree& = -1
IF LEN(Drive$) <> 1 THEN EXIT FUNCTION

InRegs.ax = &H3600
InRegs.dx = ASC(UCASE$(Drive$)) - ASC("A") + 1
CALL INTERRUPT(&H21, InRegs, Outregs)

→ IF OutRegs.ax = -1 THEN EXIT FUNCTION
     :
     :
```

Otherwise, we have to multiply ax * bx * cx to get the number of bytes free on the disk. To avoid overflows, we first load ax into a LONG variable, and then perform the multiplication:

```
    DIM InRegs AS RegType, Outregs AS RegType

    DiskFree& = -1
    IF LEN(Drive$) <> 1 THEN EXIT FUNCTION

    InRegs.ax = &H3600
    InRegs.dx = ASC(UCASE$(Drive$)) - ASC("A") + 1
    CALL INTERRUPT(&H21, InRegs, Outregs)

    IF OutRegs.ax = -1 THEN EXIT FUNCTION

→ Temp& = OutRegs.ax
    DiskFree& = Temp& * Outregs.bx * Outregs.cx
```

NOTE: bx contains the number of available allocation units (clusters), ax the number of sectors per allocation unit, and cx the number of bytes per sector. The product of these three is therefore the number of free bytes available on the drive.

That's it; we now return the resulting value as the value of DiskFree&. Listing 9-5 shows the whole function.

Listing 9-5. DiskFree& Shows — Amount of Free Disk Space 1 of 2

```
DECLARE FUNCTION DiskFree& (Drive$)

TYPE RegType
        ax      AS INTEGER
        bx      AS INTEGER
        cx      AS INTEGER
        dx      AS INTEGER
        bp      AS INTEGER
        si      AS INTEGER
        di      AS INTEGER
        flags   AS INTEGER
END TYPE

DECLARE SUB INTERRUPT (IntNo AS INTEGER, InRegs AS RegType, OutRegs AS RegType)
```

Listing 9-5.   DiskFree& Shows — Amount of Free Disk Space   2 of 2

```
FUNCTION DiskFree& (Drive$)

   DIM InRegs AS RegType, Outregs AS RegType

   DiskFree& = -1
   IF LEN(Drive$) <> 1 THEN EXIT FUNCTION

   InRegs.ax = &H3600
   InRegs.dx = ASC(UCASE$(Drive$)) - ASC("A") + 1
   CALL INTERRUPT(&H21, InRegs, Outregs)
   IF OutRegs.ax = -1 THEN EXIT FUNCTION

   Temp& = OutRegs.ax
   DiskFree& = Temp& * Outregs.bx * Outregs.cx

END FUNCTION
```

And here's a short program putting DiskFree& to work:

```
REM Example of DiskFree&

DECLARE FUNCTION DiskFree& (Drive$)

MyDrive$ = "C"

PRINT "Free space on drive ";MYDrive$; " ="; DiskFree&(MyDrive$)
```

This program simply checks drive C and reports how many bytes are free. Don't try this unless you have a C drive, without an actual drive to check, the results will be meaningless.

Continuing our DOS tour now, we come to the modern file handling services.

The DOS File Services

Starting with Version 2.0, DOS started to support pathnames, which made the old file services obsolete. The new file services, which use *file handles*, start at this point. File handles work much like the window handles we developed in Chapter 2. A file handle is just a 16-bit word that stands for a specific open file. Here are the new file services:

> Interrupt &H21   Service &H3C   Create a File
> Interrupt &H21   Service &H3D   Open a File
> Interrupt &H21   Service &H3E   Close a File Handle

Interrupt &H21	Service &H3F	Read from File or Device
Interrupt &H21	Service &H40	Write to File or Device
Interrupt &H21	Service &H41	Delete a File
Interrupt &H21	Service &H42	Move Read/Write Pointer
Interrupt &H21	Service &H43	Change File's Attribute
Interrupt &H21	Service &H44	I/O Control
Interrupt &H21	Service &H45	Duplicate a File Handle
Interrupt &H21	Service &H46	Force Duplication of a File Handle
Interrupt &H21	Service &H47	Get Current Directory on Specified Drive

The next few DOS services following these have to do with allocating or deallocating memory, and are mostly important in multiuser environments (DOS usually gives your program all available memory unless that memory is shared):

Interrupt &H21	Service &H48	Allocate Memory
Interrupt &H21	Service &H49	Free Allocated Memory
Interrupt &H21	Service &H4A	SETBLOCK (Memory Allocation)
Interrupt &H21	Service &H4B	Load or Execute a program—EXEC
Interrupt &H21	Service &H4C	Exit With Return Code
Interrupt &H21	Service &H4D	Get Return Code of Subprocess

The following two services, however, can be very useful for BASIC programmers:

Interrupt &H21	Service &H4E	Find First Matching File
Interrupt &H21	Service &H4F	Find Next Matching File

Service &H4E searches a directory for the first filename that matches a file specification that you've given. Service &H4F continues the work that service &H4E began. Using it repeatedly finds all the remaining matches (service &H4E performs initialization work that only needs to be done once). Let's add this power to BASIC.

Finding the First Matching File

Service &H4E is a serious service, and it will introduce us to the intricacies of interfacing with the DOS file services. This service lets you search a directory for a file that matches your file specification, and we can use it in a function called, say, Get-FirstMatchingFile$( ). For example, to find a match to PROGRAM.* in the subdirectory C:\ARCHIVES, just use it this way:

```
Match$ = GetFirstMatchingFile$ ("C:\ARCHIVES\PROGRAM.*")
```

Or, to find if there are any files there at all:

```
Match$ = GetFirstMatchingFile$ ("C:\ARCHIVES\*.*")
```

We can design this function to return a string made up of the first matching filename (the pathname will be omitted because service &H4E doesn't return it).

TIP: With this function, you can find files placed anywhere on disk, check to see if a file exists before overwriting it, or examine the contents of whole subdirectories.

Because service &H4E only returns the name of the first matching file, we'll need to use another function, which we can call GetNextMatchingFile$( ), to continue the search. To search a directory for multiple files, use GetFirstMatchingFile$( ) first. If it returns a matching filename (and not a null string, " ", which indicates that there was no match), use GetNextMatchingFile$( ) next, calling it repeatedly until you run out of matches (i.e., it returns " ").

Let's write the function GetFirstMatchingFile$( ). Interrupt &H21 service &H4E returns information about matching files in the *Disk Transfer Area*, or DTA. The DTA is a buffer put aside for low-level DOS file manipulations (and it is mostly obsolete, except for this service). For that reason, we need to find the address of current Disk Transfer Area, and one of the services we've already covered — interrupt &H21 service &H2F — will give us that.

As we saw in Chapter 5, addresses in the PC are made up of two 16-bit words, a segment address and an offset address. Service &H2F returns both the segment and offset address of the DTA, and we place them in DTASegment% and DTAOffset%, respectively:

```
FUNCTION GetFirstMatchingFile$ (FileSpec$)

    DIM InRegs AS RegTypeX, OutRegs AS RegTypeX

    REM Get Disk Transfer Area (DTA) address

    InRegs.ax = &H2F00
    CALL INTERRUPTX(&H21, InRegs, OutRegs)
    DTASegment% = OutRegs.es  ←
    DTAOffset% = OutRegs.bx
        :
        :
```

Now that we have the DTA address, we're ready to find the first match. Checking the BIOS and DOS appendix, we see that we must pass an ASCIIZ string holding the file specification to interrupt &H21. An ASCIIZ string is just a string of characters with a termination character of ASCII 0 — that is, CHR$(0) — at the end.

If the file specification passed to us is called FileSpec$ (e.g., this string will hold *.DAT or *.*), we can make an ASCIIZ string out of it this way: NameFile$ = FileSpec$ + CHR$(0). Now we have to pass the address of NameFile$ to interrupt &H21. We can use VARSEG( ) to get the segment address of a string, and we use the BASIC function SADD( ) (not VARPTR( )) to get its offset address.

The segment address goes into a new register called ds, which stands for data segment, and the offset address goes into dx. The ds register is one of the four *segment registers* in your PC (see Figure 9-1). These registers are designed to keep track of segment addresses. There are four segment registers: cs, ds, es, and ss. They are all used for holding segment addresses. The ds register holds the segment address of the current data segment; es holds the extra segment; ss holds the stack segment; and cs holds the code segment. We'll see them at work in Chapter 11.

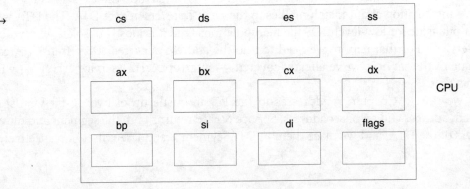

Figure 9-1

We can load the address of NameFile$ into ds and dx like this:

```
FUNCTION GetFirstMatchingFile$ (FileSpec$)

    DIM InRegs AS RegTypeX, OutRegs AS RegTypeX

    REM Get Disk Transfer Area (DTA) address

    InRegs.ax = &H2F00
    CALL INTERRUPTX(&H21, InRegs, OutRegs)
    DTASegment% = OutRegs.es
    DTAOffset% = OutRegs.bx

    REM Now find first match

    NameFile$ = FileSpec$ + CHR$(0)
    InRegs.ds = VARSEG(NameFile$) ←
    InRegs.dx = SADD(NameFile$)
        :
```

Now we have to decide what type of files we want to find; that is, what the *file attribute* to be used in the search should be. DOS uses file attribute values like this (and you can use this list for reference if you want to try using any other DOS file services):

Attribute	Means
0	Plain file
1	Read only file
2	Hidden file
4	System file
8	Volume label of a disk
16	Subdirectory name

TIP: You can search for hidden files on your disk by using this function and setting the file attribute to 2. You can even search for the system files IBMDOS.COM or MSDOS.COM to see if the current disk is a boot disk.

In other words, if we passed a file attribute of 1, we would search exclusively for read-only files. Let's use an attribute of 0 and search for only plain files. We have to pass the file attribute in cx, so we place 0 in it and call interrupt &H21:

```
FUNCTION GetFirstMatchingFile$ (FileSpec$)

   DIM InRegs AS RegTypeX, OutRegs AS RegTypeX

   REM Get Disk Transfer Area (DTA) address

   InRegs.ax = &H2F00
   CALL INTERRUPTX(&H21, InRegs, OutRegs)
   DTASegment% = OutRegs.es
   DTAOffset% = OutRegs.bx

   REM Now find first match

   NameFile$ = FileSpec$ + CHR$(0)
   InRegs.ds = VARSEG(NameFile$)      ←
   InRegs.dx = SADD(NameFile$)
   InRegs.cx = 0
   InRegs.ax = &H4E00                 ←
   CALL INTERRUPTX(&H21, InRegs, OutRegs)
         :
         :
```

When we return from interrupt &H21 service &H4E, there will be one of two possible outcomes: we will either find a matching file, or we will not. If *no* matches are found, this service sets the carry flag on return.

The carry flag is one of eight flags internal to the 80x86, and we've seen those flags as far back as Chapter 1:

OutRegs.flag bit	Flag
11	Overflow Flag
10	Direction Flag
9	Enable Interrupts Flag
8	Trap Flag
7	Sign Flag
6	Zero Flag
4	Auxiliary Carry Flag
2	Parity Flag
→ 0	Carry Flag

As we can see, the carry flag is in bit 0 of OutRegs.flags; if that bit is 1, the carry flag was set. We can read the value of the carry flag after the call to INTERRUPTX( ) by examining the value of OutRegs.flags AND 1. If there was no match, the carry flag will be set (OutRegs.flags AND 1 will equal 1), so we return a null string, " ", like this:

```
FUNCTION GetFirstMatchingFile$ (FileSpec$)

   DIM InRegs AS RegTypeX, OutRegs AS RegTypeX

   REM Get Disk Transfer Area (DTA) address

   InRegs.ax = &H2F00
   CALL INTERRUPTX(&H21, InRegs, OutRegs)
   DTASegment% = OutRegs.es
   DTAOffset% = OutRegs.bx

   REM Now find first match

   NameFile$ = FileSpec$ + CHR$(0)
   InRegs.ds = VARSEG(NameFile$)
   InRegs.dx = SADD(NameFile$)
   InRegs.cx = 0
   InRegs.ax = &H4E00
   CALL INTERRUPTX(&H21, InRegs, OutRegs)

   IF OutRegs.flags AND 1 THEN                ←
    GetFirstMatchingFile$ = " "
    EXIT FUNCTION
   END IF
        :
```

On the other hand, if there *is* a match, the DTA will be filled as shown in Figure 9-2 (according to the Appendix).

DTA begins:

> 21 bytes: Reserved.
> 1 byte: Found file's attribute.
> 2 bytes: Found file's time.
> 2 bytes: Found file's date.
> 2 bytes: Low word of file's size.
> 2 bytes: High word of file's size.

DTA ends: 13 bytes: Name of found file in ASCIIZ form   ←

Figure 9-2

Let's suppose that there is a match. In that case the matching filename will be 29 bytes into the DTA, stored as an ASCIIZ string. We can place its offset address into a variable named MatchOffset% like this:

```
FUNCTION GetFirstMatchingFile$ (FileSpec$)

   DIM InRegs AS RegTypeX, OutRegs AS RegTypeX

   REM Get Disk Transfer Area (DTA) address

   InRegs.ax = &H2F00
   CALL INTERRUPTX(&H21, InRegs, OutRegs)
```

```
    DTASegment% = OutRegs.es
    DTAOffset% = OutRegs.bx

    REM Now find first match

    NameFile$ = FileSpec$ + CHR$(0)
    InRegs.ds = VARSEG(NameFile$)
    InRegs.dx = SADD(NameFile$)
    InRegs.cx = 0
    InRegs.ax = &H4E00
    CALL INTERRUPTX(&H21, InRegs, OutRegs)

    IF OutRegs.flags AND 1 THEN
     GetFirstMatchingFile$ = " "
     EXIT FUNCTION
    END IF

    DEF SEG = DTASegment%                       ←
    MatchOffset% = DTAOffset% + 29
        :
```

All that remains is to convert that ASCIIZ string into a BASIC one, and return:

```
FUNCTION GetFirstMatchingFile$ (FileSpec$)

    DIM InRegs AS RegTypeX, OutRegs AS RegTypeX

    REM Get Disk Transfer Area (DTA) address

    InRegs.ax = &H2F00
    CALL INTERRUPTX(&H21, InRegs, OutRegs)
    DTASegment% = OutRegs.es
    DTAOffset% = OutRegs.bx

    REM Now find first match

    NameFile$ = FileSpec$ + CHR$(0)
    InRegs.ds = VARSEG(NameFile$)
    InRegs.dx = SADD(NameFile$)
    InRegs.cx = 0
    InRegs.ax = &H4E00
    CALL INTERRUPTX(&H21, InRegs, OutRegs)

    IF OutRegs.flags AND 1 THEN
     GetFirstMatchingFile$ = " "
     EXIT FUNCTION
    END IF

    DEF SEG = DTASegment%
    MatchOffset% = DTAOffset% + 29

    Match$ = " "                                ←
    FOR i = 1 TO 13                             :
     NewChar$ = CHR$(PEEK(MatchOffset% + i))    :
     IF NewChar$ = CHR$(0) THEN EXIT FOR
```

```
     Match$ = Match$ + NewChar$
     NEXT i

     DEF SEG

GetFirstMatchingFile$ = Match$
```

And that's all there is to it. If we've found a match, we return the filename in a BASIC string. Otherwise, we return a null string. In addition, the Disk Transfer Area is now set up with the information needed by GetNextMatchingFile$( ) to continue the search.

Listing 9-6 shows the whole function GetFirstMatchingFile$( ).

Listing 9-6.   GetFirstMatchingFile$ Function.   **1 of 2**

```
DECLARE FUNCTION GetFirstMatchingFile$ (FileSpec$)

TYPE RegTypeX
          ax       AS INTEGER
          bx       AS INTEGER
          cx       AS INTEGER
          dx       AS INTEGER
          bp       AS INTEGER
          si       AS INTEGER
          di       AS INTEGER
          flags    AS INTEGER
          ds       AS INTEGER
          es       AS INTEGER
END TYPE

DECLARE SUB INTERRUPTX (InNo AS INTEGER, InRgs AS RegTypeX, OutRgs AS RegTypeX)

FUNCTION GetFirstMatchingFile$ (FileSpec$)

    DIM InRegs AS RegTypeX, OutRegs AS RegTypeX

    REM Get Disk Transfer Area (DTA) address

    InRegs.ax = &H2F00
    CALL INTERRUPTX(&H21, InRegs, OutRegs)
    DTASegment% = OutRegs.es
    DTAOffset% = OutRegs.bx

    REM Now find first match

    NameFile$ = FileSpec$ + CHR$(0)
    InRegs.ds = VARSEG(NameFile$)
    InRegs.dx = SADD(NameFile$)
    InRegs.cx = 0
    InRegs.ax = &H4E00
    CALL INTERRUPTX(&H21, InRegs, OutRegs)

    IF OutRegs.flags AND 1 THEN
     GetFirstMatchingFile$ = ""
```

Listing 9-6. GetFirstMatchingFile$ Function. 2 of 2

```
    EXIT FUNCTION
    END IF

    DEF SEG = DTASegment%
    MatchOffset% = DTAOffset% + 29

    Match$ = ""
    FOR i = 1 TO 13
     NewChar$ = CHR$(PEEK(MatchOffset% + i))
     IF NewChar$ = CHR$(0) THEN EXIT FOR
     Match$ = Match$ + NewChar$
    NEXT i

    DEF SEG

    GetFirstMatchingFile$ = Match$

END FUNCTION
```

And here's how to use GetFirstMatchingFile$( ):

```
REM Example of GetFirstMatchingFile$

DECLARE FUNCTION GetFirstMatchingFile$ (FileSpec$)

FileSpec$ = "*.DAT"

MatchFile$ = GetFirstMatchingFile$(FileSpec$)

IF MatchFile$ <> "" THEN
    PRINT "First matching file is: ", MatchFile$
ELSE
    PRINT "No matches."
END IF
```

This example returns the first filename in the current directory with the extension .DAT. Keep in mind that this function only returns the name of the *first* matching file. To continue the search, use GetNextMatchingFile$( ). In addition, it only returns files that have attribute 0 (i.e., all files that are not hidden, system, or subdirectory files).

Let's continue with GetNextMatchingFile$( ).

Finding the Next Matching File(s)

Now we're going to use the next DOS service, service &H4F, to continue searching for matching files, and we can write a function named GetNextMatchingFile$( ) to do it. This function will search for all subsequent matching files after using GetFirstMatchingFile$( ).

Just keep calling GetNextMatchingFile$( ) repeatedly until it returns a null string, " ", at which point we've run out of matches.

This function is much like GetFirstMatchingFile$( ), except that it uses interrupt &H21 service &H4F to search for the *next* matching file. We start off by finding the DTA address as before, and by calling service &H4F (no input needed — everything required is already in the DTA):

```
FUNCTION GetNextMatchingFile$

    REM Get Disk Transfer Area (DTA) address

    InRegs.ax = &H2F00
    CALL INTERRUPTX(&H21, InRegs, OutRegs)
    DTASegment% = OutRegs.es
    DTAOffset% = OutRegs.bx

    REM Now find next match

    InRegs.ax = &H4F00
    CALL INTERRUPTX(&H21, InRegs, OutRegs)
        :
        :
```

If the carry flag is set on return from INTERRUPTX( ), there was no match and we have to indicate that by returning a null string, "". Otherwise, we read the filename as before from the DTA:

```
FUNCTION GetNextMatchingFile$

    REM Get Disk Transfer Area (DTA) address

    InRegs.ax = &H2F00
    CALL INTERRUPTX(&H21, InRegs, OutRegs)
    DTASegment% = OutRegs.es
    DTAOffset% = OutRegs.bx

    REM Now find next match

    InRegs.ax = &H4F00
    CALL INTERRUPTX(&H21, InRegs, OutRegs)

    IF OutRegs.flags AND 1 THEN
      GetNextMatchingFile$ = ""
      EXIT FUNCTION
    END IF

    DEF SEG = DTASegment%                    ←
    MatchOffset% = DTAOffset% + 29           :
                                             :
```

```
   Match$ = ""
   FOR i = 1 TO 13
    NewChar$ = CHR$(PEEK(MatchOffset% + i))
    IF NewChar$ = CHR$(0) THEN EXIT FOR
    Match$ = Match$ + NewChar$
   NEXT i

   DEF SEG

   GetNextMatchingFile$ = Match$
```

That's all there is to it. If there is a match, we return the filename in a BASIC string. Otherwise, we set GetNextMatchingFile$ to a null string and exit. Listing 9-7 shows the whole function.

Listing 9-7. GetNextMatchingFile$ ( ) Function.   1 of 2

```
DECLARE FUNCTION GetNextMatchingFile$ ( )

TYPE RegTypeX
          ax      AS INTEGER
          bx      AS INTEGER
          cx      AS INTEGER
          dx      AS INTEGER
          bp      AS INTEGER
          si      AS INTEGER
          di      AS INTEGER
          flags   AS INTEGER
          ds      AS INTEGER
          es      AS INTEGER
END TYPE

DECLARE SUB INTERRUPTX (InNo AS INTEGER, InRgs AS RegTypeX, OutRgs AS RegTypeX)

FUNCTION GetNextMatchingFile$

   DIM InRegs AS RegTypeX, OutRegs AS RegTypeX

   REM Get Disk Transfer Area (DTA) address

   InRegs.ax = &H2F00
   CALL INTERRUPTX(&H21, InRegs, OutRegs)
   DTASegment% = OutRegs.es
   DTAOffset% = OutRegs.bx

   REM Now find next match

   InRegs.ax = &H4F00
   CALL INTERRUPTX(&H21, InRegs, OutRegs)

   IF OutRegs.flags AND 1 THEN
    GetNextMatchingFile$ = ""
    EXIT FUNCTION
   END IF
```

Listing 9-7. GetNextMatchingFile$ ( ) Function. 2 of 2

```
    DEF SEG = DTASegment%
    MatchOffset% = DTAOffset% + 29

    Match$ = ""
    FOR i = 1 TO 13
     NewChar$ = CHR$(PEEK(MatchOffset% + i))
     IF NewChar$ = CHR$(0) THEN EXIT FOR
     Match$ = Match$ + NewChar$
    NEXT i

    DEF SEG

    GetNextMatchingFile$ = Match$

END FUNCTION
```

And here's how to use both GetFirstMatchingFile$( ) and GetNextMatchingFile$( ):

```
REM Example of GetNextMatchingFile$

DECLARE FUNCTION GetFirstMatchingFile$ (FileSpec$)
DECLARE FUNCTION GetNextMatchingFile$ ( )

FileSpec$ = "*.DAT"

MatchFile$ = GetFirstMatchingFile$(FileSpec$)

IF MatchFile$ <> "" THEN
    PRINT "First matching file is: ", MatchFile$
    MatchFile$ = GetNextMatchingFile$
    DO WHILE MatchFile$ <> ""
        PRINT "Next matching file is: ", MatchFile$
        MatchFile$ = GetNextMatchingFile$
    LOOP
ELSE
    PRINT "No matches."
END IF
```

You can see that we use GetFirstMatchingFile$( ) first, check the result, and then keep on going with GetNextMatchingFile$( ). If we got a null string from Get-FirstMatchingFile$( ), there are no matches to our file specification, and we quit. If there was a match, however, we print it out and then keep going, looping over GetNext-MatchingFile$( ) until it finally returns " ", at which point we can quit:

```
→ DO WHILE MatchFile$ <> ""
     PRINT "Next matching file is: ", MatchFile$
     MatchFile$ = GetNextMatchingFile$
  LOOP
```

We've come a long way through BIOS and DOS, and we've put some of the services we've seen to work. Now we're just about ready to wind up our DOS tour.

The Rest of DOS

The remaining interrupt &H21 services represent a hodgepodge that was added as time went on and new DOS versions appeared. Here's what they look like:

Interrupt &H21	Services &H50H-&H53	Internal to DOS
Interrupt &H21	Service &H54	Get Verify State
Interrupt &H21	Service &H55	Internal to DOS
Interrupt &H21	Service &H56	Rename File
Interrupt &H21	Service &H57	Get or Set a File's Date & Time
Interrupt &H21	Service &H58	Internal to DOS
Interrupt &H21	Service &H59	Get Extended Error DOS 3+
Interrupt &H21	Service &H5A	Create Unique File DOS 3+
Interrupt &H21	Service &H5B	Create a New File DOS 3+
Interrupt &H21	Service &H5C	Lock and Unlock Access to a File DOS 3+
Interrupt &H21	Service &H5E00	Get Machine Name DOS 3+
Interrupt &H21	Service &H5E02	Set Printer Setup DOS 3+
Interrupt &H21	Service &H5E03	Get Printer Setup DOS 3+
Interrupt &H21	Service &H5F03	Redirect Device DOS 3+
Interrupt &H21	Service &H5F04	Cancel Redirection DOS 3+
Interrupt &H21	Service &H61	Reserved
Interrupt &H21	Service &H62	Get Program Segment Prefix DOS 3+
Interrupt &H21	Service &H63-64	Reserved
Interrupt &H21	Service &H65	Get Extended Country Information
Interrupt &H21	Service &H6601	Get Global Code Page
Interrupt &H21	Service &H6602	Set Global Code Page
Interrupt &H21	Service &H67	Set Handle Count DOS 3.30

Interrupt &H21 Service &H68   Commit File (Write Buffers)
                                      DOS 3.30

Interrupt &H21 Service &H6C   Extended Open/Create DOS
                                      4.0

NOTE: If the service number is 16 bits long (e.g., &H5F03), you have to load that entire number into the ax register.

That's it for the interrupt &H21 services, and with them, we wind down interrupt &H21. As you can see, this interrupt can be very useful to BASIC programmers.

NOTE: There is more information on this interrupt in the Appendix.

The remaining DOS interrupts are not usually very useful, however, with the exception of interrupts &H25 and &H26, which read and write sectors on the disk (see the appendix for more information), and interrupt &H27, which lets you create TSR programs (although this has largely been superceded by interrupt &H21 service &H3C). Here are the remaining DOS interrupts:

Interrupt &H22   Terminate Address
Interrupt &H23   Control Break Exit Address
Interrupt &H24   Critical Error Handler
Interrupt &H25   Absolute Disk Read
Interrupt &H26   Absolute Disk Write.
Interrupt &H27   Terminate and Stay Resident
Interrupts &H28H-&H2E   Internal to DOS
Interrupt &H2F   Multiplex Interrupt
Interrupt &H30H-&H3F   DOS Reserved

The rest of the interrupts, which run to &HFF, also don't offer much utility, except for interrupt &H67, which provides support for LIM 4.0 and expanded memory:

Interrupt &H40H-&H5F   Reserved
Interrupt &H60H-&H66   Reserved for User Software
Interrupt &H67   LIM 4.0 Support

Interrupts &H68H-&H7F	Not Used
Interrupts &H80H-&H85	Reserved by BASIC
Interrupts &H86H-&HF0	Used by BASIC Interpreter
Interrupts &HF1H-&HFF Not Used	

And that's it for all the interrupts, 0 through &HFF.

Conclusion

We've completed our tour of BIOS and DOS, from interrupt 0 up through interrupt &HFF, and we've even put some of the available services to work. Now, however, it's time to really get to work on low-level programming. We start our assembly language excursion in Chapter 10.

Welcome to Assembly Language

IN THIS CHAPTER, we're going to start working with the machine on the lowest levels. Here's where we'll boost BASIC's speed and capabilities enormously. This chapter is going to be about the essentials of assembly language, and in the next chapter we'll interface it to BASIC. We'll see how to write our own BASIC subprograms and functions entirely in assembly language for unprecedented power. The most important thing is to get a good base to start from, and we'll do that in this chapter when we learn the fundamentals of assembly language programming. In fact, through our use of the INTER-RUPT( ) routine, we already have a big leg up.

Machine Language

To get a computer to do something, you have to supply machine language instructions, and these bytes are really only comprehensible to the microprocessor. Often, only part of the machine language instruction will be used to tell the computer what to do, and the rest of the instruction is data. For example, you can write an instruction to put the byte &HFF into a certain memory location. Part of the instruction will be to tell the microprocessor that you want to store a number, part of the instruction will be to tell it the location in memory you want to store the number, and part of it will be the number itself, &HFF.

Although machine language instructions can be many bytes long, data and the instruction codes never mix across byte boundaries. For example, some machine language instructions may be all instruction to the microprocessor (see Figure 10-1).

01010101
Instruction

Figure 10-1

And some will be a mix of both instruction and data (Figure 10-2).

10101010	10111010
Instruction	Data Used by the Instruction

Figure 10-2

or even mostly data (Figure 10-3).

01010101	10111010 10010101 001010100
Instruction	Data Used by the Instruction

Figure 10-3

The data used by the instruction is either memory address(es) or data, like the &HFF we wanted to store in a memory location earlier.

Reading this kind of binary code is extremely difficult. Imagine yourself confronted with a page of numbers, all 0's or 1's. Even if such instructions were to be converted to hex, you'd have to look up the meaning of each byte before understanding what was going on (there are tables in the manuals that accompany assemblers listing what binary instructions mean what). Mostly, however, what means everything to the microprocessor means nothing to us.

Assembly Language

This is where assembly language enters. It is the direct intermediary between machine language and English. For every machine language instruction, there is one assembly language instruction. Rather than using a byte like 10101010B (we'll place a B for Binary at the end of binary numbers; there is no binary type in BASIC, so we couldn't denote this number as something like &B10101010), an English language mneumonic is used such as MOV AX,5.

This instruction, MOV AX,5, may be terse, but it is still an improvement over the corresponding machine code, &HB8 &H00 &H05. What this instruction does is to direct the machine to move (the MOV part of MOV AX,5) the value of 5 into the AX register.

What an assembler does is simple. It takes the program you've written in assembly language, and converts it, instruction by instruction, directly into machine language.

The machine language is then run by the microprocessor. Let's see some assembly language examples. These examples will be assembly language instructions that were assembled (i.e., converted into machine language) so that the corresponding machine language for each instruction (all numbers are in hex) becomes the following:

MOV	DI,00B0	→	BF B0 00
MOV	COUNTER,00B0		C7 06 C3 01 B0 00
MOV	BX,0080		BB 80 00
CMP	INDEX,00		80 3F 00
JZ	0670		74 12
CMP	[SI],0D		80 3C 0D
JZ	0666		74 03
MOVSB			A4
JMP	065E		EB F8

Sometimes assembly language is hard to write, sometimes it's hard to debug; there is no escaping the fact. It has to follow the design of the microprocessor, and as we'll see, assembly language for the PC and PS/2 has many quirks.

The MOV Instruction

The most fundamental assembly language instruction is MOV, the instruction that moves data between registers and memory, or register and registers. The MOV format is this: MOV destination, source. The data gets moved from the source into the destination. If you have something stored in memory and want to work with it, you can use MOV. Here's how it works:

```
MOV     AX,0FFFFH
```

Here we are putting the number 0FFFFH (65535) into AX. 0FFFFH is the biggest number any register (all are 16 bits) can hold. Note that in assembly language, the H for Hex goes at the end of the number (0FFFFH) not at the beginning as in BASIC (&HFFFF). In addition, if any number begins with a letter, like FFFFH, you have to preface it with a 0 (0FFFFH) to let the assembler know it's really a number and not a name.

We can take the 0FFFFH in the register AX and move it into the DX register:

```
MOV     DX,AX      (Move the data from AX into DX)
```

And now DX and AX hold the same value. We could also work one byte at a time:

```
MOV     DL,AL      (Move the data from AL into DL)
```

Data can also be moved into registers from memory. Let's say we have a memory location with 0 in it. This can be moved into, say, CX, this way:

```
MOV     CX,[Memory Location]
```

Or, we can move whatever is in DX into the memory location this way:

```
MOV     [Memory Location],DX
```

However, data cannot be moved from memory directly to memory. This is one of the peculiarities of the 80×86: data cannot go directly from memory location to memory location in one instruction. If we wanted to, we could move data from memory location 1 to AX, and then to memory location 2 like this:

```
MOV AX, [Memory Location 1]
MOV [Memory Location 2], AX
```

But it cannot go like this:

```
MOV [Memory Location 2], [Memory Location 1]
```

Assembly Language Example

It's always better to see an example. There is an excellent program that comes with all DOS versions named DEBUG. DEBUG has had the ability to assemble small programs that you write on the spot, a mini-assembler is built into the program. We'll use this mini-assembler to convert our instruction MOV AX,5 into machine language, and then run it, watching the value stored in AX change from 0 to 5. Start the DEBUG program; it gives you its hyphen prompt:

```
C:\>DEBUG
-
```

The command R in DEBUG stands for Register and it lets you see the contents of all the 80×86's registers. You can pick out the registers AX, BX, CX, and DX readily (note that all numbers displayed in DEBUG are in hexadecimal, which is standard for assembly language debuggers):

```
C:\>DEBUG
-R
AX=0000  BX=0000  CX=0000  DX=0000  SP=FFEE  BP=0000  SI=0000  DI=0000
DS=0EF1  ES=0EF1  SS=0EF1  CS=0EF1  IP=0100     NV UP EI PL NZ NA PO NC
0EF1:0100 9AEC04020F     CALL     0F02:04EC
```

In addition to the registers shown:

```
C:\>DEBUG
-R
 AX=0000  BX=0000  CX=0000  DX=0000  SP=FFEE  BP=0000  SI=0000  DI=0000
 DS=0EF1  ES=0EF1  SS=0EF1  CS=0EF1  IP=0100    NV UP EI PL NZ NA PO NC
 0EF1:0100 9AEC04020F     CALL      0F02:04EC
```

The settings of the internal flags of the 80×86 are shown (there are eight flags, as mentioned in Chapter 9):

```
C:\>DEBUG
-R
AX=0000  BX=0000  CX=0000  DX=0000  SP=FFEE  BP=0000  SI=0000  DI=0000
DS=0EF1  ES=0EF1  SS=0EF1  CS=0EF1  IP=0100    NV UP EI PL NZ NA PO NC
0EF1:0100 9AEC04020F     CALL      0F02:04EC
```

We've already seen the carry and zero flags, and the notations NZ and NC tell us that, at the moment, they are not set. Flags are used in conditional jumps, and we'll work with them later in this chapter. DEBUG also tells you the current memory location. Here, we are at memory location 0EF1:0100:

```
C:\>DEBUG
-R
AX=0000  BX=0000  CX=0000  DX=0000  SP=FFEE  BP=0000  SI=0000  DI=0000
DS=0EF1  ES=0EF1  SS=0EF1  CS=0EF1  IP=0100    NV UP EI PL NZ NA PO NC
 0EF1:0100   9AEC04020F     CALL      0F02:04EC
```

The final part of the DEBUG R display indicates what is to be found at the current memory location. In our case, those are the bytes following the address in the R display:

```
C:\>DEBUG
-R
AX=0000  BX=0000  CX=0000  DX=0000  SP=FFEE  BP=0000  SI=0000  DI=0000
DS=0EF1  ES=0EF1  SS=0EF1  CS=0EF1  IP=0100    NV UP EI PL NZ NA PO NC
 0EF1:0100   9AEC04020F     CALL      0F02:04EC
```

DEBUG tries to group bytes together, starting at the current memory location (which only holds one byte), into what would be a valid machine language instruction. It then provides us with an assembly language translation of the machine language instruction that begins at our present location.

When there is in reality no machine language instruction there, as there frequently is not, the translation is meaningless. That is the case here. Having just started DEBUG, there is as yet no program to look at. It is just taking leftover bytes in the computer's memory and trying to make sense out of them. In fact, DEBUG's supplied translation means nothing:

```
C:\>DEBUG
-R
AX=0000  BX=0000  CX=0000  DX=0000  SP=FFEE  BP=0000  SI=0000  DI=0000
DS=0EF1  ES=0EF1  SS=0EF1  CS=0EF1  IP=0100    NV UP EI PL NZ NA PO NC

0EF1:0100   9AEC04020F→   CALL    0F02:04EC
```

We'll use the A (for Assemble) command to put our own program in, consisting of only one line: MOV AX,5. The A command needs an address at which to start depositing the machine language instructions it will generate in memory. Our current address is 0EF1:0100, and we will tell it to assemble the machine language right there, using the shorthand A100:

```
C:\>DEBUG
-R
AX=0000  BX=0000  CX=0000  DX=0000  SP=FFEE  BP=0000  SI=0000  DI=0000
DS=0EF1  ES=0EF1  SS=0EF1  CS=0EF1  IP=0100    NV UP EI PL NZ NA PO NC
0EF1:0100 9AEC04020F    CALL    0F02:04EC
-A100                         ← Here is the A100 command.
0EF1:0100                       DEBUG's response.
```

> **TIP:** The Assemble DEBUG command provides an easy way of testing assembly language instructions, saving you the time needed to edit a source file and assemble it. Also, if you need to find the actual machine language bytes corresponding to some assembly language instructions, just use the Assemble command and then use the memory dump command, D.

Following the A100 command, DEBUG returned with the line 0EF1:0100, showing the current address at which it will deposit assembled code. We simply type MOV AX,5 and then a carriage return:

```
C:\>DEBUG
-R
AX=0000  BX=0000  CX=0000  DX=0000  SP=FFEE  BP=0000  SI=0000  DI=0000
DS=0EF1  ES=0EF1  SS=0EF1  CS=0EF1  IP=0100     NV UP EI PL NZ NA PO NC
0EF1:0100 9AEC04020F    CALL    0F02:04EC
-A100
0EF1:0100 MOV      AX,5            ← Type "MOV AX,5<cr>"
0EF1:0103
```

DEBUG then prompts for the next instruction we wish to give with the address 0EF1:0103. There are no more instructions to assemble at this time, so we give DEBUG a carriage return. It interprets the blank line to mean that we are through assembling, and returns to its normal prompt.

That's all there is to it. We've just assembled our first line of assembly language. To see what occurred, remember that the R command displays the current memory location and instruction. Since we assembled MOV AX,5 at the current memory location, let's give the R command and take a look:

```
C:\>DEBUG
-R
AX=0000  BX=0000  CX=0000  DX=0000  SP=FFEE  BP=0000  SI=0000  DI=0000
DS=0EF1  ES=0EF1  SS=0EF1  CS=0EF1  IP=0100     NV UP EI PL NZ NA PO NC
0EF1:0100 9AEC04020F    CALL    0F02:04EC
-A100
0EF1:0100 MOV      AX,5
0EF1:0103
-R                            ←
AX=0000  BX=0000  CX=0000  DX=0000  SP=FFEE  BP=0000  SI=0000  DI=0000
DS=0EF1  ES=0EF1  SS=0EF1  CS=0EF1  IP=0100     NV UP EI PL NZ NA PO NC
0EF1:0100 B80500        MOV     AX,0005
```

We can see the instruction (note the machine language bytes corresponding to MOV AX,5 in DEBUG's display). Executing the instruction is simple. DEBUG has a trace command, and typing T once will execute the current instruction, and increment us to the next memory location:

```
C:\>DEBUG
-R
AX=0000  BX=0000  CX=0000  DX=0000  SP=FFEE  BP=0000  SI=0000  DI=0000
DS=0EF1  ES=0EF1  SS=0EF1  CS=0EF1  IP=0100     NV UP EI PL NZ NA PO NC
0EF1:0100 9AEC04020F    CALL    0F02:04EC
-A100
0EF1:0100 MOV      AX,5
0EF1:0103
```

```
-R
AX=0000  BX=0000  CX=0000  DX=0000  SP=FFEE  BP=0000  SI=0000  DI=0000
DS=0EF1  ES=0EF1  SS=0EF1  CS=0EF1  IP=0100    NV UP EI PL NZ NA PO NC
0EF1:0100 B80500          MOV     AX,0005
-T                              ← This will execute our MOV instruction.

AX=0005  BX=0000  CX=0000  DX=0000  SP=FFEE  BP=0000  SI=0000  DI=0000
DS=0EF1  ES=0EF1  SS=0EF1  CS=0EF1  IP=0103    NV UP EI PL NZ NA PO NC
0EF1:0103 020F          ADD     CL,[BX]                     DS:0000=CD
```

After the T command, DEBUG displays what the register contents and flags are now: AX holds 5.

All the flags remain unchanged. On the other hand, the memory location has changed, from 0EF1:0100 to 0EF1:0103. This is because the machine language instruction corresponding to MOV AX,5 is three bytes long in memory (0B8H 05H 00H). The instruction following it will begin three bytes later; therefore, the 100 has changed to 103.

Our First Assembly Language Program

DEBUG not only allows you to assemble programs, but to write them out to the disk as well. Let's use DEBUG to assemble our first assembly language progam. This program will simply type out the letter Z and then exit.

We'll start with the A command. As before, we will put our machine language code starting at location 0100H:

```
C:\>DEBUG
-A100                          ←
0EF1:0100
```

We're going to use interrupt 21H service 2 to print out a letter. Just type in the following assembly language instructions verbatim, followed by a carriage return after the prompt 0EF1:010A to stop assembling:

```
C:\>DEBUG
-A100
1CE1:0100 MOV AH,2
1CE1:0102 MOV DL,5A
1CE1:0104 INT 21
1CE1:0106 INT 20
1CE1:0108          ← Just type a<cr> here.
-A100
```

What our progam is doing is loading the registers AH and DL with the MOV instruction. We're asking for service 2 of interrupt 21H, and that service prints out the ASCII
code in DL. We place the ASCII code for Z there, 5AH.

Then we issue an interrupt 21H instruction directly — INT 21H — followed by INT
20H. You may recall from our BIOS and DOS tour that interrupt 20H is used to end
programs at the assembly language level and return to the DOS prompt. This is how we'll
end all our programs. We can call the program PRINTZ.COM, following its function. We
name it this way:

```
C:\>DEBUG
-A100
1CE1:0100 MOV AH,2
1CE1:0102 MOV DL,5A
1CE1:0104 INT 21
1CE1:0106 INT 20
1CE1:0108
-NPRINTZ.COM      ←
```

And now we can write it out (DEBUG will write this file in the current directory).
DEBUG needs the number of bytes to write out, and, in our case, the program goes from
locations 0100H to 0107H. Each memory location holds a byte, so that makes 8 bytes

---

TIP: DEBUG allows you to do hexadecimal math with the H, or Hex command. For
example, H 8 2 returns both the sum and difference of 8 and 2 - A and 6.

The DEBUG W command, Write, reads the number of bytes to write as a file directly
out of the CX register. This means that to write our 8 byte program PRINTZ.COM, we
will have to load the CX register with 8 and then give the W command.

To move 8 into CX, we can use the R (Register) command again. If you use the R
command without any arguments, DEBUG gives you its standard display. On the other
hand, giving the command RCX indicates to DEBUG that you wish to change the value in
CX (this will work with any register). DEBUG displays the current value in CX (which
will be 0000) and gives us a colon prompt, after which we will type our new value for CX,
8, and a carriage return. Then we can write PRINTZ.COM by giving the W command:

```
C:\>DEBUG
-A100
1CE1:0100 MOV AH,2
1CE1:0102 MOV DL,5A
1CE1:0104 INT 21
1CE1:0106 INT 20
1CE1:0108
-U100 106
1CE1:0100 B402        MOV         AH,02
1CE1:0102 B25A        MOV         DL,5A
1CE1:0104 CD21        INT         21
1CE1:0106 CD20        INT         20
-NPRINTZ.COM
-RCX                   ←
CX 0000
:8
-W                     The W command
Writing 0008 bytes
-Q
```

Now we've written a functional 8-byte (!) program to disk. Let's run it:

```
C:\>PRINTZ
Z
C:\>
```

And PRINTZ does what it's supposed to do: It types out Z and exits.

For the first time, we've reached interrupt 21H directly (that is, without INTER-RUPT( )), using service 2 to print out a character on the screen. Here are some other interrupt 21H character I/O services we'll find useful in this chapter:

Service #	Name	Set These	What Happens
1	Keyboard Input	AH = 1	ASCII code of typed key returned in AL
2	Character Output	AH = 2 Dl = ASCII Code	The character corresponding to the ASCII CODE in DL is put on the screen
9	String Output	AH=9 DS:DX = Address of string of characters to print	Prints a string of bytes from memory on the screen (we will use this service in this chapter)

Now that we have some experience, we can start putting together assembly language programs without using DEBUG. To do that, we'll have to review the way memory is accessed by the 80×86 chips. Memory usage is much more important in assembly language than it is in BASIC. In fact, knowing your way around is essential.

Memory Segmentation

The address 0EF1:0100 is made up of two hex numbers, each 16 bits long. As we've seen as long ago as Chapter 5, this is usual for addresses — two words are involved for a full address. The 0EF1H in 0EF1:0100 is the segment address of that particular memory location, and 0100H is the offset address (see Figure 10-4).

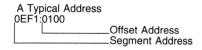

Figure 10-4

Under DOS, you can access up to one megabyte of memory, or 2^{20} bytes. To specify memory locations that big, you need numbers 20 bits long, but the largest number of bits a number can hold in the 80×86 (with the exception of the 386 and 486) is 16 bits. To make 20-bit addresses out of 16-bit numbers, you need two of them, the segment address and the offset address. This is the way it works: You move the segment address left by one hex place and add it to the offset address to get the real 20-bit address (see Figure 10-5).

```
    0EF1      ← Segment address shifted left one place
  + 0100
    0F010     ← Real 20-bit address
```

Figure 10-5

In other words, byte 0EF1:0100 really means byte 0F010H, or byte 61456, in memory. The lowest address is 0000:0000, byte 0 in memory, and the highest address is F000:FFFF, which corresponds to byte 0FFFFFH, or 1048575. Using these 20-bit addresses, we can refer to 1 megabyte, 1,024K (see Figure 10-6 below).

Segmented Address		Real Address	
F000:FFFF	1 Byte	FFFFFH	← The top of memory
F000:FEEE	1 Byte	FFFFEH	(FFFFFH = 1 MB − 1)
F000:FFFD	1 Byte	FFFFDH	
F000:FFFC	1 Byte	FFFFCH	
	.		
	.		
	.		
C000:AAAA	1 Byte	CAAAAH	
C000:AAA9	1 Byte	CAAA9H	
C000:AAA8	1 Byte	CAAA8H	
C000:AAA7	1 Byte	CAAA7H	

1 MB

⋮

0000:0003	1 Byte	00003H
0000:0002	1 Byte	00002H
0000:0001	1 Byte	00001H
0000:0000	1 Byte	00000H ← The bottom of memory

Figure 10-6

Segments in Memory

A segment is the memory space that can be addressed with one particular segment address, and a segment can go from xxxx:0000 to xxxx:FFFF, 64K. For example, the segment that starts at the bottom of memory, segment 0000, can extend from 0000:0000 to 0000:FFFF (keeping the segment address, 0000, unchanged). Once you choose a segment address, like 0000, you have a 64K workspace you can use without having to change the segment address again.

On the other hand, even though segments can describe such a large area, they can overlap. The next possible segment after segment 0000 is segment 0001. This segment extends from 0001:0000 to 0001:FFFF. Converting these numbers to 20-bit addresses gives 00010H to 1000FH.

Segment 0001 starts just 16 bytes (called a *paragraph*) after segment 0000. Segment 0002 starts just 16 bytes after segment 0001, and so on. Choosing a segment gives you a 64K work space, but that 64K work space overlaps with many other segments too (see Figure 10-7).

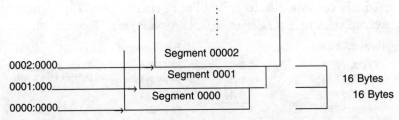

Figure 10-7

To let you set the segment that you want to choose as your work area, the 80×86 provides four *segment registers* (which we originally saw in Chapter 9). You set these segment registers typically at the beginning of a program, or let them be set automatically for you. Keep in mind, however, that they only define a 64K area. If you want something outside that area, you'll have to take care of setting them as required.

The four segment registers are CS, DS, ES, and SS. They stand for Code Segment, Data Segment, Extra Segment, and Stack Segment:

Segment Register	Means	Used With
CS	Code Segment	Your program's instructions
DS	Data Segment	The data you want to work on
ES	Extra Segment	Auxilary data segment register
SS	Stack Segment	Set by DOS; holds the "stack"

The code segment is where the instructions of your program will be stored. When your program is loaded, the code segment is chosen for it by the program loader. We will not have to set this segment register, CS, for the things we are going to do in this book. (See Figure 10-8.)

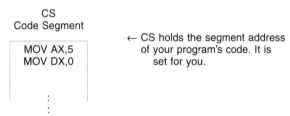

Figure 10-8

The DS register holds the value of the data segment. We've seen this register and even loaded values into it already in Chapter 9. Anything that you want to store as data, and not have the computer execute (cell entries in a spreadsheet, for example, or text in a word processor), can be stored here.

You usually set DS, the data segment register (if ever) at the beginning of the program and then leave it alone. If, however, we want to read bytes from faraway places in memory — to examine the screen buffer, or the keyboard buffer, for example — we'll have to set DS before we can address them (just as we use DEF SEG in BASIC). Using DS as the high word of our addresses, we can reach and read, or write any byte in memory.

Let's say that our program code is in the segment 2000H, and data in the segment at 3000H (see Figure 10-9).

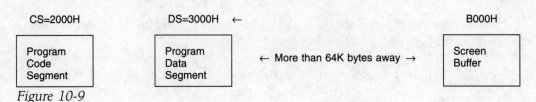

Figure 10-9

Now let's say that we wanted to change data in the video buffer (i.e., the letters that appear on the screen), which is at segment B800H for most monitors. We'd have to change the data segment that we're using, in DS, to B800H (see Figure 10-10).

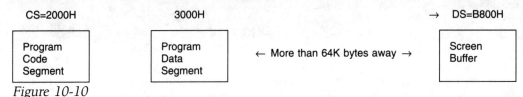

Figure 10-10

And then we could reference any data there with our instructions.

Whenever we read data from memory, the 80×86 checks the value of DS for the segment part of the address. Instructions that reference memory locations (like the MOV we used earlier) automatically mean that DS will be used as the segment address.

The Extra Segment can be used as another data segment, and we won't make much use of it here. There's also the Stack Segment. DOS stores the return address for function and subprogram calls on the *stack*, a special section of memory storage, and BASIC will pass parameters to us on the stack. We'll learn more about the stack both in this chapter and the next.

TIP: You can use the extra segment as well as the data segment when you want to specify both a source and a destination for data, as in copying.

Segment Registers in Use: .COM Files

The first programs we write will be .COM files. The default for .COM files is to set all four segment registers to the same value, the Code Segment. We will do this expressly so that we do not have to worry about the segment registers just at the time when we are being introduced to our first programs.

Everything that goes on in a .COM file will be limited to one 64K workspace. And when the program is loaded, DOS sets that segment address for us. That means in practice that we will not have to be careful about how the segment registers are set for .COM files. Here, CS = DS = ES = SS, and DOS will set them for us.

A .COM file is the simplest working program you can write on the PC or PS/2 (although the .COM format is no longer supported under OS/2). This file is, quite literally, just machine language instructions, ready to be executed. Setting these files up is going to give us the expertise we need to link assembly language into BASIC.

Assembler Directives

When you write an assembly language source file (which ends with the letters .ASM), to be turned into a .COM file, you have to specify where you want the code to be placed in the code segment, whether you will have a separate data segment and other things. The way you set up your segments is with *assembler directives*. These directives do not generate any code. What they do is give directions to the assembler (and only that). They work much like the SUB or FUNCTION statements in BASIC.

You can set up either code or data segments when you are writing a program, and you use assembler directives to do it. If you are setting up a code segment, the program instructions themselves will go there. If you are setting up a data segment, you are predefining some variables or constants that your program will later use, or you are just setting aside some blank space that the program will use. The assembler will make sure that this information is loaded into the correct segments in memory if you specify them with segment directives.

The .CODE Directive

Everything we put into our .ASM files will be enclosed inside a segment definition. We can add the code segment definition to the source code for the program PRINTZ we wrote earlier:

```
.CODE   ←

        MOV     AH,2
        MOV     DL,5AH
        INT     21H
        INT     20H
        :
```

From this point on, everything we write will be put into the code segment until the file ends, or until the assembler finds another segment directive, such as .DATA to start a data segment (which we'll explore later in this chapter). However, since there is only one segment in .COM files, everything goes into the code segment, and this is the only segment directive we'll need.

Labels

We can label our data byte by byte, or word by word; labels are also directives. And, as in BASIC, we can label an instruction in our program itself so that we can jump from the current instruction to the labeled one, which may be some distance away.

For example, when MOV AH,2 is translated into machine language, it will be 3 bytes. We can give a label to that instruction. Let's call it Start, and we can also give a label to the last instruction (INT 20H). Let's call it Exit:

```
    .CODE

Start:  MOV     AH,2        ←
        MOV     DL,5AH
        INT     21H
Exit:   INT     20H
```

As in BASIC, to label an instruction, just use a name followed by a colon. If, during our program, we wanted to leave quickly, we could just go the label Exit, and the INT 20H instruction would be executed, causing us to finish and quit. If we did decide to go there, the assembler would have to know the address of the Exit instruction, and it finds this by counting the number of machine language bytes it has produced from the beginning of the code segment (what we have labeled Start).

TIP: Be careful with long labels in asssembly language — the assembler only reads the first 31 characters, so labels must differ during those characters.

Positioning Code in the Code Segment

When .EXE files are loaded, they are put at the beginning of the code segment they have been given, at CS:0000. Their first instruction can start right there. .COM files, on the other hand, are supplied with a header that is loaded in before they are, and it is the header that is put at CS:0000, not the first instruction of the .COM file. This header is 100H — 256 decimal — bytes long. The header therefore runs from CS:0000 to CS:00FF, and the .COM file, now loaded into memory, starts exactly at CS:0100. (See Figure 10-11.)

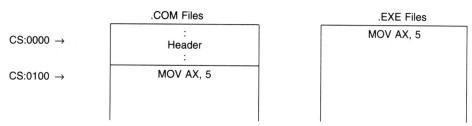

Figure 10-11

This means that we are going to have to start the code in PRINTZ.ASM at offset 0100H in the code segment. This is why we started assembling at 0100H in our DEBUG example (using A100). In a .COM file, machine language instructions must start at offset 0100H inside the program.

We can set our location in the code segment with the directive ORG (for origin):

```
.CODE
        ORG     100H     ←
Start:  MOV     AH,2
        MOV     DL,5AH
        INT     21H
Exit:   INT     20H

        END     Start
```

This tells the assembler to make the offset of Start (the line immediately after the ORG directive) 0100H. The assembler now treats the instruction MOV AH,2 as though it will be placed at CS:0100, and not at CS:0000 (and everything to follow gets treated as though it were placed after this instruction). In this way, we have made the correct allowance for the .COM file header that is automatically created for the .COM file.

The END Directive

The last thing that is required is to set an *entry point* for the program. In BASIC, the entry point is set when you define the main procedure — control is always passed to it first. In assembly language, you can set the entry point anywhere in your program with the END directive. Every .ASM file needs to end with END so the assembler knows when to stop. At the same time, you can set the entry point by adding its label after END.

In our case, we want the entry point to be at 0100H in the code segment. We have labeled that instruction as Start already, so our final directive will be END Start. And that's it. Our program PRINTZ.ASM shown in Listing 10-1 is finished.

Listing 10-1.   PRINTZ.ASM Program.

```
 .CODE

        ORG     100H
Start:  MOV     AH,2
        MOV     DL,5AH
        INT     21H
Exit:   INT     20H
        END     Start    ←
```

Assembling PRINTZ.ASM

If you have a word processor or editor, use it to type our program into a file that you name PRINTZ.ASM; now we're ready to use an assembler. If you have the Microsoft assembler (we will be using Microsoft MASM version 5.1), type this command:

```
R:\>MASM PRINTZ;  ←
```

And the macro assembler will do this:

```
R\:>MASM PRINTZ;
Microsoft (R) Macro Assembler Version 5.10
Copyright (C) Microsoft Corp 1981, 1988.  All rights reserved.

  50144 + 31277 Bytes symbol space free

     0 Warning Errors
     0 Severe  Errors
```

We've assembled the program, but, so far, all we have is an .OBJ file. The next step is stripping off some information left by the assembler in the .OBJ file. Although the linker is normally used for combining .OBJ files into big executable files, even single .OBJ files have to go through the linker before becoming .COM files.

The linker checks all segments, among other things. Since this is going to be a .COM file, there is only one segment, the code segment. Programs that are not .COM files need all segments to be explicitly spelled out, and the linker is going to give us a warning here that we have no stack segment. This is the normal warning you recieve when you are producing .COM files. Use LINK like this:

```
R:\>LINK PRINTZ;            ←
Microsoft (R) Overlay Linker   Version 3.64
Copyright (C) Microsoft Corp 1983-1988.  All rights reserved.

LINK : warning L4021: no stack segment
```

The warning is there, and we are now almost ready: the linker has taken the .OBJ file, PRINTZ.OBJ, and produced an .EXE file, PRINTZ.EXE. We did not set this up as a .EXE file, however; it's a .COM file. For the final step, stripping off the header that the linker left in the .EXE file, we run a DOS program called EXE2BIN. Run this on output from LINK. This is the last step in the process, and it converts the .EXE file into .COM format:

```
R:\>EXE2BIN PRINTZ PRINTZ.COM
```

Finally, our .COM file is there, ready to go. Give PRINTZ.COM a try. It does indeed print out Z, just as our DEBUG version did. Now we've made another advancement. We've got a working .ASM file.

Adding Data to Assembler Programs

On the other hand, this is really only half the story. As it stands, PRINTZ.ASM is a working program, but it is very primitive. In almost all .COM files, some data will be stored.

Every variable used in a program is data. We might want to read a file from the disk and store it in the data area, treating it as data. Or we might have program messages like "Hello, world." in the data area.

Let's look at an example. It turns out that we can use variables in assembly language — just as in BASIC — and we'll use the DB, *define byte*, and DW, *define word*, directives to set them up.

The DB and DW Directives

We use the DB directive to set bytes apart in memory so that we can store data in them. To define a byte named, say, VALUE, use DB like this:

```
VALUE DB 5
```

If you wanted to put this data into a data segment, the code might look like this:

```
    .CODE
    MOV     AL,VALUE
            :

    .DATA
→   VALUE   DB 5
            :
```

We ended the code segment and began the data segment by using the .DATA directive. You can't use .DATA in .COM files, but you can when designing .EXE files. Everything that follows .DATA will go into the data segment. In memory, the code and data segments might then look something like Figure 10-12.

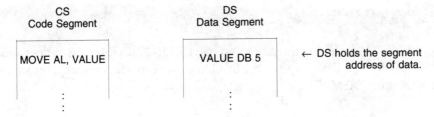

Figure 10-12

Now we are free to read the data in VALUE in the program:

```
MOV AL, VALUE
```

This is the way to use memory in the PC or PS/2: Set aside locations for it with DB and give variable names to all the bytes you set aside. Then, you can use these names just like variables in BASIC.

We can also store data a word at a time with the DW, or define word, directive like this:

```
    .CODE
    MOV       AX,WORD_VALUE
               :

    .DATA
  → WORD_VALUE      DW &H1234
               :
```

In this case, we could work with WORD_VALUE like this:

```
MOV       AX, WORD_VALUE
```

Let's see how all this works by adding data to PRINTZ.ASM. In this case, we'll have to put it into the code segment because there is only one segment available. The only data we have is the character we're going to print out, Z, so let's store that in memory:

```
    .CODE

              ORG       100H
              Our_Character    DB "Z"   ←
    Start:    MOV       AH,2
              MOV       DL,5AH
              INT       21H
    Exit:     INT       20H


              END       Start
```

DB tells the assembler that the data that follows is to be put in the program without interpretation: It is data. We have set aside a location, one byte, that we've called Our_Character, and initialized it by putting the character Z in it. The assembler will translate the Z for us into the ASCII code that the machine needs: 5AH. (Alternatively, we could have Our_Character DB 5AH. It is the same thing to the assembler.) Here are some DB examples:

```
Flag7     DB 0
Char_Z    DB "Z"
Numbers   DB 1,2,3,4,5,0 ← 6 bytes are put aside.
Prompt    DB "How long has it been since you called "
          DB "your mother?"
```

When we refer to the names Flag7, Char_Z, Numbers, or Prompt, we are actually referring to the first byte that follows DB. For example, if we were to say:

```
MOV       AH,Numbers
```

The 1, that is, the first number after DB, would be loaded into AH.

In PRINTZ.ASM, here is how we load our character into DL, just before printing it out:

```
.CODE

        ORG     100H
        Our_Character   DB "Z"
Start:  MOV     AH,2
        MOV     DL,Our_Character   ←
        INT     21H
Exit:   INT     20H

        END     Start
```

Now we've been able to label and use a memory location. However, we've left our-selves with a problem. The label Start is supposed to be at 100H in the code segment, and now that we've added 1 byte of memory space just before it, it will be at the wrong location (specifically, 101H). To solve this problem, we do what most .COM files with data do. We set aside a data area at the beginning of the program, and add a *jump instruction*, so that when things start at 100H, the first thing the microprocessor will do is jump over the data area and to the first instruction. Listing 10-2 shows the program.

Listing 10-2. PRINTZ.ASM Program.

```
.CODE

        ORG     100H
Start:  JMP     PrintZ    ←
        Our_Character   DB "Z"
PrintZ: MOV     AH,2
        MOV     DL,Our_Character
        INT     21H
Exit:   INT     20H

        END     Start
```

We've moved the label Start to point to a new instruction that is at 100H, but that instruction says: JMP PrintZ. This instruction lets control jump over the data area to the label PrintZ and then continue; JMP is an assembly language instruction that is exactly like a GOTO in BASIC. To use JMP, just provide it with a label to jump to, as we've done here (JMP PrintZ).

And that's it; PRINTZ.ASM — updated to hold data — is done. It's ready to be assembled and run. If we want to fit in more data, we can insert it right after Our_

Character. That's it for setting up .COM files. In general, Figure 10-13 shows how a .COM file shell looks.

```
.CODE

        ORG     100H
Start:  JMP     PROG
            This the data area. Use DB here.
PROG:
            And this is where the program goes.
Exit:   INT     20H

        END     Start
```

Figure 10-13

There is an area set aside for data (using DB or DW) and a part for the program code. Now let's develop a few more skills that we'll need.

Strings in Memory

We still have not resolved how to store character strings in memory. A character string — like a STRING in BASIC — is just a number of characters, one after the other, that makes sense to us but not to the computer. We want to keep them together: the computer only sees a number of bytes with no apparent relation.

Strings in assembly language are just stored as bytes, as they are in BASIC. In assembly language, they have a terminator to mark the end of the string. Although strings usually end with 0 (in what we've seen is called ASCIIZ format), this is not always the case. Strings are stored like PROMPT above, and if you want the string to end with a 0 byte, it is your responsibilty to put it in:

```
Prompt   DB "How long has it been since you called "
         DB "your mother?", 0
```

The assembler lets you store strings this way, using the quotation marks as shorthand (otherwise, you'd have to use DB for each letter).

INT 21H Service 9 — Print a String

The string printing service, service 9, of interrupt 21H prints out strings. It's the PRINT of assembly language. To terminate the string for this service, a $ (not a 0 byte) is added as the last character. This is an indication to service 9 to stop printing and is one of the times strings are not terminated with a 0 byte. Here's how it might look if we wanted to start changing our program to PRINTXYZ:

```
.CODE
        ORG     100H
Start:  JMP     PrintZ
        Our_Characters  DB "XYZ$"  ←
PrintZ: MOV     AH,2
        MOV     DL,Our_Character
        INT     21H
Exit:   INT     20H

        END     Start
```

Notice the $ terminating character, the last byte in the string. We still have to tell service 9 where to find this string in memory, and change the call from service 2 to service 9. This service requires the address of the string in DS:DX. If the address was 0EF1:0105, for example, we'd have to load 0EF1H into DS, and 0105H into DX.

Since we are dealing with a .COM file, the value of DS never changes, so DS is already set for service 9. When the program runs, DS will be pointing at the code segment (i.e., the only segment). To get the offset address of Our_Characters into DX, we use the *OFFSET* directive like this:

```
.CODE
        ORG     100H
Start:  JMP     PrintZ
        Our_Characters  DB "XYZ$"
PrintZ: MOV     AH,9
        MOV     DX, OFFSET Our_Characters          ←
        INT     21H
Exit:   INT     20H

        END     Start
```

The OFFSET directive gives you a label's offset value from the beginning of the data segment (which is the same as the code segment here). You can think of it as returning a pointer to that object like VARPTR( ). For example, our line (below)

```
MOV     DX, OFFSET Our_Characters
```

will load the offset of the first byte of Our_Characters into DX. OFFSET is a handy directive that we'll use often (especially in the next chapter), since many interrupt services require that we pass them the address of data.

That's all there is to it. Now we have a working .ASM file that prints out XYZ instead of just Z.

Using Comments

Before we leave PRINTXYZ, let's discuss commenting our code. Comments can be added in assembly language by preceding them with a semi-colon (;) as shown in Listing 10-3.

```
Listing 10-3.  PRINTXYZ.ASM — Prints "XYZ."

  .CODE

          ORG     100H              ;Set up for a .COM file.
  Start:  JMP     PrintZ            ;JmP over data area.
          Our_Characters  DB "XYZ$"        ;We will print out this string.
  PrintZ: MOV     AH,9              ;Request INT 21H service 9.
          MOV     DX, OFFSET Our_Characters     ;Point to our string.
          INT     21H               ;And print it out here.
  Exit:   INT     20H               ;End the program.

          END     Start             ;Set entry point to label Start.
```

By reading the comments, you can see what was intended in each line. Comments are often more important in assembly language than in BASIC, and they can be a great help.

Now that we have the fundamentals of program writing down, let's broaden our library of instructions and start to read some keys from the keyboard. Working with keyboard input will give us some experience in a vital assembly language topic: conditional jumps (the IF...THEN statements of assembly language).

Accepting Keyboard Input

The most basic of the interrupt 21H services is service number 1, which reads keyboard input. This is assembly language's INKEY$ (except that it waits for keyboard input). This is really the primary input service. When a key is typed, it is echoed on the screen and its ASCII code is returned in the AL register. Let's put this service to use.

The Program CAP.COM

The following example program will accept a letter that you type, capitalize it, and print it on the screen. For the first time, we will get our assembly language program to accept input from us. Let's start with the .COM file shell:

```
     .CODE

          ORG 100H
Start:    JMP CAP
          ;Data Area
CAP:
          ;Program will go here.

Exit:     INT    20H

          END Start
```

And add the instructions that will let us accept input:

```
     .CODE

          ORG 100H
Start:    JMP CAP
          ;Data Area
CAP:      MOV    AH,1     ;Request keyboard input ←
          INT    21H      ;From INT 21H

Exit:     INT    20H

          END Start
```

After the INT 21H instruction is executed, the ASCII code of the typed character is in AL. The program's job is to capitalize the letter and print it out. There is an easy way to capitalize letters — ASCII codes for lowercase letters, (e.g., a) have higher values than the ASCII codes for uppercase letters (e.g., A). The ASCII codes for A to Z run from 65 to 90; for a to z from 97 to 122. To capitalize a letter we just have to subtract a number from its ASCII code to move the code from its place in the a...z part of table to its corresponding place in the A...Z part:

Uppercase	Code		Lowercase	Code
A	65	←subtract 32—	a	97
B	66	←subtract 32—	b	98
C	67	←subtract 32—	c	99
.			.	
.			.	
.			.	
Z	90	←subtract 32—	z	122

The number we have to subtract is just equal to ASCII(a) − ASCII(A), which is 97 - 65 = 32, the distance between the two parts of the table. Here's how we capitalize the ASCII value in AL, introducing the new instruction, SUB, for subtract:

```
    .CODE

          ORG 100H
 Start:   JMP CAP
          ;Data Area
 CAP:     MOV     AH,1    ;Request keyboard input
          INT     21H     ;From INT 21H
 →        SUB     AL,"a"-"A"      ;Capitalize the typed key
          :
          :
 Exit:    INT     20H

          END Start
```

The SUB and ADD Instructions

The SUB instruction is used this way:

```
 SUB    AL,5
```

Here, 5 is subtracted from the contents of AL. AL is changed. In the same way, you could do this:

```
 SUB    AX,DX
```

This subtracts the contents of DX from AX. AX is changed, DX is not. Besides the SUB instruction, there is ADD, the built-in add instruction, which works like this:

```
 ADD    AL,5
 ADD    AX,DX
```

We will use ADD and SUB frequently. In addition, the assembler lets you use expressions like "a" − "A". For instance, we can use a line like this:

```
 SUB    AL,"a"-"A"
```

which makes what we are doing much clearer than if we simply said:

```
SUB    AL,32
```

Similarly, expressions like "a"+"A" are allowed.

TIP: The assembler understands expressions that include operators like +, -, /, and *. It's often a good idea to use them to make your code clearer.

Now that we've read a character and capitalized it by subtracting a from A, we have to print it out. Interrupt 21H service 2, which prints a character on the screen, expects the ASCII code of the character that it is to print in DL. In CAP.ASM so far, the ASCII code is still in the AL register (because service 1 returned it there). We move that code from AL to DL and then print the character out (see Listing 10-4).

Listing 10-4. CAP.ASM Program.

```
.CODE
        ORG 100H
Start:  JMP Cap
        ;Data Area
Cap:    MOV    AH,1     ;Request keyboard input
        INT    21H      ;From INT 21H
        SUB    AL,"a"-"A"       ;Capitalize the typed key
        MOV    DL,AL    ;Set up for service 2.
        MOV    AH,2     ;Request character output ←
        INT    21H      ;Type out character.
Exit:   INT    20H

        END Start
```

And that's it; CAP.ASM is complete. We read in a typed key with INT 21H service 1, capitalize it ourselves, and then print it out with INT 21H service 2. Type it in, assemble and produce CAP.COM. Give it a try. When you run it, you see this:

```
D:\>CAP
```

The program waits for a key to be typed. As soon as you type a letter, say s, it echoes it and prints out a capital S. Then it simply exits:

```
D:\>CAP
sS        ←
D:\>
```

Although it is gratifying to get the result we expected, there are a number of problems with this progam. Perhaps the most serious one is what happens if you type in some character other than a lowercase letter? Odd characters will be printed, since we are only ready to handle lowercase letters.

This problem may be fixed if we check the incoming ASCII code to make sure that it actually represents a lowercase letter. In other words, we have to check that the ASCII code is between the values for a and z. This type of checking brings us to the topic of conditional jumps, which are extremely important in assembly language, since they are almost the only branching instructions available.

Conditional Jumps

We want to augment CAP.ASM to check that the incoming ASCII code is between a and z. If it is not, we exit. To make this check, we divide the process into two steps. First, we check whether the character is greater than or equal to a; next, we check whether it's less than or equal to z. If bothh tests pass, we capitalize the letter, type it, and exit.

The CMP Instruction

Checking a value against some known comparison value is done with the assembly language instruction compare, CMP. To branch on the results of the comparison, we then use a *conditional jump* immediately after the CMP instruction. Unlike BASIC, comparisons are a two-step processes in assembly language. For example, here is the code to check whether the value in AL (i.e., the ASCII code read from the keyboard) is above or equal to a:

```
    .CODE

        ORG  100H
  Start:  JMP  Cap
          ;Data Area
  Cap:    MOV  AH,1    ;Request keyboard input
          INT  21H     ;From INT 21H
  →       CMP  AL,"a"   ;Compare the incoming ASCII code to "a".
          JB   Exit    ;If the letter is not lower case, exit.
```

```
            SUB      AL,"a"-"A"        ;Capitalize the typed key
            MOV      DL,AL     ;Set up for service 2.
            MOV      AH,2      ;Request character output
            INT      21H       ;Type out character.
Exit:       INT      20H

            END Start
```

Here, we've compared AL to the ASCII value for a and then immediately followed with a JB — Jump if Below — instruction:

```
CMP      AL,"a"   ;Compare the incoming ASCII code to "a".
JB       Exit     ;If the letter is not lower case, exit.
```

If the comparison indicates that the value in AL was below a in value, we will jump to the label Exit at the end of the program and leave without capitalizing it. What actually happens is this. First, the microprocessor's flags are set by the CMP instruction, and then the JB instruction checks these internal flags and acts accordingly:

TIP: Besides CMP, all the math instructions like ADD, SUB, or MUL set the flags too, so you can use conditional jumps after these instructions without a CMP.

```
CMP      AL,"a"    ←  Sets Flags
JB       Exit         Reads Flags
```

The next step is to check whether the ASCII code is below or equal to z. This is done with an instruction named, as you could probably guess, JA for Jump if Above. That completes the program CAP.ASM (shown in Listing 10-5), our first real assembly language program. It accepts input, and generates output, and even checks for errors.

Listing 10-5. CAP.ASM Program. 1 of 2

```
.CODE
        ORG 100H
Start:  JMP Cap
        ;Data Area
Cap:    MOV      AH,1      ;Request keyboard input
        INT      21H       ;From INT 21H
        CMP      AL,"a"    ;Compare the incoming ASCII code to "a".
        JB       Exit      ;If the letter is not lower case, exit.
   →    CMP      AL,"z"    ;Compare the incoming ASCII code to "z".
```

Listing 10-5.   CAP.ASM Program.   2 of 2

```
          JA      Exit    ;If the letter is not lower case, exit.
          SUB     AL,"a"-"A"       ;Capitalize the typed key
          MOV     DL,AL   ;Set up for service 2.
          MOV     AH,2    ;Request character output
          INT     21H     ;Type out character.
  Exit:   INT     20H

          END Start
```

More Conditional Jumps

At this point, we've seen the two instructions JA and JB. These follow a CMP (for compare) instruction, and, depending on the result, a jump may be made. There are actually many conditional jumps. In fact, there are even variations of JA and JB. In addition to these two, there are JAE (Jump if Above or Equal); JBE (Jump if Below or Equal); JNA (Jump if Not Above); JNB (Jump if Not Below); JNAE (Jump if Not Above or Equal); and JNBE (Jump if Not Below or Equal). All of these can be used after a CMP instruction. Here are a number of conditional jumps and their meanings:

Conditional Jump	Means
JA	Jump if Above
JB	Jump if Below
JAE	Jump if Above
JBE	Jump if Below
JNA	Jump if Not Above
JNB	Jump if Not Below
JNAE	Jump if Not Above
JNBE	Jump if Not Below
JE	Jump if Equal
JNE	Jump if Not Equal
JZ	Jump if result was Zero
JNZ	Jump if result was Not Zero
JCXZ	Jump if CX = 0 (Used at end of loops)

You can see that there is a rich selection of jump instructions. Without such a selection of conditional jumps, assembly language would be very difficult to use. As it is, there are conditional jumps that meet most needs. If you are new to assembly language, it might take you a while to become practised in their use.

Now let's put our assembly language expertise to work with the final example of the chapter, a program that converts hex numbers to decimal numbers.

An Assembler Program to Convert Hex to Decimal

The next step after CAP.ASM will be to write a program that's slightly more substantial. Let's develop a program that will change four digit hex numbers to decimal numbers. We start with the .COM file shell:

```
.CODE

        ORG 100H
ENTRY:  JMP DEHEXER

        ;Data will go here.

DEHEXER:

        ;Program will go here.

        INT     20H
        END     ENTRY
```

First, we'll have to read the hex number from the keyboard. DOS provides special input services to read strings, and we can use them by setting up a buffer in memory with the DB directive like this:

```
BUFFER DB #, 0, 0, 0, 0, 0, 0, 0, 0, 0, 0, 0
```

To fill this buffer, we will use INT 21H, service 0AH — get string. This is the LINE INPUT of assembly language. We set the number (# above) in the beginning of the buffer to the length of the buffer. (Service 0AH needs that number so it won't return too many bytes.)

TIP: Service 0AH always sets the last byte of the buffer to ASCII 13 (a carriage return) as an end-of-string marker, so you must leave room for one more than the number of characters you expect as input.

The second byte in the buffer will be filled by service 0AH with the number of bytes actually typed. If we're careful, we can set up our buffer with some foresight by expressly labeling the important bytes in it:

```
     .CODE

             ORG 100H
     ENTRY:  JMP DEHEXER
        →    BUFFER          DB 5
             NUM_TYPED       DB 0
             ASCII_NUM       DB 3 DUP (0)
             END_NUM         DB 0
             CRLF            DB 0
     DEHEXER:MOV     AH,9
             MOV     DX,OFFSET PROMPT
             INT     21H
             MOV     AH,0AH
             MOV     DX,OFFSET BUFFER
             INT     21H

             INT     20H
```

You might notice the use of the directive DUP:

```
             BUFFER          DB 5
             NUM_TYPED       DB 0
        →    ASCII_NUM       DB 3 DUP (0)
             END_NUM         DB 0
             CRLF            DB 0
```

This directive saves us time. This expression is equal to ASCII_NUM DB 0, 0, 0, not such a big saving for 3 bytes, but it is if you need to reserve space for 32,000. Now we've set up and labeled our buffer as shown in Figure 10-14.

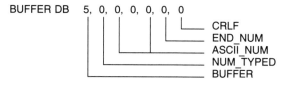

Figure 10-14

We can also add a prompt to the code — Type in a 4 digit hex number:$ — to be typed out with service 9, the string printer. In order to print out our prompt, we have to pass service 9 an offset address in DX:

```
        .CODE

                ORG 100H
        ENTRY:  JMP DEHEXER
            →   PROMPT              DB "Type in a 4 digit hex number:$"
                BUFFER              DB 5
                NUM_TYPED           DB 0
                ASCII_NUM           DB 3 DUP (0)
                END_NUM             DB 0
                CRLF                DB 0
        DEHEXER:MOV     AH,9
            →   MOV     DX,OFFSET PROMPT
                INT     21H
                :
```

This is what the prompt will look like on the screen:

```
Type in a 4 digit hex number:
```

Next, we use can service 0AH to read the four-digit hex number from the keyboard. This is the number that we'll convert to decimal and print out. We just have to pass the offset of the beginning of the buffer to service 0AH in DX, and that looks like this:

```
        .CODE

                ORG 100H
        ENTRY:  JMP DEHEXER
                PROMPT              DB "Type in a 4 digit hex number:$"
                BUFFER              DB 5
                NUM_TYPED           DB 0
                ASCII_NUM           DB 3 DUP (0)
                END_NUM             DB 0
                CRLF                DB 0
        DEHEXER:MOV     AH,9
                MOV     DX,OFFSET PROMPT
                INT     21H
                MOV     AH,0AH
            →   MOV     DX,OFFSET BUFFER
                INT     21H
                :
                :
                INT     20H
```

Next we issue an INT 21H instruction and accept the hex number.

> **NOTE:** If you try to type more than the number of characters we can accept in the buffer, the computer will beep. This is the same beep that DOS uses, and for that matter, the same internal service (0AH) that it uses to accept keyboard input at the DOS prompt.

After the buffer has been filled with input from the keyboard, the ASCII string extends from the locations ASCII_NUM to END_NUM. The <cr>— CHR$(13) — at the end of the returned string will go into the byte marked CRLF, and we can ignore it. The first step is to convert our character string into a number. If the number typed was 1234H, then the buffer now looks like Figure 10-15.

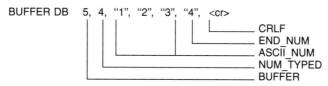

Figure 10-15

We can just point to the last number, 4, convert it from ASCII to binary, then point to the next number, 3, convert it to binary, multiply by 16, add it to the 4 we already have, and keep going to higher places. In this way we loop over all characters.

We have labeled the last ASCII digit as END_NUM, so we can read the ASCII character at that location with the instruction MOV AL, END_NUM. But how do we point to the previous digits?

We can use a register as a pointer. In assembly language, the BX register was designed explictly to be used as a pointer; let's examine how that's done. We'll need a loop to read all four digits, so we start off by loading BX with the offset address of END_NUM:

```
    .CODE

          ORG 100H
    ENTRY:  JMP DEHEXER
          PROMPT          DB "Type in a 4 digit hex number:$"
          BUFFER          DB 5
          NUM_TYPED       DB 0
          ASCII_NUM       DB 3 DUP (0)
          END_NUM         DB 0
          CRLF            DB 0
    DEHEXER:MOV     AH,9
          MOV     DX,OFFSET PROMPT
          INT     21H
```

```
        MOV     AH,OAH
        MOV     DX,OFFSET BUFFER
        INT     21H

        MOV     CX, 0
        MOV     AX,0
→       MOV     BX, OFFSET END_NUM
LOOP1:
        :
        :
        JB      LOOP1

        INT     20H
        END     ENTRY
```

Now we'll load the ASCII character into the DL register. We can do that like this:

```
    .CODE

        ORG 100H
ENTRY:  JMP DEHEXER
        PROMPT          DB "Type in a 4 digit hex number:$"
        BUFFER          DB 5
        NUM_TYPED       DB 0
        ASCII_NUM       DB 3 DUP (0)
        END_NUM         DB 0
        CRLF            DB 0
DEHEXER:MOV     AH,9
        MOV     DX,OFFSET PROMPT
        INT     21H
        MOV     AH,OAH
        MOV     DX,OFFSET BUFFER
        INT     21H

        MOV     BX, OFFSET END_NUM
LOOP1:  MOV     DL, [BX]                    ←
        DEC     BX
        :
        :

        JB      LOOP1

        INT     20H
        END     ENTRY
```

Putting BX inside square brackets, [BX], means that the microprocessor will use the value in BX as an address. This is called *indirect addressing*, and it's practically going to be the foundation of Chapter 11. [BX] stands for the byte at location END_NUM right now because BX holds that byte's offset address (see Figure 10-16).

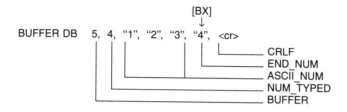

Figure 10-16

And we can move that byte into DL like this: MOV DL, [BX]. After moving the byte into DL, we decrement the pointer BX by 1 with the DEC instruction, which is just like SUB BX,1. (The corresponding instruction for incrementing by 1 is INC.) This points us to the previous ASCII character in preparation for the next time through the loop (see Figure 10-17).

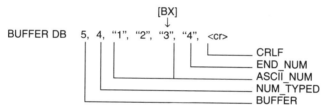

Figure 10-17

And that is how indirect addressing [BX] works. BX holds the offset address (in the data segment) of the byte or word we want to locate.

Now that the last ASCII character (4) is in DL, we have to convert it into binary. If it's in the range 0 to 9, we have to subtract the ASCII value for 0 from it (i.e., 0 will become 0, 1 will become 1, and so on). If it's in the range A to F, we have to subtract A and add 10 to it. We do that this way:

```
        .CODE

        ORG 100H
ENTRY:  JMP DEHEXER
        PROMPT          DB "Type in a 4 digit hex number:$"
        BUFFER          DB 5
        NUM_TYPED       DB 0
        ASCII_NUM       DB 3 DUP (0)
        END_NUM         DB 0
        CRLF            DB 0
DEHEXER:MOV     AH,9
        MOV     DX,OFFSET PROMPT
```

```
        INT     21H
        MOV     AH,0AH
        MOV     DX,OFFSET BUFFER
        INT     21H

        MOV     BX, OFFSET END_NUM
LOOP1:  MOV     DX,0
        MOV     DL, [BX]
        DEC     BX
        CMP     DL,"9"                        ←
        JBE     UNDER_A
        SUB     DL, "a" - "0" - 10
UNDER_A:SUB     DL, "0"
        :
        JB      LOOP1

        INT     20H
        END     ENTRY
```

DL now holds the numerical value of the current hex digit. To convert the entire four-digit number to decimal, we have to multiply each digit by the appropriate power of 16 and add it to a running total. And, to multiply by 16, we can *shift* the value in DL left.

There is an assembly language instruction called SHL, for shift left (and there's also SHR for shift right). Every time we shift an operand left by one binary place, it's the same as multiplying by 2. We load the number of places to shift left into CL and shift the value in DL left like this:

```
SHL     DL, CL
```

For example, if CL held 2 and DL held 00000001B, then after SHL DL,CL, DL would hold 00000100B. Shifting left by four binary places is the same as multiplying by 16, and each time through our loop, we'll add 4 to CL so that SHL DL,CL will produce the next hex digit. Note that when we shift DL left by more than two hex places, however, the result will be bigger than a byte can hold. Instead, we will use the whole DX register, not just DL:

```
SHL     DX, CL
```

TIP: The MUL instruction in the 80×86 microprocessors is comparatively slow, so programmers often cobble their own multiplications out of left shifts and additions. For example, to multiply AX by 5, make a copy of it in BX, shift AX left two places, and add BX to it. This is about ten times faster than MUL.

After it is shifted, we have to add this current hext digit to the running total. Let's keep the running total in, say, AX, and add DX to it each time we loop through. (See Listing 10-6.)

Listing 10-6. DEHEXER.ASM Program — Converts Hex to Decimal.

```
        .CODE

             ORG 100H
ENTRY:       JMP DEHEXER
             PROMPT              DB "Type in a 4 digit hex number:$"
             BUFFER              DB 5
             NUM_TYPED           DB 0
             ASCII_NUM           DB 3 DUP (0)
             END_NUM             DB 0
             CRLF                DB 0
DEHEXER:MOV      AH,9
        MOV      DX,OFFSET PROMPT
        INT      21H
        MOV      AH,0AH
        MOV      DX,OFFSET BUFFER
        INT      21H

   →    MOV      CX, 0
        MOV      AX,0
        MOV      BX, OFFSET END_NUM
LOOP1:  MOV      DX,0   ←
        MOV      DL, [BX]
        DEC      BX
        CMP      DL,"9"
        JBE      UNDER_A
        SUB      DL, "a" - "0" - 10
UNDER_A:SUB      DL, "0"
   →    SHL      DX, CL
        ADD      AX, DX
        ADD      CL,4
        CMP      CL,16
        JB       LOOP1

        INT      20H
        END      ENTRY
```

Every time through the loop, we load the ASCII value into DL, make it into a binary number, shift it to the left, and add it to the running total in AX. We only loop four times, one for each digit.

At this point, the ASCII string has been converted into binary, and its value is in AX. We still have to convert it back to decimal ASCII digits. The way to do that is to peel off successively the decimal digits by dividing the number in AX by 10. Each time we divide by 10, the remainder is a decimal digit. For example, if we divided the number 21 by 10, the result would be 2 with a remainder of 1.

The DIV and MUL Instructions

There is a divide instruction in assembly language, named DIV. If you load the number to divide into AX and divide by a byte-long register like this:

```
DIV BL
```

then the instruction divides AX by BL. AX is assumed to hold the number to divide when you divide by a byte. The quotient is returned in AL and the remainder in AH.

On the other hand, if you give this instruction (with a 16-bit register):

```
DIV BX
```

then the microprocessor assumes that you are dividing the double word number in DX:AX by the specifed register, BX.

NOTE: The terminology DX:AX is an unfortunate way of specifying double words, since addresses are also specifed with a colon; however, when segment registers are used, you can be sure it's an address.

Similarly, MUL BL will multiply AL by BL and leave the result in AX. MUL BX will multiply BX by AX and leave the result in DX:AX.

TIP: It's a good idea to plan ahead with your use of registers so that instructions like MUL will leave the results in the registers you want, and you don't have to move data from register to register too much. You'll often see this in assembly language programs.

If we use the DIV BX instruction, the number in DX:AX will be divided by BX, so let's load DX with 0 and BX with 10. AX already holds the number to convert. After the division is through, AX will hold the quotient (ready to be divided by 10 again in the next pass to peel the next decimal digit off) and DX holds the remainder:

```
      .CODE

              ORG  100H
      ENTRY:  JMP  DEHEXER
              PROMPT           DB "Type in a 4 digit hex number:$"
              BUFFER           DB 5
              NUM_TYPED        DB 0
              ASCII_NUM        DB 3 DUP (0)
              END_NUM          DB 0
              CRLF             DB 0
      DEHEXER:MOV  AH,9
              MOV  DX,OFFSET PROMPT
              INT  21H
              MOV  AH,0AH
              MOV  DX,OFFSET BUFFER
              INT  21H

              MOV  CX, 0
              MOV  AX,0
              MOV  BX, OFFSET END_NUM
      LOOP1:  MOV  DX,0
              MOV  DL, [BX]
              DEC  BX
              CMP  DL,"9"
              JBE  UNDER_A
              SUB  DL, "a" - "0" - 10
      UNDER_A:SUB  DL, "0"
              SHL  DX, CL
              ADD  AX, DX
              ADD  CL,4
              CMP  CL,16
              JB   LOOP1

              MOV  CX,0
              MOV  BX, 10
      LOOP2:  MOV  DX,0
              DIV  BX           ← After this, DX holds current decimal digit.
                  :
              INT  20H
              END  ENTRY
```

The remainder in DX is what we want. It's the current decimal digit. Note that we are peeling the digits off in backwards order. For example, if we had the number 4,321 (decimal) in AX, the first time we divided by 10 we would get a remainder of 1, the next time a remainder of 2, and so on:

To store these decimal digits now in DX, we push them on the stack, using the instruction PUSH DX. The stack is a part of memory specially reserved to hold data, and, in the next chapter, BASIC will PUSH values onto the stack for us to read. Let's see how the stack works. If there was a value of 5 in DX, and we executed the instruction PUSH DX, the stack would look like Figure 10-18 (we can only PUSH words, not bytes).

→ | 5 |

Figure 10-18

Next we might push CX, which might hold a value of 3 (see Figure 10-19).

5
3

→

Stack "Grows" downwards — towards
↓   lower memory locations

Figure 10-19

After that, we might push AX, which holds 0 (see Figure 10-20).

5
3
0

→

Figure 10-20

Then we could give the instruction *POP* BX to retrieve values from the stack. The value placed on the stack last — 0 — will be popped into BX, and the stack will look like Figure 10-21.

→

Figure 10-21

Another POP, say POP DX, would place 5 into DX and the stack would look like Figure 10-22.

Figure 10-22

POP CX would load that value into CX, and the stack would be empty. Notice that values come off the stack in opposite order of going on (this is going to be valuable to us). In our example DEHEXER, we'll strip each decimal digit off the value now in AX and PUSH it onto the stack. A decimal value of 8,573 would be pushed onto the stack as 3, 7, 5, and 8 (we'll also keep track of how many numbers we've pushed so we can POP them later — a four-digit hex number may give from 1 to 5 decimal digits).

NOTE: When we pop them, these digits will come off in the order we want to print them: 8, 5, 7, and 3.

Here's the way we load each decimal digit onto the stack:

```
    .CODE

            ORG 100H
ENTRY:      JMP DEHEXER
            PROMPT          DB "Type in a 4 digit hex number:$"
            BUFFER          DB 5
            NUM_TYPED       DB 0
            ASCII_NUM       DB 3 DUP (0)
            END_NUM         DB 0
            CRLF            DB 0
DEHEXER:MOV     AH,9
            MOV     DX,OFFSET PROMPT
            INT     21H
            MOV     AH,0AH
            MOV     DX,OFFSET BUFFER
            INT     21H

            MOV     CX, 0
            MOV     AX,0
            MOV     BX, OFFSET END_NUM
LOOP1:      MOV     DX,0
            MOV     DL, [BX]
            DEC     BX
            CMP     DL,"9"
            JBE     UNDER_A
            SUB     DL, "a" - "0" - 10
UNDER_A:SUB .    DL, "0"
            SHL     DX, CL
            ADD     AX, DX
            ADD     CL,4
            CMP     CL,16
            JB      LOOP1

            MOV     CX,0
            MOV     BX, 10
LOOP2:      MOV     DX,0
            DIV     BX
            PUSH    DX
            INC     CX          ← ;CX holds the number of digits pushed
            CMP     AX,0           ;Anything left to strip digits off of?
            JA      LOOP2          ;IF yes, loop again
                    :
            INT     20H
            END     ENTRY
```

At this point, we're almost done. The decimal digits are on the stack, and the number of digits is in CX. Let's print out a message saying "That number in decimal is:" with service 9 of INT 21H:

```
     .CODE
              ORG   100H
     ENTRY:   JMP   DEHEXER
              PROMPT          DB  "Type in a 4 digit hex number:$"
              BUFFER          DB  5
              NUM_TYPED       DB  0
              ASCII_NUM       DB  3 DUP (0)
              END_NUM         DB  0
              CRLF            DB  0
   →          ANS_STRING      DB  13, 10, "That number in decimal is: $"
     DEHEXER: MOV   AH,9
              MOV   DX,OFFSET PROMPT
              INT   21H
              MOV   AH,0AH
              MOV   DX,OFFSET BUFFER
              INT   21H

              MOV   CX, 0
              MOV   AX,0
              MOV   BX, OFFSET END_NUM
     LOOP1:   MOV   DX,0
              MOV   DL, [BX]
              DEC   BX
              CMP   DL,"9"
              JBE   UNDER_A
              SUB   DL, "a" - "0" - 10
     UNDER_A: SUB   DL, "0"
              SHL   DX, CL
              ADD   AX, DX
              ADD   CL,4
              CMP   CL,16
              JB    LOOP1

              MOV   CX,0
              MOV   BX, 10
     LOOP2:   MOV   DX,0
              DIV   BX
              PUSH  DX
              INC   CX
              CMP   AX,0
              JA    LOOP2

   →          MOV   AH,9
              MOV   DX,OFFSET ANS_STRING
              INT   21H
                    :
              INT   20H

              END   ENTRY
```

And then we can just print out the digits using service 2 of INT 21H and POP DX. Note that since we peeled the digits off in reverse order, and that since using the stack has reversed that order once again, we can just print digits as we POP them. In other words, if the number was 1,234, we would have peeled the digits off and pushed them in the order of 4, 3, 2, and 1, so the stack looks like Figure 10-23.

4
3
2
1

Figure 10-23

The first digit to be popped, and printed, is 1, followed by 2, and so on, meaning that we'll print 1,234. Each digit still has to be converted to ASCII. For example, if we pop 1 off the stack, that's still not ASCII "1". To convert them to ASCII, we have to add the ASCII value for "0" to them; i.e., 0 will become "0", 1 will become "1", and so on.

Here's the loop where we pop the digits. We'll pop them into DX since service 2 expects the ASCII character to print to be in DL, and use the new LOOP instruction:

```
      .CODE

              ORG 100H
      ENTRY:  JMP DEHEXER
              PROMPT          DB "Type in a 4 digit hex number:$"
              BUFFER          DB 5
              NUM_TYPED       DB 0
              ASCII_NUM       DB 3 DUP (0)
              END_NUM         DB 0
              CRLF            DB 0
              ANS_STRING      DB 13, 10, "That number in decimal is: $"
      DEHEXER:MOV     AH,9
              MOV     DX,OFFSET PROMPT
              INT     21H
              MOV     AH,0AH
              MOV     DX,OFFSET BUFFER
              INT     21H

              MOV     CX, 0
              MOV     AX,0
              MOV     BX, OFFSET END_NUM
      LOOP1:  MOV     DX,0
              MOV     DL, [BX]
              DEC     BX
              CMP     DL,"9"
              JBE     UNDER_A
              SUB     DL, "a" - "0" - 10
      UNDER_A:SUB     DL, "0"
              SHL     DX, CL
              ADD     AX, DX
              ADD     CL,4
              CMP     CL,16
              JB      LOOP1

              MOV     CX,0
```

```
            MOV     BX, 10
LOOP2:      MOV     DX,0
            DIV     BX
            PUSH    DX
            INC     CX
            CMP     AX,0
            JA      LOOP2
            MOV     AH,9
            MOV     DX,OFFSET ANS_STRING
            INT     21H

            MOV     AH,2                    ←
LOOP3:      POP     DX
            ADD     DX,"0"
            INT     21H
            LOOP    LOOP3

            INT     20H
            END     ENTRY
```

The LOOP Instruction

The LOOP instruction is just like a FOR...NEXT loop in BASIC. Here we use LOOP to loop over the pushed digits, pop them, and print them out. In order to use LOOP, just fill CX with the number of times you want to loop, define a label, and loop like this:

```
            MOV     CX,5
LOOP_1:
            :
            :
            LOOP    LOOP_1
```

In this case, the body of LOOP_1 will be executed five times.

In DEHEXER, the previous loop (where we stripped the decimal digits off the value in AX) left the number of digits in CX already, so the loop index CX is all set. All we have to do is to use LOOP, printing out each digit as we pop it off the stack:

```
            MOV     AH,2
LOOP3:      POP     DX
            ADD     DX,"0"
            INT     21H
            LOOP    LOOP3
```

And that's it. We've read in a hex number, converted it to binary by multiplying each digit by a power of 16, peeled decimal digits off by successively dividing it by 10, reversed their order, and now printed them out. We've made tremendous progress.

The program works. Give it a try. It accepts four-digit hex numbers and prints out the correct decimal version. On the other hand, there is still one difference between it and most .ASM files. Most .ASM files have at least one procedure defined inside them. This will be the final topic of this chapter, and it's crucial to know about procedures for Chapter 11.

Procedures in Assembly Language

In BASIC, we can write subroutines, subprograms, and functions. In assembly language, all we can write are procedures. We can make DEHEXER into a single procedure by adding the PROC and ENDP directives so that they straddle our code like this:

```
    .CODE

        ORG 100H
ENTRY:  JMP DEHEXER
        PROMPT          DB "Type in a 4 digit hex number:$"
        :
DEHEXER PROC                      ←
        MOV     AH,9
        MOV     DX,OFFSET PROMPT             The DEHEXER Procedure
        :
        INT     20H
DEHEXER ENDP                      ←

        END     ENTRY
```

Here's how the whole program looks now:

```
    .CODE

        ORG 100H
ENTRY:  JMP DEHEXER
        PROMPT          DB "Type in a 4 digit hex number:$"
        BUFFER          DB 5
        NUM_TYPED       DB 0
        ASCII_NUM       DB 3 DUP (0)
        END_NUM         DB 0
        CRLF            DB 0
        ANS_STRING      DB 13, 10, "That number in decimal is: $"
DEHEXER PROC            ←
        MOV     AH,9
        MOV     DX,OFFSET PROMPT
        INT     21H
        MOV     AH,0AH
```

```
        MOV     DX,OFFSET BUFFER
        INT     21H
        MOV     CX, 0
        MOV     AX,0
        MOV     BX, OFFSET END_NUM
LOOP1:  MOV     DX,0
        MOV     DL, [BX]
        DEC     BX
        CMP     DL,"9"
        JBE     UNDER_A
        SUB     DL, "a" - "0" - 10
UNDER_A:SUB     DL, "0"
        SHL     DX, CL
        ADD     AX, DX
        ADD     CL,4
        CMP     CL,16
        JB      LOOP1

        MOV     CX,0
        MOV     BX, 10
LOOP2:  MOV     DX,0
        DIV     BX
        PUSH    DX
        INC     CX
        CMP     AX,0
        JA      LOOP2

        MOV     AH,9
        MOV     DX,OFFSET ANS_STRING
        INT     21H

        MOV     AH,2
LOOP3:  POP     DX
        ADD     DX,"0"
        INT     21H
        LOOP    LOOP3

        INT     20H
DEHEXER ENDP                         ←

        END     ENTRY
```

We have added the PROC and ENDP directives, which define procedures. The PROC directive lets the assembler know that you want to define a procedure, and the ENDP directive indicates that the procedure definition is finished.

And, unless you are in the main procedure, you have to end the procedure with a return, or RET instruction. Let's break DEHEXER into two procedures to see how this is done. We can, for example, print out the decimal answer in a new procedure called PRINT_NUM.

As soon as we've decoded the typed hex number into a binary value in AX, we can call PRINT_NUM to do the job of stripping decimal digits from AX, placing them on the stack, and then printing them out. We call Print_Num with the instruction CALL Print_Num, and return at the end with a RET instruction (just like RETURN at the end of a BASIC subroutine). (See Figure 10-24.)

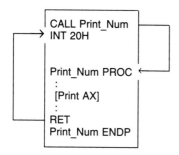

Figure 10-24

Here's how it looks in outline:

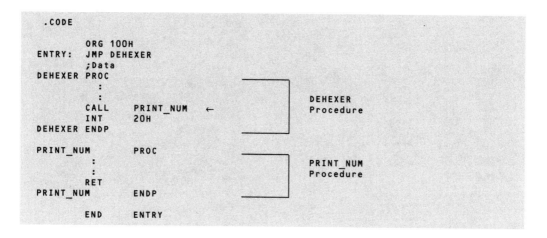

This works as you'd expect it to. When you CALL PRINT_NUM, control is transferred to the first line there. Execution continues until the return instruction, RET, is reached, and control returns to the line just after the CALL PRINT_NUM instruction in the main procedure. You never call procedures with arguments (like CALL PRINT_NUM(AX)). Instead, you pass values in the registers. The whole program is shown in Listing 10-7.

Listing 10-7.   DEHEXER.ASM with a Subroutine.   1 of 2

```
          .CODE

                  ORG  100H
ENTRY:    JMP  DEHEXER
          PROMPT           DB "Type in a 4 digit hex number:$"
          BUFFER           DB 5
          NUM_TYPED        DB 0
          ASCII_NUM        DB 3 DUP (0)
          END_NUM          DB 0
          CRLF             DB 0
          ANS_STRING       DB 13, 10, "That number in decimal is: $"
DEHEXER PROC
          MOV     AH,9
          MOV     DX,OFFSET PROMPT
          INT     21H
          MOV     AH,0AH
          MOV     DX,OFFSET BUFFER
          INT     21H

          MOV     CX, 0
          MOV     AX,0
          MOV     BX, OFFSET END_NUM
LOOP1:    MOV     DX,0
          MOV     DL, [BX]
          DEC     BX
          CMP     DL,"9"
          JBE     UNDER_A
          SUB     DL, "a" - "0" - 10
UNDER_A:SUB       DL, "0"
          SHL     DX, CL
          ADD     AX, DX
          ADD     CL,4
          CMP     CL,16
          JB      LOOP1

          CALL    PRINT_NUM               ←

          INT     20H
DEHEXER ENDP

PRINT_NUM        PROC
          MOV     CX,0
          MOV     BX, 10
LOOP2:    MOV     DX,0
          DIV     BX
          PUSH    DX
          INC     CX
          CMP     AX,0
          JA      LOOP2

          MOV     AH,9
          MOV     DX,OFFSET ANS_STRING
          INT     21H

          MOV     AH,2
LOOP3:    POP     DX
```

Listing 10-7. **DEHEXER.ASM with a Subroutine.**   2 of 2

```
            ADD     DX,"0"
            INT     21H
            LOOP    LOOP3
            RET                          ←
PRINT_NUM       ENDP

        END     ENTRY
```

Procedures in assembly language don't specifically return any values, as functions can in BASIC. Instead, information is returned in the registers, or, in some cases, in the flags.

TIP: There is no such thing as a formal local variable in assembly language. All variables in the same module are shared. You can, however, make variables local by putting them into another file.

That's how PROC and ENDP work, and we'll see much more of them soon.

Conclusion

That's it for our assembly language primer. Now that we've reached this point, we're up to speed in assembly language, and we're ready to press on. We can start putting all our knowledge to work when we interface BASIC to assembly language, and we'll do that next, in Chapter 11, BASIC/Assembly Language Interface.

BASIC/Assembly
Language Interface

IN THIS CHAPTER, we'll learn about these topics:

- How to link assembly language procedures into BASIC
- How to work with BASIC data in assembly language
- How to read parameters passed from BASIC
- How to return values to BASIC

By linking in your own assembly language code into BASIC, you can streamline your programs and add raw computing power. We will present many assembly language examples for both BASIC functions and subprograms. To BASIC, these will look like normal BASIC subprograms and functions although they will actually be written in assembly language. For example, Listing 11-1 shows what a BASIC function that adds two integers looks like in assembly language.

Listing 11-1.   Assembly Language Version of a BASIC Function That Adds Two Integers.

```
.MODEL MEDIUM, BASIC
.CODE
.286

          PUBLIC Addem
Addem     PROC FAR USES DI SI DS ES, VALUE1:WORD, VALUE2:WORD

          MOV BX, VALUE1  ;Pick addr of VALUE from stack (BASIC passes ref.)
          MOV AX, [BX]
          MOV BX, VALUE2
          ADD AX, [BX]

          RET
Addem     ENDP
          END
```

If you wish, you can use the examples in this chapter as templates, keeping the BASIC interface of the assembly language code intact and adapting the body of that code to suit your needs.

Keep in mind, however, that this is an advanced topic. A good deal of the programming that follows is not exactly straightforward.

Linking into BASIC

To make use of this chapter, you must have a Microsoft assembler, such as MASM 5.1, to assemble the code we develop. For example, you might have a file named A.ASM that contains an assembly language procedure named PrintString( ). The first thing you'll have to do is to assemble the file:

```
D:\>MASM A;
Microsoft (R) Macro Assembler Version 5.10
Copyright (C) Microsoft Corp 1981, 1988.  All rights reserved.

   49894 + 311895 Bytes symbol space free

        0 Warning Errors
        0 Severe  Errors
```

This produces A.OBJ. If you are using QuickBASIC, there's only one way to make PrintString( ) available to your programs. You have to link A.OBJ into a Quick Library and load that library when you start QuickBASIC.

Let's produce a quick library named A.QLB. That process works like this:

```
D:\>LINK /Q A.OBJ QB.LIB, A.QLB,, BQLB45.LIB;
```

Now that we've created A.QLB, we can just start QB this way (where the program you want to call PrintString( ) from is in PROGRAM.BAS):

```
D:\>QB PROGRAM /L A
```

The /L command loads the Quick Library A.QLB into memory, ready for use. In extended QuickBASIC, you build the Quick Library like this:

```
D:\>LINK /Q A.OBJ QBX.LIB, A.QLB,, QBXQLB.LIB;
```

And now that you've created A.QLB, you start QBX this way:

```
D:\>QBX PROGRAM /L A
```

You can also use use the command line compiler, BC.EXE (any version — 4.5 or 7.10, for example). In that case, you'd begin by assembling A.ASM, the assembly language source for PrintString( ):

```
D:\>MASM A;
Microsoft (R) Macro Assembler Version 5.10
Copyright (C) Microsoft Corp 1981, 1988.  All rights reserved.

  49894 + 311895 Bytes symbol space free

      0 Warning Errors
      0 Severe  Errors
```

This creates A.OBJ. Then, you would compile the BASIC program that calls PrintString( ):

```
D:\>BC PROGRAM;

Microsoft (R) QuickBASIC Compiler Version 4.50
(C) Copyright Microsoft Corporation 1982-1988.
All rights reserved.
Simultaneously published in the U.S. and Canada.

43997 Bytes Available
43722 Bytes Free

      0 Warning Error(s)
      0 Severe  Error(s)
```

This creates PROGRAM.OBJ. Next, we link the two .OBJ files together with LINK (note that you'll also have to add any other libraries required by the code in PROGRAM):

```
D:\>LINK PROGRAM + A;
IBM Linker/2  Version 1.10
(C) Copyright IBM Corporation 1984, 1988
(C) Copyright Microsoft Corp 1983, 1988.  All rights reserved.
```

And this creates a file named PROGRAM.EXE, which is ready to run.

NOTE: A tool named the Programmer's Work Bench (PWB) comes with the BASIC PDS 7.10. The PWB is designed to facilitate working in multiple language environments. Unfortunately, support has only been offered so far for connecting BASIC with C, not with assembly language.

Before beginning, we should also note that the QBX.EXE compiler occasionally handles data (strings and arrays) a little differently than either BC.EXE or QB.EXE. For that reason, some of the examples below will be split into two parts, one for BC.EXE and QB.EXE and one for QBX.EXE.

Receiving Parameters from BASIC

Like all languages, BASIC passes parameters to subprograms and functions on the stack. Each parameter is pushed in the order it appears in the call; for example, if you used MID$( ) like this:

```
MyChar$ = MID$(MyString$, Place%, Num%)
```

Then, before control is passed to MID$( ), MyString$ is pushed onto the stack, followed by Place%, and then Num%. Pushing parameters in this order is called the *BASIC calling convention.*

Each parameter passed is actually passed by *near reference* (unless you use the BYVAL or SEG keywords). This means that what BASIC actually passes is the one-word offset address of the variable in memory. For example, if we had a function named Add5%( ), which adds 5 to a passed integer, and called it this way:

```
Val% = 9
PRINT "9 + 5 ="; Add5%(Val%)
```

then BASIC pushes the *offset address* of Val% (from the beginning of the data segment) onto the stack before calling Add5%( ). As soon as we get to Add5%( ), the stack looks like Figure 11-1.

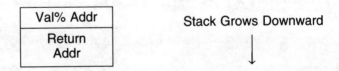

Figure 11-1

Here Return Addr is the (two-word) address that control returns to when Add5%( ) is done. Let's see how we can read the argument passed to us, Val%.

In the old days, the assembly language programmer had to read values like Val% Addr directly off the stack, but the new, extended PROC directive (under MASM 5.1) saves us the trouble. Instead, we can start the assembly language code for Add5 like this, with the new, extended PROC definition:

```
Add5    PROC FAR USES DI SI DS ES, VALUE1:WORD  ←
        :
        :
```

Here we tell the assembler we're going to use the DI, SI, DS, and ES registers in our program (we do not actually use them; this is only for the purposes of demonstration). The assembler then automatically adds code at the beginning to push and at the end to pop these registers so that the original values in them that BASIC was using are preserved. We also indicate that the parameter VALUE1, a word, will be passed to our program.

From now on, we can refer to VALUE1 as we would to any other variable. That is, to get the address of the integer that's been passed to us into BX, we only need to do this:

```
Add5    PROC FAR USES DI SI DS ES, VALUE1:WORD

  →     MOV BX, VALUE1  ;Pick addr of VALUE from stack (BASIC passes ref.)
        :
        :
```

Remember that what BASIC passes is the *address* of the parameter, not the actual parameter itself. Since each address is an offset address, that is, one word, all passed parameters will be one word long. We use that offset address to get the actual parameter into AX, and then we can add 5 to it:

```
Add5    PROC FAR USES DI SI DS ES, VALUE1:WORD

        MOV BX, VALUE1  ;Pick addr of VALUE from stack (BASIC passes ref.)
  →     MOV AX, [BX]
        ADD AX, 5
        :
```

Our next job is to return the result to BASIC, and we'll see more about this process in the next section. Briefly, it turns out that you return INTEGER values to BASIC from a function in the AX register. Our result is already in AX, so we just have to add a return instruction:

```
Add5      PROC FAR USES DI SI DS ES, VALUE1:WORD

          MOV BX, VALUE1  ;Pick addr of VALUE from stack (BASIC passes ref.)
          MOV AX, [BX]
          ADD AX, 5

  →       RET
Add5      ENDP
          END
```

And that's it. We've loaded the value being passed to us into AX, added 5 to it, and left it in AX as the return value of our function. The calling program will read this values from that register.

We'll make use of the extended PROC definition frequently in this chapter to pick the parameters passed to us off the stack. In fact, the extended PROC definition will make the our procedures very simple. Now let's see how to return values to BASIC.

Returning Values to BASIC

Another question is how do BASIC functions return values to the calling program? This is actually pretty easy. Here's how they return values, by data type:

Data type	Returned
INTEGER	In AX
LONG	In DX:AX (high word in DX, low in AX)
All others	Offset address in AX

In other words, to return an INTEGER value, place the integer in the AX register and exit. To return a LONG integer, place the upper word in DX, the lower word in AX, and exit.

For all other data types, you must return the offset address of the data in AX. This can be a little tricky. If you plan to return a non-INTEGER or non-LONG type, you must follow certain steps. BASIC passes you the address to store your return data at on the stack when it calls your function. This address is at [BP+6] on the stack when you gain control, where BP is special register, called the *base pointer*.

We've seen how the addressing mode [BX] works in the last chapter. [BP] works in the same way, except that BP will point us to some location in the stack section of memory. It turns out that we actually don't want the value at [BP], but at the address six bytes later; that is, at BP + 6. The assembler allows us to refer to that value like this: [BP+6] (negative values like [BP-6] or [BX-2] are also allowed). Here, then, are the steps that we'll follow to return values other than INTEGERs or LONGs:

1. When we gain control, we'll store the value at [BP+6] — the return value offset — for later use. For example, we can load that offset into DX this way: MOV DX, [BP+6].

2. When we're ready to return data, we'll place our return value at that offset in memory.

3. Then we place that offset into AX, and return.

We'll see how this works in the section *Function Returning a String* below. In the meantime, let's see how to work with the actual BASIC data that we receive.

BASIC's Internal Representation of Data

The real difficulty for the assembly language programmer is not so much in receiving or returning data as it is in decoding the values that have been passed. For example, if we get passed a SINGLE and read the value &H23110000 from memory, how do we know what number those four bytes represent? To be able to read and pass data to and from BASIC, you must know exactly what the internal representation of data in BASIC is; that is, how BASIC stores its data.

Here are the data types that are most standard in BASIC:

Type	Symbol	Bytes	Range
INTEGER	%	2	-32,768 to 32,767
LONG	&	4	-2,147,483,648 to 2,147,483,647
SINGLE	!	4	-3.402823E+38 to -1.40129E-45
DOUBLE	#	8	-1.79769313486232D308 to -2.2250738585072D-308
CURRENCY	@	8	-$922337203685477.5808 to $922337203685477.5807
STRING	$	32K	Strings can range up to 32K characters (bytes)

Let's get more familiar with each of these data types. To do advanced work with data stored in these formats, we'll have to know the details of how they're stored inside BASIC. In particular, this information will be crucial to interface BASIC to assembly language. Unless we understand each data type at the byte-by-byte level, we won't be able to work with it.

Let's work through the different BASIC data formats, beginning with the easiest format, integers.

INTEGERs and LONGs

The INTEGER and LONG formats are simple: INTEGERs are stored as one word and LONGs as two words. For example, here's how some INTEGERs are stored:

Value	Stored As
1	&H0001
29	&H001D
32,767	&H7FFF

On the other hand, here's how some negative INTEGERs are stored:

Value	Stored As
-1	&HFFFF
-219	&HFF25
-32,768	&H8000

> **NOTE:** The top bit, bit 7, is always equal to 1 in negative INTEGERs and LONGs.

> **TIP:** What BASIC calls an INTEGER, assembly language calls a word. You can provide space in memory for a BASIC INTEGER just by using the DW directive.

These negative numbers are stored in what is called *two's complement notation*, which was mentioned as long ago as Chapter 3, and we should understand it before continuing.

Two's Complement Notation

The whole scheme of signed numbers in computers comes from the simple fact that 1 + (-1) = 0. We realize that if we want to do any calculation with negative numbers in the PS/2 or PC, the number we choose to be -1, when added to 1, has to give 0. Yet this seems impossible. Let's say we were working with INTEGERs. Can you think of a 16-bit number which, when added to 1, will give a result of 0? It seems as though the result must always be 1 or greater.

In fact, however, there is an answer. Figure 11-2 shows what happens. If we take &HFFFF, which is 1111111111111111B in binary, and add 1 to it.

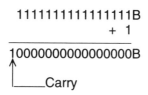

Figure 11-2

The result is 1000000000000000B. That is, the INTEGER is left holding 0000000000000, or 0, and there is a carry since the 1 is in the 2^{16} place (65,536), more than the integer's capacity to hold. If we ignore this carry, and only look at the 16 bits that fit into the integer, we are left with 0000000000000000B. In other words, &HFFFF + 1 = 0. That's exactly what happens when we're working with two's complement notation. We ignore the carry. That means that &HFFFF is the two's complement of 1 in INTEGER format. In LONG format, this number would be &HFFFFFFFF.

If you take a number like 5, which is 0000000000000101B in INTEGER format, then flip all its bits, 1111111111111010B (= &HFFFA), and add the two together, you get all ones (see Figure 11-3).

```
  0000000000000101B ← 5
+ 1111111111111010B    5 with bits flipped [ &HFFFA ]
  1111111111111111B  = &HFFFF
```

Figure 11-3

And adding 1 to this sum gives us 0 with a carry (see Figure 11-4)

```
  0000000000000101B ← 5
+ 1111111111111010B    5 with bits flipped &HFFFA
+                 1
 10000000000000000B  = 0 with a carry
  ↑
  └────Carry
```

Figure 11-4

Since we ignore the carry, this result is 0. Therefore, -5, the two's complement of 5, must equal &HFFFA + 1, which is &HFFFB. And this is how negative numbers are found.

For example, to find -1, start with +1, which is stored in INTEGER format as 0000000000000001B (16 bits). First, reverse all the bits. Zeros become ones and ones become zeros: 1111111111111110B. Now, add 1 to the result to get 1111111111111111B. This is the two's complement of 1; that is, -1 is stored as the binary number 1111111111111111B in INTEGER format, which is &HFFFF (&HFFFFFFFF in LONG format).

The process is the same for any other number whose sign you want to change. Now we can work with both positive and negative INTEGERs and LONGs on a bit-by-bit level.

SINGLEs and DOUBLEs

Floating point numbers, however, are considerably more complex. For example, a number like 10.5 is stored as &H41280000 in BASIC, and this number has little resemblance to the original value. What's going on?

We have to keep in mind that the computer is a binary machine, which means it uses base 2, so a number like 10.5 must be stored as 1×2^3 plus 1×2^1 plus 1×2^{-1}, which is 1010.1, where the point is a binary point. It is possible to store any number in binary that can be stored in decimal (it just takes more places). For instance, 0.75 can be broken down into 1/2 + 1/4, or $2^{-1} + 2^{-2}$, so .75 = .11B.

The numbers stored as floating point are all *normalized*, which means they appear with the binary point near the beginning. For example, 1010.1B is this in exponent form: 1.0101×2^3. To expand this, just move the binary point three places to the right, giving 1010.1B again. You can see that the first digit in any normalized binary number is always 1. Under BASIC floating point format, the leading 1 is *implicit*. In other words, all that is stored of the *significand* is 0101B. The exponent is still 3, but, to make matters even more complex, all exponents are stored after being added to some offset or *bias*.

For a SINGLE, this bias is &H7F, or 127. For DOUBLEs, this number is &H3FF, or 1,023. In other words, if our number, 1010.1B, is going to be stored as a SINGLE, the exponent will be 3 + 127 = 130 = &H82.

Finally, the first bit of any floating point number is the sign bit. Floating point numbers are not stored in two's complement notation. If the sign bit is 1, the number is negative; if it is 0, the number is positive. That's the only distinction between positive and negative numbers. The SINGLE format (4 bytes) is shown in Figure 11-5.

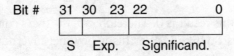

Figure 11-5

So 10.5 = 1010.1B will look like Figure 11-6.

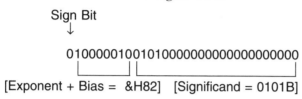

Figure 11-6

This can be made into Hex by grouping every four binary digits together since four binary digits represent exactly one hex digit (see Figure 11-7).

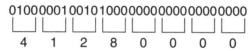

Figure 11-7

So 10.5 is stored as &H41280000.

The format for DOUBLEs (8 bytes) is shown in Figure 11-8.

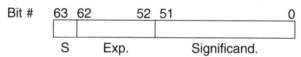

Figure 11-8

It's worth noting that the format for both SINGLEs and DOUBLEs is the standard IEEE format, which is the same format used by the 80×87 co-processors, so you can interface with them easily.

TIP: The easiest way of handling BASIC's floating point numbers from assembly language is to let BASIC handle all floating point math and then pass both mantissa and exponent to your assembly language code as integers, avoiding the need to decode them.

CURRENCY

The currency type is pretty easy. It's just an 8-byte two's complement integer, scaled by 10,000. That is, to find the amount represented by a variable of type CURRENCY, just treat the eight bytes as one number and divide it by 10,000. The fractional part represents the cents (since that's four digits, it's accurate down to 1/100 of a cent), and the whole number represents the dollar amount. For example, if you had one dollar, that would be stored as 10,000, which is &H2710, so it would be stored like this:

```
&H00  &H00  &H00  &H00  &H00  &H00  &H27  &H10
```

Let's finish up by covering the last of the standard data types, STRINGs.

Strings and Arrays

Strings and arrays are stored with *descriptors*; however, we can only work here with the descriptors used by BC.EXE and QB.EXE. String and array descriptors used by QBX.EXE are proprietary, and we'll have to use some special BASIC routines to work with them in other ways. Under BC.EXE or QB.EXE, a *string descriptor* looks like Figure 11-9.

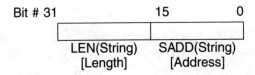

Figure 11-9

Where LEN(String) is the string's length, stored in two bytes, and SADD(String) is the address of the string data, also stored in bytes (i.e., an offset address). What BASIC will pass to us is the address of this descriptor, not the address of the actual string data. To find the string data, we must read the string's offset address from the descriptor (as we'll do later).

In extended QuickBASIC, QBX.EXE, we'll have to find the string's length and address in a different fashion. QBX.EXE has two internal routines that it uses itself to find a string's address and length, named StringAddress( ) and StringLength( ). When BASIC passes us a string descriptor, we'll pass it to these two internal routines to find the string's actual length and address.

In addition, when we pass a string back to a program under QBX, we'll have to put together a string descriptor that it will recognize, and we'll use QBX's own internal subroutine named StringAssign( ) to do that.

Array descriptors are considerably more complex than string descriptors. However, it is still useful to know how BASIC stores the elements of an array. For example, even if we know the address of Array(1, 1), where is Array(5, 1)? If we fill an array like this (from Chapter 7):

TIP: Instead of trying to decode array descriptors, the best thing to do is to simply pass the address of the first element of the array to your assembly language code.

```
DIM Array(10, 2) AS CURRENCY

REM Fill Array(n,1) with today's sales:

Array(1, 1) = 10.00      ←
Array(2, 1) = 53.00
Array(3, 1) = 7.17
Array(4, 1) = 9.67
Array(5, 1) = 87.99
Array(6, 1) = 14.00
Array(7, 1) = 91.19
Array(8, 1) = 12.73
Array(9, 1) = 1.03
Array(10, 1) = 5.04

REM Fill Array(n,2) with yesterday's sales:

Array(1, 2) = 9.67
Array(2, 2) = 3.5
Array(3, 2) = 8.97
Array(4, 2) = 10.00
Array(5, 2) = 78.33
Array(6, 2) = 17.00
Array(7, 2) = 91.36
Array(8, 2) = 12.73
Array(9, 2) = 16.12
Array(10, 2) = 7.98
          :
          :
```

Figure 11-10 shows the array produced.

Col 1	Col 2	
10.00	9.67	← Row 1
53.00	3.5	← Row 2
7.17	8.97	
9.67	10.00	
87.99	78.33	
14.00	17.00	
91.19	91.36	
12.73	12.73	

Col 1	Col 2
1.03	16.12
5.04	7.98

Figure 11-10

Internally, BASIC stores arrays in *column major* order as its default, which means that the numbers in column 1 are all stored before the numbers in column 2, and so on. You'll find the above numbers in ascending order in memory, like this:

```
Col 1
10.00   ←    Row 1 (that is, Array(1, 1))
53.00        Row 2
 7.17        :
 9.67
87.99
14.00
91.19
12.73
 1.03
 5.04
Col  2
 9.67   ←    Row 1
 3.5         Row 2
 8.97        :
10.00
78.33
17.00
91.36
12.73
16.12
 7.98
```

TIP: Using column major order, you can work up an array to find the entry you want. For example, for an integer array, each entry is a word long. If you know where the array begins in memory, you can now find any element you want directly, instead of relying on BASIC.

Now let's start writing some code and interfacing to BASIC.

A Function with No Parameters

Our first example is a function that takes no parameters and returns an integer. The example program here is called Return5%( ), and it simply returns 5 whenever called. All this procedure does is to act like a BASIC function which returns an integer value of 5. We begin by declaring the standard *memory model* for BASIC.

When you write a program, it's not necessary to restrict yourself to one segment. In fact, it's not necessary to restrict either the data or the code to a single segment either. However, if you wish to use multiple segments for data or code, labels need to be stored by the assembler as two words; that is, as segment:offset, not just as an offset address. Microsoft has defined various memory models corresponding to the possible sizes of the code and data sections of a program, and Microsoft BASIC uses the *MEDIUM* model, which means that there can be more than 64K of code, but less than 64K of data.

We'll always use the default memory model here, the MEDIUM model. All we have to do is to specify that model to the assembler with a .MODEL directive, and then we can forget it. In the same line, we inform the assembler that the BASIC calling convention will be used by the program that calls ours (i.e., parameters are pushed in order of appearance):

```
.MODEL MEDIUM, BASIC    ←
        :
        :
```

Next we start the code segment with .CODE:

```
.MODEL MEDIUM, BASIC
.CODE   ←
    :
    :
```

Now we must declare the procedure Return5 as *PUBLIC*. This means that the assembler will put the name Return5 into the .OBJ file's header, where LINK.EXE can find it (without the PUBLIC statement, we could not link Return5 into BASIC). We also start defining the procedure:

```
.MODEL MEDIUM, BASIC
.CODE

        PUBLIC Return5          ←
Return5 PROC                    :
    :                           :
    :
        RET
Return5 ENDP
        END
```

Finally, we're ready to write the procedure itself. We'll be using several of the registers, and it's good programming practice to preserve the original contents of those registers and restore them later in case BASIC was relying on them. We can do that by pushing the original contents of the registers we'll use onto the stack (and we'll pop them back when we leave):

```
        .MODEL MEDIUM, BASIC
        .CODE

                PUBLIC Return5
Return5 PROC
    →           PUSH BX          ;Should save all registers
                PUSH CX
                PUSH ES
                PUSH DS

                ;Do work here.
                :
                :
                RET
Return5 ENDP
                END
```

Since we want to return an integer value of 5, we have to load 5 in AX after restoring the other registers, and then we return. Listing 11-2 shows the whole function.

Listing 11-2.   Return5 Function.

```
        .MODEL MEDIUM, BASIC
        .CODE

                PUBLIC Return5
Return5 PROC
                PUSH BX          ;Should save all registers
                PUSH CX
                PUSH ES
                PUSH DS

                ;Do work here.

                POP DS           ;Restore registers
                POP ES
                POP CX
                POP BX

    →           MOV AX,5         ;Return integer value of 5

                RET
Return5 ENDP
                END
```

To BASIC, Return5%( ) looks just like a normal BASIC function. We just declare it and use it this way:

```
DECLARE FUNCTION Return5%( )        ←

PRINT "Value from Return5:";Return5%
```

And that's all there is to it: you can link Return5%( ) into this BASIC program and run it.

A Function with One Parameter

Next we can develop a program to read one integer parameter and return another integer parameter. For example, we discussed the function Add5%( ) in the beginning of the chapter, and we can review it here. This function simply adds 5 to the incoming integer and returns the result. We start with the extended PROC definition like this:

```
         PUBLIC Add5
Add5     PROC FAR USES DI SI DS ES, VALUE1:WORD  ←
         :
         :
```

Now we get the address of the integer that's been passed to us into BX:

```
         PUBLIC Add5
Add5     PROC FAR USES DI SI DS ES, VALUE1:WORD
  →      MOV BX, VALUE1  ;Pick addr of VALUE from stack (BASIC passes ref.)
         :
         :
```

BASIC passes the address of the parameter, not the actual parameter itself. We use that address to get the actual parameter, and add 5 to it this way:

```
        PUBLIC Add5
Add5    PROC FAR USES DI SI DS ES, VALUE1:WORD

        MOV BX, VALUE1  ;Pick addr of VALUE from stack (BASIC passes ref.)
→       MOV AX, [BX]
        ADD AX, 5
        RET
Add5    ENDP
        END
```

Since we have to return the value in AX, we're all set. Listing 11-3 shows the whole thing:

Listing 11-3. Add5 Function.

```
.MODEL MEDIUM, BASIC
.CODE

        PUBLIC Add5
Add5    PROC FAR USES DI SI DS ES, VALUE1:WORD

        MOV BX, VALUE1  ;Pick addr of VALUE from stack (BASIC passes ref.)
        MOV AX, [BX]
        ADD AX, 5

        RET
Add5    ENDP
        END
```

Here's how to use Add5%( ), which is, to BASIC, just another function:

```
REM Example of Assembly Language interface -- Add5 adds 5 to an integer

DECLARE FUNCTION Add5%(V%)

PRINT "9 + 5 =";Add5%(9%)
```

A Function with One Long Integer Parameter

Now let's see how to recieve a LONG integer as a parameter by changing Add5%( ) into Add5Long&( ). Even though we're reading a LONG value, its offset address is still passed as a one word value. We load the LONG into the DX:AX register pair like this:

```
            PUBLIC Add5Long
Add5Long PROC FAR USES DI SI DS ES, LONG_VALUE:WORD

  →         MOV BX, LONG_VALUE   ;Pick Addr of LONG_VALUE from stack (BASIC passes
            MOV AX, [BX]         ; by reference)
            MOV DX, [BX+2]
            :
            :
```

Since a LONG is two words, we read the value at [BX] and then the next word (that is, 2 bytes later) as well: [BX+2]. We load those values into DX:AX. Now we have to add 5 to this LONG integer, and we can do that like this:

```
ADD       AX, 5
ADC       DX, 0
```

Here we're using the ADD instruction to add 5 to the value in AX, but this might produce a carry, which we have to add to the high word in DX. We do that with the assembly language instruction *ADC*, or add with carry. We just use ADC DX, 0, which adds 0 to DX, along with any possible carry from the previous instruction. Breaking additions up with ADD and ADC let us generate results of high accuracy. Here's how we put those two instructions to work:

```
            PUBLIC Add5Long
Add5Long PROC FAR USES DI SI DS ES, LONG_VALUE:WORD

            MOV BX, LONG_VALUE   ;Pick Addr of LONG_VALUE from stack (BASIC passes
            MOV AX, [BX]         ; by reference)
            MOV DX, [BX+2]
  →         ADD AX, 5            ;Add 5 to DX:AX
            ADC DX, 0

            RET
```

NOTE: In addition to ADC, there is also SBB, subtract with borrow.

And that's it: we're supposed to return a LONG in DX:AX, and those registers are already loaded. Listing 11-4 shows the whole function.

Listing 11-4. Add5Long Function.

```
.MODEL MEDIUM, BASIC
.CODE
        ;This picks a LONG off the stack

        PUBLIC Add5Long
Add5Long PROC FAR USES DI SI DS ES, LONG_VALUE:WORD
        MOV BX, LONG_VALUE   ;Pick Addr of LONG_VALUE from stack (BASIC passes
        MOV AX, [BX]         ; by reference)
        MOV DX, [BX+2]
        ADD AX, 5            ;Add 5 to DX:AX
        ADC DX, 0

        RET
Add5Long ENDP
        END
```

A Function Returning a String

Now we can develop a example that returns the string "QQQ" to BASIC. Let's call it GetQQQ$( ). This function takes no parameters, but just returns a string.

QBX keeps string and array data in a special segment separate from the rest of the data, while the BC and QB compilers keep it in the same segment. For that reason, they have different types of string descriptors, and we'll handle QBX separately.

GetQQQ$( ) with QB.EXE and BC.EXE

In this version of GetQQQ$( ), we'll put together our own string descriptor to return to BASIC. That string descriptor looks like Figure 11-11.

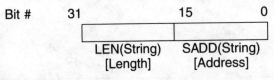

Bit #   31   15   0

LEN(String)   SADD(String)
[Length]   [Address]

Figure 11-11

To return a string, we have to place the descriptor we make at the offset address BASIC specifies (as well as returning that address itself in AX).

When we receive control, BASIC has already passed the return value's offset address at [BP+6]. We load that address into both BX (so we can use BX as an indirect index) and AX (since we have to return that address in AX to BASIC anyway):

```
              PUBLIC GetQQQ
      GetQQQ  PROC FAR USES BX

              MOV     BX, [BP+6]              ;Return value offset
              MOV     AX, BX                  ;Must also be returned in AX
              :
              :
```

Now we have to set up our string descriptor at that address. The first word will be 3, the length of the "QQQ" string:

```
              PUBLIC GetQQQ
      GetQQQ  PROC FAR USES BX

              MOV     BX, [BP+6]              ;Return value offset
              MOV     AX, BX                  ;Must also be returned in AX
      →       MOV     WORD PTR [BX], 3        ;String length
              :
              :
```

The expression WORD PTR deserves note here. Those special keywords are necessary for a situation that arises only in assembly language: the case when we exchange data between two operands, and neither of them have a defined size.

In BASIC, all variables have an assigned type, like INTEGER or LONG, so this problem never arises. Even in assembly language, there is no problem most of the time, for example, if we had this instruction:

```
MOV AX, 3
```

then there is no problem. The assembler knows that, since AX is one word long, we intend to fill that whole word with the value 3. Similarly, if we have defined MY_NUMBER like this: MY_NUMBER DB 5, then we could change that number to 3 like this:

```
MOV MY_NUMBER, 3
```

There would be no problem because the assembler knows that the variable MY_NUMBER stands for 1 byte. On the other hand, if we used this instruction:

```
MOV [BX], 3
```

then the assembler, which can handle either byte- or word-sized values, is unsure what to do: do we want to fill the word or the byte pointed to by [BX] with 3? In this case, the assembler will give you an error because neither operand has a well-defined size. The correct thing to do is specify the size with either BYTE PTR:

```
MOV BYTE PTR [BX], 3
```

In which case, the byte at location [BX] is filled with 03H, or WORD PTR:

```
MOV WORD PTR [BX], 3
```

In which case, the word at [BX] is filled with 0003H.

The next word in the string descriptor will hold the offset address of the string data. Let's store the string data immediately after the string descriptor itself (i.e., we have to add 4 bytes to the present value of BX to skip over the descriptor). This is a common place to store string data in BASIC. We can point to the byte right after the string descriptor, and also place that address in the descriptor itself like this:

```
          PUBLIC GetQQQ
GetQQQ    PROC FAR USES BX

          MOV    BX, [BP+6]            ;Return value offset
          MOV    AX, BX               ;Must also be returned in AX
          MOV    WORD PTR [BX], 3     ;String length
  →       ADD    BX, 4
          MOV    [BX-2], BX      ;Put string data address into descriptor
          :
          :
```

The next thing we have to do here is to store the string, "QQQ." But as we just saw, we can't do that like this:

```
          MOV    WORD PTR [BX], 3          ;String length
          ADD    BX, 4
          MOV    [BX-2], BX      ;Put string data address into descriptor
  →       MOV    [BX], "Q"
          MOV    [BX+1], "Q"
          MOV    [BX+2], "Q"
```

Because "Q" is just a numeric value, 51H, to the assembler, which sees this:

```
          MOV      WORD PTR [BX], 3            ;String length
          ADD      BX, 4
          MOV      [BX-2], BX                 ;String data address
  →       MOV      [BX], 51H
          MOV      [BX+1], 51H
          MOV      [BX+2], 51H
```

In this case, neither operand has a defined size (do we mean 51H or 0051H?), so we have to store the string like this, and then we can return:

```
GetQQQ   PROC FAR USES BX

          MOV      BX, [BP+6]                 ;Return value offset
          MOV      AX, BX                     ;Must also be returned in AX
          MOV      WORD PTR [BX], 3           ;String length
          ADD      BX, 4
          MOV      [BX-2], BX                 ;String data address
  →       MOV      BYTE PTR [BX], "Q"         ;Store string
          MOV      BYTE PTR [BX+1], "Q"
          MOV      BYTE PTR [BX+2], "Q"

          RET
GetQQQ   ENDP
```

And that's it: we've returned a string from a function in BASIC under BC.EXE or QB.EXE. Listing 11-5 shows the whole listing.

Listing 11-5.   GetQQQ Function.

```
.MODEL MEDIUM, BASIC
.CODE

          PUBLIC GetQQQ
GetQQQ   PROC FAR USES BX

          MOV      BX, [BP+6]                 ;Return value offset
          MOV      AX, BX                     ;Must also be returned in AX
          MOV      WORD PTR [BX], 3           ;String length
          ADD      BX, 4
          MOV      [BX-2], BX                 ;String data address
          MOV      BYTE PTR [BX], "Q"         ;Store string
          MOV      BYTE PTR [BX+1], "Q"
          MOV      BYTE PTR [BX+2], "Q"

          RET
GetQQQ   ENDP
          END
```

Here's how to use GetQQQ$( ), just like any other BASIC function that returns a string:

```
REM Example of Assembly Language interface -- GetQQQ$ returns the string 'QQQ'.
DECLARE FUNCTION GetQQQ$()
PRINT GetQQQ$
```

GetQQQ$( ) with QBX.EXE

QBX's string descriptors, however, have to be made by QBX — they're not in the same simple form used by BC.EXE or QB.EXE. Instead, we'll use the same internal subprogram that QBX itself uses to make a string descriptor for a string. This subprogram is called StringAssign( ), and you call it like this:

```
CALL StringAssign(SourceStrAddr, SourceStrLen%, DescAddr, DescLen%)
```

In this case, all these values are passed by value, not reference. Here, SourceStrAddr is the address of the string we want a descriptor for; SourceStrLen% is the length of that string; DescAddr is the address we want the descriptor to be placed at; and DestStrLen% will be set to 0 (indicating that we are creating a BASIC string).

To begin, we set up our data in the *data segment* (since the final executable code will be an .EXE file, we can use both code and data segments here). When the program is linked together, our data will automatically go into the data segment of the whole .EXE file.

This is how we'll store data in code that we link into BASIC — in the data segment. We'll need to store the string itself in memory, as well as provide space for a two word string descriptor, so let's set up a data segment with the directive .DATA:

```
.MODEL MEDIUM, BASIC
.DATA
        Ret_Str         DB      "QQQ"
        Ret_Desc_1      DW      0
        Ret_Desc_2      DW      0
        :
```

We've defined the return string Ret_Str as "QQQ," and two words (using the DW directive), Ret_Desc_1 and Ret_Desc_2, to hold the descriptor that StringAssign( ) will give us. Now we can start the code segment with .CODE. As with BC.EXE or QB.EXE, we save the return value's offset as passed to us:

```
.MODEL MEDIUM, BASIC
.DATA
        Ret_Str         DB      "QQQ"
        Ret_Desc_1      DW      0
        Ret_Desc_2      DW      0
.CODE

        PUBLIC GetQQQ
GetQQQ  PROC FAR USES BX

   →    MOV     BX, [BP+6]              ;Return value offset
        MOV     AX, BX                 ;Must also be returned in AX
        :
```

Then we have to call StringAssign( ) to get a descriptor for "QQQ" — i.e., Ret_str — so that we can pass that descriptor back to the calling program as the return value of our function. Here's what the call to StringAssign( ) looks like:

```
CALL StringAssign(SourceStrAddr, SourceStrLen%, DescAddr, DescLen%)
```

To call StringAssign( ), we'll have to place parameters on the stack just as if we were a BASIC program. The first parameter to pass to StringAssign( ) is the address of "QQQ," the string we want to return. We have to push the segment address (in DS), followed by its offset (OFFSET Ret_Str). Then we have to pass the length of our string, which is 3:

```
.MODEL MEDIUM, BASIC
.DATA
        Ret_Str         DB      "QQQ"
        Ret_Desc_1      DW      0
        Ret_Desc_2      DW      0
.CODE

        PUBLIC GetQQQ
GetQQQ  PROC FAR USES BX

        MOV     BX, [BP+6]              ;Return value offset
        MOV     AX, BX                 ;Must also be returned in AX
   →    PUSH    DS                     ;Address of QQQ string
   :    MOV     DX, OFFSET Ret_Str
        PUSH    DX
        MOV     DX, 3                  ;Length of QQQ string
        PUSH    DX
        :
```

Next we have to pass the address we want BASIC to write the string descriptor to. We've set aside two words named Ret_Desc_1 and Ret_Desc_2 for that purpose. We pass the address of the first of these words, and then a word equal to 0 to indicate that we want to make this string a BASIC string. Now we're ready to call StringAssign( ):

```
      .MODEL MEDIUM, BASIC
      .DATA
            Ret_Str         DB        "QQQ"
            Ret_Desc_1      DW        0
            Ret_Desc_2      DW        0
      .CODE

            PUBLIC GetQQQ
GetQQQ  PROC FAR USES BX

            MOV     BX, [BP+6]             ;Return value offset
            MOV     AX, BX                 ;Must also be returned in AX
            PUSH    DS                     ;Address of QQQ string
            MOV     DX, OFFSET Ret_Str
            PUSH    DX
            MOV     DX, 3                  ;Length of QQQ string
            PUSH    DX
            PUSH    DS                     ;Address of descriptor to be filled
            MOV     DX, OFFSET Ret_Desc_1
            PUSH    DX
            MOV     DX, 0                  ;0 for variable length string
            PUSH    DX
            EXTRN   StringAssign: PROC
  →         CALL    StringAssign
            :
```

Note that we also used the statement EXTRN StringAssign: PROC. This is much like a DECLARE statement in BASIC; EXTRN tells the assembler that we're going to link in a procedure named StringAssign( ) later, but we don't have the address for it right now. In this way, the assembler leaves space for that address in the assembled code, and the linker will fill it in. And that's it.

When we return from StringAssign( ), the two words of the descriptor will be in Ret_Desc_1 and Ret_Desc_2. This is the descriptor we have to pass to BASIC as the return value of our function.

QBX has already given us the return value's offset, so we place the descriptor there and then we're done. Listing 11-6 shows the whole program (QBX version).

Listing 11-6.   GetQQQ$ (QBX Version) Program.

```
REM Example of QBX interface -- GetQQQ$ returns the string ''QQQ''.
DECLARE FUNCTION GetQQQ$()

PRINT GetQQQ$

.MODEL MEDIUM, BASIC
.DATA
        Ret_Str         DB      "QQQ"
        Ret_Desc_1      DW      0
        Ret_Resc_2      DW      0
.CODE

        PUBLIC GetQQQ
GetQQQ  PROC FAR USES BX

        MOV     BX, [BP+6]              ;Return value offset
        MOV     AX, BX                  ;Must also be returned in AX
        PUSH    DS                      ;Address of QQQ string
        MOV     DX, OFFSET Ret_Str
        PUSH    DX
        MOV     DX, 3                   ;Length of QQQ string
        PUSH    DX
        PUSH    DS                      ;Address of descriptor to be filled
        MOV     DX, OFFSET Ret_Desc_1
        PUSH    DX
        MOV     DX, 0                   ;0 for variable length string
        PUSH    DX
        EXTRN   StringAssign: PROC
        CALL    StringAssign
        MOV     DX, Ret_Desc_1          ;Return descriptor
        MOV     [BX], DX
        MOV     DX, Ret_Desc_2
        MOV     [BX+2], DX

        RET
GetQQQ  ENDP
        END
```

It's a little extra work, but if you're using QBX.EXE, this is the way you have to do it.

A Function with Two Parameters

Now let's expand a little. We can read two parameters from BASIC almost as easily as one. Let's write a function called Addem%( ), which takes two integers, adds them, and returns the sum. Here, we want to read two parameters (both integers), and we can do that using PROC like this:

```
        PUBLIC Addem
Addem   PROC FAR USES DI SI DS ES, VALUE1:WORD, VALUE2:WORD        ←
        :
        :
```

Now VALUE1 and VALUE2 hold the addresses of the two integers. We can load and add them like this:

```
        PUBLIC Addem
Addem   PROC FAR USES DI SI DS ES, VALUE1:WORD, VALUE2:WORD
→       MOV BX, VALUE1  ;Pick addr of VALUE from stack (BASIC passes ref.)
        MOV AX, [BX]
        MOV BX, VALUE2
        ADD AX, [BX]

        RET
Addem   ENDP
```

The result is returned in AX, and that's it. Listing 11-7 shows the whole thing.

Listing 11-7.   ADDEM.ASM — Adds Two Integers.

```
.MODEL MEDIUM, BASIC
.CODE

        PUBLIC Addem
Addem   PROC FAR USES DI SI DS ES, VALUE1:WORD, VALUE2:WORD

        MOV BX, VALUE1  ;Pick addr of VALUE from stack (BASIC passes ref.)
        MOV AX, [BX]
        MOV BX, VALUE2
        ADD AX, [BX]

        RET
Addem   ENDP
        END
```

And here is an example of Addem%( ) at work:

```
REM Example of Assembly Language interface -- Addem() adds two integers

DECLARE FUNCTION Addem%(V1%,V2%)

PRINT "9 + 5 =";Addem%(5,9)
```

A Function Using the Data Segment

We've seen briefly how to use a data segment in the QBX string example. Let's take a closer look at that now. We can modify the procedure Addem%( ), which we've already written, to store data in the data segment. This data segment will be placed in the common data segment of the .EXE file, along with all the BASIC variables, when the file is linked.

To store data in memory, we need to reach the data segment, which we do with the .DATA directive. Nothing could be easier. To store the two integers we are to add in the memory words VAL1 and VAL2, we use .DATA this way:

```
.MODEL MEDIUM, BASIC

        PUBLIC Addem
.DATA                        ←

        VAL1 DW 0
        VAL2 DW 0
        :
        :
```

Now we can refer to VAL1 and VAL2 as normal assembly language variables in our code:

```
.MODEL MEDIUM, BASIC

        PUBLIC Addem
.DATA

        VAL1 DW 0
        VAL2 DW 0

.CODE
Addem   PROC FAR USES DI SI DS ES, VALUE1:WORD, VALUE2:WORD

        MOV BX, VALUE1   ;Pick addr of VALUE from stack (BASIC passes ref.)
        MOV CX, [BX]
    →   MOV VAL1, CX
        MOV BX, VALUE2
        MOV CX, [BX]
        MOV VAL2, CX

        ;Now data is in the data group

        MOV AX, VAL1
        ADD AX, VAL2

        RET
Addem   ENDP
        END
```

And that's all there is to it. We can store and retrieve data in the data segment this way. Listing 11-8 shows the entire listing.

Listing 11-8. ADDEM.ASM Using the Data Segment.

```
.MODEL MEDIUM, BASIC

        PUBLIC Addem
.DATA
        VAL1 DW 0
        VAL2 DW 0

.CODE
Addem   PROC FAR USES DI SI DS ES, VALUE1:WORD, VALUE2:WORD

        MOV BX, VALUE1  ;Pick addr of VALUE from stack (BASIC passes ref.)
        MOV CX, [BX]
        MOV VAL1, CX
        MOV BX, VALUE2
        MOV CX, [BX]
        MOV VAL2, CX

        ;Now data is in the data group

        MOV AX, VAL1
        ADD AX, VAL2

        RET
Addem   ENDP
        END
```

A Subprogram with Parameters

Now let's develop an assembly language version of a subprogram, not a function, that takes one parameter. Let's write a subprogram named PrintChar( ) that takes a character's ASCII code and prints it out.

From assembly language's point of view, a BASIC subprogram is just like a BASIC function, except that we don't have to load AX (and possibly DX) with a return value. Here, we just read the ASCII code passed to us and use interrupt &H21 service 2 to print it out:

```
PrintChar PROC FAR USES DI SI DS ES, The_Char:WORD

→       MOV BX, The_Char  ;Pick addr of The_Char from stack (BASIC passes ref.)
:       MOV DX, [BX]      ;Load into DL
:       MOV AH, 2
        INT 21H
```

Listing 11-9 shows the whole thing.

Listing 11-9.   PRINTCHAR.ASM.

```
.MODEL MEDIUM, BASIC
.CODE

        PUBLIC PrintChar
PrintChar PROC FAR USES DI SI DS ES, The_Char:WORD

        MOV BX, The_Char   ;Pick addr of The_Char from stack (BASIC passes ref.)
        MOV DX, [BX]       ;Load into DL
        MOV AH, 2
        INT 21H

        RET
        PrintChar ENDP
        END
```

You can use PrintChar( ) this way:

```
REM Example of Assembly Language interface -- Add5 adds 5 to an integer

DECLARE SUB PrintChar(V%)

CALL PrintChar(ASC("a"))
```

In the same way as with functions, we can receive two parameters. Here's a quick example of a subprogram named PrintSum%( ), which accepts two integers and prints the result out (as long as that result is a single digit, 0-9):

```
.MODEL MEDIUM, BASIC
.CODE

        PUBLIC PrintSum
PrintSum PROC FAR USES DI SI DS ES, VALUE1:WORD, VALUE2:WORD

        MOV BX, VALUE1   ;Pick addr of VALUE from stack (BASIC passes ref.)
        MOV DX, [BX]
        MOV BX, VALUE2
        ADD DX, [BX]
        ADD DX, "0"
        MOV AH, 2
        INT 21H

        RET
PrintSum ENDP
        END
```

We just read two parameters, which are both integers, convert the result (which must be in the range 0 - 9) to an ASCII character, and print it out with interrupt &H21 service 2.

A Subprogram with a String Parameter

Now let's get a little fancy. We can develop a subprogram that reads a string passed from BASIC (as opposed to GetQQQ$( ), which was a function that returned a string to BASIC). For example, let's develop a subprogram named PrintString( ) that prints a string which has been passed as an argument, like this:

```
REM Example of Assembly Language interface -- Prints a string

DECLARE SUB PrintString(Strg$)

CALL PrintString("This is a test.")      ←
```

TIP: String handling is one of the most common uses for assembly language. The 80×86 microprocessors have a number of built-in string instructions with names like MOVS, CMPS, and SCAS. They are much faster than the comparable instructions in BASIC.

Again, since QBX.EXE handles string descriptors differently, we'll have to split the example up into two versions, one for BC.EXE and QB.EXE and one for QBX.EXE.

PrintString( ) with BC.EXE and QB.EXE

We'll start off by examining the process under BC.EXE and QB.EXE. In this case, the calling program passes us the address of the string descriptor when it makes the call CALL PrintString("This is a test."). To decode that descriptor, we load the length of the string (the first word in the string descriptor) into CX, and the address of the string data (the second word in the descriptor) into BX like this:

```
PrintString PROC FAR USES DI SI DS ES, The_String:WORD

        MOV AH, 2
        MOV BX, The_String  ;Addr of str_len:word, str_data_addr:word
        MOV CX, [BX]      ;String Length
        MOV BX, [BX+2]   ;String data addr
        :
        :
```

Now we only need to loop over the string data, loading each byte into DL and printing it out with service 2 like this:

```
PrintString PROC FAR USES DI SI DS ES, The_String:WORD

        MOV AH, 2
        MOV BX, The_String  ;Addr of str_len:word, str_data_addr:word
        MOV CX, [BX]      ;String Length
        MOV BX, [BX+2]   ;String data addr
Print_Loop:
→       MOV DX, [BX]
→       INT 21H
        INC BX
        LOOP Print_Loop

        RET
PrintString ENDP
        END
```

That's it; we're done. Listing 11-10 shows the whole listing.

Listing 11-10. PRINTSTRING. ASM

```
.MODEL MEDIUM, BASIC
.CODE

        PUBLIC PrintString
PrintString PROC FAR USES DI SI DS ES, The_String:WORD

        MOV AH, 2
        MOV BX, The_String  ;Addr of str_len:word, str_data_addr:word
        MOV CX, [BX]      ;String Length
        MOV BX, [BX+2]   ;String data addr
Print_Loop:
        MOV DX, [BX]
        INT 21H
        INC BX
        LOOP Print_Loop

        RET
PrintString ENDP
        END
```

PrintString( ) with QBX.EXE

It's a little more complicated with QBX. Instead of being able to read the string's length and address from the string descriptor, we have to use two internal functions internal to QBX to find that information. These functions are called StringLength(Descriptor) and StringAddress(Descriptor), and the argument you pass is the string descriptor that you want to decode.

We'll start the code segment by using StringLength( ) to find the length of the string we've been passed. Keep in mind that what was passed to us was not the string's descriptor but the address of the string's descriptor. That's fine, however, because we'll want to pass that address to StringLength( ) and StringAddress( ) anyway. We start off by calling StringLength( ) with the address of the string descriptor we just got from the calling program:

```
.MODEL MEDIUM, BASIC

        PUBLIC PrintString

.CODE
PrintString PROC FAR USES DI SI DS ES, The_String:WORD
        PUSH   The_String
        EXTRN StringLength: PROC
        CALL   StringLength
        MOV    CX, AX     ;Load string length into CX for LOOP
        :
```

The length of the string is returned in AX. Like the version of PrintString( ) we developed before, we'll move that value into CX so we can use the LOOP instruction to print the string out.

Next, we have to pass the address of the descriptor to StringAddress( ). This function returns the two-word address of the string data. Since that return value is two words long, DX will hold the high word (segment address), and AX will hold the low word (offset address):

```
.MODEL MEDIUM, BASIC

        PUBLIC PrintString

.CODE
PrintString PROC FAR USES DI SI DS ES, The_String:WORD
        PUSH   The_String
        EXTRN StringLength: PROC
```

```
        CALL    StringLength
        MOV     CX, AX     ;Load string length into CX for LOOP

→       PUSH    The_String
        EXTRN   StringAddress: PROC
        CALL    StringAddress
        :
```

Now we want to read the string, character by character. To do that, we must first make the segment address returned by StringAddress( ) into our data segment by loading it into DS. Then we can load BX with the string's offset address and read characters like this: MOV DL, [BX]. (As we saw in Chapter 10, in the [BX] method of addressing, BX holds the offset from the beginning of the data segment.)

The string's segment address is in DX right now, and its offset is in AX, so we first save the original data segment address and we can load DS and BX like this:

```
.MODEL MEDIUM, BASIC

        PUBLIC PrintString

.CODE
PrintString PROC FAR USES DI SI DS ES, The_String:WORD
        PUSH    The_String
        EXTRN   StringLength: PROC
        CALL    StringLength
        MOV     CX, AX     ;Load string length into CX for LOOP

        PUSH    The_String
        EXTRN   StringAddress: PROC
        CALL    StringAddress
→       PUSH    DS                      ;Save    DS
        MOV     DS, DX                  ;DS ←    String's segment
        MOV     BX, AX                  ;BX      String's offset
        :
```

Now we're free to use the same printing loop as we've developed in the earlier version of PrintString:

```
.MODEL MEDIUM, BASIC

        PUBLIC PrintString

.CODE
PrintString PROC FAR USES DI SI DS ES, The_String:WORD
        PUSH    The_String
        EXTRN   StringLength: PROC
        CALL    StringLength
```

```
        MOV    CX, AX     ;Load string length into CX for LOOP

        PUSH   The_String
        EXTRN  StringAddress: PROC
        CALL   StringAddress
        PUSH   DS                    ;Save    DS
        MOV    DS, DX                ;DS ←    String's segment
        MOV    BX, AX                ;BX      String's offset

        MOV    AH, 2         ←
Print_Loop:                  :
        MOV    DL, [BX]      :
        INT    21H
        INC    BX
        LOOP   Print_Loop
        :
```

At the end, we have to restore the original value of DS, and then we can return. Listing 11-11 shows the complete version of PrintString set up for QBX.EXE.

Listing 11-11.   PRINTSTRING.ASM (QBX.EXE Version).

```
.MODEL MEDIUM, BASIC

        PUBLIC PrintString

.CODE
PrintString PROC FAR USES DI SI DS ES, The_String:WORD
        PUSH   The_String
        EXTRN  StringLength: PROC
        CALL   StringLength
        MOV    CX, AX     ;Load string length into CX for LOOP

        PUSH   The_String
        EXTRN  StringAddress: PROC
        CALL   StringAddress
        PUSH   DS                    ;Save    DS
        MOV    DS, DX                ;DS ←    String's segment
        MOV    BX, AX                ;BX      String's offset

        MOV    AH, 2
Print_Loop:
        MOV    DL, [BX]
        INT    21H
        INC    BX
        LOOP   Print_Loop

        POP    DS                    ;Restore DS

        RET
PrintString ENDP
        END
```

And that's it. Again, it's a little more work to use string under QBX.EXE, but if you use that compiler, it's your only option.

A Subprogram with an Array Parameter

As our last example, we're going to see how to pass arrays to a subprogram. As mentioned earlier, array descriptors are complex to work with. It is far better to pass the actual address of the first element of the array.

This process also differs with QBX.EXE, but this time, QB.EXE and QBX.EXE operate the same way. Arrays can be stored anywhere in memory with both of them, so we'll need to pass both the segment and offset address of the first array element to our assembly language routine. In BC.EXE, arrays are just stored in the data segment, so we'll only need to pass a single word address (the data segment address is already in DS).

Let's write a subprogram to print out the first element of an array, called PrintFirstElement( ), and see how this works.

PrintFirstElement with BC.EXE

We have to pass PrintFirstElement( ) the address of the first element of an array we can call A( ). To do that, we don't want to just pass VARPTR(A(1)). That would pass the address of the address of A(1), since arguments are passed by reference. To avoid that, we'll use BYVAL in the declaration of PrintFirstElement( ) so that our program passes parameters by value and not by reference. Then we're ready to call PrintFirstElelement( ) with an argument of VARPTR(A(1)):

```
REM Example of PrintFirstElement
REM Arrays have complex descriptors -- have to pass addr of first element
REM Note use of BYVAL in SUB declaration.

DECLARE SUB PrintFirstElement (BYVAL Addr AS INTEGER)    ←
DIM A(1 TO 6) AS INTEGER

A(1) = 1
A(2) = 2
A(3) = 3
A(4) = 4
A(5) = 5
A(6) = 6

PRINT "A(1) = ";
CALL PrintFirstElement(VARPTR(A(1)))                         ←
```

Now we have to write the assembly language procedure PrintFirstElement( ). We will receive the address of the first element of the array. All we have to do is to load that element into DL and print it (assuming that it is in the range 0 to 9):

```
PrintFirstElement PROC FAR USES DI SI DS ES, The_Array_Addr:WORD

→         MOV BX, The_Array_Addr
:         MOV DX, [BX]
          ADD DX, "0"
          MOV AH,2
          INT 21H
```

And that's it. Listing 11-12 shows the whole procedure (BC.EXE version).

Listing 11-12. PrintFirst Element (BC.EXE Version).

```
.MODEL MEDIUM, BASIC
.CODE

        PUBLIC PrintFirstElement
PrintFirstElement PROC FAR USES DI SI DS ES, The_Array_Addr:WORD

        MOV BX, The_Array_Addr
        MOV DX, [BX]
        ADD DX, "0"
        MOV AH,2
        INT 21H

        RET
PrintFirstElement ENDP
        END
```

PrintFirstElement with QB.EXE and QBX.EXE

Arrays can be stored anywhere in memory with QBX.EXE and QB.EXE, so we have to pass the element's segment address and its offset to PrintFirstElement( ):

```
REM Example of PrintFirstElement with QBX
REM Arrays have complex descriptors -- have to pass addr of first element
REM Note use of BYVAL in SUB declaration.

DECLARE SUB PrintFirstElement (BYVAL Addr1 AS INTEGER, BYVAL Addr2 AS INTEGER)
DIM A(1 TO 6) AS INTEGER

A(1) = 1
A(2) = 2
A(3) = 3
A(4) = 4
A(5) = 5
A(6) = 6

PRINT "A(1) = ";
CALL PrintFirstElement(VARSEG(A(1)), VARPTR(A(1)))        ←
```

Then, in the procedure PrintFirstElement, we place the segment address into DS (after saving the original value on the stack), the offset address into BX, and read the first element of the array like this: MOV DX, [BX]. We can add ASCII "0" to this value to convert it to an ASCII digit (assuming its value was 0 – 9), and print it out. Listing 11-13 shows the QB.EXE and QBX.EXE version.

Listing 11-13.   PrintFirstElement (QB.EXE and QBX.EXE Version).

```
.MODEL MEDIUM, BASIC
.CODE

        PUBLIC PrintFirstElement
PrintFirstElement PROC FAR USES DI SI DS ES, Array_Seg:WORD,Array_Offset:WORD

→       PUSH DS
:       MOV  BX, Array_Offset
:       PUSH Array_Seg
        POP  DS
        MOV  DX, [BX]
        POP  DS
        ADD  DX, "0"
        MOV  AH,2
        INT  21H

        RET
PrintFirstElement ENDP
        END
```

That's all there is to it, and that's the end of our last assembly language example.

Conclusion

We've come far in this book, and we've ranged widely over the computer, from screen control to menus, from the keyboard to the mouse, from our own paint program to our own database program. We've become experts in interfacing BASIC to assembly language, in sorting data, and in drawing windows. We've even toured through the operating system and put it to use for us as well.

In fact, we've become experts in almost all areas of BASIC. We've seen how professional programs get things done and had the chance to peek behind the scenes. And that's it. The only thing that remains now is to put all this knowledge to use. Good luck — and happy programming!

BIOS and DOS Reference

This appendix is intended for use as a reference. We will work through all the interrupts that are available, from 0 to FFH, reviewing the ones that are useful.

Interrupt 0 Divide by 0

This is the first of the BIOS interrupts. BIOS uses interrupts 0 to 1FH, and DOS continues from 20H upward. Interrupt 0 is the divide by zero routine. If a divide by zero occurs, then this interrupt is called. It prints out its message, "Divide Overflow," and usually stops program execution.

Interrupt 1 Single Step

No one, except a debugger, uses this interrupt. It is used to single step through code, with a call to this interrupt between executed instructions.

Interrupt 2 Nonmaskable Interrupt (NMI)

This is a hardware interrupt. This interrupt cannot be blocked off by using STI and CLI. It always gets executed when called.

Interrupt 3 Breakpoint

This is another debugger interrupt. DEBUG uses this interrupt with the Go command. If you want to execute all the code up to a particular address and then stop, DEBUG will insert an INT 3 into the code at that point and then give control to the program. When the INT 3 is reached, DEBUG can take control again.

Interrupt 4 Overflow

This is similar to INT 0. If there is an overflow condition, this interrupt is called. Usually, though, no action is called for, and BIOS simply returns.

Interrupt 5 Print Screen

This interrupt was chosen by BIOS to print the screen out. If you use the PrtSc key on the keyboard, this is the interrupt that gets called. Needless to say, your program can also issue an INT 5 by just including that instruction in the program. There are no arguments to be passed.

Interrupts 6 and 7 Reserved

Interrupt 8 Time of Day

This is another hardware interrupt. This interrupt is called to update the internal time of day (stored in the BIOS data area) 18.2 times a second. If the date needs to be changed, this interrupt will handle that too.

This interrupt calls INT 1CH as well. If you want to intercept the timer and do something 18.2 times a second, it is recommended you intercept INT 1CH instead of this one.

Interrupt 9 Keyboard

This hardware interrupt may be intercepted by memory resident programs.

Interrupt 0AH Reserved

Interrupts 0BH-0FH

These interrupts point to the BIOS routine D_EOI, which is BIOS' End of Interrupt routine. All this routine does is to reset the interrupt handler at port 20H and return.

INT 10H Service 0 Set Screen Mode

Input

AH=0

AL=Mode

Mode (in AL)	Display Lines	Number of Colors	Adapters	Maximum Pages
0	40x25	B & W text	CGA, EGA, VGA	8
1	40x25	Color text	CGA, EGA, VGA	8
2	80x25	B & W text	CGA, EGA, VGA	4 (CGA) 8 (EGA, VGA)
3	80x25	Color text	CGA, EGA, VGA	4 (CGA) 8 (EGA, VGA)
4	320x200	4	CGA, EGA, VGA	1
5	320x200	B & W	CGA, EGA, VGA	1
6	640x200	2 (on or off)	CGA, EGA, VGA	1
7	80x25	Monochrome	MDA, EGA, VGA	1 (MDA) 8 (EGA, VGA)
8	160x200	16	PCjr	1
9	320x200	16	PCjr	1
AH	640x200	1	PCjr	1
BH	Reserved for future use.			
CH	Reserved for future use.			
DH	320x200	16	EGA, VGA	8
EH	640x200	16	EGA, VGA	4

Mode (in AL)	Display Lines	Number of Colors	Adapters	Maximum Pages
FH	640x350	monochrome	EGA, VGA	2
10H	640x350	16	EGA, VGA	2
11H	640x480	2	VGA	1
12H	640x480	16	VGA	1
13H	320x200	256	VGA	1

INT 10H Service 1 Set Cursor Type

Input

AH=1

CH = Cursor Start Line

CL = Cursor End Line

Output

New Cursor

INT 10H Service 2 Set Cursor Position

Input

DH,DL = Row, Column

BH = Page Number

AH=2

Output

Cursor position changed

NOTE: DH,DL = 0,0 = Upper Left

INT 10H Service 3 Find Cursor Position

Input

BH=Page Number

AH=3

Output

DH,DL=Row, Column of Cursor.

CH,CL=Cursor Mode currently Set.

INT 10H Service 4 Read Light Pen Position

Input

AH=4

Output

AH=0→Light pen switch not down.
AL=1   DH,DL=Row, Column of Light Pen position.
          CH Raster line (Vertical) 0-199
          BX Pixel Column (Horizontal) 0-319,639

INT 10H Service 5 Set Active Display Page

Input

AL=0-7 (Screen modes 0,1)
    0-3 (Screen modes 2,3)
AH=5

Output

Active Page Changed

NOTE: Different pages available in alphanumeric modes only (graphics adapters).

INT 10H Service 6 Scroll Active Page Up

Input

AL=#Lines blanked at bottom (0→Blank whole area).
CH,CL=Upper Left Row,Column of area to scroll.
DH,DL=Lower Right Row,Column of area to scroll.
BH=Attribute used on blank line.
AH=6

INT 10H Service 7 Scroll Active Page Down

Input

AL=#Lines blanked at bottom (0→Blank whole area).
CH,CL=Upper Left Row,Column of area to scroll.
DH,DL=Lower Right Row,Column of area to scroll.
BH=Attribute used on blank line.
AH=7

INT 10H Service 8 Read Attribute and Character at Cursor Position

Input

BH = Page Number

AH=8

Output

AL=Character read (ASCII).

AH=Attribute of character (Alphanumerics only).

INT 10H Service 9 Write Attribute and Character at Cursor Position

Input

BH=Page Number

BL→Alpha Modes=Attribute;

    Graphics Modes=Color

CX=Count of characters to write

AL=IBM ASCII code

AH=9

Output

Character written on screen at Cursor Position

INT 10H Service A Write Character ONLY at Cursor Position

Input

BH=Page Number

CX=Count of characters to write

AL=IBM ASCII code

AH=0AH

Output

Character written on screen at Cursor Position

INT 10H Service B Set Color Palette

Input

BH=Palette Color ID

BL   BH=0→BL=Background Color

    BH=1→BL=Palette Number; (0=Green/Red/Yellow); (1=Cyan/Magenta/White)

AH=11

INT 10H Service C Write Dot
Input
DX=Row Number(0-199)   [0,0] is upper left.
CX=Column Number(0-319,639)
AL=Color Value (0-3)
AH=12

NOTE: If bit 7 of AL is 1, the color value is XORed with the current value of the dot.

INT 10H Service D Read Dot
Input
DX=Row Number(0-199)
CX=Column Number(0-319,639)
AH=13

Output
AL=Color Value (0-3)

NOTE: [0,0] is upper left. If bit 7 of AL is 1, the color value is XORed with the current value of the dot.

INT 10H Service E Teletype Write to Active Page
Input
AL=IBM ASCII code
BL=Foreground Color (Graphics mode).
AH=14

INT 10H Service FH Return Video State
Input
AH=15

Output
AH=Number of alphanumeric columns on screen
AL=Current mode (See INT 10H Service 0)
BH=Active display page

INT 10H Service 10H Set Palette Registers
Default Palette Colors (0-15) on EGA

Color Value	Color	rgbRGB
0	Black	000000
1	Blue	000001
2	Green	000010
3	Cyan	000011
4	Red	000100
5	Magenta	000101
6	Brown	010100
7	White	000111
8	Dark gray	111000
9	Light blue	111001
10	Light green	111010
11	Light cyan	111011
12	Light red	111100
13	Light magenta	111101
14	Yellow	111110
15	Intense white	111111

INT 10H Service 10H Function 0 Set Individual Palette Register
Input
AH = 10H
AL = 0
BL = Palette register to set (0-15)
BH = Value to set (0-63)

INT 10H Service 10H Function 1 — Set Overscan (Border) Register
Input
AH = 10H
BH = Value to set (0-63)

INT 10H Service 10H Function 2 — Set All Palette Registers
Input
AH = 10H
AL = 2

ES:BX = Address of a 17-byte table holding color selections (0 - 63)
   Bytes 0 - 15 hold color selections for palette registers 0 - 15
   Byte 16 holds the new overscan (border) color

INT 10H Service 10H Function 7 — Read Individual Palette Register

Input
AH = 10H
AL = 7
BL = Register to read (color value)

Output
BH = Register setting.

INT 10H Service 10H Function 8 — Read Overscan (Border) Register

Input
AH = 10H
AL = 8

Output
BH = overscan setting.

INT 10H Service 10H Function 10H — Set DAC Register

Input
AH = 10H
AL = 10H
BX = Register to set (0 - 255)
CH = Green Intensity
CL = Blue Intensity
DH = Red Intensity

INT 10H Service 10H Function 12H — Set DAC Registers

Input
AH = 10H
AL = 12H
BX = First register to set (0 - 255)
CX = Number of registers to set (1 - 256)
ES:DX = Address of a table of color intensities. Three bytes are used for each
   DAC register (use only lower 6 bits of each byte). Table is set up: red,
   green, blue, red, green, blue....

INT 10H Service 10H Function 13H — Select Color Page Mode
Input
AH = 10H
AL = 13H
BL = 0 Select Color Paging Mode
        BH = 0 Selects 4 DAC register pages of 64 registers each
        BH = 1 Selects 16 DAC register pages of 16 registers each
BL = 1 Select Active Color Page
    For use with 4 page mode:
    BH = 0 Selects the first block of 64 DAC registers
    BH = 1 Selects the second block of 64 DAC registers
    BH = 2 Selects the third block of 64 DAC registers
    BH = 3 Selects the fourth block of 64 DAC registers
    For use with 16 page setting:
    BH = 0 Selects the first block of 16 DAC registers
    BH = 1 Selects the second block of 16 DAC registers
    :
    :
    BH = 15 Selects the 15th block of 16 DAC registers
    BH = 16 Selects the 16th block of 16 DAC registers

INT 10H Service 11H — Character Generator

INT 10H Service 12H — Alternate Select
Input
AH = 12H
BL = 30H
AL = 0 $\rightarrow$ 200 screen scan lines
    = 1   350 screen scan lines
    = 2   400 screen scan lines

INT 11H Equipment Determination
Output
Bits of AX
15,14 = Number of Printers
13 Not used
12 Game Adapter attached
11,10,9 Number of RS232 cards installed
8 Unused.

7,6 Number of Diskette Drives.
(00→1;01→2;10→3;11→4 If Bit 0 = 1)
5,4 Video Mode (00 Unused; 01=40x25 Color Card;
10=80x25 Color Card, 11=80x25 Monochrome)
3,2 Motherboard RAM:
(00=16K,01=32K,10=48K,11=64K)
1 Not used
0 = 1 if there are diskette drives attached

INT 12H Determine Memory Size

Output
AX=Number of Contiguous 1K Memory Blocks

INT 13H Service 0 Reset Disk

Input
AH=0

Output
No carry → AH=0, Success
Carry →   AH=Error Code (see Service 1)

NOTE: Hard disk systems: DL=80H→reset diskette(s); DL=81H→reset hard disk.

INT 13H Service 1 Read Status of Last Operation

Input
AH=1

Output (Disk Error Codes)
AL=00   No Error
AL=01   Bad Command passed to controller
AL=02   Address Mark not found
AL=03   Diskette is Write Protected
AL=04   Sector not found
AL=05   Reset failed
AL=07   Drive parameters wrong
AL=09   DMA across segment end

AL=0BH   Bad track flag seen
AL=10H   Bad error check seen
AL=11H   Data is error corrected
AL=20H   Controller failure
AL=40H   Seek operation has failed
AL=80H   No response from disk
AL=0BBH Undefined error
AL=0FFH   Sense operation failed

NOTE: DL = Drive number; set bit 7 to 1 for hard disks. For hard disks, drive number in DL can range from 80H to 87H.

INT 13H Service 2 Read Sectors into Memory

Input
AH=2

DL=Drive Number
DH=Head Number
CH=Cylinder or Track (Floppies) Number
CL=bits 7,6 high 2 bits of 10-bit cylinder number.
CL=Sector Number (bit 0-5)
AL=Number of Sectors to Read (Floppies 1-8; Hard disks 1-80H; Hard disks read/write Long 1-79H)
ES:BX=Address of buffer for reads and writes

Output
No Carry→ AL = Number of sectors read (diskette)
Carry→   AH=Disk Error Code (see Service 1)

NOTE: DL = Drive number; set bit 7 to 1 for hard disks. For hard disks, drive number in DL can range from 80H to 87H.

INT 13H Service 3 Write Sectors to Disk

Input
AH=3

DL=Drive Number

DH=Head Number
CH=Cylinder or track (floppies) number
CL=bits 7,6 high 2 bits of 10-bit cylinder number
CL=Sector Number (bits 0-5)
AL=Number of Sectors to Write (floppies 1-8; Hard disks 1-80H; hard disks read/write Long 1-79H).
ES:BX=Address of buffer for reads and writes

Output
No carry→AL = No. sectors written (diskette)
Carry→   AH=Disk Error Code (see Service 1)

NOTE: DL = Drive number; set bit 7 to 1 for hard disks. For hard disks, drive number in DL can range from 80H to 87H.

INT 13H Service 4 Verify Sectors
Input
AH=4
DL=Drive Number
DH=Head Number
CH=Cylinder or Track (Floppies) Number
CL=Bits 7,6 high 2 bits of 10-bit cylinder number
CL=Sector Number (bits 0-5)
AL=Number of Sectors (Floppies 1-8; Hard Disks 1-80H; Hard Disks Read/Write Long 1-79H).

Output
No Carry→AH=0, Success
Carry→   AH=Disk error code (see Service 1)

NOTE: DL = Drive number; set bit 7 to 1 for hard disks. For hard disks, drive number in DL can range from 80H to 87H.

INT 13H Service 8 Return Drive Parameters

This service works only on hard disks and PS/2s.

Input
AH=8
DL=Drive number (0 based)

Output
DL=Number of drives attached to controller
DH=Maximum value for Head Number
CH=Maximum cylinder value
CL=bits 7,6 high 2 bits of 10-bit cylinder No.
CL=Maximum value for sector number (bits 0-5)
BL (For PS/2 diskettes only)
    = 1 → 360K drive
    = 2 → 1.2 MB drive
    = 3 → 720K drive
    = 4 → 1.44 MB drive

NOTE: DL = Drive number; set bit 7 to 1 for hard disks. For hard disks, drive number in DL can range from 80H to 87H.

INT 13H Services 0AH and 0BH Reserved

INT 13H Service 0CH Seek

This service works ONLY on hard disks.

Input
AH=0CH
DH=Head Number
DL=Drive number (80H-87H allowed)
CH=Cylinder Number
CL=Sector Number; bits 7,6 of CL = high 2 bits of 10-bit cylinder No.

Output
No Carry→AH=0, Success
Carry→   AH=disk Error Code (see Service 1)

NOTE: DL = Drive number; set bit 7 to 1 for hard disks. For hard disks, drive number in DL can range from 80H to 87H.

INT 13H Service 0DH Alternate Disk Reset

INT 13H Services 0EH and 0FH Reserved

INT 13H Service 10H Test Drive Ready

INT 13H Service 11H Recalibrate Hard Drive

This service works ONLY on hard disks.

Input

AH=11H (Read)

DL=Drive number (80H-87H allowed)

Output

No Carry→AH=0, Success
Carry→ AH=Disk Error Code (see Service 1)

NOTE: DL = Drive number; set bit 7 to 1 for hard disks. For hard disks, drive number in DL can range from 80H to 87H.

INT 13H Diagnostic Services

These services work ONLY on hard disks.

Input

AH=12H (RAM diagnostic)
AH=13H (Drive diagnostic)
AH=14H (Controller diagnostic)
DL=Drive Number (80H-87H allowed)

Output

No carry→AH=0, Success
Carry→ AH=Disk Error Code (see Service 1)

NOTE: DL = Drive number; set bit 7 to 1 for hard disks. For hard disks, drive number in DL can range from 80H to 87H.

INT 13H Service 19H Park Heads PS/2 Only

Input (PS/2)

DL = Drive Number

Output

Carry = 1 → Error, AH = Error code

    = 0 → Success

NOTE: DL = Drive number; set bit 7 to 1 for hard disks. For hard disks, drive number in DL can range from 80H to 87H.

INT 14H, AH=0 Initialize RS232 Port

Input

AH=0

Bits of AL:

0,1	Word Length 01→7 Bits, 11→8 Bits
2	Stop Bits 0→1, 1→2 stop bits.
3,4	Parity. 00→None, 01→Odd, 11→Even
5,6,7	Baud Rate. 000→ 110
	001→ 150
	010→ 300
	011→ 600
	100→1,200
	101→2,400
	110→4,800
	111→9,600

INT 14H, AH=1 Send Character through Serial Port

Input

AH=1

AL=Character to send

Output
If Bit 7 of AH is set, failure
If Bit 7 is not set, bits 0-6 hold status (see INT 14H, AH=3)

INT 14H, AH=2 Receive Character from Serial Port
Input
AH=2

Output
AL=Character Received
AH=0, success
Otherwise, AH holds an error code (see INT 14H, AH=3)

INT 14H, AH=3 Return Serial Port's Status
Input
AH=3

Output
AH Bits Set:
    7→Time Out
    6→Shift Register Empty
    5→Holding Register Empty
    4→Break detected
    3→Framing error
    2→Parity error
    1→Overrun error
    0→Data Ready
AL Bits Set:
    7→Received Line signal Detect
    6→Ring Indicator
    5→Data Set Ready
    4→Clear to Send
    3→Delta Receive Line Signal Detect
    2→Trailing Edge Ring Detector
    1→Delta Data Set Ready
    0→Delta Clear to Send

INT 15H Cassette I/O

Input

AH=0 → Turn Cassette Motor On.

AH=1 → Turn Cassette Motor Off.

AH=2 → Read one or more 256-byte blocks. Store data at ES:BX. CX=Count of Bytes to read.

AH=3 → Write one or more 256-byte blocks from ES:BX. Count of bytes to write in CX.

Output

DX=Number of bytes actually read.

Carry flag set if error.

If Carry, AH=01→CRC Error.

         =02→Data transitions lost.

         =04→No Data Found

NOTE: In recent BIOS versions, new items have been added to this interrupt, such as joystick support, the ability to switch processor mode (protected or not), mouse support, and some BIOS parameters.

INT 16H, Service 0 Read Key from Keyboard

Input

AH = 0

Output

AH=Scan Code AL=ASCII code

INT 16H, Service 1 Check if Key Ready to be Read

Input

AH = 1

Output

Zero Flag=1 → Buffer Empty

Zero Flag=0 → AH=Scan Code

                 AL=ASCII Code

INT 16H, Service 2 Find Keyboard Status
Input
AH = 2

Output
AL=Keyboard Status byte.

INT 17H Service 0 Print character in AL
Input
AH=0
AL=Character to be printed.
DX=Printer Number (0,1,2)

Output
AH=1 → Printer Time Out.

INT 17H Service 1 Initialize Printer Port
Input
AH=1
DX=Printer Number (0,1,2)

Output
AH=Printer Status:
Bits Set of AH:
    7→Printer Not Busy.
    6→Acknowledge.
    5→Out of Paper.
    4→Selected.
    3→I/O Error.
    2→Unused.
    1→Also Unused.
    0→Time Out.

INT 17H Service 2 Read Printer Status into AH
Input
AH=2
DX=Printer Number (0,1,2)

Output
AH Set to Status Byte as in INT 17H, AH=1.

INT 18H Resident BASIC
This interrupt starts up ROM resident BASIC in the PC.

INT 19H Bootstrap
This interrupt is the one that boots the machine (try it with DEBUG).

INT 1AH Service 0 Read Time of Day
Input
AH=0

Output
CX=High Word of Timer Count.
DX=Low Word of Timer Count.
AL=0 If Timer has not passed 24 hours since last read.

NOTE: Timer count increments by 65,536 in one hour.

INT 1AH Service 1 Set Time of Day
Input
AH=1
CX=High Word of Timer Count
DX=Low Word of Timer Count

NOTE: Timer count increments by 65,536 in one hour.

INT 1BH Keyboard Break Address

INT 1CH Timer Tick Interrupt

INT 1DH Video Parameter Tables

INT 1EH Diskette Parameters

INT 1FH Graphics Character Definitions

DOS Interrupts

Interrupt 1FH is the last BIOS Interrupt, and DOS starts with INT 20H.

INT 20H Terminate

Programs are usually ended with an INT 20H.

Interrupt 21H

Interrupt 21H is the DOS service interrupt. To call one of these services, load AH with the service number, and the other registers as shown.

INT 21H Service 0 Program Terminate

Input
AH = 0

INT 21H Service 1 Keyboard Input

Input
AH = 1

Output
AL = ASCII code of struck key does echo on screen

NOTE: Checks for ^C or ^Break.

INT 21H Service 2 Character Output on Screen

Input
AH=2
DL=Character's ASCII code.

INT 21H Service 3 Standard Auxiliary Device Input

Input
AH=3

Output
Character in AL

INT 21H Service 4 Standard Auxiliary Device Output

Input
AH=4
DL=Character to output

INT 21H Service 5 Printer Output

Input
AH=5
DL=Character to output.

INT 21H Service 6 Console I/O without Echo

Input	Output
AH = 6	
DL = FFH	→ Zero flag set if no character was ready. Otherwise, AL holds character's ASCII code.
DL < FFH	→ Type ASCII code in DL on screen.

NOTE: Does NOT check for ˆC or ˆBreak.

INT 21H Service 7 Console Input without Echo

Input
AH = 7

Output
AL = ASCII code of struck key NO Echo on screen.

NOTE: Does NOT Check for ˆC or ˆBreak.

INT 21H Service 8 Console Input w/o Echo with ˆC Check

Input
AH = 8

Output
AL = ASCII code of struck key. Does NOT echo the typed key.

NOTE: Checks for ˆC or ˆBreak.

DOS INT 21H Service 9 String Print
Input
DS:DX point to a string that ends in '$'
AH=9

INT 21H Service A String Input
Input
AH = 0AH
[DS:DX]=Length of buffer

Output
Buffer at DS:DX filled
Echo the typed keys

NOTE:	Checks for ^C or ^Break.

INT 21H Service 0BH Check Input Status
Input
AH = 0BH

Output
AL = FF → Character ready
AL = 00 → Nothing to read in

NOTE:	^Break is checked for.

INT 21H Service 0CH Clear Keyboard Buffer and Invoke Service
Input
AH = 0CH
AL = Keyboard Function #

Output
Standard Output from the selected Service

NOTE:	^Break is checked for.

INT 21H Service 0DH Disk Reset

Input
AH=0DH

INT 21H Service 0EH Select Disk

Input
AH=0EH
DL=Drive Number (DL=0→A; DL=1→B; and so on)

INT 21H Service 0FH Open Preexisting File

Input
DS:DX points to an FCB
AH=0FH

Output
AL=0   → Success
AL=FF → Failure

INT 21H Service 10H Close File

Input
DS:DX points to an FCB.
AH=10H

Output
AL=0   → Success
AL=FF → Failure

INT 21H Service 11H Search for First Matching File

Input
DS:DX points to an unopened FCB
AH=11H

Output
AL=FF → Failure
AL=0   → Success. DTA holds FCB for match

NOTE: Note DTA is at CS:0080 in .COM files on startup.

INT 21H Service 12H Search for Next Matching File
Input
DS:DX points to an unopened FCB
AH=12H

Output
AL=FF → Failure
AL=0 → Success. DTA holds FCB for match

NOTE: Use this Service after Service 11H.

INT 21H Service 13H Delete Files
Input
DS:DX points to an unopened FCB
AH=13H

Output
AL=FF → Failure
AL=0 → Success

INT 21H Service 14H Sequential Read
Input
DS:DX points to an opened FCB.
AH=14H
Current Block and Record Set in FCB.

Output
Requested Record put in DTA
AL=0 Success
    1 End of File, no data in record.
    2 DTA Segment too small for record.
    3 End of File; record padded with 0

NOTE: Record address increased.

INT 21H Service 15H Sequential Write

Input
DS:DX points to an opened FCB
AH=15H
Current Block & Record Set in FCB

Output
One record read from DTA and written.
AL=0 Success.
   1 Disk full.
   2 DTA Segment too small for record.

NOTE: Record address increased.

INT 21H Service 16H Create File

Input
DS:DX points to an unopened FCB.
AH=16H

Output
AL=0 success
   =FF directory full

INT 21H Service 17H Rename File

Input
DS:DX points to a MODIFIED FCB.
AH=17H

Output
AL=0 success
   =FF failure

NOTE: Modified FCB → Second file name starts 6 bytes after the end of the first file name, at DS:DX+11H.

INT 21H Service 18H Internal to DOS

INT 21H Service 19H Find Current Disk
Input
AH=19H

Output
AL=Current Disk (0=A, 1=B, and so on).

INT 21H Service 1AH Set the DTA Location
Input
DS:DX points to new DTA address
AH=1AH

NOTE: DTA= Disk Transfer Address, the data area used with FCB services. Default DTA is 128 bytes long, starting at CS:0080 in the PSP.

INT 21H Service 1BH FAT Information for Default Drive
Input
AH=1BH

Output
DS:BX points to the "FAT Byte"
DX=Number of Clusters
AL=Number of Sectors/cluster
CX=Size of a Sector (512 bytes)

NOTE: Files are stored in clusters, the smallest allocatable unit on a disk.

INT 21H Service 1CH FAT Information for Specified Drive
Input
AH=1CH
DL=Drive Number (0=Default; 1=A...)

Output
DS:BX points to the "FAT Byte"
DX=Number of Clusters
AL=Number of Sectors/Cluster
CX=Size of a Sector (512)

NOTE: Files are stored in clusters, the smallest allocatable unit on a disk.

INT 21H Services 1DH - 20H Internal to DOS

INT 21H Service 21H Random Read

Input
DS:DX points to an opened FCB.
Set FCB's Random Record field
  at DS:DX+33 and DS:DX+35

AH=21H

Output
AL=00 success.
   =01 end of file, no more data
   =02 not enough space in DTA segment
   =03 end of file, partial record padded with 0s

INT 21H Service 22H Random Write

Input
DS:DX points to an opened FCB.
Set FCB's Random Record field
  at DS:DX+33 and DS:DX+35

AH=21H

Output
AL=00 success.
   =01 disk is full.
   =02 not enough space in DTA segment.

INT 21H Service 23H File Size

Input

DS:DX points to an unopened FCB.
AH=23H

Output

AL=00 Success.
=FF No file found that matched FCB. Random Record Field set to file length in records, rounded up.

INT 21H Service 24H Set Random Record Field

Input

DS:DX points to an opened FCB
AH=24H

Output

Random Record Field set to match Current Record and Current Block.

INT 21H Service 25H Set Interrupt Vector

Input

AH=25H
AL = Interrupt Number
DS:DX = New Address

NOTE: This service can help you intercept an interrupt vector.

INT 21H Service 26H Create a New Program Segment (PSP)

INT 21H Service 27H Random Block Read

Input

DS:DX points to an opened FCB.
Set FCB's Random Record field
    at DS:DX+33 and DS:DX+35

AH=27H

Output

AL =00 Success.

   =01 end of file, no more data

   =02 not enough space in DTA segment

   =03 end of file, partial record padded with 0s

CX =Number of records read

   Random Record Fields set to access next record

NOTE: The data buffer used in FCB services is the DTA, or disk transfer area.

INT 21H Service 28H Random Block Write

Input

DS:DX points to an opened FCB

Set FCB's Random Record field

   at DS:DX+33 and DS:DX+35

CX=number of records to write.

AH=28H

Output

AL=00 success

   =01 disk is full

   =02 not enough space in DTA segment

Random Record Fields set to access

   next record.

NOTE: CX=0 → file to set to the size indicated by the Random Record field. The data buffer used iin FCB services is the DTA, or disk transfer area.

INT 21H Service 29H Parse Filename

Input

DS:SI = Command line to parse.

ES:DI = Address to put FCB at.

AL =   Bit 0=1 →Leading separators are scanned off command line.
        Bit 1=1 → Drive ID in final FCB will be changed ONLY if a drive was
        specified.
        Bit 2=1 → Filename in FCB changed ONLY if command line includes
        filename.
        Bit 3=1 → Filename extension in FCB will be changed ONLY if
        command line contains a filename extension.
AH=   29H

Output
DS:SI = 1st character after filename.
ES:DI = Valid FCB

NOTE: If the command line does not contain a valid filename, ES:[DI+1] will be a blank.

INT 21H Service 2AH Get Date
Input
AH=2AH

Output
CX = Year - 1980
DH = Month (1=January, etc.)
DL = Day of the month

INT 21H Service 2BH Set Date
Input
CX = Year - 1980
DH = Month (1=January, etc.)
DL = Day of the month.
AH=2BH

Output
AL = 0 Success
AL = FF Date not valid

INT 21H Service 2CH Get Time

Input
AH=2CH

Output
CH = Hours (0-23)
CL = Minutes (0-59)
DH = Seconds (0-59)
DL = Hundredths of seconds (0-99)

INT 21H Service 2DH Set Time

Input
AH=2DH
CH = Hours (0-23)
CL = Minutes (0-59)
DH = Seconds (0-59)
DL = Hundreds of seconds (0-99)

Output
AL = 0 Success
AL = FF Time is Invalid

INT 21H Service 2EH Set or Reset Verify Switch

Input
AH=2EH
DL=0
AL=1 → Turn Verify On
   =0 → Turn Verify Off

INT 21H Service 2FH Get Current DTA

Input
AH=2FH

Output
ES:BX = Current DTA address

NOTE: The data buffer used in FCB services is the DTA, or Disk Transfer Area.

INT 21H Service 30H Get DOS Version Number

Input
AH=30H

Output
AL=Major Version Number (3 in DOS 3.10)
AH=Minor Version Number (10 in DOS 3.10)
BX=0
CX=0

NOTE: If AL returns 0, you are working with a version of DOS before 2.0.

INT 21H Service 31H Terminate Process and Keep Resident

Input
AH=31H
AL=Binary Exit Code
DX=Size of memory request in paragraphs

NOTE: Exit code can be read by a parent program with Service 4DH. It can also be tested by ERRORLEVEL commands in batch files.

INT 21H Service 32H Internal to DOS

INT 21H Service 33H Control-Break Check

Input
AH=33H
AL=0 → Check state of ˆBreak checking
  =1 → Set the state of ˆBreak checking (DL=0→ Turn it Off;DL=1→ Turn it On)

Output
DL=0 → Off
DL=1 → On

INT 21H Service 34H Internal to DOS

INT 21H Service 35H Get Interrupt Vector
Input
AH=35H
AL=Interrupt Number

Output
ES:BX = Interrupt's Vector

INT 21H Service 36H Get Free Disk Space
Input
AH=36H

DL=Drive Number (0=Default; 1=A...)

Output
AX=0FFFH→Drive Number invalid
AX=Number of Sectors/cluster
BX=Number of available clusters
CX=Size of a Sector (512)
DX=Number of Clusters

NOTE: Files are stored in clusters, the smallest allocatable unit on a disk.

INT 21H Service 37H Internal to DOS

INT 21H Service 38H Returns Country Dependent Information
Input
AH=38H
DS:DX = address of 32-byte block
AL=0

The 32-byte block looks like this:

2 Bytes DATE/TIME Format.
1 Byte of currency symbol (ASCII)
1 Byte set to 0.
1 Byte thousands separator (ASCII)

1 Byte set to 0.
1 Byte decimal separator (ASCII)
1 Byte set to 0.
24 Bytes used internally.

The DATE/TIME format has these values:

0 = USA (H:M:S M/D/Y)
1 = EUROPE (H:M:S D/M/Y)
2 = JAPAN (H:M:S D:M:Y)

Output
Filled in 32-byte block (see below)

NOTE: In DOS 3+ you can set, as well as read, these values.

INT 21H Service 39H Create a Subdirectory
Input
AH=39H
DS:DX point to ASCIIZ string with directory name

Output
No Carry→ success
Carry→ AH has error value
      AH=3 path not found
      AH=5 access denied

INT 21H Service 3AH Delete a Subdirectory
Input
AH=3AH
DS:DX point to ASCIIZ string with directory name.

Output
No Carry→ Success

Carry→   AH has error value
          AH=3 Path Not Found
          AH=5 Access denied or
          Subdirectory not empty.

INT 21H Service 3BH Change Current Directory

Input

AH=3BH

DS:DX point to ASCIIZ string with directory name.

Output

No Carry→ Success

Carry→   AH has error value.
          AH=3 path not found.

INT 21H Service 3CH Create a File

Input

DS:DX points to ASCIIZ filename.

CX=Attribute of File.

AH=3CH

Output

No carry → AX=File Handle

Carry →   AL=3 Path not found
          AL=4 Too many files open
          AL=5 Directory full, or previous
          Read Only file exists

INT 21H Service 3DH Open a File

Input

DS:DX points to ASCIIZ filename

AL=Access code. ⌐
AH=3DH   ↓

Access Codes: AL=0   File Opened for Reading.
                AL=1   File Opened for Writing.
                AL=2   File Opened for Reading and Writing.
Access Code DOS 3+: isssraaa

i = 1 → file is not to be inherited by child processes
i = 0 → file handle will be inherited
sss = 000 → Compatibility Mode
sss = 001 → Deny All
sss = 010 → Deny Write
sss = 011 → Deny Read
sss = 100 → Deny None
r = reserved
aaa = 000 → Read Access
aaa = 001 → Write Access
aaa = 010 → Read/Write Access

Output
No Carry → AX=File Handle
Carry → AL=Error Code
        (Check Error Table)

INT 21H Service 3EH Close a File Handle
Input
BX holds a valid File Handle
AH=3EH

Output
Carry → AL=6 → Invalid handle

INT 21H Service 3FH Read from File or Device
Input
DS:DX = Data Buffer Address
CX=Number of bytes to read
BX=File Handle
AH=3FH

Output
No Carry→ AX=Number of bytes read
Carry→   AL=5 Access Denied
          AL=6 Invalid Handle

INT 21H Service 40H Write to File or Device

Input

DS:DX = Data Buffer Address

CX=Number of bytes to write
BX=File Handle
AH=40H

Output

No Carry→ AX=Number of bytes written
Carry→   AL=5 Access Denied
            AL=6 Invalid Handle

NOTE: Full disk is NOT considered an error: check the number of bytes you wanted to write (CX) against the number actually written (returned in AX). If they do not match, the disk is probably full.

INT 21H Service 41H Delete a File

Input

DS:DX = ASCIIZ filename
AH=41H

Output

No Carry→ Success
Carry→   AL=2 File Not Found
            AL=5 Access Denied

NOTE: No wildcards allowed in filename.

INT 21H Service 42H Move Read/Write Pointer

Input

BX=File Handle
CX:DX=Desired offset.
AL=Method Value———┐
AH=42H   ↓

Method Values (AL):
    AL=0 → Read/Write Pointer moved to CX:DX from the start of the file
    AL=1 → Pointer incremented CX:DX bytes
    AL=2 → Pointer moved to end-of-file plus offset (CX:DX)

Output
No Carry→ DX:AX=New Location of Pointer.
Carry→   AL=1 Illegal Function Number.
           AL=6 Invalid Handle.

INT 21H Service 43H Change File's Attribute

Input
DS:DX = ASCIIZ Filestring
AL=1→ File attribute changed; CX holds new attribute
AL=0→ File's current attribute returned in CX
AH=43H

Output
No carry→ success.
Carry→   AL=2 File Not Found.
           AL=3 Path Not Found.
           AL=5 Access Denied.
If AL was 0, CX returns the attribute.

INT 21H Service 44H I/O Control

INT 21H Service 45H Duplicate a File Handle

Input
BX=File Handle to duplicate
AH=45H

Output
No Carry→ AX=New, duplicated Handle
Carry→   AL=4 Too many files open
           AL=6 Invalid Handle

INT 21H Service 46H Force Duplication of a File Handle

Input
BX=File Handle to duplicate

CX=Second File Handle
AH=46H

Output
No carry→ Handles refer to same "stream"
Carry→   AL=6 Invalid handle

INT 21H Service 47H Get Current Directory on Specified Drive
Input
AH=47H
DS:SI point to 64 byte buffer.
DL=Drive Number.

Output
No carry→ Success, ASCIIZ at DS:SI
Carry→   AH=15 Invalid Drive Specified.

NOTE: Drive letter is NOT included in returned ASCIIZ string.

INT 21H Service 48H Allocate Memory
Input
AH=48H

BX=Number of paragraphs

Output
No carry→AX:0000 memory block address
Carry→   AL=7 memory control blocks destroyed
              AL=8 Insufficient memory, BX contains maximum allowable request

INT 21H Service 49H Free Allocated Memory
Input
AH=49H
ES=Segment of block being freed

Output

No carry →   success

Carry →   AL=7 memory control blocks destroyed

              AL=9 incorrect memory block address

INT 21H Service 4AH SETBLOCK

Input

AH=4AH

ES=Segment of block to modify

BX = Requested size in paragraphs

Output

No carry → success.

Carry →   AL = 7 memory control blocks destroyed

              AL = 8 insufficient memory; BX holds maximum possible request

              AL = 9 invalid memory block address

INT 21H Service 4BH Load or Execute a Program — EXEC

Input

AH=   4BH

DS:DX=ASCIIZ string with drive, pathname, filename.

ES:BX= Parameter Block Address (See Below)

AL=   0 → Load and execute the program

          3 → Load but create no PSP, don't run (Overlay)

          See Below

Parameter Block for AL = 0:

Segment Address of environment to pass (Word)

Address of command to put at PSP+80H (DWord)

Address of default FCB to put at PSP+5CH (DWord)

Address of 2nd default FCB to put at PSP+6CH (DWord)

Parameter Block for AL = 3:

Segment Address to load file at (Word)
Relocation Factor for image (Word)

Output
No Carry → Success
Carry →   AL=1 Invalid Function Number
               AL=2 File Not Found on Disk
               AL=5 Access Denied
               AL=8 Insufficient Memory for requested operation
               AL=10 Invalid Environment
               AL=11 Invalid Format

INT 21H Service 4CH Exit
Input
AH=4CH
AL=Binary Return Code.

NOTE: This service can end a program.

INT 21H Service 4DH Get Return Code of Subprocess
Input
AH=4DH

Output
AL=Binary Return Code from Subprocess
AH=0 If subprocess ended normally
     1 If subprocess ended with a ˆBreak
     2 If it ended with a critical device error
     3 If it ended with Service 31H

INT 21H Service 4EH Find First Matching File
Input
DS:DX→ASCIIZ filestring.

CX=attribute to match.
AH=4EH

Output
Carry→   AL=2 No Match Found
           AL=18 No More Files
No carry→DTA filled as follows:
        21 bytes reserved.
        1 byte found attribute.
        2 bytes file's time.
        2 bytes file's date.
        2 bytes low word of size.
        2 bytes high word of size.
        13 bytes name and extension of found file in ASCIIZ form (NO
            pathname).

NOTE: The data buffer used in FCB services is the DTA, or disk transfer area. See earlier services.

INT 21H Service 4FH Find Next Matching File
Input
Use Service 4EH BEFORE 4FH.
AH=4FH

Output
Carry→AL=18 no more files
No carry→DTA filled as follows:
        21 bytes reserved.
        1 byte found attribute.
        2 bytes file's time.
        2 bytes file's date.
        2 bytes low word of size.
        2 bytes high word of size.
        13 bytes name and extension of found file in ASCIIZ form (NO
            pathname).

NOTE: The data buffer used in FCB services is the DTA, or Disk Transfer Area. See earlier services.

INT 21H Services 50H-53H Internal to DOS

INT 21H Service 54H Get Verify State
Input
AH=54H

Output
AL=0→ verify is OFF
    1→ verify is ON

INT 21H Service 55H Internal to DOS

INT 21H Service 56H Rename File
Input
DS:DX=ASCIIZ filestring to be renamed.
ES:DI= ASCIIZ filestring that holds the new name.
AH=   56H

Output
No Carry→   success.
Carry→   AL=3 Path Not Found.
               AL=5 Access Denied.
               AL=17 Not Same Device.

NOTE: File CANNOT be renamed to another drive.

INT 21H Service 57H Get or Set a File's Date & Time
Input
BX=File handle.
AL=0→Get Date & Time

AL=1→Set Time to CX.
     Set Date to DX.

Output
No Carry:

> CX returns Time
> DX returns Date

File's date and time set

Carry→AL=1 Invalid Function Number

> 6 Invalid Handle

The time and date of a file are stored like this:

$$\text{Time} = 2048 \times \text{hours} + 32 \times \text{minutes} + \text{Seconds}/2$$
$$\text{Date} = 512 \times (\text{Year} - 1980) + 32 \times \text{Month} + \text{Day}$$

INT 21H Service 58H Internal to DOS

INT 21H Service 59H Get Extended Error DOS 3+
Input
AH = 59H
BX = 0

Output
AX = extended error
BH = error class
BL = suggested action
CH = locus

NOTE: This error handling service is very lengthy, and involves the many DOS 3+ extended errors.

INT 21H Service 5AH Create Unique File DOS 3+
Input
AH = 5AH
DS:DX = Address of an ASCIIZ path (ending with "\")
CX = File's attribute

Output
AX = Error if Carry is set
DS:DX = ASCIIZ path and filename

INT 21H Service 5BH Create a New File DOS 3+

Input
AH = 5BH
DS:DX = Address of an ASCIIZ path (ending with "\")
CX = File's attribute

Output
AX = Error if Carry is set
= Handle if Carry is not set

INT 21H Service 5CH Lock and Unlock Access to a File DOS 3+

Input
AH = 5CH
AL = 0 $\rightarrow$ lock byte range
1 $\rightarrow$ Unlock byte range
BX = File handle
CX = byte range start (high word)
DX = byte range start (low word)
SI = No. bytes to (un)lock (high word)
DI = No. bytes to (un)lock (low word)

Output
If Carry = 1, AX = Error

INT 21H Service 5E00H Get Machine Name DOS 3+

Input
AX = 5E00H
DS:DX = Buffer for computer name

Output
DS:DX = ASCIIZ computer name
CH = 0 $\rightarrow$ Name not defined
CL = NETBIOS number
AX = Error if carry set

INT 21H Service 5E02 Set Printer Setup DOS 3+

Input

AX = 5E02H

BX = Redirection list index

CX = Length of Setup String

DS:DI = Pointer to printer setup buffer

Output

AX = Error if carry is set

INT 21H Service 5E03 Get Printer Setup DOS 3+

Input

AX = 5E03H

BX = Redirection list index

ES:DI = Pointer to printer setup buffer

Output

AX = Error if Carry is set

CX = Length of data returned

ES:DI = Filled with printer
       setup string

INT 21H Service 5F03 Redirect Device DOS 3+

Input

AX = 5F03H

BL = Device type

    = 3 → Printer Device

    = 4 → File Device

CX = Value to save for caller

DS:SI = Source ASCIIZ device name

ES:DI = Destination ASCIIZ network path with password

Output

AX = Error if Carry is set

INT 21H Service 5F04H Cancel Redirection DOS 3+

Input
AX = 5F04H
DS:SI = ASCIIZ device name or path

Output
AX = Error if Carry is set

INT 21H Service 62H Get Program Segment Prefix DOS 3+

Input
AX = 62H

Output
BX = Segment of currently
        executing program.

INT 21H Service 67H Set Handle Count DOS 3.30

Input
AX = 67H
BX = Number of allowed open handles (up to 255)

Output
AX = Error if Carry is set

INT 21H Service 68H Commit File (Write Buffers) DOS 3.30

Input
AX = 68H

Output
BX = File Handle

NOTE: 68H is the last of the DOS 3.3 INT 21H services.

INT 22H Terminate Address

INT 23H Control Break Exit Address

INT 24H Critical Error Handler
AH filled this way:

> 0 Diskette is write protected
> 1 Unknown Unit
> 2 The requested drive is not ready
> 3 Unknown command
> 4 Cyclic redundancy check error in the data
> 5 Bad request structure length
> 6 Seek error
> 7 Media type unknown
> 8 Sector not found
> 9 The printer is out of paper
> A Write fault
> B Read fault
> C General failure

If you just execute an IRET, DOS will take an action based on the contents of AL. If AL=0, the error will be ignored. If AL=1, the operation will be retried. If AL=2, the program will be terminated through INT 23H.

INT 25H Absolute Disk Read
Input
AL=Drive Number
CX=Number of Sectors to Read.
DX=First logical sector.
DS:BX=Buffer address.

Output
No Carry→ Success
Carry→   AH=80H Disk didn't respond.
            AH=40H Seek Failed.
            AH=20H Controller Failure
            AH=10H Bad CRC error check.
            AH=08 DMA overrun.
            AH=04 Sector not found.
            AH=03 Write protect error.

AH=02 Address Mark missing.
AH=00 Error unknown.

NOTE: Flags left on stack after this INT call because information is returned in current flags. After you check the flags that were returned, make sure you do a POPF. Also, this INT destroys the contents of ALL registers.

INT 26H Absolute Disk Write

Input
AL=Drive Number
CX=Number of Sectors to write
DX=First Logical Sector
DS:BX=Buffer address

Output
No Carry→   Success
Carry→AH=80H Disk didn't respond
          AH=40H Seek failed
          AH=20H Controller failure
          AH=10H Bad CRC error check
          AH=08 DMA overrun
          AH=04 Sector not found
          AH=03 Write protect error
          AH=02 Address Mark missing
          AH=00 Error unknown

NOTE: Flags left on stack after this INT call because information is returned in current flags. After you check the flags that were returned, make sure you do a POPF. Also, this INT destroys the contents of ALL registers.

INT 27H Terminate and Stay Resident

Input
DS:DX = point directly after end of code which is to stay resident.

INTs 28H-2EH Internal to DOS

INT 2FH Multiplex Interrupt

INT 30H-3FH DOS Reserved

INT 40H-5FH Reserved

INT 60H-67H Reserved for User Software

INTs 68H-7FH Not Used

INTs 80H-85H Reserved by BASIC

INTs 86H-F0H Used by BASIC Interpreter

INTs F1H-FFH Not Used

Index

CUSTOMER SUPPORT

It is important that you register your purchase of any Simon & Schuster software package. By completing and returning your Owner Registration Card, you become eligible for:

- Software support directly from S & S.
- Diskette replacement when applicable.
- Purchase of future product upgrades at special prices.
- Subscriptions to Hint Books and newsletters where applicable.

Software Support

S & S will provide support to registered owners. Our technical support number is (900) 990-2778. It is staffed on working days during normal business hours, 10:00 am to 6:00 pm, Eastern time. There is a charge of $1.00 per minute charged to your phone for each minute after the first.

Mail-in Support Service—Registered owners may write to us with questions. We will respond in writing. There is no additional charge for this service.

We realize that our software packages are put to a wide variety of uses, however, we can only answer questions about the software package itself. We cannot support the hardware and operating system required to run our software packages.

Before Calling Customer Support

Before calling our Technical Support Department, please make sure you have followed the steps in the "Pre-call Checklist" below.

Pre-call Checklist

1. If you are having difficulty understanding the program, have you read and performed the suggestions listed in the manual?

2. If you are not sure how to operate the program, have you used the help system (where available) to find the answer?

3. If there seems to be a problem in the software, can you reproduce the problem by following your steps again?

4. If the program displayed an error message, please write down the exact message.

5. You should be familiar with the hardware configuration you are using. We may need to know the brand/model of your computer, printer, the total amount of memory available, what video adaptor(s) you have in the system, the operating system version, etc.

6. When you call our Technical Support Department, please be at your computer or be prepared to repeat the sequence of steps leading up to the problem.

Services and Prices

The above services and prices are subject to change without prior notice.

Important! Read before Opening Sealed Diskette
END USER LICENSE AGREEMENT

Advanced BASIC
REPLACEMENT ORDER FORM

Please use this form when ordering a 3.5-inch disk or a replacement for a defective diskette.

A. If Ordering within Thirty Days of Purchase
If a diskette is reported defective within thirty days of purchase, a replacement diskette will be provided free of charge. *The back of this card must be totally filled out and accompanied by the defective diskette and a copy of the dated sales receipt.* In addition, please complete and return the Limited Warranty Registration Card.

B. If Ordering after Thirty Days of Purchase but within One Year
If a diskette is reported defective after thirty days, but within one year of purchase and the Warranty Registration Card has been properly filed, a replacement diskette will be provided to you for a nominal fee of $5.00 (send check or money order only). *The back of this card must be totally filled out and accompanied by the defective diskette, a copy of the dated sales receipt, and a $5.00 check or money order made payable to Simon & Schuster, Inc.*

C. If ordering 3.5 inch replacement disks
If you wish to order 3.5-inch disks for this product, please complete the back of this card and mail it with your original 5.25-inch diskettes along with a nominal fee of $5.00 to cover shipping and handling (send check or money order only). In addition, please complete and return the Limited Warranty Registration Card.

Advanced BASIC
LIMITED WARRANTY REGISTRATION CARD

In order to preserve your rights as provided in the limited warranty, this card must be on file with Simon & Schuster within thirty days of purchase.

Please fill in the information requested:

NAME _____ PHONE NUMBER ( ) _____

ADDRESS _____

CITY _____ STATE _____ ZIP _____

COMPUTER BRAND & MODEL _____ DOS VERSION _____ MEMORY _____ K

Where did you purchase this product?

DEALER NAME? _____ PHONE NUMBER ( ) _____

ADDRESS _____

CITY _____ STATE _____ ZIP _____

PURCHASE DATE _____ PURCHASE PRICE _____

How did you learn about this product? (Check as many as applicable.)

STORE DISPLAY_____ SALESPERSON_____ MAGAZINE ARTICLE_____ ADVERTISEMENT_____

OTHER (Please explain) _____

How long have you owned or used this computer?

LESS THAN 30 DAYS_____ LESS THAN 6 MONTHS_____ 6 MONTHS TO A YEAR_____OVER 1 YEAR_____

What is your primary use for the computer?

BUSINESS_____ PERSONAL_____ EDUCATION_____ OTHER (Please explain)_____

Where is your computer located?

HOME_____ OFFICE_____ SCHOOL_____ OTHER (Please explain) _____

67-65875

Get the Spark. Get *BradyLine*.

Published quarterly, beginning with the Summer 1990 issue. Free exclusively to our customers.

☐ Check here to begin your subscription.

Advanced BASIC

Please fill out the information below and return it to the address listed with your *original* 5.25-inch diskettes. Please print clearly.

☐ I am ordering replacement diskettes within 30 days. I have enclosed my original diskettes and a copy of the dated sales receipt.   ISBN 0-13-658758-5

☐ I am ordering replacement diskettes after 30 days but within one year. I have enclosed my original diskettes, a copy of the dated sales receipt and check or money order for $5.00 made out to Simon & Schuster, Inc.   ISBN 0-13-658758-5

☐ I am ordering 3.5-inch disks. I have enclosed my original 5.25-inch diskettes along with a check or money order for $5.00 made out to Simon & Schuster, Inc.
ISBN 0-13-663071-5

NAME _____ PHONE NUMBER ( ) _____

ADDRESS _____

CITY _____ STATE _____ ZIP _____

Please mail this request to: MICROSERVICES, 200 Old Tappan Road, Old Tappan, NJ 07675.
For more information, call (201) 767-5054.

PUT
FIRST
CLASS
STAMP
HERE

College Marketing Group
50 Cross Street
Winchester, MA 01890

ATTN: **CHERYL READ**